Naval Science 3

3
Naval Science

An Illustrated Text for the NJROTC Student

by Captain Wilbur A. Sundt USN (Ret.)

NAVAL INSTITUTE PRESS · ANNAPOLIS, MARYLAND

Contents

Preface

The purpose of the new NJROTC Naval Science series is essentially threefold:

1) To improve the academic status of the naval science course throughout the participating high school community.

2) To develop texts of high school language and content level which will, in fact, provide a sound academic background for both leadership and citizenship growth of high school youth.

3) To cut textbook acquisition and training costs to the Navy and give stability, continuity, and uniformity to the total NJROTC program across the nation.

It is the author's hope that all these objectives will be met by this and the succeeding texts of the series. It is my way to continue service to my Navy which gave me the opportunity to serve my country for over 30 years. Helping the youth of today so they will be better prepared to serve the Navy and the nation tomorrow seems to be the right way to extend that service.

The cooperation of many people helped in the making of this first text. To Tom Epley, editorial director of the Naval Institute Press, goes my special gratitude for his confidence in my ability and his overall support for the series at its inception. To Ward Brown, educational specialist in the Navy Youth Programs Office of the Chief of Naval Education and Training, goes my thanks for coordinating the project at the Navy's end. Without the patience and competence of Bill McClay, the Institute's manuscript editor for my beginning work, it is doubtful that my efforts would ever have made print. The wonderful cooperation of Patty Maddocks, director of the Naval Institute library and photographic service, made possible the fine photography used to illustrate the text. Exceptionally fine photographic support also was given by Mr. Ed Wilson, publications officer at the U. S. Naval Academy; Mr. Frank Pritchard, public affairs officer at the Navy Education Training Center at Newport, Rhode Island; *The Keel*, Navy Exchange publication at the Naval Training Center, Great Lakes, Illinois; and the Public Affairs Office at the Recruit Training Command, Great Lakes, Illinois. Very special photographic assistance was graciously provided by Bill Wedertz.

The voluminous input from many naval science instructors across the country through CNET helped crystallize many ideas. I trust that my efforts will assist them in making their important task more organized, interesting, and meaningful for those whom we serve.

And finally, I want to acknowledge the special support and perserverance of my wife Jean, who willingly put up with my concentration on things to do with the book during every spare moment for over a year. As she stood stalwartly by me during my active naval service, so has she continued to encourage my efforts in teaching naval science at Harlem High School in Loves Park (Rockford), Illinois, and in the writing of these books for the NJROTC program.

Naval Science 3

1

Sea Power Today

Chapter 1. What is Sea Power?

There are many definitions of "sea power." Perhaps the most useful is this one: sea power means controlling the seas for one's own use, and denying the use of the seas to one's enemy. This is a quite fundamental definition, however; let's expand on it by looking at some others.

One Chief of Naval Operations defined sea power as "the sum of a nation's capabilities to implement its interests by using the ocean areas for political, economic, and military activities in peace or war in order to attain national objectives." He went on to say that "the principal components of sea power are naval power, ocean science, ocean industry, and ocean commerce." This definition makes the term much clearer, showing the broadness of its scope. We now see that sea power has a profound effect upon nearly every aspect of national security, commercial prosperity, and social welfare.

A former Commander in Chief, Pacific, Admiral John S. McCain, Jr., wrote, "Sea power is the ability of a nation to use the waters of the earth and their depths for its own political, economic, and military interests by the application of pressures, direct and indirect, any place on the globe through commercial and naval activities on, over, under, and from these waters." This definition points to the many ways sea power can be projected—on, over, under, and from the seas—and states the

broader strategic goals of American naval and maritime policy.

It is clear, then, that sea power is of basic importance to the United States. It encompasses the merchant marine, oceanography, ocean engineering, marine research and technology, and naval power itself. The sea has played a vital role in our history since our very beginning, and since our country will continue to champion the cause of freedom in the world, the future will offer an even greater challenge. It is imperative that the men and women of today's Navy become thoroughly familiar with the expanding scope of sea power. It is equally important that all Americans understand the importance of sea power as it relates to the future of our country.

MAHAN'S CONCEPT OF SEA POWER

The originator of the term "sea power" was Alfred Thayer Mahan, who published *The Influence of Sea Power Upon History* in 1890. Mahan observed that the great maritime nations of the world have six things in common: (1) geographical position (2) physical similarity, including natural abundance and climate (3) size (4) population (5) character of the people, and (6) character of the government, including its national institutions.

He felt that geographical position was a very significant factor in the exercise of sea power. He believed that England's rise to world prominence during the sixteenth to twentieth centuries was mainly due to her

Sea power is the ability of a nation to use the oceans for its own political, economic, and military interests. Pacific Fleet ammunition ship USS *Shasta* provides underway replenishment to the nuclear-powered attack carrier USS *Enterprise* and the escort ship USS *Bagley*.

being situated along major European trade routes. He felt that the United States, too, could eventually rise to such a commanding position if our nation acquired overseas bases, a powerful fleet in each ocean, and a Panama Canal to allow rapid transit between oceans.

Mahan also stressed the fact that England is an island; this has protected her from invasion by land forces. But he pointed out that the right geographical position was not enough; a good coastline with fine harbors was also necessary. Further, he believed that if the land had a natural abundance of food and minerals, there would be less inclination for a nation to look seaward. Indeed, England had taken to the seas and to colonization because her own land lacked such abundance.

Mahan could not have known that the United States, so blessed with abundance at the turn of the century, would be facing the critical shortages it does today, particularly in petroleum products. He recognized the necessity of ocean commerce, but could not have foreseen how essential it would become. While he recognized the great worth of the seas as a barrier to invasion of North America, he could not have foreseen that the sea would become crucial to the deployment of our principal deterrent against nuclear war—our submarine missile systems.

Mahan also pointed out that territory and population are closely related; the larger the nation, the more people are needed for its defense. Seacoasts and harbors need to be defended, for they are not only routes for expansion, but routes for penetration as well.

By referring to a people's character, Mahan implied that any nation striving to become a sea power needs to have an aptitude for commercial enterprise and an understanding of the seas. Of course, he believed in the free enterprise system—capitalism—which was an essential ingredient in the phenomenal growth of America.

Finally, Mahan believed that the government must make its people see the need for maritime strength. It is in this area that the United States Navy fights a continual "battle" to maintain strength, improve capabilities, and provide for national defense.

Traditionally, the Navy and the other services have been hit with drastic reductions in funds and personnel during times of peace. During these periods, the nation has devoted its attentions to other projects and problems. But in the past, when the U. S. Navy has been allowed to dwindle, potential aggressors have grown stronger and bolder. We only have to look at the rise of Japan before World War II, and the significant Soviet challenge on all of the world's seas today. While all of Mahan's "characteristics of a great sea power" are important, in the final analysis it is the will of the people that determines whether a nation will maintain its security and strength—and its independence.

SEA POWER AND HISTORY

Mahan's doctrine of sea power was welcomed by those who wanted the United States to be among the world's great maritime powers. Mahan had shown that maritime strength was a decisive factor in history. It had given victory to Athens at Salamis, enabling Western civilization to survive and flourish. It had determined the supremacy of England after her defeat of the Spanish Armada in 1588. It had given America her independence at Yorktown in 1781, after the French defeat of the British naval squadron off the Virginia Capes. And, he reasoned, it allowed England to build the world's greatest colonial empire after her victory over the French at Trafalgar in 1805.

Our principal deterrent against nuclear war is our fleet of ballistic missile submarines. The USS *Henry Clay* (SSBN-625) surfaces near her home port. Once submerged, she will not surface during an entire patrol on the high seas.

There is little doubt that Mahan's concepts of sea power influenced the thinking of American expansionists in the Spanish-American War of 1898. As the result of that war, the United States became a world power with possessions and bases overseas. Our powerful Navy had defeated a major European power, and we had gained the necessary impetus to build the Panama Canal.

Much has happened since the time of Mahan to confirm his theories. British sea power, augmented by American naval strength, defeated the German U-boat menace in World War I. The two navies combined to repeat the feat in World War II, proving conclusively that Germany had erred in underestimating the importance of sea power. Japan recognized the importance of sea power, but American industrial might, superior training, and vast naval surface, air, and submarine superiority devastated the Japanese Navy. As a result, most of the Japanese armies received no supplies and were thus rendered helpless.

Naval forces in readiness enabled the United States to come to the aid of Lebanon in 1957 and to bolster a friendly regime in the Dominican Republic in 1961. The U. S. naval quarantine around Cuba in 1962 forced the Soviets to withdraw their missiles from that island. In 1950–53, U. S. naval forces made extensive contributions to the United Nations' efforts to stop North Korean and Chinese Communist advances into the Republic of Korea. And the U. S. Navy played a vital role in offensive, defensive, and logistic operations in Vietnam during American involvement in that war from 1964 to 1973. In each instance, control of the sea was established and maintained for the sustained benefit of U. S. and allied forces.

Chapter 1. Study Guide Questions

1. What is the fundamental definition of sea power?

2. What national objectives may be attained by full use of the seas?

3. What are the principal components of sea power?

4. What are Mahan's six characteristics of a great maritime nation?

5. What did Mahan think was necessary for the United States to rise to a prominent world position?

6. What factors are considered important in assessing the strength of geographical position?

7. What factors relative to the geography of the United States have changed since Mahan's original writings on sea power?

8. How did Mahan's interpretation of "national character" influence his concept of sea power?

9. Which of Mahan's characteristics is the factor which will ultimately determine whether a major nation remains strong and independent?

10. What naval battles did Mahan consider in arriving at his theory that sea power was a decisive factor in determining the trend of civilization in the world?

11. How did Mahan's theory influence American involvement in the Spanish-American War?

12. What three factors brought about Japanese defeat in World War II?

13. When and how has U. S. naval power influenced world history since World War II?

Vocabulary

sea power	free enterprise
components of sea	system
power	maritime strength
merchant marine	potential aggressor
inevitability	characteristics of a
dedication	sea power
imperative	Battle of Salamis
geographical position	Spanish Armada
national institutions	Battle of Yorktown
dominant world posi-	Battle of Trafalgar
tion	expansionist
world prominence	Lebanon crisis
natural abundance	Cuban quarantine
deterrent force	control of the sea
national character	balanced weapons
	system

Chapter 2. Geopolitics: Opposing Theories

Geopolitics is the relationship between politics and geography as they affect strategic planning. Alfred Thayer Mahan's theories concerning sea power actually are part of the study of geopolitics. As you would expect, geopolitical strategies other than those of Mahan have also been developed. The various theories are the subject of this chapter. Geopolitical thinking is the foundation of all government policy concerning international relations. Thus there is no way that leaders in our country can ignore geopolitics.

Mahan's Theory

According to Mahan's geopolitical theory, the nation controlling the seas, straits, principal sea lanes, and harbors would control the

Mahan's theory of geopolitics contends that a strong sea power can control the commerce and lifeblood of the world. Factors necessary to support sea power include strong overseas bases and good harbors. This is an aerial view of the fine U. S. Ship Repair Facility at Subic Bay, Philippines, the major base for the U. S. Seventh Fleet in the Far East.

commerce and lifeblood of the world. He advocated an arrangement in which a mother country would be supported and made wealthy by her colonies; but this concept has largely disappeared with industrialization, world trade, and the independence of all major nations. Mahan did not necessarily envision military conquest and occupation of the world's land areas by sea power. But he did see that sea power could give a nation political and commercial dominance in the world.

There are flaws in the details of some of Mahan's concepts, because of changes in the world and in military equipment. But he was right about one thing—sea power is steadily growing in importance in today's world, and will continue to do so in the future. No nation has ever been economically self-sufficient. Nations will always need the natural resources and manufactured goods of other nations. Transporting these resources and products across the oceans in ships is the most economi-

cal and practical means of trade. In time of peace or war, over 99 percent of all international trade moves on the seas.

To use the sea for transportation, we must control it, and not allow other nations to interfere with our use of it. We are thus back to the primary mission of our Navy—to gain control of the sea and, if necessary, deny the use of the sea to enemies. This mission is as important today as it has always been. Without sea power, our national prosperity and security would be in jeopardy. If control of the seas were lost, not only would our allies and our forces overseas be cut off, but our perimeter of defense would shrink to our own shores, and our industry would lack the resources necessary to manufacture essential goods.

MACKINDER'S THEORY

Mahan's doctrine did not go unchallenged. The opposite theory, of course, is that a centralized land power which controls vast natural resources and population will be the most powerful type of nation. Sir Halford J. Mackinder, a noted English geographer, formally presented that view in 1904, in a paper entitled "The Geographical Pivot of History."

Mackinder's basic theory was this: the nation controlling Eurasia's heartland (Russia and Eastern Europe) could, with improved overland communications and a developing industry, expand to the coastlines of the continent and capture the European sea bases from the landward side. Having accomplished this, it would be an easy matter to capture Africa. Together, he said, Eurasia and Africa make up the "World Island," and they control enough resources and manpower to swing the balance of power in the world. Thus, in time, the rest of the world—North and South America, England, Japan, and Australia—would fall under the domination of the heartland power. He predicted that this dominant land power would have political, military, and economic control of the world.

Mackinder assumed certain events and changes that have not yet occurred. He took for granted that the heartland would develop extensive modernized overland communications, transportation, and industrial might. Certainly there have been significant advances since Mackinder's time, but much of the Soviet Union is still a vast wasteland with primitive railways and roads. Russia's industry cannot support the needs of its own people, who in many areas live as Americans and Western Europeans lived a hundred years ago. Because of its harsh climate and poor agriculture, the Soviet Union annually imports millions of bushels of grain to sustain its people and its livestock animals. Consumer-goods shortages are part of everyday life there.

The development of modern nuclear and missile weapons is of great significance in comparing the sea-power and land-power geopolitical theories. The "safe" heartland envisioned by Mackinder is now no more than 30 minutes away from undersea or silo-based nuclear missiles, and only hours away from penetration by supersonic aircraft. To be sure, the bases and cities of the seaside nations are no more secure from this threat. But it is this balance of threat, if maintained, that is the greatest possible insurance for world peace.

Historically, land powers controlling the heartland have come out second best in conflicts with maritime nations and their allies. One only has to study the numerous wars of Europe over the last 500 years to see that land-oriented nations, though they were often victorious in battles and campaigns at the outset of a war, generally ended up suing for peace. The maritime power could then dictate terms and acquire territories "beyond the seas" to further broaden its control of the sea lanes.

THE NEW SOVIET GEOPOLITICS

In 1962 President John F. Kennedy established a naval quarantine around Cuba. This act was made necessary by the discovery that Soviet missile bases were nearing completion barely 90 miles from our country. The quarantine was a dramatic test of the readiness and ability of our naval forces to respond. The Soviets had to withdraw their missiles, submit to searches, and, in general, "lose face" by backing away from U. S. naval strength.

Flushed with the victory of the day, President Kennedy said, "Events of October 1962, indicated, as they have all through history, that control of the sea means security. Control of the seas can mean peace. Control of the seas can mean victory. The United States must control the seas if it is to protect our security." These words are both true and prophetic. Yet, since that time, the U. S. Fleet has declined in size. This is due to a combination of factors— inflation of shipbuilding costs, deactivation of aging ships, and inadequate Congressional appropriations.

Looking back at their own history, the Russians have realized that it was their defeat in

The Soviet carrier *Kiev* in the Mediterranean. The ship is 925 feet long and displaces 40,000 tons; it is also a missile cruiser forward and carries antiaircraft and antisubmarine missiles, as well as the long-range cruise missiles. The *Kiev* operates VTOL aircraft and helicopters.

the naval Battle of Tsushima Straits in 1905 that had lost them the Russo-Japanese War. During World War II, sea lanes to Murmansk—kept open only by the valiant efforts of Allied naval and merchant ships—were the Russian defenders' principal source of supply when all else appeared lost to Hitler's armies. When the Cuban quarantine showed once again that the Russian Navy was not equal to its task, the Soviets coldly analyzed the facts. They finally realized what the United States, Britain, ancient Greece, Spain, Germany, and Japan had already discovered—that control of the sea is essential to success in a war between powerful nations. They formulated a positive plan to change the Soviet Union into a major sea power, as well as a major land power.

Though the Soviet fleet had already started to build up in the late 1950s, it was the Cuban quarantine which really gave it impetus. Never again, said Soviet Premier Khrushchev, would the Soviet Union lack naval power in time of crisis. This fundamental change in Soviet policy has had far more impact on our national defense posture today than did the Cuban missiles in 1962.

Soviet sea power has grown steadily and positively since the Cuban crisis. Every aspect of sea power has been considered by the Soviet hierarchy. Many high-capacity shipyards have been built. Fishing fleets have been greatly expanded. Major emphasis has been given to oceanography, and a large force of research vessels is continuously at sea. The Soviet merchant fleet has expanded eightfold. Research on weapons systems and ship design has developed sleek, well-armed fleets of submarines and surface ships. The naval air arm has been expanded to include helicopter, vertical take-off and conventional aircraft, and aircraft carriers. The amphibious forces have been vastly improved with new ships, amphibious vehicles, and trained marines. The greatest achievement of all is the obvious improvement in the training, morale, and effectiveness of their naval personnel. If this trend continues, the effect on our future could be profound.

The Soviets follow a "new" geopolitical policy, one which combines the heartland theory of Mackinder with Mahan's concept of sea power. They have secured the heartland and expanded its strategic frontiers into Eastern Europe, Cuba, and North Korea. Now they are building and training a worldwide navy which already exceeds the U. S. Navy in at least one principal ship type—submarines. It is clear that the goal is to exceed the United States in *all* aspects of naval and maritime power. Soviet strategists have not spared any resources in striving for this goal.

The U. S. Secretary of Defense stated in 1977 that there can be only one reason for this buildup—the Russians intend to overtake the United States and establish a position of dominance in the world. It remains for the American people, through their Congress, to reverse this trend.

GEOPOLITICS: A HISTORY OF THE WORD

The term "geopolitics" came into being during World War I in a political-science paper prepared by Rudolf Kjellen, a Swedish author. He believed that national governments functioned much like biological organisms—in other words, a state has powers independent of and superior to the human beings who make up that state. Kjellen's theory provided ambitious leaders with the right kind of propaganda to initiate aggressive national policies in their countries. These leaders claimed that their state had a "manifest destiny," and it would "inevitably" grow, just as organisms evolve.

In Germany and Japan, and to a lesser extent in Italy, this theory was adopted as the foundation for policies of war and conquest. These countries claimed that it was their "natural right" to expand and conquer surrounding "inferior" nations. Kjellen's book became the foundation for the political and military resurgence of Hitler's Germany between the two World Wars.

A group of German army officers and politicians, led by retired General Karl Haushofer, developed the German version of geopolitics. Haushofer modified Mackinder's theory to fit German "requirements." He made it his mission to regenerate the defeated German state by a form of political propaganda which appealed to almost all Germans. According to their theory, Germany was a "growing" state. Although it had been temporarily set back by World War I, it would continue to grow and take over more and more territory, until it conquered the whole earth. Adolph Hitler called conquered lands "Lebensraum," living space, and justified the conquest of Germany's European neighbors as providing more lands and food for the "superior German race."

Haushofer believed that Germany should ally herself with the Soviet Union to help fulfill Mackinder's prophecy of world domination by the heartland. When Hitler and Stalin united their countries to invade and divide Poland at the beginning of World War II, Haushofer was elated and foresaw certain victory. But when Hitler invaded Russia, Haushofer was silenced.

When Germany was defeated in Russia, Haushofer's ideas were confirmed in the minds of German expansionists. There are strategists today in East Germany and the Soviet Union who think that a German–Russian alliance is necessary for the heartland to attain world domination.

Haushofer's geopolitical theories were also widely published in Japan. The love of military conquest made Haushofer's brand of geopolitics appealing to Japanese militarists of the 1920s and 1930s. They believed that the conquest of Asia was the natural right of the Emperor. He would develop a "Greater East Asia Co-Prosperity Sphere," which had Japan as its undisputed military and economic leader.

GEOPOLITICS TODAY

The term "geopolitics" is another way of saying "global thinking." Such thinking is essential to every nation in this modern era. As populations grow, transportation becomes quicker, communications become almost instantaneous, and the world's natural resources become scarcer, geopolitics become more important in the planning requirements of every government.

Geopolitics is the planning "science" which aids governments in determining their foreign policy. Modern geopoliticians believe that a nation should formulate its national policy only after looking closely at the natural environment—the geography—as it relates to the government and people. Geopolitics today provides the systematic and detailed knowledge that governments need. The Geographic Survey of the World, an ongoing research project of the U. S. government, has immense value, in both peace and war.

Geopolitics, then, is the study of how national policy (politics) is affected by the natural environment (geography). Governments depend on geopolitics to make decisions involving national security and foreign policy. Geopolitics has also influenced military procedures, in two ways: (1) by adding a political dimension to military strategy; (2) by adding environmental study and conditioning to the training of military personnel. This extra training prepares servicemen for the natural problems met in various theaters of war (for example, in arctic or jungle operations).

Chapter 2. Study Guide Questions

1. What is geopolitics?
2. What is Mahan's geopolitical theory?
3. What has caused the part of Mahan's sea-power theory dealing with colonization to change?
4. Why is it that nations are not self-sufficient?
5. Why is the mission of a maritime nation's navy so important today?
6. What is meant by "perimeter of defense," and how does sea power influence it?
7. What is Mackinder's geopolitical theory?
8. What is the basic difference, as to "degree of control," between the sea-power and heartland theories?
9. Which of Mackinder's assumptions concerning Russia have not yet been fully realized? What factors will probably continue to hinder this development?
10. What weapons developments have drastically weakened heartland security, which was so important to Mackinder's theory?
11. What is the purpose of maintaining a "balance of threat?"
12. What did the Cuban quarantine prove as far as our own Navy was concerned?
13. What appears to have been the major long-range effect of the Cuban quarantine on the Soviet Union?
14. What factors have combined to cause a decline in U. S. naval strength since the Cuban quarantine?
15. What major change in Soviet policy concerning sea power has taken place since 1962? Why is this change in policy so important to the United States?

16. What is the greatest achievement of the Soviet Navy in the implementation of their new national policy?
17. What is the "new" Soviet geopolitical policy? What appears to be the objective of this policy?
18. What was the basic idea in Kjellen's fundamental theory of geopolitics? Do you believe this idea has merit? Explain.
19. What is meant by the term "manifest destiny" as it relates to geopolitical expansion?
20. What was General Karl Haushofer's geopolitical theory? How did Hitler use that theory?
21. How did the Soviet Union figure into Haushofer's concept of geopolitics?
22. How did the Japanese use Haushofer's theory? What did they plan to develop in Asia?
23. What factors make geopolitics a necessity in government planning today?
24. What does geopolitical research accomplish for governments today? Why is this a valuable service? What two aspects of government are dependent upon this research for sound judgements?
25. How has geopolitics influenced military procedures?

Vocabulary

geopolitics
sea lanes
industrialization
commercial domination
political subordination
self-sufficient
jeopardy
heartland
World Island
political repression
balance of threat
inflation
deactivation
prophetic

Congressional appropriations
national, foreign, and naval policy
conventional weapons
"manifest destiny"
military resurgence
political propaganda
"Lebensraum"
Japanese militarists
"Greater East Asia Co-Prosperity Sphere"
environmental study
war theater

Chapter 3. The Expanding Scope of Sea Power

Today the United States faces a challenge on all of the world's seas. This challenge has direct impact upon our political, economic, psychological, and military well-being.

The United States is, first and foremost, a maritime nation. We have depended upon free use of the seas since the Revolutionary War. After World War II, we were in a position of unquestioned leadership on the seas. Since the mid-1970s, however, that leadership has been challenged by the ambitious long-range program of the Soviet Union—a program encompassing all facets of sea power.

Only by the careful maintenance of our sea power can we meet this challenge. As the Soviets have recognized, sea power means more than a strong navy. All aspects of maritime endeavor fit within the total program—merchant marine, fishing industry, oceanography, and the exploitation of the ocean depths for vital minerals and other resources.

Our future and that of generations to come depend upon how well we meet this Soviet challenge. The youth who are in school today will have to assume a considerable part of this burden; the problem will not be solved in a few years. It will continue to grow as a national problem each year of the foreseeable future. How well we grasp the significance of the oceans and how well we learn to use them will determine our future as a nation.

The Increasing Importance of the Oceans

Four major developments since World War II have increased the importance of the oceans. Two of these developments are political and two are technological.

The first major political development has been the rapid increase in the number of new nations since World War II. Only 51 nations formed the original United Nations; but by

"Inland reach" includes the use of supersonic jet aircraft launched from a carrier at sea.

1977 there were 149 members. Most of these nations previously were colonial dependencies. Most are underdeveloped—economically, socially, and politically—and are tempting targets for aggressor nations. Subversion, insurrection, and direct military intervention are all used by these aggressors.

The second political development is the fact that the United States has more commitments—in more places, with more nations, and involving more people—than any nation in history. We are committed to the defense of over 60 nations by treaty or agreement. Most of these nations border on oceans or seas. Thus the seas are the means by which this confederation is held together.

The first of the technological developments is the capability of sea power to reach far inland. The sea is no longer just an avenue of attack for a surface force or a shield against invasion from overseas. It has become a vast arena from which new and awesome weapons of mass destruction can strike any target, anywhere. This has changed military strategy profoundly, for there is now no place on earth beyond the range of direct, immediate attack from the sea. Any strategy must include naval forces as a factor in land hostilities—in both offense and defense.

This "inland reach" includes long-range ballistic missiles launched from huge nuclear-powered submarines far below the surface of the sea. It means supersonic jet aircraft launched from a distant carrier. It also includes the improved amphibious capability of the Navy–Marine Corps Team. Helicopters can carry combat-equipped Marines to inland strong points and transportation chokepoints. This tactic, called *vertical envelopment*, makes it possible to seize a beachhead before enemy reinforcements can arrive.

Added to the inland reach of sea power is nuclear power—the second technological development. Nuclear energy has both destructive and constructive uses. From the destructive side there is the thermonuclear warhead or bomb, which can be launched by a surface ship, aircraft, or submarine. On the constructive side are the nuclear reactors used in the propulsion of ships and submarines. Full utilization of nuclear energy as a propulsion and power source is still in its infancy. Important developments are sure to occur in the future.

For the present the United States has 41 Polaris/Poseidon ballistic missile submarines and more than 60 nuclear-powered attack submarines. The new Trident submarine weapons system will be with the fleet before 1980. On the surface, a growing number of nuclear-powered guided missile cruisers, frigates, and aircraft carriers are being added to the fleet. The USS *Eisenhower* (CVN-69), our third nuclear carrier and the largest and most powerful warship in the world, joined the U. S. Atlantic Fleet in October 1977.

These ships have unequalled endurance, effectiveness, and versatility. They can steam at 20 knots for months, without ever slowing down and without requiring logistic support. The ships can operate for more than a year without replenishment of their nuclear fuel.

Such a mobile threat extends the Navy's attack strength to the farthest corners of the earth. Defensively, it expands the protective frontier of the United States. But more important than either of these purely military considerations is the deterrent effect of these powerful ships. With such strength present and ready, the likelihood of nuclear war between the world's great powers is greatly lessened.

THE FOUR-OCEAN CHALLENGE

In the past, the Navy's radius of action was limited to the enemy's coastline and inland areas within the range of ships' guns. The development of high-performance aircraft and missiles has greatly expanded the Navy's radius. Ships, because of their mobility, are not as vulnerable as shore bases are. Mobility is the fleet's greatest protection against modern weapons; consequently, dispersal and mobility have become part of fleet operational doctrine.

Thus, the challenge our nation is faced with encompasses the three-fourths of the earth's surface covered by water. It is a "four-ocean" challenge. The Navy has been forced to face challenges in the four main ocean areas ever since World War II. This fact alone is sufficient reason for maintaining a strong Navy.

The Navy's radius of action was always limited to the enemy's coastline plus the range of ship's guns, until the development of high-performance aircraft and missiles. Now the radius extends from continent to continent. A Tartar missile is fired from the guided missile destroyer USS *Sampson* during a firing exercise in the Mediterranean Sea.

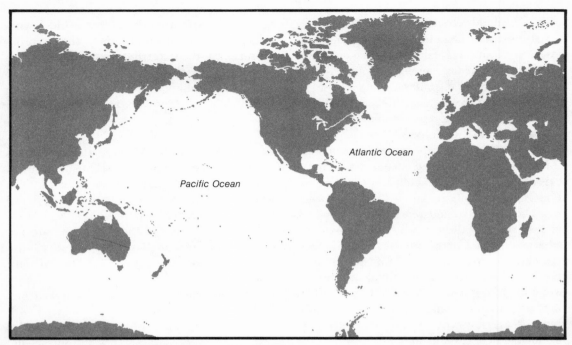

Map of the world, showing the Atlantic and Pacific Oceans.

The Four Ocean Areas

Ocean number one is the Atlantic, which includes the Mediterranean Sea, the North Atlantic, and the western approaches to Europe. This is the North Atlantic Treaty Organization's area of responsibility, and the United States plays a major role in its defense.

Ocean number two is the Pacific, extending from the Bering Strait which separates Alaska and the Soviet Union, to the Strait of Malacca separating Malaysia from Indonesian Sumatra. It includes the China seas and Sea of Japan—the eastern approaches to the Asian continent.

The third ocean is the Arctic Ocean, which lies north of our own continent of North America and separates Canada and Alaska from Siberia. Only since the advent of nuclear power has this frozen ocean become a naval operating area. In 1962 the nuclear submarines *Sea Dragon* and *Skate* moved underneath the polar ice to effect a rendezvous near the North Pole. It now is common for our nuclear sub-

marines to exercise in the Arctic Ocean, periodically breaking through the polar ice for a look at the top of the world.

The fourth ocean area is the vast Afro-Asian Ocean which includes the broad reaches of the South Atlantic and Indian Oceans. Traditional geography has tended to view these two oceans as separate entities, but they must be considered one strategic area today.

Major sea lanes cut through these oceans, carrying petroleum products from the Middle East around the Cape of Good Hope or through the Suez Canal. Many of the nations bordering on the Afro-Asian Ocean produce raw materials vital to our industrial economy.

Over forty new nations representing every political alignment lie adjacent to these sea lanes. We have few bases here and little prospect of gaining any. Naval communications stations have been created at Diego Garcia in the central Indian Ocean, and at North Cape, Western Australia, to serve the Navy's interests in the area. Our former allies in the area—

South Africa, Rhodesia, and India—often are at odds with our government because of their racial policies or aggressive military behavior.

MOBILITY OF SEA POWER

Because our fleets actually serve as mobile sea bases, we gain a fourfold mobility from the oceans. This is essential because we must be capable of meeting challenges in widely separated areas of the world. Because the Navy is able to travel freely on the high seas, its ability to range close to any potential enemy improves its offensive power.

First, we gain a geographical mobility, since the sea is a vast highway on which we can steam at will. Secondly, we gain political mobility by using international waters (wherever there are no problems of national sovereignty). Third, the oceans give us tactical mobility. We can move quickly wherever we wish, and disperse whenever and however necessary. We can blockade the enemy, a tactic which is designed to break down his economic system. Our far-ranging fleet can provide a defense line far from our own shores, which can readily shift from defense to offense.

And fourth, we have sustained mobility, since we can replenish fuel, stores, and ammunition at sea. Our nuclear-powered vessels are virtually self-sustaining. Additionally, the presence of mobile sea forces near certain land areas may act as a deterrent. Sea-based forces are on the scene, combat-ready and able to anticipate problems. Their timely arrival in an area of tension may be sufficient to cool down a potential conflict.

HOTSPOTS AND BOTTLENECKS

The Caribbean Sea/Gulf of Mexico is an area vital to the defense of the United States. It provides a water avenue to our southern and midwestern states. Our trade route through the Panama Canal is crucial, for the canal-bound sea lanes could be interdicted from Cuban bases. Our training base at Guantanamo Bay,

Cuba, is important to the Atlantic Fleet, and perhaps even more important to the stability and security of the Caribbean area.

The Caribbean "hotspot" has economic and political problems which encourage the expansion of communism—for example, overpopulation and unemployment in Puerto Rico, political instability in Jamaica, labor and racial problems in Guyana, and insurgency in Co-

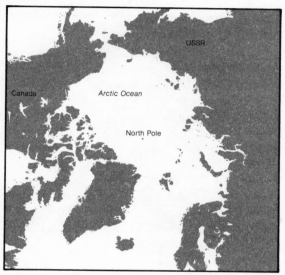

The Arctic Ocean.

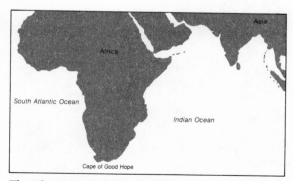

The Afro-Asian Ocean area includes the South Atlantic and Indian Oceans, and especially concentrates attention on the sea lanes around Africa and the trade route between the Persian Gulf and the Strait of Malacca. Strategically, it is considered one area today.

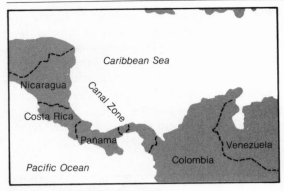

The Panama Canal.

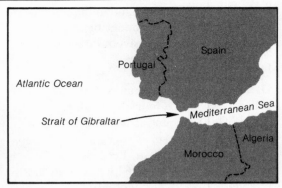

The Strait of Gibraltar.

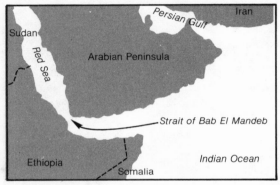

The Strait of Bab El Mandeb.

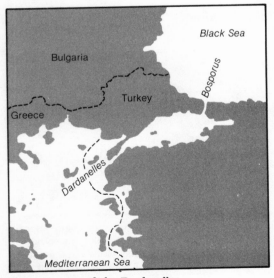

The Bosporus and the Dardanelles.

lombia and Guatemala. This hotspot and the Panama Canal bottleneck are almost certain to be trouble spots in the future. Naval sea power and the Navy–Marine Corps Team are the surest means of responding to immediate problems in the area. Moreover, a strong presence may reduce (or even eliminate) the need for our direct military involvement.

The Mediterranean Sea has been an area of contention since the dawn of history, and it is no less so today. Gibraltar, the front door to the Mediterranean, is a vital commercial chokepoint, or bottleneck. Controlled for two centuries by Great Britain, "The Rock" is claimed by Spain and is a major reason for the poor relations between those two countries. The destiny of all nations is affected by whether this doorway is open or closed. Nor should it be forgotten that there is a side door to the Mediterranean, through the Bosporus and Dardanelles in Turkey. The ships of the Soviet Union come through these straits, from Soviet bases and seaports on the Black Sea.

The eastern end of the Mediterranean becomes the focus of ships steaming between Europe and Asia. These ships must transit the Suez Canal, the Red Sea, and the Strait of Bab El Mandeb before entering the Indian Ocean. This same area is probably the most explosive area of the world, since it includes Israel and her Arab neighbors. The United States, Soviet Union, the United Nations, and the several

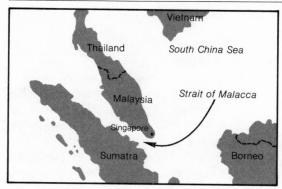

The Strait of Malacca.

states involved all have a stake in the peaceful settlement of the Arab–Israeli dispute. The major powers recognize that a war could break out there at any time—a war which could easily escalate into a direct confrontation between the nuclear powers.

The Soviet Mediterranean Squadron roves that sea now—just as the U. S. Sixth Fleet has done since World War II, in support of the southern flank of NATO. The two fleets are roughly equivalent in numbers. The United States has the edge in carriers and carrier aircraft, while the Soviets are stronger in destroyers and cruisers with a surface-to-surface guided-missile capability. Both navies deploy extensive submarine, amphibious, and service forces in the area.

A fourth major bottleneck in the world's sea lanes is the Strait of Malacca, the ocean highway between the Indian Ocean, the South China Sea, and the Pacific. The port of Singapore sits at the strait's southern entrance. Although relatively stable at present, after the defeat of communist insurgent forces in Malaysia and Indonesia, the area is threatened by communist expansion. Fresh from victories in Cambodia, Laos, and Vietnam, communist insurgents press into Thailand and keep a smoldering guerrilla effort going in the Malay States. The Seventh Fleet uses the Strait of Malacca to enter the Indian Ocean, showing the flag in areas of growing Soviet influence.

The Danish Straits—Skagerrak and Kattegat—guard the entrance to the Baltic Sea and the Soviet Union's largest port city, Leningrad. Denmark, Norway, and West Germany control the straits; all three are in NATO. Control of these waters would be a primary objective of both sides in any conflict. In event of a war between NATO and the Soviet-dominated Warsaw Pact countries, the Soviet Union would have to gain control of these straits before her Baltic Fleet could transit to the North Sea and the Atlantic Ocean.

TWO POWERFUL NAVIES

Today there are two powerful world navies—ours and the Soviet Union's. Once a relatively small force, the huge Soviet fleet of over 400 submarines and hundreds of new ships is now a formidable rival. The real importance

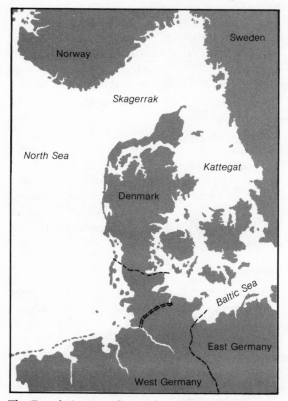

The Danish Straits—Skagerrak and Kattegat.

of this fleet is not so much its size, but the strategy behind it. There is little doubt now that the Soviet Union plans to exploit the world's dependence on the seas by developing a powerful naval and merchant fleet which will dominate the world's oceans.

Naval power is only one facet of sea power. But only the Navy can guarantee that we will continue to use the oceans freely and fully, for the benefit of all our citizens. We are challenged by numerically superior forces, which have greater natural resources and great industrial potential. Our biggest advantage, now and in years to come, lies in our use of the seas.

Sea power must have its roots in public understanding and in the public's determination to guard the heritage given us by our nation's founders. Those men saw the necessity of a strong maritime posture and insisted that we have that power.

Today we face a choice. We can show the national determination and provide the necessary resources to maintain our position on the seas. If we do, our country will have free and continuous access to some 85 percent of the world's surface. Or we can lose this capability and lose our guarantee of free passage on the seas. That would reduce us to an island, isolated from allies and resources overseas. Under those circumstances we could be starved out by forces surrounding us—even if no missile were ever detonated above our cities. A nation can die quickly in a nuclear holocaust, but it can die just as surely through strangulation of its sea lanes.

MERCHANT MARINE

A strong merchant marine is a vital element of sea power. This belief was part of Mahan's doctrine of sea power. The merchant fleet must be kept competitive if it is to meet the growing needs of industry and provide logistic support to our forces overseas.

The Department of Defense has actively supported programs to update the U. S. Mer-

chant Marine. The Navy and the Department of Commerce have cooperated in the development of the world's fastest cargo freighters. They are conducting research on a cargo-carrying surface-effect vessel and a cargo submarine. The Military Sealift Command and the maritime industry have worked out arrangements to ensure that U. S. merchant ships are available to the Department of Defense when needed. Such ships carried 97 percent of the logistic support required by our military forces in Vietnam.

Increased foreign competition in the shipping industry has hurt our Merchant Marine, however. Because of corporate income taxes, insurance rates, shipbuilding costs, and labor costs, U. S.-flag ships move only about 7 percent of our total ocean commerce. We use foreign-flag vessels to handle the remainder. Congress appears reluctant to continue subsidizing our merchant fleet companies, and it is only through subsidies that they can continue to operate.

The United States has about 14 percent of the world's gross tonnage in merchant ships, compared with Russia's 6 percent. However, 80 percent of our ships are more than 20 years old. Most of the Soviet merchant ships are far younger. Recognizing the importance of a viable merchant fleet, the Soviet Union is now building ships at a rapid rate. Soviet merchant ships have mechanized equipment for loading and unloading, and are faster and more modern than two-thirds of our merchant fleet. The total world fleet is, however, expanding at about the same rate as the Russian fleet, so it appears possible that the free world can continue to dominate world shipping, despite Soviet expansion.

MARITIME COMMERCE

There was a time in American life when we had a boundless supply of raw materials. We believed we were completely self-sufficient and did not need to purchase raw materials abroad. But our increasing population and growing rate of consumption has changed that situation. In fact, we are dependent on other nations for much of what we need to keep our economy strong, keep our people at work, and manufacture what we need.

There are about 80 resources that the United States cannot do without if we are to maintain our present economy. We must import 85 percent of our manganese to make steel. We import 86 percent of the bauxite from which

A strong, modern merchant marine is a vital element of sea power. 99% of the world's trade goes by sea to its destination. The United States' survival depends upon its ability to use the seas for trade.

aluminum is refined. We import more than 99 percent of the tin we need and over 90 percent of the chromite used to toughen steel. Ninety percent of the columbite used to construct nuclear reactors, make stainless steel, and manufacture rockets and missiles is imported. By 1977 we were importing 46 percent of our total petroleum needs; this meant we annually consumed over one-third of the entire world supply of oil. Almost half of our total annual trade deficit was the result of foreign oil purchases.

The doctrine of freedom of the seas is understood by all nations under international law. But in wartime, a belligerent nation will do all in its power to disrupt the passage of commercial shipping to its opponents. Throughout history, whenever powerful nations have lost control of the seas, they have fallen. There is no reason to believe that things will be different in the future.

For this reason a strong American defense must include a strong merchant marine. The flow of raw materials must not be halted by any enemy if we are to maintain our national security as well as the health and stability of our domestic economy. Keeping the sea lanes open is a vital mission of the U. S. Navy, for these lanes are the lifelines of America.

OCEANOGRAPHY

Within the depths of the oceans is a wealth of animal and plant life. Every mineral known to man can be found on the sea bottom or suspended in the sea water. The sea is the last great storehouse of food and minerals on earth—and every nation on earth knows it. Oceanography is the science which will find ways to properly exploit this wealth for the benefit of mankind. We must learn to use these resources fully, without depleting sea life or polluting the sea environment.

Many littoral nations—those with ready access to the seas—are engaged in oceanographic research, but the United States and the Soviet

Union are the ones most deeply involved. The Russians have by far the largest oceanographic research fleet. But the United States is also awakening to the need for oceanographic research, and has conducted many major projects in the past twenty years.

We know that we must increasingly turn to the sea for resources that we previously obtained on land—food, fresh water, minerals, energy, and maybe even living space. Vast new resources have already been discovered in the continental shelf (a narrow belt around the continents), and these finds may bring the world a momentary reprieve from the growing shortage of oil. An international agreement at the 1958 Geneva Conference on the Seas gave littoral nations exclusive rights to develop the resources in the continental shelf adjacent to their own shores.

Minerals of all kinds can be extracted from sea water, but as yet this is economically feasible only for certain chemical fertilizers and magnesium. Refinement of fresh water for city water supplies and for irrigation is already being done in a few areas around the world where natural fresh water is in insufficient supply. Harnessing the tides for energy—an endless supply of energy—is done only in Holland and France in two large-scale projects. But it could be done on nearly every seacoast where tidal range is sufficient, in the North and South Temperate Zones.

Commercial fisheries have just begun to harvest the food potential of the seas. The Soviet Union ranks fourth and the U. S. ranks fifth in the fishing industry, but the Soviets are quickly widening their lead over us. Their factory ships are the most modern in the world. They service the catch of a fleet of busy trawlers, canning the catch and delivering the product to the customer nations in an extremely efficient operation.

The science of aquaculture—farming the sea—may in time make it possible to cultivate plants and fish which can produce a considerable portion of the protein products needed by the world's people. The Navy's oceanographic fleet of surface ships and submersibles is studying every aspect of the sea—from fish culture to the effects of salinity on sonar used in antisubmarine warfare.

Commercial fisheries have not begun to realize the potential of the ocean harvest. They have concentrated on only 20 varieties of fish out of more than 20,000 known species. Almost all sea life is edible. Even tiny high-protein plankton and algae are being investigated as possible sources of food. The Japanese have already begun harvesting plankton in the seas of the Antarctic for commercial food use.

The United States has always had a relatively large fishing industry, but it is falling far behind that of other nations today. We now rank fifth behind Japan, Peru, Communist China, and Russia. Our catch is less than half that of Japan. Of the fish consumed in the United States, 62 percent is imported. This represents an annual cash outflow of $500 million. Moreover, the Russians are rapidly widening their lead over us. Their modern factory ships can process the catch from a fleet of trawlers while still at sea, with the most scientific canning operation ever devised. These ships can deliver their product directly to the customers, thus eliminating any competition from American land-based processing plants.

Man has barely begun his search for knowledge of the ocean's depths. The United States' efforts to step up basic and applied research in oceanography are quite recent. Our progress, when compared with that of the Soviets, is entirely too slow. There is no question that the United States has the capability and scientific know-how for this effort. What it must develop is a national understanding of the importance of the seas, and the will to move ahead boldly with its program.

The United States leads the world in the number and variety of its deep submergence research vessels. The *Alvin*, a scientific research submarine sponsored by the Office of Naval Research, was designed to explore depths of up to 6,000 feet. It is used primarily to investigate the continental shelves.

As early as the mid-1960s the Russians had twice as many oceanographers, nearly four times as many oceanographic technicians, and ten times the number of oceanographic research vessels as the United States. Except in the category of deep-sea research vehicles, the Soviets have expanded their lead in the 1970s. In view of the acknowledged fact that the seas are the last frontier on earth, students in high school and college today should be thinking seriously of careers in the wide-open field of oceanography.

GAZING INTO SPACE
BRINGS MAN BACK TO EARTH

No one denies the importance of outer space. But even as we gaze toward the stars, dreaming of space ships and distant planets, we must still live on earth. While expeditions to outer galaxies and colonies on the planets or the moon may happen someday, it is far more practical to consider the proper use of the earth for the sustenance of future generations.

With more than three-fourths of the globe covered by water, it is inevitable that the oceans will play a vital role in the future of the human race.

As mankind turns seaward for fresh water, food, oil, natural gas, and raw materials, it becomes abundantly clear that no country can live in isolation from the rest of the world. The trade routes of the seas become the arteries of life for mankind. And sea power becomes the essential ingredient in sustaining life, political independence, and economic prosperity.

Balanced sea power makes possible a flexible national strategy. With sea power we can easily make a show of force or a show of the flag. We can project our power from mobile bases at sea, and can bring positive pressure to bear with amphibious forces. We can prevent trouble from erupting, and suppress it when it does, with the Navy–Marine Corps Team. We can send our sailors and Marines ashore as ambassadors of good will, making our friends and allies confident of our ability to support them in times of trouble. Our reassuring presence lends stability to an otherwise troubled world. In short, sea power makes it possible for the United States to carry out a defense policy which fosters peace in the world.

Sea power, however, depends on people—highly trained and dedicated people who believe in their mission. Dedicated men and women are the ones who, through their own standards of excellence and professionalism, make the other elements of sea power work. We depend upon these people to respond rapidly and decisively to changing world events. It is these sailors and Marines, with their qualities of vision, judgement, and willpower, who actively support American sea power. But it's up to *all* Americans—service people, civilians, professional people, and students—to learn about the importance of sea power. There is one fact that the American public must never be allowed to forget: the sea and the United States are inseparable.

Chapter 3. Study Guide Questions

1. What aspects of American life are affected by the Soviet challenge on the seas?

2. What aspects of sea power have the Soviets recognized as important parts of their expanding maritime program?

3. What two major political developments since World War II have increased the importance of the oceans?

4. What are the identifying characteristics of most of the newly independent nations of the world?

5. What does "insurrection" or "insurgency" mean?

6. How does sea power affect our worldwide political alliances?

7. What two principal technological developments have occurred since World War II?

8. What does "inland reach" mean as related to sea power? What are some examples of sea power's inland reach?

9. What two aspects of nuclear technology have affected sea power?

10. What three U. S. nuclear-powered ballistic missile submarine systems will be operational by 1980?

11. How is ship "endurance" affected by nuclear propulsion?

12. What is meant by the "strategic frontier?" Where is the United States' strategic frontier today?

13. What is meant by "deterrent effect?"

14. What is the U. S. Fleet's best protection against modern weapons? How has fleet operational doctrine been modified to meet this impact?

15. In what four ocean areas is the U. S. Navy now facing the Soviet naval challenge?

16. What is unique about naval operations in the Arctic Ocean?

17. What two naval communications stations have been built in the Indian Ocean area?

18. What four kinds of mobility do our fleets

possess because of their ability to move fully on the high seas?

19. What is the "periphery of defense?"

20. Why is sustained mobility so important to world peace?

21. What are the names of the world's most strategic straits or "bottlenecks" for world trade?

22. What particular naval and maritime interests does the United States have in the Caribbean area?

23. Through which strategic water route must Soviet Black Sea shipping pass?

24. What makes the outbreak of an Arab–Israeli war so potentially dangerous to the world?

25. What great seaport is located on the Strait of Malacca? Why is this area so important now?

26. What is the strategic importance to the NATO alliance of the Danish Straits?

27. What is the apparent goal of the Soviets' increasing sea power?

28. From where must U. S. sea power obtain its fundamental support if it is to continue to guard our heritage and our future?

29. What alternatives does the United States have concerning our future maritime strength?

30. What factors make it almost impossible for the U. S. Merchant Marine to compete with other world maritime fleets?

31. What factors have changed the United States' former self-sufficiency in raw materials?

32. How does a belligerent nation regard the doctrine of freedom of the seas?

33. What is the importance of oceanographic research to mankind?

34. What was the purpose of the 1958 Geneva Conference on the Seas concerning natural resources?

35. What benefits can man derive from harnessing the tides?

36. Why is the ocean fishing industry so important in oceanographic research and maritime power?

37. Why are Russian and Japanese fishing fleets so successful in meeting world competition with their products?

38. In what area of oceanographic research has the United States maintained a lead over the Soviets?

39. How does balanced sea power allow national strategy to be flexible?

40. How does U. S. naval power lend stability to a troubled world?

41. Upon whom does the maintenance of U. S. sea power depend?

42. Who must learn about the importance of the sea in America today?

Vocabulary

scope of sea power
ocean exploitation
technological
  developments
subversion
insurrection
insurgency
aggressor
international com-
  mitments
vertical envelopment
Polaris/Poseidon/
  Trident
ship endurance
strategic frontier
mobility
dispersal
fleet operational
  doctrine
performance radius
encompass
Strait of Malacca
rendezvous
political alignment
national sovereignty
periphery of defense
political stability
Caribbean Sea
Guantanamo Bay

Gulf of Mexico
Gibraltar
Bosporus
Dardanelles
Strait of Bab el
  Mandeb
escalation
confrontation
NATO Allies
Danish Straits
Warsaw Pact nations
national determina-
  tion
nuclear holocaust
attrition
merchant marine
Military Sealift
  Command
subsidize
infinity
manganese
bauxite
aluminum
freedom of the seas
domestic economy
littoral country
aquaculture
oceanographic
  research

2

The Naval Service:
A Rewarding Way of Life

Chapter 1. The Challenge of Navy Life

A naval career is a demanding way of life, calling for complete loyalty and dedication. It is a unique undertaking. Of its many features, there are four which are particularly representative:

First, Navy life gives you a unique opportunity to further your personal goals.

Second, it gives you the opportunity to lead others and contribute to the Navy and your society.

Third, it gives you an opportunity to share experiences with people from all over the nation and the world, to an extent unattainable elsewhere.

And fourth, your Navy career will give you operational skill in modern technologies—skill on a level that you couldn't achieve in most professional areas.

There are pleasant assignments and those that are not so pleasant; but any billet can be an opportunity for learning. Sometimes it takes a very mature and observant person to see all of the many opportunities—but they are always there.

The military lifestyle is patterned around the mission and purpose of the U. S. Armed Forces: to defend the United States. It is a unique experience which cannot be duplicated in civilian life.

The U. S. Navy needs young men and women with a strong desire to succeed. These people have to be willing to work for success, and they must believe that the Navy is a good place to achieve their goals.

The Navy today is a force made up of young people who have chosen to accept the ultimate challenge of an American citizen: defense of the nation. That is why the Navy wants only the best young citizens. That is why it provides the best schools and teachers, and insists that its people get the finest training and education for their jobs.

The Navy learned long ago that the most important factor aboard any ship or station is the *people,* not the equipment. In the days of sailing ships, good men were needed to man both helm and sails. And it's the same today, even with computers, radar, and instant communications. Today's complex equipment is only as good as the judgment of its operators.

Everyone who joins the Navy gets the chance to prove his ability, stamina, and initiative. Every person, man or woman—regardless of race, color, religion, or national origin—gets an equal opportunity. Advancement is based on ability and performance. Navy people are encouraged to use their abilities to move into areas of greater responsibility.

Applicants for enlistment must have enough education to participate in the training pro-

The Navy today is a force composed of people who have chosen to accept the ultimate challenge of an American citizen: defense of the nation. That is why the Navy provides the best schools and teachers and insists on the finest training and education to fill its positions. The assistant navigator trains a quartermaster seaman in the use of the stadimeter.

gram. A high school diploma is required for certain technical programs. The Navy urges prospective recruits to get all the education they can and to make every effort to complete high school. The better educated they are, the better equipped they'll be to serve their country.

Officers in the Navy must be mature individuals capable of assuming a wide variety of duties at sea and ashore. Officers must be superior individuals, who accept a full measure of responsibility and show exceptional dedication to duty. They must be professional, in the truest sense of the word, and competent to solve complex problems quickly. Officers must set an example of honesty and integrity. They must be versatile, resourceful, and adaptable to changing circumstances.

Officers must be in good health, with the physical stamina and stability to perform their jobs well under trying and tiring conditions. In addition, they must have a thorough education. The Navy wants only the best persons for its officer corps.

Everybody wants to be someone in life. And everyone can be someone special in the Navy—whether as a specialist in an interesting enlisted rating, or as a commissioned officer in a role of responsible leadership.

THE NAVY'S JOB

The Navy is *big*—it operates over 460 major ships, about 2,500 small craft, and some 7,000 aircraft. It employs a force of nearly a million men and women, as officers, enlisted personnel, and civilian employees. About 535,000 men and women wear the Navy uniform—63,000 officers and 472,000 enlisted personnel. The Navy is one of the top employers in the United States. It's an ideal place for a young man or woman with ambition, dedication, and intelligence to learn an important occupation and find a rewarding career.

The Navy's job today is bigger and more important than ever before. The Navy must carry out national policies, and support our forces and our allies wherever they may be. It must protect the right of our maritime ships to move about freely on the oceans. It must provide a first line of defense in protecting our country against aggressors.

The Navy's job requires it to function smoothly in many different environments—on, under, and over the seas, and on shore stations. The ships of the fleet must operate as self-sufficient communities. They require their own telephone repairmen, firemen, cooks, and computer operators. There must be people who know how to operate laundries, run barber shops, manage post offices, and handle medical needs. Many must have the technical and military skills necessary to defend and support themselves and other ships of the fleet. The Navy's men and women represent a broader range of occupations and skills than ever before.

Most of the jobs performed by Navy people have the same technical requirements as those performed by civilians. But the environment and equipment of the Navy make those jobs unique. It is the difference in lifestyle that makes the Navy "not just a job, but an adventure."

LIFE AT SEA

The Navy is a sea service. Men who join the Navy can expect to have the opportunity to spend some time at sea. (At present, Congress prohibits the assignment of women to combatant ships; but most other jobs in the Navy are open to qualified women. Women may be assigned to shore stations both in the United States and overseas.) Assignment to sea duty usually depends upon the current needs of the Navy, though a sailor's personal needs are also considered. The Navy is striving for the best possible team effort to accomplish its mission.

Sea duty means assignment to a ship or deployable unit, whether that ship is at sea or in port. Assignment to a ship doesn't mean that a sailor will be "at sea" all the time. Navy ships are assigned to a home port, either in the United States or overseas, and normally spend about 10–14 days at sea during a month of local or regional training operations.

Deployments away from home port are usually about six months long. During that time, a ship will usually be at sea about half the time, but rarely more than three weeks at a stretch. Ships will normally pull into a port in the general area of deployment to give their crews rest and recreation, and to have periodic repairs and upkeep.

Every sailor, on whatever level, looks forward to the completion of training and assignment to a ship of the fleet. Whether aboard a sleek destroyer, a nuclear-powered cruiser, an aircraft carrier, a submarine, or one of the new multi-purpose amphibious or service ships, life at sea is a far cry from duty ashore. All of an individual's training, skill, and determination are put to the test.

Picture yourself in this shipboard role. You will be given all the responsibility and challenge you can handle. You'll be doing an important job that you are particularly qualified to do. You will be serving your country in a way only you, with your training, can do, and you'll feel the pride and satisfaction of having done an important job well.

The special opportunity for the sailor on sea duty is travel. The Navy gets around. Wherever Navy duty may take you—to the Mediterranean, Europe, Hawaii, or the Western Pacific—you'll have the chance to see places, meet people, and do things that most people just dream about. And in some Navy programs you can choose the foreign land or area in which you'd like to serve.

Even in our own country the Navy gets around. There are Navy bases everywhere—from Norfolk to San Diego. A tour of duty in any one place will probably be about three years, with shorter tours normally involved with duty under instruction in schools. Requests for extension or reassignment within the same area will usually be honored if they best meet the needs of the Navy and the individual concerned. Wherever you go, wherever you serve, you'll be richer for the experience.

ADDITIONAL BENEFITS FOR NAVAL PERSONNEL

We have talked about many of the challenging and interesting aspects of Navy life. To help round out the picture, you should also know about some of the benefits which service members receive.

FINANCES

People need enough salary to afford the many requirements of modern life, whether in the Navy or in civilian life. When comparing Navy pay with civilian pay you must consider benefits which are additional to your base pay—allowances, medical care, retirement, and others. Taking all into consideration, a Navy career is competitive with any comparable civilian job; in many instances, the Navy benefits are superior to what you could get in civilian life.

As in civilian life, higher education and longevity (time in service) will mean more pay; another way of saying this is that with greater responsibility and higher rate or rank, you'll reach higher pay levels. Since pay scale, allowances, and benefits are adjusted to keep up with the rising cost of living, Navy personnel and their dependents can look forward to a life that is reasonably relaxed and free from financial worries.

Because a person's well-being is essential to a successful career, complete medical, dental, and hospital care—including regular physical checkups for preventive health care—are available to service personnel at all times, free of charge. If there are dependents, they are entitled to medical, surgical, and hospital care under a medical care program, on a space-available, minimal-cost basis at military or civilian hospitals.

Service personnel pay Federal income taxes and Social Security taxes just as other employed Americans do. State income taxes are paid in accordance with state laws which pertain in the individual's home of record. How-ever, many allowances paid to service people are not taxable. Among these are: subsistence allowances for meals; sums authorized for quarters, clothing, travel, and transportation; and allowances for housing and cost of living.

Room and board are provided for all service personnel, though officers must pay for their food from their subsistence allowance. Service personnel who are married can save money on household goods, clothing, and food by using the base commissary, exchanges, and service stores—like the laundry and dry cleaning, tailor shop, cobbler shop, gas station, barber shop, and clubs and snack bars.

Special pay is generally awarded to individuals who serve in unusual or hazardous duty, such as aviation, submarine service, underwater demolition, explosive ordnance disposal, and diving. Bonuses are offered to certain qualified people who enlist in special skills or reenlist in critical ratings. Officers in critical programs such as nuclear propulsion and medical fields are given financial incentives for extensions of obligated service.

Retirement pay and disability benefits are other significant financial considerations for the career person and for those persons with family responsibilities. Retirement pay is very substantial: 50 percent of base pay after 20 years is the base retirement rate for both officers and enlisted personnel. This goes to a maximum of 75 percent after 30 years of satisfactory service.

INSURANCE

Anyone entering active duty is automatically insured for $20,000 at a minimal $3.40 monthly premium under the Servicemen's Group Life Insurance program. An individual may select less coverage, but this is generally inadvisable. Upon separation from service, this insurance may be converted to a renewable term life insurance policy, or to a civilian policy with a company participating in the program.

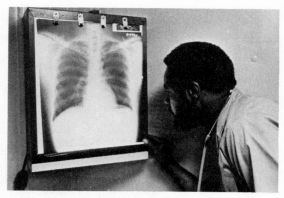

A hospital corpsman checks over a patient's X-ray during his regular duties. Shipboard medical facilities are superb aboard all larger ships, and smaller vessels have immediate access to the finest medical treatment on service force tenders and bases.

One of the more attractive benefits of military service is the opportunity for further education, both civilian and military. A great many educational programs are available to fulfill service requirements or increase the general educational level of the service member. Other programs provide financial assistance for medical, dental, and law students, in exchange for a tour of active duty.

For many enlisted ratings, advanced training in Class "C" schools provides specialty training in specific equipments and tasks. Schools range from cargo-handling to nuclear propulsion, heavy equipment operation, utility and electrical repair, electronics, air conditioning and refrigeration, machinery repair, precision instruments, supply packaging and transportation, aviation technology, management control, pharmacy, and police investigation.

A new program is now in effect in the Navy which enables enlisted men and women to plan for advanced education with cooperating colleges and technical schools. Called the Navy Campus for Achievement (NCFA), the program helps an individual work toward a college degree or earn a technical certificate or license. In partnership with the Navy, the participating school will allow the individual to take academic or technical courses in many locations without losing credit toward the degree. NCFA also will provide counseling and placement services for military specialization schools, civilian colleges, vocational schools, and various programs leading to a commission, such as NROTC, the Naval Academy, and other college programs financed by the Navy.

Professional education for officers is designed to develop leadership at every level of operations and management. It also provides the professional, scientific, and technical skills needed at sea and ashore. Service colleges—such as the Naval War College, Industrial College of the Armed Forces, National War College, and Armed Forces Staff College—play a

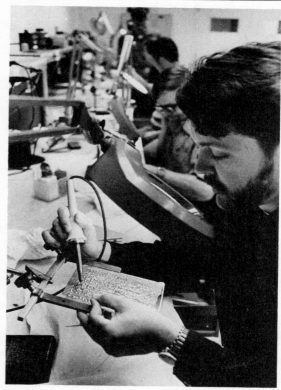

Advanced training in technical schools is offered to many enlisted ratings. Technical repair courses, such as this one in electronic circuits, train petty officers in special equipments using the latest training devices and methods. These men will truly be experts in their field when returning to the fleet for duty.

large part in the education of officers destined to attain senior rank.

Every officer must meet professional requirements for the corps or warfare specialty in which he or she was commissioned. Examples of these specialties: oceanography, meteorology, intelligence, engineering, cryptology, and public information. A growing number of officers attain their masters degrees in the Navy Postgraduate School and cooperating civilian educational institutions. The officers' educational program is wide and varied, but all facets are designed to improve service by instilling pride, professionalism, and performance.

ASSIGNMENTS

The type and location of duty to which a service member may be assigned are dependent on two things: (1) the missions and needs of the service, and (2) that member's qualifications and desires. There are certain specific requirements for most types of duty, such as: the proper rank or rating, specialty training, sufficient time left on current enlistment or tour of obligated service, past record of conduct and performance of duty, and eligibility for transfer. Service members' time overseas is determined by the type and location of duty, and whether dependents will accompany them.

LEAVE

Service members, regardless of rank or length of service, earn 30 days of paid leave or vacation each year, accrued at the rate of $2\frac{1}{2}$ days per month. During recruit training and special schooling, leaves are granted only for emergencies verified by the American Red Cross.

UNIFORMS

International law requires that military personnel wear uniforms to distinguish them from civilians. Enlisted personnel must maintain and replace uniform items from a monthly clothing allowance. Officers receive an initial monetary clothing allowance to purchase their uniforms. There are three basic classes or types of uniforms: *utility* or "working" for manual work, *service* for everyday military wear, and *dress* for formal, social, or liberty wear.

Personnel are normally required to wear appropriate uniforms while on duty. Civilian clothing is usually worn during off-duty time.

VETERANS' ASSISTANCE

Veterans who serve on active duty for at least 181 consecutive days are eligible to receive certain VA benefits while still on active duty. Probably the best known VA benefit is the Veterans' Educational Assistance Act, usually called the "G. I. Bill." Anyone entering active service since December 31, 1976 is eligible to participate in a voluntary contributory education fund. A participant makes a monthly contribution which the VA matches, 2 for 1. In 1978 a maximum contribution of $2,700 by the service person would mean a VA contribution of $5,400 or a total educational fund of $8,100. This amount can easily be attained within one 4-year enlistment.

Additional VA benefits available to qualified persons include educational monetary aid, loans (home, farm, and business), disability compensation, medical and dental care, home and life insurance, employment and reemployment aid, unemployment compensation, veterans' points for Civil Service employment, funeral expenses, and other considerations.

Chapter 1. Study Guide Questions

1. What are four particular features of Navy life which set it apart from most other professions?

2. What is the basic mission of the U. S. Armed Forces?

3. What three fundamental characteristics does the Navy want in its young men and women?

4. Why are people the most important ingredient aboard any ship or station?

5. What is the Navy's outlook on a high school education?

6. What characteristics are essential if true professionalism is to be attained by an officer?

7. What percentage of the Navy's total personnel strength is made up of officers? of enlisted people? What is the ratio of officers to enlisted personnel in today's Navy?

8. Name four national policy missions of the U. S. Navy.

9. Why must ships of the fleet be able to operate as self-sufficient communities?

10. What two basic factors make Navy life different from civilian life?

11. What is present Congressional law concerning assignment of women in the Navy?

12. How does the Navy decide who is assigned to sea duty?

13. How does "sea duty" differ from being "at sea"?

14. What do the terms "home port" and "deployment" mean?

15. What is the ultimate objective that a Navy person trains for?

16. Explain the statement "Join the Navy and see the world."

17. What is meant by a "tour of duty"?

18. When comparing Navy and civilian pay for comparable jobs, what pay factors must be considered?

19. What factors in both Navy and civilian life result in higher pay?

20. How does medical care play an important part in figuring Navy pay and benefits?

21. Do Navy people and civilians pay the same taxes? Explain.

22. How is "special pay" earned by Navy personnel? What are some ways of earning "bonus" pay?

23. How is retirement pay figured?

24. What insurance program is offered to all military personnel?

25. What are some of the educational benefits offered by the Navy today?

26. What is the purpose of professional education for officers?

27. Upon what two factors do duty assignments depend?

28. How much leave do Armed Forces personnel earn each year?

29. What are the three classes of uniforms worn by service personnel?

30. How does the G. I. Bill help the active duty person or military veteran?

Vocabulary

duty assignment	subsistence (allowance)
equal opportunity	
advancement	commissary store
professionalism	base exchange
physical stamina	retirement (pay)
national policy	disability benefit
self-sufficiency	insurance coverage
camaraderie	Navy Campus for Achievement
sea duty	
deployment	sub-specialty
tour of duty	Navy Postgraduate School
rotation of duty	
basic pay	contributory education fund
allowances	

Chapter 2: Enlisted Programs

The Navy is a large and complex organization, offering job opportunities at many different levels of responsibility. Navy recruiters have to find people capable of filling these jobs. Recruiters also have the important task of acquainting potential enlistees with the rewards and benefits of Navy life. They provide information on the wide variety of Navy education and training programs. Then they test and counsel applicants to find the right persons to fill the jobs.

To enlist in the Navy, men and women must be between 17 and 31 years of age. Consent of parents or guardian is required for 17-year-olds. They must be U. S. citizens, or immigrant aliens with immigration and naturalization forms which prove that they are legal residents. Applicants must show a birth certificate, Social Security card, and either a high school diploma or equivalent.

After preliminary processing at the recruiting station, the applicant is sent at government expense to an Armed Forces Examining and Entrance Station (AFEES) in a major city serving the recruiting area. There the applicant has a thorough physical examination and is given the Armed Services Vocational Aptitude Battery (ASVAB) Test. An applicant may also be given other special tests to determine aptitude for special programs. The ASVAB is often waived for persons who have already taken the test in high school. The Navy is anxious to match each person's desires and capabilities with the right job. This offers the best chance of success for all concerned.

Most enlistees enter active service as seamen recruits, paygrade E-1. However, some advanced paygrades (E-2 or E-3) are available to persons who, on the basis of their ASVAB, are selected for a specialty field. Advanced paygrades are available to high school students who have successfully completed the Naval Junior Reserve Officer Training Corps (NJROTC) program. An advanced grade is also available to certain vocational school graduates and to enlistees who have completed one or more years of college education.

Delayed Entry Program

The Navy allows enlistees time between signing up and reporting for active duty, to take care of previous commitments. It is especially important to the Navy that every applicant finish high school, so this is the most common reason for delayed entry agreements. It makes good sense for the future Navy person to join up five or six months prior to graduation. This ensures a smooth transition into recruit training a few weeks after graduation.

Under the delayed entry program, the new recruit can be allowed as much as a full year of delay. The exact length of delay depends upon the field the enlistee is entering. Another benefit of an early sign-up is the establishment of a "pay entry base date (PEBD)." This is the date from which longevity is determined. Longevity concerns automatic pay increases of 5 percent for each two years of service.

Basic Training

Before recruits can begin learning about a special occupational field, they must receive basic or recruit training. This process gives young men and women the fundamental knowledge and physical conditioning necessary for effective military service. The recruits learn about the heritage and traditions of the Navy, how it operates, and how each individual and job fits into the overall mission of a unit. In basic training, recruits learn the importance of doing the job assigned, on time, within the Navy environment. They must learn to be ready for combat or emergencies. Basic training teaches Navy men and women to carry out their responsibilities under conditions of stress.

The Navy provides seven weeks of basic training, usually called "boot camp," with a full schedule of military and technical training. Male trainees go to one of three sites: Great Lakes, Illinois; San Diego, California; or Orlando, Florida. All women report to Orlando. Enlistees may request a certain training site, but usually they are sent to the training base nearest their homes.

Instruction will cover military topics, administration, and processing; but one-third of the course is devoted to technical subjects such as seamanship, survival at sea, ship structure, damage control, and fire-fighting instruction. Classes also cover service regulations, handling and care of weapons, rules of conduct, military courtesy, proper care and wear of uniforms, drill ceremonies, military justice, hygiene, first aid, and personal services available to the Navy person. Classroom work is mixed with practical experience.

Physical fitness and stamina are developed and maintained through daily calisthenics, competitive sports, and marching drills. Tests are used to measure the degree of physical fitness each trainee has attained. Careful medical examinations and required innoculations are also administered.

The Navy organizes each recruit company from a group of about 80 enlistees. These persons train together and learn teamwork, under a company commander who is a top senior petty officer. Selected recruits are appointed to leadership positions within their units and perform under the supervision of these instructors.

NAVY EDUCATION AND SCHOOLING

In today's Navy, people can go as far as their ability and initiative will take them. Upon completion of recruit training, many will proceed to Class "A" schools for training in specific job skills. Others will be ordered to the fleet for duty and on-the-job training, after a short apprenticeship course. The Class "A" schools begin shortly after the 10- to 14-day leave following boot camp.

The Class "A" school is a top school in a particular rating specialty; these schools are

Class "A" schooling provides training in specific job skills. This is a class in an engineering rating.

located all over the country. With the "quals" and ambition, the Navy person can enter the more demanding and rewarding training programs, like advanced electronics, advanced technical fields, or nuclear propulsion. Navy training in radar, electronics, and computers is unequaled in the civilian community. In fact, most of the nuclear propulsion technicians in the nation received their initial training in the Navy.

Special training is also necessary for submarine programs and other undersea operations. Persons who enter the advanced training areas must have a sound background in mathematics and sciences. These programs call for a lot of serious studying, for as much as two years.

Qualified candidates in the advanced training areas will start ahead of their contemporaries in pay and rating. They also can advance more rapidly during their service careers. But they have an added obligation, because of the extra training and immediate personal benefits they receive. Candidates must agree to extend their enlistments to six years upon acceptance of their third-class petty officer rate when they finish Class "A" schooling. These new advanced skills are of great importance to the Navy during the member's term of service, and will be very helpful to the member later—either in the Navy or in a civilian career.

ENLISTED ADVANCEMENT IN THE NAVY

Navy advancement in a rating specialty is based on an individual's performance of duty, competitive Navy-wide examination marks, recommendations of supervisors based on ability to do the job, length of service, and time in present level of work. Because there are so many factors involved, it is not possible to determine exactly when an advancement will occur.

Typically, however, a recruit will be advanced to apprentice after six months of service; then, after the requirements are fulfilled, to paygrade E-3 (seaman, fireman, construc-

Navy personnel with the qualifications and ambition can enter the demanding and rewarding Advanced Electronics Field Program.

tionman, airman, hospitalman, or dentalman); then, within the next 18 months, on to petty officer third class. Thereafter, the recruit's performance and other factors will determine advancements up to chief petty officer in from 10 to 14 years. Advancement may be accelerated if the enlistee has entered the service via NJROTC or the special advanced technical programs. For advancement to the senior enlisted paygrades (chief, senior chief, and master chief—E-7 through E-9), individual records must be reviewed. The advancement is approved by a selection board on a competitive basis, in accordance with the number of vacancies in each field.

NAVY RATINGS AND CAREER FIELDS

The U. S. Navy currently has nearly 70 career rating specialties available to enlisted personnel. There is something for virtually everyone in the Navy's wide variety of specialties.

It is impractical to discuss here the duties, requirements, training, and job opportunities in each of these ratings. However, every year the Naval Recruiting Command publishes a *Navy Career Guide* which discusses the opportunities in each Navy rating. Naval science instructors and all Navy Recruiting offices have this document available.

The *Career Guide* groups the Navy's ratings according to the clustering system used by the Occupational Outlook Handbook published by the U. S. Department of Labor Statistics. The occupational groupings are as follows:

Clerical and Administrative Occupations
Communications Occupations
Construction Occupations
Data Processing Occupations
Health Occupations
Manufacturing Occupations
Mechanical and Repair Occupations
Scientific and Technical Occupations
Service Occupations
Social Science Occupations
Transportation Field Occupations

This same guidebook lists civilian occupations which are related to one or more Navy occupation. It is extremely helpful to those who are interested in furthering their careers through the Navy's enlisted service and training program.

Chapter 2. *Study Guide Questions*

1. What are the two principal tasks of a Navy recruiter?

2. What three documents must every applicant show the recruiter prior to enlistment?

3. What takes place at the AFEES?

4. What is the purpose of the Armed Forces Vocational Aptitude Battery test? Where is this test administered most often today? Who may enlist in the Navy at paygrades higher than E-1? What is the purpose of the delayed entry program?

5. What is meant by the term "pay entry base date"? How does longevity affect basic

pay? How does the delayed entry program benefit the individual's base pay?

6. What are the main goals of recruit training?

7. What are some of the technical subjects taught in recruit training?

8. What is a Class "A" school?

9. In what field is Navy technical training considered superior to similar civilian instruction?

10. What are the advantages of qualifying for advanced special technical training?

11. What are the principal factors determining advancement in a rating specialty?

12. What are the six recruit categories from which enlisted personnel advance to petty officer?

13. How does the *Navy Career Guide* assist individuals planning their future?

Vocabulary

enlistment	boot camp
ASVAB	recruit company
aptitude	competitive Navy-
delayed entry pro-	wide examination
gram	accelerated advance-
PEBD	ment
Class "A" school	contemporaries
longevity	recruit categories
recruit	career option

Chapter 3. Officer Programs

Why does an outstanding young man or woman aspire to become a naval officer? There is no single answer, of course. Many different factors may motivate an individual to make this decision. Among these factors are patriotism, the desire to serve, and a special dedication to the Navy and the nation.

The young officer will need character, personality, and maturity to master the art of leadership and the complexities of the sea. An officer has a deep sense of responsibility, for it is the officer who is accountable for action taken in difficult situations. The officer corps must lead Navy enlisted personnel effectively, to accomplish the tasks assigned to the Navy by national leaders.

Professional knowledge and competence—gained in college, in the Navy's officer training schools, and in the fleet—will provide the foundation for a commission.

Maybe you think that all a naval officer does is fight heroic battles. But the real Navy is a lot more complex and diverse than the stirring words spoken in the heat of combat. Our large, modern Navy is like many businesses and industries rolled into one. If you make a list of every kind of leadership position you can think of in the civilian world—executive, managerial, professional, scientific, and technical— you can usually find a comparable occupation for a naval officer.

In general, naval officer occupations fall into two major categories: (1) Operations and Management, which includes every kind of executive and managerial position, at sea and ashore; (2) Scientific and Technical, which includes all areas of professional expertise: physicians, engineers, mathematicians, lawyers, comptrollers, supply specialists, and nurses.

Officer occupations are divided into "unrestricted line," "restricted line," and "staff corps" designations. The unrestricted line officers are trained to command the operating forces—ships, submarines, aircraft squadrons, and operational staffs and fleets—that carry out the Navy's mission. Restricted line officers perform specialized duties in technical fields such as ship engineering, meteorology, intelligence, and oceanography. Staff corps officers have specialized duties in a professional corps, such as the Supply, Civil Engineering, Judge Advocate General (Law), Medical, Dental or Chaplain Corps.

The basic requirement for a commission

today is a college degree. Commissioned officers in the armed forces come from several training sources—the U. S. Service Academies, Reserve Officers' Training Corps programs, Marine Platoon Leaders' Classes, and Flight Training Programs. We will talk principally about the Naval Academy and the Naval Reserve Officer Training Corps programs in this text.

The Naval Academy

The Naval Academy in Annapolis, Maryland offers a full four-year scholarship leading to a commission in the Navy or Marine Corps. In return for the scholarship, the individual agrees to give five years of service to the nation. There is no obligation beyond those five years of service, but a midshipman is expected to seriously consider naval service as a career when applying for entry. Dedication to the idea of service to country must be high among reasons for coming to Annapolis if one hopes to take a place in the entering class.

A candidate for the Naval Academy must be nominated for an appointment as a midshipman. Most candidates receive nominations from members of the U. S. Congress. Other sources include Presidential nominations (available to children of career military members), and nominations by regular and reserve military units, honor military and naval schools, ROTC, JROTC, and various categories from other governmental units. Children of deceased or disabled veterans are also eligible for nomination.

Appointments are awarded to the best qualified applicants. This decision is based on the candidate's entire scholastic record, performance in physical aptitude tests, and record of extracurricular activities, including athletics, leadership potential, and medical examination.

Congressional members determine their nominees on their own competitive scale, then list their selectees in order of preference—a principal nomination and up to nine alter-

All service academies are now open to qualified young women. These plebes learn the manual of arms during their first summer indoctrination session.

nates. Congressional nominees must meet all Academy qualification standards prior to appointment, just as do nominees from all other sources.

Procedures for Nomination

Applications for Congressional nominations should be made during January or February of the junior year in high school. Candidates should send letters to their local U. S. representative and the two U. S. senators from their state. They also should request a pre-candidate questionnaire from the Naval Academy in order to start their admission file there.

Second or third-year NJROTC cadets will have made sufficient progress within their unit for the naval science instructor to have determined their eligibility. The instructor will advise any candidates about the Academy's scholarship program, and will ensure that qualified, genuinely interested individuals take all necessary administrative steps toward nomination. The Academy provides the naval science instructor with separate pre-candidate forms for the NJROTC cadet to fill out. The NSI will also send a detailed recommendation to the Academy Admissions Review Board.

ELIGIBILITY

In order to be eligible for admission to the Naval Academy, an applicant must be at least 17 but not more than 22 before 1 July of the year of entrance. The applicant must be a citizen of the United States, of good moral character, and able to meet the academic, physical, and medical requirements. Applicants must not be married, and if appointed, may not marry while in attendance at the Academy.

The overall academic and physical preparation of a candidate is of vital importance at the Academy. This is called the whole-person concept of qualification. An above-average academic record in high school is absolutely necessary. Also, active participation in athletics, student government, school publications, debate, music, clubs, and scouting is very important. Some part-time work in the business world and in the management of funds is also encouraged. But this should not be at the expense of academics and extracurricular activities. Selection to attend Boys' State, Boys' Nation, or the Presidential Classroom for Young Americans, awards in state or national essay contests, and awards by civic and veterans' organizations are constructive experiences.

Being a cadet officer in an NJROTC unit is an outstanding indicator of leadership potential. Participation in varsity athletics is indicative of physical fitness and leadership ability in teamwork and stress conditions.

About 75 percent of the candidates receiving appointments are in the top 20 percent of their high school classes. Candidates are urged to have the following subjects in their high school curriculum: math (4 years), English (4 years), modern language (2 years), chemistry (1 year), and physics (1 year).

A candidate's academic qualification for admission to the Academy is determined by results on the Scholastic Aptitude Test (SAT) or the American College Testing (ACT) program, and by the candidate's high school grades. In a recent year the new class entering the Academy had average SAT scores of 644 (math) and 558 (verbal); the same class averaged 30 (math) and 23 (English) in the ACT. Because the Academy uses only the highest scores attained by a candidate, it may be a good idea to take the test more than once. Some prospective applicants take the tests first during the early spring of their junior year. They then schedule to take the tests again, either in early June or in October, trying to improve their scores.

Applicants must pass a very thorough medical examination to ensure that they possess the physical and mental fitness necessary for the rigorous Academy program and service life. All medical examinations are scheduled by the Department of Defense Medical Examination Review Board in Colorado Springs, Colorado. The examination itself may be given at any military medical facility near the candidate's home. Only one medical examination is necessary, regardless of the number of applications made to academies or for ROTC scholarships.

Eyesight deficiencies are the most common cause for disqualification of candidates who otherwise would meet high medical standards. All of the sea services—Navy, Coast Guard, and Merchant Marine—require 20/20 vision, as does the Air Force pilot program. Outstanding candidates with minor variances from perfect eyesight can still be appointed on medical waiver, if their vision is correctable to 20/20.

Naval Academy Program

Leadership, scholarship, fellowship; this is the Naval Academy. A sound college education is the foundation of every profession in American society today. The naval profession is no exception. The Academy is dedicated to providing a sound education for its students. The growing complexity of the Navy has required that undergraduate education at the Academy be broadened beyond the normal professional naval subjects. The Academy curriculum includes over 20 additional areas—from engineering, oceanography, and mathematics to history, economics, and political science. The needs of the Navy require that at

Midshipmen at the U. S. Naval Academy learn to handle the Academy's patrol craft in Chesapeake Bay.

least 80 percent of the midshipmen in each class have engineering, scientific, or math majors. Upon graduation, a newly commissioned ensign will hold a Bachelor of Science degree and will be ready to serve as a line officer in any of the principal naval specialties.

The Naval Academy does much more than simply offer midshipmen a sound college education. The program includes military training, physical training, and instruction in the goals of the naval profession. The purpose of the overall program at Annapolis is to produce self-confident leaders who accept responsibility and are fully ready to carry out their duties.

The ultimate objective of the leadership training that begins at Annapolis is to produce officers who can command—professional officers who are physically strong, intelligent, and knowledgable. Officers must show unflinching honesty and forthrightness, with a commitment to high standards of honor, duty, and responsibility. They must relish a challenge and thrive on accomplishment.

The four years at Annapolis are not easy ones. The challenge is total, mental and physical. The plebe year, the first year, is especially tough. Thereafter, the Academy regulations are not as severe. But an upperclassman has more responsibility in running the Brigade of Midshipmen and other activities. Two of four summers will be taken up by cruises to foreign ports in ships of the Navy. There's a balance between practical work at sea and academic work, between training and education, that is at the heart of the Academy program. By graduation, midshipmen have developed their scholastic knowledge, physical conditioning, and leadership ability to the greatest possible extent. Few achievements are so satisfying.

Naval Reserve Officer Training Corps (NROTC)

Naval ROTC trains college students to become naval officers while they are earning their degrees. The various NROTC programs

The Staff of the Brigade of Midshipmen, U. S. Naval Academy, pass in review in a dress parade. Such new young officers must develop the highest standards of honor, duty, and responsibility.

are the largest single source of newly commissioned officers entering the Navy each year. Because the Navy needs technically trained officers, it prefers degrees in engineering, physics, math, and chemistry. But many other course majors are acceptable. Those majoring in these other fields must earn some credits in calculus and physics. NROTC students must complete their course work in naval science prior to graduation. NJROTC cadets who enter the college-level NROTC may have up to one year of college naval science waived if they have successfully completed three years of NJROTC.

NROTC programs have been established in about 60 leading universities and colleges across the United States. The program includes four years of naval science subjects, in addition to the curriculum for a college major.

There are two scholarship programs. The first is a four-year scholarship which pays full tuition, books, fees, uniforms, and a monthly cash allowance for the entire 40-month educational period, including summer cruises. In addition to regular classes, the scholarship student attends scheduled campus drills while earning the bachelor's degree. Upon graduation the midshipman is commissioned as an ensign in the Navy, and serves for four years on active duty.

A two-year scholarship program is particularly geared toward men and women majoring

Naval Reserve Officer Training Corps midshipmen join their Naval Academy brethren during summer cruises. This midshipman looks at the submarine which will be his laboratory for learning during part of his summer cruise.

in math, science, or engineering. Selected applicants attend a naval science course in the summer preceding their junior year at the Naval Science Institute in Newport, Rhode Island. In order to become eligible for the two-year program, qualified sophomores must meet all requirements for entrance into NROTC, including the physical examination and several aptitude tests which will be used by a selection board. Successful completion of the Naval Science Institute course qualifies the student for appointment as a NROTC midshipman for the final two years of college. The student receives the same pay and allowances as do those in the regular four-year program. Students who complete all the requirements for the two-year program are commissioned as ensigns in the Navy and have a four-year active duty obligation.

NROTC students are selected on the basis of their college aptitude tests, and other documents in the applicant's file. Those who qualify on either the SAT or ACT are given the same thorough medical examination as for an Academy scholarship. Selectees are offered appointments as midshipmen and are simultaneously enlisted in the Naval Reserve. Appointees may indicate their choices as to which colleges they prefer and are willing to attend. The Navy then nominates them to those colleges. Admission must be accomplished by the individual through the regular application procedures of the college.

There also are two- and four-year NROTC College Programs leading to a commission in the Naval Reserve upon graduation. There is no scholarship assistance in these programs, but qualified students receive a monthly cash allowance during their junior and senior years of college. They may apply for transfer to full NROTC scholarship status as freshmen or sophomores, if their performance is outstanding. Anyone interested in the four-year college program should apply to the professor of Naval Science upon enrolling at a college hosting an NROTC unit. Applicants for the two-year program should apply during their sophomore year. Selection for a college program is on the basis of personal interviews, school and community reputation, scholastic record, and results of an aptitude test, as well as the recommendation of the professor of Naval Science at the participating college.

Many other variations of these programs exist for the qualified student with initiative and desire for a commission. Among these are various Nuclear Propulsion Candidate Scholarships and a number of Naval Aviation Officer programs. Brochures and other information on these programs are available from Recruiting District offices, professors of Naval Science at participating colleges, and NJROTC naval science instructors.

Officer Candidate School (OCS)

The Navy's Officer Candidate School, located at Newport, Rhode Island, provides a concentrated program of about 16 weeks that trains recent college graduates to become naval officers. It is an intensive program, focusing on the study of naval science and management. Candidates who successfully complete the course will graduate with the gold bars of an ensign in the line of the Naval Reserve.

Qualified young men and women may apply for OCS after successful completion of their junior year in college. This will allow them to begin the program shortly after graduation. It is necessary to apply well in advance of graduation because openings are limited and the quotas are filled quickly each year. The active duty obligation is for three or four years,

depending upon the specialty in which the officer is commissioned.

Chapter 3. Study Guide Questions

1. What factors may motivate an individual to seek an officer's commission?

2. What qualities must officers possess in today's Navy?

3. What is the basic requirement for a commission?

4. Into what two major categories do naval officers' occupations fall?

5. What are the three different designations into which officers' occupations are divided? What does each grouping do, in general?

6. What is the most basic preparatory requirement for a commission today?

7. What are the principal sources of newly commissioned officers for the U. S. Armed Forces?

8. What is the mission of the U. S. Naval Academy?

9. What service obligation is incurred with an Academy scholarship?

10. What must any candidate obtain in order to be considered for an appointment to the Academy?

11. What is the difference between a nomination and an appointment to the Academy?

12. From what source do most candidates receive Academy nominations? How are these nominees selected?

13. What important factors are considered when selecting candidates for appointments to the Academy?

14. How does the naval science instructor select NJROTC nominees and how does he help them obtain an appointment?

15. What is the whole-person concept of determining qualifications of a candidate for appointment? Why should this concept serve to select excellent persons for appointment?

16. What is the function of the SAT and ACT?

17. Why are all candidates required to pass

a thorough physical examination for scholarship programs?

18. What is the most common cause for medical disqualification among scholarship candidates?

19. What educational degree is awarded the graduating midshipman from Annapolis? In what officer rank is the graduating midshipman commissioned?

20. What is the ultimate objective of the leadership training at Annapolis?

21. How would you characterize the total program at Annapolis? How does the disciplinary, academic, and activity approach change during the course of the four-year program?

22. What is the purpose of the various NROTC programs? What courses of study are emphasized? From what commissioning source are the largest number of new officers obtained each year?

23. What does the four-year NROTC scholarship program provide the midshipman? How does the two-year program differ? What rank is attained upon graduation in these programs?

24. What is the NROTC College Program? How are applicants selected for the college programs?

25. Who is eligible to attend the Navy's Officer Candidate School? Where is the school located? How long does OCS instruction last?

Vocabulary

commission
character
maturity
competence
unrestricted line
restricted line
staff corps
scholastic record
physical aptitude
leadership potential
pre-candidate questionnaire
admission file
supersonic jet

U. S. Naval Academy
academic scholarship
nomination (Academy)
appointment
whole-person concept
medical waiver
Brigade of Midshipmen
tuition
bachelor's degree
NROTC
OCS

3

Naval History:
Global War at Sea

Chapter 1. Movement Toward
World War II (Part I)

Prussian General Karl von Clausewitz, one of history's great philosophers on the subject of war, called it "the continuance of politics by other means." War is by no means just that, nor can it be defined by any single phrase, such as "hostilities between nations." War includes both these definitions, and many others. In a study of World War II, however, it is necessary to look at the political events which occurred in the years between the close of World War I in 1918 and the beginning of World War II in 1939. Such a study would indeed lend much weight to von Clausewitz's definition. As you will see, World War II grew out of a progressive series of treaties, negotiations, and economic actions between nations. It was, in a sense, a "continuance of politics."

The study of history has one practical purpose: to learn from mankind's previous errors in order to ensure that these mistakes will not be repeated again. If men and governments could learn and apply the lessons of history, the world would not find itself so often on the brink of disastrous crises. Historians well know the factors that have led nations into wars and economic catastrophies. They can point to mistakes in philosophy and action which have propelled countries into war, again and again. When the people in governments are unaware

of history, they are condemned to repeat it, thus bringing their nations into ever more destructive wars.

Educated citizens in a democracy must understand their nation's history so the past's errors are not repeated. The NJROTC has as its foremost objective the training and development of leaders and citizens who will be able to make the intelligent decisions required of America in the future. Learning about the nation's history—and that includes its errors—should make every new generation of citizens and leaders stronger than the generation before.

Washington Disarmament Treaties

The armistice which stopped the fighting of World War I came at the eleventh hour on the eleventh day of the eleventh month in 1918. After the war was over, the victorious Allies conferred at Versailles. They imposed their demands on a defeated Germany the following June. This war had been called "war to end all wars." But it was not long before the economic and political problems of the day forced a "reassessment" of America's defense needs.

The headlong rush "back to normalcy" had quickly made itself felt across the United States. Congress rejected United States membership in the League of Nations, as isolationism gained in favor. Naval building projects were vetoed as the country listened to the demands of pacifists to cut military spending. In 1921 came a business recession, felt not only in the United States but in other major industrial nations. It seemed to President Harding that it was time for the Allies to come to an agreement on arms limitations.

Britain, France, Italy, and Japan were invited to send representatives to a conference in Washington on naval armament. The United States astounded the conferees with sweeping proposals to drastically reduce the standing navies of each of the major naval powers. Among other things, the United States, Britain, and Japan would agree to a 5:5:3 ratio in battleship tonnage. After several weeks of negotiations the Naval Disarmament Treaty was signed. This limited the total tonnage of capital ships—battleships and carriers—and placed limitations on the tonnage and armament of these ships and cruisers. It was this treaty that limited battleships to nine 16-inch guns and cruisers to 8-inch guns. No limitations on total tonnage of cruisers were included, however.

Other treaties were concluded in which:

1) The United States agreed not to fortify Pacific bases west of Hawaii;

2) The British agreed not to strengthen bases north of Australia or east of Singapore;

3) The territorial integrity of China was "guaranteed." All of these provisions were designed to placate the Japanese, who felt that the treaty relegated them to a third-rate naval status.

There were, of course, some who voiced opposition to these treaties. The United States would not remain the strongest naval power in the world if it adhered to the agreements. An economy-minded country could not be persuaded otherwise, however. As might have been expected, all countries except the United States almost immediately embarked on a major heavy-cruiser building program. It was not long before U. S. intelligence sources determined that both Japan and Italy were exceeding the 10,000-ton size limitation. The

Japanese proceeded to fortify major island bases in the Pacific, now that they knew Britain and the United States would do nothing to contest such construction.

Additional treaties were signed on several occasions in the succeeding years, but none really accomplished anything. Presidents Coolidge and Hoover, faced by the aggressive building programs of the Europeans and Japan, reluctantly put construction bills before Congress. Sometimes, however, they suspended usage of funds that had been authorized for naval building. At other times the pacifists, isolationists, and taxpayers' groups raised such protests that Congress reduced the programs to virtually nothing. The United States, trusting in the Kellogg–Briand Pact of 1924 which "outlawed war," seemed to believe that other countries would abide by the treaties, or would stop their building programs, if the United States "set a good example" by not building!

Such an assumption was naive, as history was soon to prove. Indeed, the most amazing fact of diplomatic and military history is that many countries, including the United States, have repeatedly made the same kind of decisions concerning military preparedness. This, in spite of a world history which conclusively has proven that it is (1) impossible to negotiate successfully from a position of relative military weakness, and (2) that there is no such thing as a perpetual power vacuum in any part of the globe; some stronger nation will move into that "vacuum" as quickly as they are able to do so.

RISE OF DICTATORSHIPS

Wavering economies in much of the world, including the United States, had characterized the 1920s. Periods of recession and labor unrest alternated with almost dizzying heights of prosperity. Europe's precarious economy collapsed because of widespread inflation, first in Germany, and then quickly spreading into the other major nations. Revolution swept across

Russia and riots and strikes erupted throughout Europe. Finally, in 1929 the U. S. stock market collapsed. The great world depression was on.

In this climate of worldwide despair, anyone with a radical panacea to end the depression—and a voice loud enough to speak out—could move crowds of disillusioned people to follow. Benito Mussolini had come into power in Italy in 1922, reawakening the grandeur of ancient Rome in the eyes of his followers. He inspired Italian workers to build up the country's military might, so that he could reestablish Rome as the center of Mediterranean power. At the same time, Adolph Hitler, playing on the theme of German superiority, founded the Nazi Party in Germany; by 1932 the Party dominated the German government. When unrest swept Berlin in 1933, Hitler was named Chancellor.

During the early 1920s Japanese moderates were fairly successful in keeping the militarists out of political control. However, in 1924 the U. S. Congress passed an immigration bill classing the Japanese as undesirable Orientals. The bill prohibited them from entering the United States under any circumstances. The militarists were now able to arouse national resentment against the United States, and political support for themselves. Once in control, the militarists selectively assassinated their political opposition and began to build up the Imperial Armed Forces.

By the time the early 1930s arrived, the military dictatorships in Italy, Germany, and Japan sought to regain prosperity for their peoples by conquering their neighbors. The democracies—Britain, France, and the United States—refused to take effective countermeasures against these aggressive acts. This lack of military preparedness helped bring on World War II.

By 1931 the Japanese leaders felt themselves sufficiently strong to invade China from their Korean bases. The United States and Britain protested the move as a violation of the Wash-

ington Treaty, but did nothing. A protest by the League of Nations did nothing to stop Japan's three-month conquest of Manchuria. Japan went her own way, and simply withdrew from the League. The militarists recognized that they had achieved the naval superiority to do whatever they wished in the Western Pacific. And they had; the treaties had ensured that they would.

In 1935 Hitler withdrew Germany from the League and denounced all treaty limitations imposed on German armaments and military service. The Italians invaded Ethiopia, annexing that country in 1936 as Italian East Africa. When the League denounced the act as "bald aggression" and imposed some economic sanctions, Italy purchased war supplies from Germany, withdrew from the League, and with Germany formed the Rome–Berlin Axis.

THE U. S. NAVY IN THE PRE-WAR YEARS

Weak presidents, politically motivated Congressmen, and loud-speaking isolationists and pacifists did much to weaken the United States' military position during this period. But there also were military leaders and Congressmen who managed to keep the best interests of the nation in mind.

Because of additional treaties and insufficient funds, the Navy's plans for equality in fleet size were thwarted. Thus, strategists devoted their time to the development of new weapons systems and operational doctrines. Funds from the meager allocations were used to develop naval aviation, amphibious warfare, and overall logistics doctrine. The methods worked out in these areas during the 1920s and 1930s provided the margin of victory in World War II.

After the Washington Treaties, Navy strategists changed their planning. Their new operational plans envisioned the necessity of making a comeback from an initial loss of bases in the Philippines and Guam. They saw that the Navy would probably have to fight its way back across the Pacific, operating for long periods far from permanent bases, while seizing and converting enemy bases. The Navy faced a threefold problem: (1) how to free the fleet from dependence on established bases, (2) how to isolate and attack enemy bases protected by land-based air units, and (3) how to invade and occupy heavily defended enemy bases.

The Marines took on the task of working out number 3. From this effort came the amphibious doctrine which was put into effect in World War II. Amphibious exercises emphasized the concepts of command and control, close air support, naval gunfire support, patrol tactics, and the development of new amphibian vehicles and landing craft. This amphibious capability, when expanded to meet the needs of the war, proved to be an irresistible assault force. Many historians regard these amphibious tactics as the most far-reaching tactical innovations of the war.

During the same time, naval aircraft and aircraft carriers came into use on a sophisticated scale. Naval aviation was originally looked upon as merely a reconnaissance arm of the fleet. But this all changed in 1921 when General Billy Mitchell proved that an airplane could sink a battleship with bombs. Mitchell's feat finally convinced tactical planners to convert a collier into the Navy's first aircraft carrier, the *Langley,* and to get the treaty powers to consent to the United States' building the carriers *Lexington* and *Saratoga.*

Along with the carrier, of course, came a continuous parade of improved airplanes, used for an increasing number of purposes: reconnaissance, dive-bombing, fighter patrol, and attack (including torpedo bombing). The techniques of dive-bombing worked out during this time proved to be decisive in the major Pacific air–sea battles. Even though exercises had proven that the carrier could be used as an attack vessel, fleet doctrine still dictated that its aircraft be used mainly for reconnaissance.

Finally, with carriers, their aircraft, and

An aircraft takes off from the *Langley,* the U. S. Navy's first aircraft carrier.

amphibious forces working far from established home bases, a logistic support system had to be devised which would keep these forces in operation. First there was the problem of mobile fuel and supply support. This problem was solved by the highly versatile underway replenishment operation, in which support ships moved with the fleet. This innovation is sometimes regarded as "the secret weapon" which won the Pacific war.

When a Marine amphibious force captured new areas from the enemy, new Allied bases on that captured territory would have to be built rapidly. For this task the Naval Construction Battalions (NCBs) were developed. The "Sea-Bees" were trained to create operating bases out of any environment, from jungle to atoll. These bases included all the materials and personnel needed to set up various kinds of facilities. Depending upon the needs of the area commander, the bases could be delivered and assembled as soon as the land was cleared. Shortly thereafter the base would be in full operation.

The Final Steps Toward War

By 1936 the League of Nations was little more than a squabbling group, neither able nor willing to halt the inevitable drift toward world war. The aggressive dictatorships had withdrawn their memberships. In 1936 Germany remilitarized the Rhineland, in defiance of the Versailles Treaty. In 1937 Japan launched a full-scale invasion of China, quickly conquering most of the eastern half of the country. During these Chinese operations Japan repeatedly bombed U. S. missions, schools, churches, and hospitals, and even sank the U. S. Navy gunboat *Panay*. The United States limited its response to verbal and written protests. In 1938 Hitler invaded Austria; betrayed by traitors from within, that nation became a province of Germany.

British Prime Minister Neville Chamberlain now decided that the only way to avert war was to come to some agreement with Italy and Germany. He launched what has become known as a policy of "appeasement," wherein Britain and France would make a series of concessions to Hitler and Mussolini in return for "promises of peace." In one of these deals Britain persuaded the League to recognize the Italian conquest of Ethiopia, an act which effectively destroyed the League. Next, Britain and France agreed to the dismemberment and annexation of Czechoslovakia by Germany.

But when Hitler's next demand was for the Free City of Danzig and a large segment of western Poland, Britain and France finally drew the line, abandoned the policy of appeasement, and aligning themselves with Poland. Russia, which had been angered by the Allied sellout on Czechoslovakia, now signed a non-aggression pact with Germany. Hitler was thus free of the Soviet threat from the east. On 1 September 1939 his armies invaded Poland in a massive offensive. Britain and France declared war on Germany two days later. World War II had begun.

Chapter 1. Study Guide Questions

1. What are two simple definitions of "war?"

2. What is one practical purpose of the study of history?

3. In a democracy, what should be the result if its citizens and leaders know and understand their nation's history?

4. What is isolationism? How did this philosophy affect the United States' relationship to the League of Nations?

5. What were the five major naval powers invited to the Naval Disarmament talks in Washington in 1921? What did the 5:5:3 ratio agreement mean?

6. What were the significant concessions made to Japan in return for her signing of the 5:5:3 agreement?

7. How did the various nations which signed the Naval Disarmament Treaty live up to their agreement?

8. What two facts has history proven about the relationship between international negotiations and military preparedness?

9. How did the world's economic problems of the 1920s allow the military dictatorships to rise in Europe?

10. How did the militarists gain control of the Japanese government in 1924?

11. What factor really enabled the dictatorships to drag the world into World War II?

12. Why were the Japanese able to proceed with their conquest of Chinese Manchuria without opposition?

13. What was the Rome–Berlin Axis?

14. What three broad areas of military doctrine and tactics did U. S. naval strategists concentrate on in the 1920s and 1930s?

15. In the Pacific what particular problems did the Navy and Marines have to solve?

16. What did Billy Mitchell's test sinking of a battleship by aerial bombing cause Navy planners to do?

17. Why was development of a mobile logistic system so important to the naval strategy in the Pacific?

18. Who are the Seabees and what is their task?

19. What was the British "policy of appeasement" with Germany and Italy? Did it work?

20. What was the act which finally caused Britain and France to declare war on Germany?

Vocabulary

negotiations
armaments
Rome–Berlin Axis
League of Nations
isolationism
disarmament
territorial integrity
pacifist
power vacuum
appropriations
parity
doctrine
tactics
reconnaissance
depression
business recession
inflation
Japanese militarists
dictatorship
flexibility
versatile
NCB, "Seabees"
appeasement
annexation

Chapter 2. Movement Toward World War II (Part II)

The United States had retreated into isolationism when the Washington Disarmament Treaties began to collapse. In 1935 the Congress passed laws forbidding the sale or delivery of munitions to belligerent nations. Loans to belligerents were forbidden in 1936. In 1937 the Congress passed the "Cash-and-Carry" Act; this required that all sales to belligerents be paid for in cash before export, and then carried away in foreign-flag ships. America appeared to retreat from the seas in order to avoid being challenged on the seas.

When the Europeans declared war on each other, President Roosevelt established a Neutrality Patrol which had as its task the reporting and tracking of belligerent ships and aircraft approaching the United States or the West Indies. Actually, President Roosevelt regarded the Neutrality Patrol as a means of preparing for the war he saw coming. The Patrol enabled him to refit some ships, and recall reserves to active duty for training and assignment at sea.

The American people were certainly opposed to the totalitarian moves of the Axis powers and Japan, even though they wanted to stay out of the war. As the Nazi blitzkrieg (lightning war) rolled over Poland and conquered Belgium, Holland, Luxembourg, Norway, Denmark, and France—all by June of 1940—President Roosevelt began to see the defeat of Britain as a possibility. He asked for assurances that the British Fleet would not be turned over to Hitler in that event. Prime Minister Churchill replied that he could not guarantee this since he probably wouldn't be Prime Minister following a British defeat.

Faced then with the potential loss of the Royal Navy as the first line of American defense, Congress finally recognized the necessity of expanding the U. S. Navy as Roosevelt had requested. They passed the Two-Ocean Navy Bill, authorizing the President to build for each ocean a fleet sufficient to meet America's defense needs.

Things started to move faster for the United States now. In September of 1940 Roosevelt concluded a deal with Churchill in which Britain gave the United States bases in the West Indies, Newfoundland, and Bermuda. In return, Britain received 50 old destroyers and 10 Coast Guard cutters. In March of the following year, the famous Lend-Lease Act was passed, enabling the United States to "loan" war materials to Britain. This put U. S. industry on a wartime production level, because, as Roosevelt declared, we had became the "arsenal of democracy." The United States later seized Axis ships in American ports, froze German and Italian assets in the United States, occupied Greenland, and took over the defense of Iceland from Britain.

In 1941 high-ranking American and British

officers met secretly in Washington and drew up what was called the ABC-1 Staff Agreement. This agreement, in effect, put the U. S. Navy in the war, since the Navy would be sharing escort duties for transatlantic convoys to Britain. The agreement also called for American and British chiefs of staff, in order to make strategic plans. A key decision to come out of the meeting was that the United States would make its principal military effort in the European theater, even if Japan made war on America. This decision was made because of Germany's greater military potential and because of the immediate danger then faced by Britain.

In the meantime, the situation in the Pacific had also deteriorated. When France fell in 1940 the Japanese quickly declared a protectorate over Indochina, taking control of the valuable rice crop and occupying the air and naval bases there. They also informed the Dutch authorities in the East Indies that the oil resources on those islands would henceforth be developed "jointly" with them. It was clear that the Japanese were out to dominate the East Indies and its mineral resources.

In reaction to this aggressive behavior, President Roosevelt immediately placed an embargo on the sale of aviation gasoline and scrap iron to Japan. Steel was added to the embargo two months later.

The next step—an embargo on oil—was sure

Pearl Harbor, Hawaii, before the Japanese attack of 7 December 1941. Ford Island lies in the center of the harbor. Hickam Field is off toward the upper left on the main shore. Battleship row lies along the left side of Ford Island.

to be the next United States move. It came in July of 1941, along with a freeze on all Japanese assets in the United States. Thus the Japanese could no longer pay in cash for Dutch East Indies oil. War was now inevitable. Japanese militarists would accept nothing less than full cooperation in their effort to conquer China—and America would not give it to them.

Though earlier exchanges had taken place between German submarines and U. S. naval escorts, it was not until 16 October 1941 that the first casualties were sustained by the two undeclared enemies. On that date a U. S. destroyer was damaged by a torpedo, with the loss of eleven men. In early November a naval tanker and the destroyer USS *Reuben James* were sunk with heavy losses. That caused Congress to remove the last feature of the U. S. neutrality policy. American merchant ships were now armed and authorized to carry lend–lease goods directly to Britain.

However, it remained for the Japanese to bring the United States into the war totally. On 7 December 1941 the Japanese launched a carefully planned surprise carrier attack on Pearl Harbor, Hawaii. The following day Congress declared war on Japan. On 11 December, Germany and Italy declared war on the United States; the United States declared war on those countries that same day.

JAPANESE PLANNING

When the United States restricted the sale of oil to Japan, the war was inevitable. The Japanese had to find an alternative source of oil, or their efforts on the Chinese mainland would grind to a halt. The Dutch East Indies were the only possible source of supply. When the Japanese moved into Indochina it became obvious that the Indies were their ultimate target. And when the United States froze all Japanese assets to prevent purchase of Dutch oil, a Japanese military move into the Indies became the logical next step.

American strategists anticipated the Japanese moves, but believed Japan would confine herself to the Indies. At most, she might try to seize British Singapore and the Philippines to protect her communications lines there. No one believed she would take the risk of attacking Pearl Harbor, which was 3,500 miles from her objective.

Actually, the Japanese Naval General Staff had not originally planned to attack Pearl Harbor either. However, Admiral Yamamoto, Commander in Chief of Japan's Combined Fleet, persuaded them that unless the U. S. Pacific Fleet was destroyed, Japan could not be assured of success elsewhere in the Southwest Pacific. The General Staff agreed in November, and the Pearl Harbor Striking Force moved into the Kurile Islands to await orders.

In late November Japanese leaders, seeing no progress in negotiations to unfreeze Japanese assets, decided on war with the United States. The timing looked right. In Europe, their Axis partners had the Russians at the gates of Moscow and the British retreating toward Alexandria and Suez, while the United States had become involved in an undeclared war against the German U-boats in the Atlantic. On 1 December Admiral Yamamoto radioed the Striking Force commander, Vice Admiral Nagumo, to "Climb Mount Niitaka," meaning "Proceed with the attack."

THE ATTACK

Success of the attack depended on complete surprise. This was achieved, for the movement of the Striking Force to the launch area had been obscured by stormy seas and heavy rains. American planes were on the ground and the fleet was generally unprepared. Shortly before launching his first wave, Nagumo learned from intelligence reports that the American carriers were not at Pearl. He quickly made his primary targets the U. S. battleships and the parked aircraft on the nearby airfields. A few minutes after 0800 the radio report from the first strike sent back word, "Tora . . . tora . . . tora." These code words meant that surprise had been achieved. By 1300, all but 29 of the attacking aircraft were back aboard the Japanese carriers and they retired toward Japan. There was no American counterattack.

When the Japanese attacked, most American sailors were finishing breakfast, lining up for liberty call at Waikiki, moving toward church services, or just relaxing. The attack struck all parts of the harbor at once, because the Japanese pilots had pre-designated targets. Within moments the battleship *Arizona* exploded after a bomb set off her ammunition magazines. She settled into the mud, taking down over 1,100 officers and men. Before the smoke of battle lifted, all eight battleships of the line had been sunk or badly damaged. A total of 18 ships had been sunk, and 230 aircraft destroyed.

Though the casualties were severe, an assessment of the damages quickly revealed that some very important targets had not been attacked. First, all the carriers had been at sea,

The USS *Arizona* burning and sinking after being hit by Japanese carrier planes on the morning of 7 December 1941. Over 1,100 sailors aboard her were killed.

so none were caught in the attack. Secondly, important repair yards and machine shops were practically untouched. It was in these facilities that the greatest salvage feats of all history began to take place. All but two of the battleships were repaired and saw extensive action later in the war. Furthermore, the temporary loss of the battleships freed thousands of trained personnel for the carrier and amphibious forces, where they were badly needed.

The attacking planes had also missed the tank farm where over 4½ million barrels of fuel oil had been stored. Loss of this fuel would have been a more serious blow to subsequent naval operations in the Pacific than the actual fleet damage.

AFTERMATH OF PEARL HARBOR

The loss of the battleships actually caused a complete reassessment of U. S. naval policy. With the battleships out of commission, the carriers became the queens of the fleet. They became attack ships with their own escorts, including both new and repaired battleships when they joined the fleet.

This change in naval operational policy proved to be decisive in the Pacific War. Yamomoto had believed that air operations would merely be the preliminary to a conflict between battleships. Many of his American counterparts had believed the same thing— until Pearl Harbor. While American tactics developed the carrier task force out of necessity, the Japanese still held to the traditional battleship "line doctrine." This miscalculation was to play an important part in their navy's defeat at sea.

A second miscalculation by the Japanese was their assessment of submarine operations. They had counted heavily on subs in the attack; but except for a couple of merchant ships sunk off California, the Japanese submarines were totally unsuccessful. In the months immediately following the attack, their subs were unable to halt the flow of reinforcements to

Hawaii and Australia. Due to these failures, the Japanese deduced that submarines were of relative insignificance, and little effort went into improving their submarine fleet or training their crews for subsequent operations.

A third miscalculation concerned the psychological effect of the raid on the U. S. Navy and the American people. The Japanese fully believed that they had established superiority and were invincible. They believed that the Americans would lose hope and give up, rather than face certain defeat on the seas and battlefields. Precisely the opposite reaction occurred. The U. S. Navy's reaction was one of fury and determination to avenge Pearl Harbor. The American people, though saddened by their losses, resolved to carry the war to the homelands of the Axis Powers. The rallying cry of the American people became "Remember Pearl Harbor!"

Fleet Admiral Ernest J. King, USN. Commander in Chief, U. S. Fleet, and Chief of Naval Operations during World War II.

With the American fleet crippled in Pearl Harbor, the other parts of the Japanese master plan swung into action. Japanese forces landed on the Malay Peninsula to begin their successful push toward the great British base at Singapore. They took Thailand without resistance. Their planes bombed U. S. air bases in the Philippines, and they occupied Wake, Guam, and Hong Kong.

On 9 December Cavite Naval Base near Manila was wrecked in a Japanese air attack. On that same day, the two most powerful British ships in the Indies, HMS *Repulse* and HMS *Prince of Wales,* were sunk off Malaya by Japanese land-based aircraft. Luzon, the main island of the Philippines, was also invaded on the 9th and the march on Manila began; the city would fall to the invaders on 2 January. Guam fell on 10 December with little resistance. Movement into the Dutch Indies started on 17 December with a landing at the oil fields in Borneo. Wake put up a spirited fight but was overwhelmed on 24 December.

A reorganization of Navy commands followed the Pearl Harbor attack and declarations of war. Admiral Ernest J. King became Commander in Chief, U. S. Fleet. He would also become the Chief of Naval Operations in March 1942.

Into the confusion of successive defeat in the Pacific came the new Commander in Chief, Pacific Fleet (CINCPAC), Admiral Chester W. Nimitz. He arrived at Pearl Harbor on Christmas Day and assumed command in a brief ceremony aboard a submarine, on 31 December. It was up to him to win the biggest naval war the United States had ever faced. Nimitz was quiet and unruffled, inspiring confidence; there was no question who was running the show. Nimitz was to prove equal to the monumental task he had been assigned.

Admiral King's first instructions to Nimitz were clear: (1) cover and hold the Hawaii–Midway line and maintain communications with the U. S. west coast; (2) maintain commu-

Fleet Admiral Chester W. Nimitz, USN. Commander in Chief, U. S. Pacific Fleet, and Commander in Chief Pacific Ocean Area, in World War II.

1. What is meant by the statement, "America appeared to retreat from the seas in order to avoid being challenged on the seas."?

2. What was the real purpose of the Neutrality Patrol and the "safety zone" established by President Roosevelt in 1939?

3. What cold fact finally prompted Congress to pass President Roosevelt's Two-Ocean Navy Bill? What did this bill authorize?

4. What was the real purpose of the Lend-Lease Act?

5. What was the effect of the ABC-1 Staff Agreement on the U. S. Navy?

6. What was the key decision to come out of the ABC-1 Staff Agreement?

7. What was the immediate U. S. reaction to the Japanese occupation of French Indochina in 1940? Why was this U. S. action so important?

8. From where did the Japanese plan to get oil resources to support their war effort?

9. What were the final U. S. economic acts which made war with Japan inevitable?

10. What did Congress do as the result of the sinking of the USS *Reuben James?*

11. What did the Japanese do to cause the U. S. to enter World War II as an active belligerent?

12. Who was the Japanese admiral who convinced the Japanese General Staff to attack Pearl Harbor? Why did he believe this was necessary from the military standpoint?

13. What was essential to Japanese success in the attack?

14. What U. S. targets were successfully put out of action? What three key targets were not attacked?

15. What new U. S. naval operational policy developed as the result of Pearl Harbor? How did this policy differ from that of the Japanese? What other two important Japanese miscalculations occurred at Pearl Harbor?

16. Who were the top new U. S. naval lead-

nications between the west coast and Australia, by holding a line drawn north to south from Dutch Harbor in the Aleutian Islands of Alaska, through Midway to Samoa, then southwest to New Caledonia and Port Moresby, New Guinea. The order was to hold the line against any further Japanese advance. Available forces were to be sacrificed in delaying Japanese advances in the Dutch East Indies in order to hold that defense line. Forces would be sent to the Pacific to reinforce as they became available.

In the meantime the United States was going to have to put forth a primary effort in the Atlantic in order to keep the sealanes open to Britain and thwart the massive German threat facing the British and Russian allies.

ers named in the reorganization following Pearl Harbor? What were their positions?

17. What were Admiral King's orders to Admiral Nimitz? Where was the line of defense drawn?

18. What was to be the task of U. S. forces in the Indies?

Vocabulary

munitions
belligerent

foreign-flag ship
neutrality

blitzkrieg
arsenal
Joint Staff
Combined Staff
embargo
Day of Infamy
objective
"freeze" assets
intelligence report
counterattack
sustain damage

ammunition
  magazine
miscalculation
assessment
reinforcements
psychological effect
invincible
avenge
aftermath
reorganization
communications lines

Chapter 3. World War II: Atlantic and European Theaters (Part I)

Admiral Karl Dönitz, German submarine commander, was surprised by the Japanese attack on Pearl Harbor. Not until mid-January was he able to get five U-boats into the Atlantic waters off the American east coast. But then his boats began the slaughter of defenseless tankers and cargo ships. These losses often totaled over 50 ships a month. Such sinkings represented a greater setback to the American war effort than the attack on Pearl Harbor.

The Battle of the Atlantic, as it came to be known, was a concerted effort by the United States and Britain to keep the sea lanes open to Europe. Against the Allies the Germans made a determined onslaught. At the onset, our forces were meager indeed; in fact, the British had to provide us with trawlers and corvettes (small antisubmarine ships) to help against the U-boat peril.

The Germans started their offensive quickly, sinking ships with little opposition. Often the merchantmen were silhouetted by bright lights ashore from large cities and the Florida resorts. Blackouts of waterfront lights and dim-outs of all port cities were ordered. But by March, the Germans reached a peak in their attacks, sinking 800,000 tons of Allied shipping. German successes made such a dent into oil supplies

that fuel rationing had to be imposed in the whole northeastern area of the United States. The situation was desperate.

President Roosevelt and Prime Minister Churchill realized that little could be done against the Germans in Europe until the submarine menace had been eliminated in the Atlantic. Every effort was made to defeat the U-boat. By May a regular coastal convoy system was in operation and nearly 200 planes were on antisubmarine patrols along the east coast. The Germans were unable to cope with this concentration of aircraft and blimps and the increasing number of surface vessels sent against them. They retreated to the Caribbean, where they continued to wreak havoc until late 1942.

By this time merchant ship sinkings had caused Brazil to enter the war against Germany. Antisubmarine bases and convoy patrols were extended all the way south to Rio de Janeiro. Convoy lanes now extended from the United Kingdom to Halifax, New York, Trinidad, Aruba, and Recife (Brazil), in addition to the east coast routes.

In May 1943 Allied teamwork, with long-range planes, surface ships, and baby flat-tops, succeeded in sinking 43 German U-boats. This stunning defeat was the turning point in the Battle of the Atlantic. After that, the initiative passed to the Allies and the war began to go in their favor.

COUNTERMEASURES AGAINST THE U-BOATS

Mentioned in the summarization above are some of the methods used to defeat the U-boats in the western Atlantic and Caribbean. It was the combination of these methods which brought ultimate success to the Allies.

1) *Coastal convoys.* Assisted by the protected refuges for night anchorage, ships clustered until the daylight hours, when they would make a dash to the next anchorage. These anchorages were protected by minefields and surface patrols, as well as blimps and aircraft. During the daylight hours, submarines could quite easily be sighted by the blimps which then called surface vessels and aircraft for depth-charge attacks. The Germans could not concentrate enough submarines to counter the increased number of surface escorts around the convoys; so they had to retreat after severe losses.

2) *Air patrols.* The United States started making large "flying boats," the PBYs and

Depth-charge attack on a German submarine in the North Atlantic. A Coast Guard ship aids in clearing the seas of the U-boat menace.

Catalinas, which carried radar and depth charges. Ranging far at sea, and using magnetic detection devices, the big aircraft could cruise all day or night. This caused great stress on the submarines, which had to surface periodically to recharge batteries and change their air supplies. The flying boats sank as many German submarines as any other weapons system used by the Allies to stop the threat.

3) *Destroyer escorts.* These ships, somewhat smaller than destroyers, were designed particularly for escort and antisubmarine duties. They came to be the most prevalent convoy escort vessels. Quick and quite cheap to build, but having much the same weapons capability as the larger destroyer, the DEs were very effective in their role. They carried 3-inch guns, some antiaircraft weapons, and depth charges. In the forecastle they mounted a hedgehog, a weapon which threw a salvo of rocket-propelled antisubmarine bombs at a U-boat. These bombs exploded only on contact with a submarine, so there was no doubt as to the result of a hedgehog attack; if a bomb exploded, a U-boat had been hit.

4) *Escort carriers.* Often called "baby flat-tops," these ships were developed to provide antisubmarine protection across the Atlantic beyond the range of the patrol aircraft and blimps. Usually built on merchant ship hulls, over 120 of these CVEs were built, bringing aircraft into the antisubmarine conflict far from shore. These radar-equipped planes could either attack with depth bombs or call for surface attack support from the DEs. The two ships, working together with their aircraft, became known as "hunter-killer groups." Their effectiveness was decisive in the Battle of the Atlantic.

5) *Building yards.* These were basic to the entire antisubmarine program. In addition to building the surface attack ships, American shipyards applied the mass-production methods of auto manufacturing to merchant ship-building. Cargo and tanker ships were made

from prefabricated parts, and the shipyards became assembly lines, turning out Liberty and Victory ship hulls at amazing rates. Despite the severe losses inflicted by the U-boats in the early months of the war, by September of 1942 U. S. shipyards were already turning out more new ships than the Germans sank. By November 1943, ten times as many were made as were sunk.

6) *Technology.* This was one of the key factors in defeating the U-boats. Sonar, an electronic underwater sound-listening device, sent out impulses that were reflected by the metal hull of a submarine, indicating its distance and direction. An advance over the triangulation methods developed in World War I, sonar attacks were generally made by two or more ships.

Even more effective were the new radar devices. Radar uses electric pulses in the air, measuring their reflection when they bounce back from an encountered obstacle. Used on both surface ships and aircraft, radar could determine range and bearing of surfaced submarines, enabling pinpoint attacks which could be followed up with depth charges if the sub managed to submerge before being damaged or sunk.

Finally there were the sonobuoys, sensitive sound devices dropped by a plane in a circle around an unsuspecting submarine. These devices picked up the sub's engine and propeller noises and broadcast them by radio to both surface and air antisubmarine units, enabling them to zero in on the sub. All of these technical devices, kept secret for much of the Battle of the Atlantic, served to shorten the days of U-boats.

7) *Mass training.* The mass training of technicians and crews to use the new ships, planes, and devices was nothing short of astounding. A system of Navy training schools for both officers and enlisted men trained thousands of men in every aspect of antisubmarine warfare. Trained well as individuals first, the men were then trained in teams before assignment to their ships and planes. Knowing each other well and working as a team with the best equipment of the day, there were few subs that could stand up against them when the chips were down.

As the antisubmarine measures proved more and more effective in the western Atlantic, Admiral Dönitz decided to quit the area and lie in wait with his U-boats in the northern and central areas of the ocean. He developed the "wolfpack" tactic, wherein groups of six or more U-boats would converge on a convoy from all directions, hoping to cause widespread confusion for merchantmen and escorts alike. This tactic was initially successful in the area southeast of Greenland known as the "Black Pit," because of its distance from Allied land-based air. But the wolfpacks were eventually defeated by radar, high-frequency direction finding equipment, the escort carrier, and the hunter-killer groups.

With the defeat of his wolfpack tactic, Dönitz called off his attack in the mid-Atlantic and sent his U-boats to widely scattered areas—the Barents Sea, the Cape Town region off South Africa, and even the Indian Ocean. With this new strategy, the Germans had conceded the battle of the Atlantic.

Particularly notable among these U. S. antisubmarine group operations was one conducted by Captain Dan Gallery, and his group led by the escort carrier USS *Guadalcanal.* The American force blasted the German submarine *U-505* to the surface with depth charges and hedgehogs, causing the crew to set demolition charges and abandon ship. But a specially trained boarding party quickly moved onto the boat. They plunged down the conning tower hatch, disconnected the demolition charges, closed the sea valves, and captured the ship and her entire crew. Towed back to the United States, *U-505* has been restored, and is now on display at the Museum of Science and Industry in Chicago, Illinois.

A boarding party from the USS *Guadalcanal*, under the command of Captain Dan Gallery, captures the Nazi *U-505* in a hunter-killer antisubmarine action on 4 June 1944. This was the first boarding and capture in battle since 1815.

A particularly difficult phase of the North Atlantic sea war was that involving the convoys to the Russian port of Murmansk on the Barents Sea north of the Arctic Circle. During the 1942 and 1943 German offensives into the Soviet Union, Allied assistance to Soviet forces was slowed to a trickle. Most assistance came through the port of Murmansk. (Smaller amounts managed to get through over the Trans-Siberian Railway from the port of Vladivostok; some also came northward, on a precarious road across the desert and mountains of Iran from the Persian Gulf ports.)

Despite terrible seas and storms and ferocious attacks by German air, surface, and sub-marine forces based in Norway, supplies came through to aid the Soviet allies. Sometimes less than 40 percent of a given convoy made it, but the persistence of the Allied merchantmen and British escorting ships finally managed to break the German attacks. Some historians believe that the supplies received through Murmansk were a decisive factor in enabling the Soviet forces to hold out against the German offensives.

The Germans continued the attacks on Allied shipping throughout the world until the end of the war. But the Allies' ability to combat the U-boats directly and the productivity of American shipyards effectively contained the Germans' efforts. In all, the Allies lost 2,775 merchant ships amounting to 23,351,000 tons; 14,573,000 tons were sunk by German U-boats. The Germans entered 1,175 U-boats into the war, of which they lost 781; American forces accounted for 191.

Chapter 3. Study Guide Questions

1. What was the "Battle of the Atlantic?" Why was it so important?

2. What seven countermeasures were used to combat the U-boat?

3. How did the air patrols and DEs coordinate their attacks?

4. What was the purpose of the escort carrier?

5. What American manufacturing technique was applied to shipbuilding and how did this affect the outcome of the Battle of the Atlantic?

6. What technological advances were developed to combat the U-boats?

7. What Navy training methods proved to be so successful in antisubmarine warfare?

8. What was the German "wolfpack" tactic?

9. What was the name given to a combination of antisubmarine forces which proved effective against U-boats in far-flung reaches of the oceans? What was probably the most famous exploit of one of these groups?

10. What was the significance of the dangerous Murmansk run?

Vocabulary

U-boat	salvo
concerted effort	mass-production
onslaught	prefabricate
silhouette	sonar
concentration	radar
wreak havoc	obstacle
convoy lanes	sonobuoy
initiative	technician
refuge	blimp
"Flying boat"	hunter-killer group
demolition	Murmansk
hedgehog	productivity

Chapter 4. World War II: Atlantic and European Theaters (Part II)

In the spring of 1942 the German armies were consolidating their positions in France, opening a massive assault to regain territories lost in the Soviet winter campaign, and driving on Alexandria from Libya in North Africa. Nowhere were things going well for the Allies. American military leaders wanted to bring the war directly to Hitler with an invasion in Europe. But cooler British heads prevailed, convincing President Roosevelt that the Allies were not ready for such a major undertaking in the face of Hitler's superior forces.

Still, the Allies had to do something in order to recover the initiative. Winston Churchill proposed an invasion of French North Africa in order to take the pressure off British forces in Egypt. Field Marshall Erwin Rommel, the "Desert Fox" commanding the elite German Afrika Korps, was heading toward Suez, the loss of which would be extremely serious for the Allies. Churchill believed an Allied invasion would draw German forces away from the beaches of Europe. At the same time, it would detach them from the continent so that they could not be reinforced at a later date, because of Allied control of the Mediterranean Sea.

Operation Torch was planned for 8 November 1942. This became the first Allied offensive operation against the Axis in the European–North African theater. American amphibious forces making up the Western Naval Task Force were to come from east-coast ports and converge on French Morocco. They were to land on three beaches near the primary objective, the port of Casablanca.

Combined British and American forces

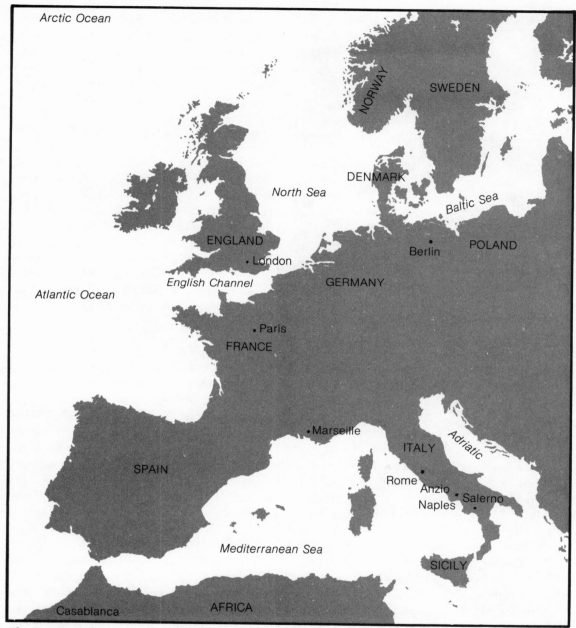

The European Theater

making up the Central Naval Task Force would invade Oran, in Algeria. A third combined contingent, called the Eastern Naval Task Force, would seize Algiers itself. Lieutenant General Dwight Eisenhower was the supreme commander, and Admiral Kent Hewitt, USN, was the Amphibious Task Force Commander.

The big question mark of Operation Torch concerned the Vichy French forces, which had

Operation Torch, the invasion of North Africa by the Allies. Arrows show the landing sites. American amphibious forces landed at the three beachheads in Morocco, while combined British and American forces landed at the two Algerian cities.

aligned themselves with the Axis. Would they resist the landings? The invasion thus became a political problem as well as a military one. If the French decided to offer serious resistance, they might well be able to hold off the Allies until German reinforcements arrived. This could have doomed the invasion and set up a major disaster for the Allies in North Africa.

As it turned out, the French Navy and some shore batteries put up a spirited defense at Casablanca, but this was quickly eliminated by U. S. Navy gunfire. Little resistance was met in either Oran or Algiers. The French quickly surrendered and joined forces with the Free French under General Charles DeGaulle (in accordance with secret orders from Marshal Petain, the French leader in Vichy). Hitler's armies immediately occupied France itself.

Operation Torch, though anything but smooth, was completely successful in meeting all of its objectives. It did show, however, that the Allies were by no means ready to invade Hitler's Europe; much more training, larger forces, and better equipment would be necessary.

The North African operations set up the first major defeat for the Axis. Shortly before the Allied landings in Morocco and Algeria, British Field Marshal Montgomery's Eighth Army routed the Afrika Korps at El Alamein, thus removing the threat to Suez. The Allies then squeezed the Germans and Italians between them into Tunisia. In May the fighting in North Africa ended with the defeat and capture of the entire Afrika Korps, about 275,000 troops and all of their remaining equipment. (Rommel escaped to Germany in the closing days of the campaign.)

ON THE EASTERN FRONT

Earlier in the winter of 1942–43 the Russians had surrounded and defeated an entire German army at Stalingrad, an industrial city on the Volga River. The Russians took 330,000 prisoners in one of history's most savage battles. The Battle of Stalingrad turned the tide on the Eastern Front. The Soviet advance begun in February of 1943 would not stop until the Red Army entered the German capital of Berlin two years later.

CASABLANCA CONFERENCE

In January 1943 President Roosevelt and Prime Minister Churchill met in the famous Casablanca Conference. They decided that before any major offensives were to succeed elsewhere, antisubmarine warfare in the Atlantic had to be given top priority. This was when merchant shipping losses along the U. S. east coast were at their peak.

Secondly, the Allied leaders agreed that the next offensive operation against the Axis would be an invasion of Sicily in July. The Mediterranean sea lanes were now reasonably secure, except from land-based air attack.

Finally, the leaders announced that the Allies would demand nothing short of unconditional surrender of Germany, Italy, and Japan.

OPERATION HUSKY: SICILY

With the success of North Africa still fresh in the minds of all, Allied forces under the command of General Eisenhower prepared for the massive invasion of Sicily. This was to be the first major attempt to take home territory of an Axis nation. On 9 July 1943 the invasion took place on beaches on the southern side of the island. Admiral Hewitt again commanded the American amphibious forces while Field Marshal Montgomery commanded the British Eighth Army. Over 580 ships landed and supported some 470,000 Allied troops on the island.

A force of newly developed amphibious ships took part—LSTs, DUKWs, LCIs, LCTs, and LCVPs. Axis tanks leading strong armored counterattacks were driven off the field by effective naval gunfire, thus allowing the Americans and British to advance. Soon the 350,000 troops of Italian General Guzzoni were in full retreat, chased by General George Patton's tanks and Montgomery's forces. Patton proved to be a masterful field commander, rapidly moving his armor to best advantage and chasing the retreating Axis armies toward Messina and an evacuation of the island. Only about one-third of the Axis armies escaped to Italy with their equipment.

By 17 August Sicily was under Allied control. To be sure, our forces had sustained some heavy casualties at the hands of the German Luftwaffe. But the new amphibian ships, detailed training, planning, and rehearsals paid off handsomely.

The Sicilian campaign was a major triumph for the Allies, for it largely eliminated Italy from the war. King Victor Emanuel II deposed Mussolini and put him into "protective custody." Marshal Pietro Badoglio, the new head of government, said publicly that he would continue the war against the Allies; but in private he began negotiations which would lead to surrender. In the meantime Eisenhower's staff began immediate planning for the invasion of Italy itself.

OPERATION AVALANCHE

On the eve of 8 September, just before the invasion of Italy at Salerno, the Italian government signed an armistice. Much of the Italian Fleet steamed out of northern ports of Genoa and La Spezia for surrender at Malta.

But the Allies still had the Germans to contend with. Montgomery's army had crossed the Straits of Messina to the mainland on 3 September without much opposition. But the Germans had sensed a landing planned for Salerno and had mined and fortified the beaches accordingly. When the landings occurred on 9 September, the amphibious forces of Admiral Hewitt and General Mark Clark met fierce German resistance.

German forces had the beaches zeroed in, and motorized vehicles and tanks were positioned overlooking the landing sites. The Luftwaffe was standing by to turn the beaches into an inferno. In spite of these adverse odds, a precarious beachhead was secured, but with heavy losses. The beachhead was repeatedly saved by naval gunfire support. Noting the reliance of Allied forces on the supporting warships, the Nazis hurled the bulk of their air power at these ships. The Germans introduced radio-controlled glide bombs which caused severe damage to a number of British and American cruisers. Three destroyers were sunk and many more ships were damaged.

But the beachhead held. German tactical errors in the field halted their counterattacks in mid-September. A strategic error by Field Marshal Rommel withheld German reinforcements from the north—when they could probably have made the difference. On 16 September Montgomery's Eighth Army joined forces with Clark's Fifth Army, and the Germans withdrew to a new defense line north of Naples. That great port city was occupied by the Fifth Army on 1 October. The port was a shambles, and the harbor was cluttered with sunken, booby-trapped ships scuttled by the Germans. Clearance of the harbor was a task assigned to the Seabees. They managed to do it, despite incredible obstacles, within four months. Meanwhile the Allies began their buildup for further movement northward.

Anzio

The Germans had consolidated their forces at the Gustav Line, about halfway between Naples and Rome. The Allies immediately planned an "end run," with an amphibious assault on Anzio beach, some 37 miles south of Rome. By this time, however, Allied forces were beginning to be transferred from the Mediterranean theater to England, in preparation for the great invasion of France across the

The cruiser USS *Philadelphia* points her antiaircraft guns skyward while making a smoke screen to shield ships off Anzio beachhead from German artillery.

English Channel. Consequently, General Eisenhower did not think that the forces available in Italy were strong enough to bridge the German defenses at Anzio. But, when Eisenhower left the area for his command headquarters in London, Churchill prevailed on the new British commander in Italy and President Roosevelt to revive the Anzio landing, in order to break the German stranglehold on Rome and the Italian peninsula.

The landing was made on 22 January 1944, with only two divisions reinforced. The initial assault was made with little resistance, but the Germans quickly moved in to stop any forward movement by the relatively small Allied invasion force. Allied reinforcements poured into the small area, but the Germans kept reinforcing their surrounding forces at a similar rate, building up powerful artillery defenses which continuously pounded the enclosed Allies. A major seaborne supply route was established between Anzio and Naples over the next several months. As forces on both sides grew, Allied casualties rose to 59,000 men, a third lost from disease, exhaustion, and stress, due to severe battle fatigue and continuous rains.

The Allied force eventually grew to 90,200 Americans and 35,500 British, packed into a small beachhead. They were surrounded by 135,000 Germans who had placed their artillery so it could reach any part of the invasion site. It wasn't until the rains ceased in May that the Allies finally broke the German hold on Monte Cassino, the key fortress on the Gustav Line, and surged northward. The Germans broke off all contact at Anzio when this happened, and the victorious Allies swept unopposed into Rome on 4 June.

Two days later the focus of attention in Europe was coastal France, as the great cross-channel operation against Hitler's "Fortress Europe" began. The rest of the Italian campaign received little public attention. Nevertheless the fighting went on, as the Germans slowly but steadily retreated northward.

OPERATION OVERLORD

Hitler had calculated that the Allies would be invading his "Festung Europa" not later than the spring of 1944. He ordered the commander on the Western Front, Field Marshal von Rundstedt, and his deputy, Field Marshal Rommel, to build a great "Atlantic Wall" of concrete fortifications to keep the Allies out. Von Rundstedt felt that static defenses were useless against naval gunfire, so he organized highly mobile inland divisions, which could rush to any spot an invasion occurred. Rommel, on the other hand, felt that Allied air power would prevent the mobile divisions from getting to the sea coast. So he concentrated his efforts on beach defenses, counting heavily on mines. He also had concluded that the Allies probably would invade at the Nor- mandy beaches, rather than directly across the English Channel at Pas-de-Calais. He was right.

In the early spring Eisenhower had launched a concerted strategic air attack against Germany, designed to eliminate aircraft factories and ruin the Luftwaffe. By April the raids had decimated the German Air Force to the point where the Allies could count on a 30:1 superiority over the Normandy beaches. Next, the Allied air forces struck at the railroad marshaling yards, bridges, and the trains and tracks themselves, wreaking such havoc that it was almost impossible for any military traffic to move by rail anywhere in France. These air attacks assisted the amphibious assault; in fact, the Allied air strikes in France and Germany *had* to be successful if the D-Day invasion was to be a success.

Invasion of Normandy. Troops wade ashore from LCVPs into a hail of deadly German machine-gun fire. The invasion of Hitler's "Fortress Europe" was the largest military operation ever.

D-Day in Normandy

The invasion was originally set for 1 May 1944. This date was decided upon by Roosevelt, Churchill, and Stalin at their Teheran Conference in November 1943. Eisenhower postponed the date to 1 June in order to get an additional month's production of landing craft.

The physical conditions of tide, visibility, and weather all were of utmost importance to the planners. The tide was especially crucial. It had to be rising at the time of the initial

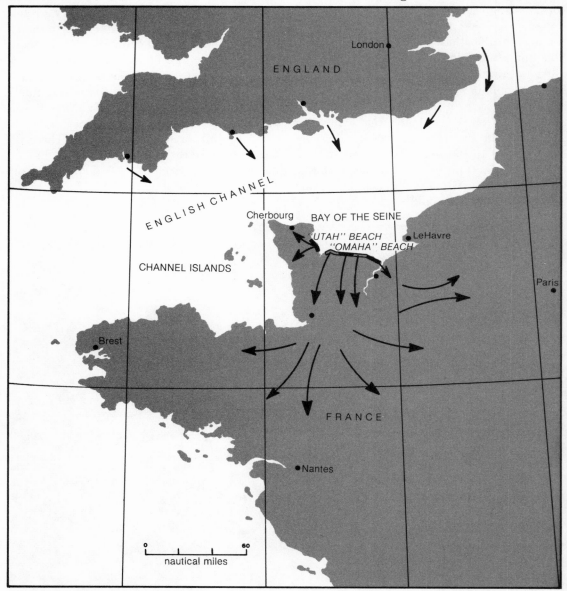

Allied landing areas on D-Day in Normandy. U. S. forces landed on Utah and Omaha beaches, British and Canadians on Gold, Juno, and Sword. Breakout occurred in mid-August, and Paris fell on August 24th.

landings so the landing craft could unload and retract without becoming stranded. At the same time, the tide had to be low enough to expose emplaced obstacles so the underwater demolition teams could destroy them.

The Allies finally selected one hour after low tide for the first landings. This meant that each succeeding wave of boats would come in on higher tides, with less beach to cross. Since only three successive days each month would give them the precise conditions required to satisfy the plan, the closest dates to 1 June were picked: 5, 6, and 7 June. Eisenhower selected 5 June as his first choice for D-Day, and then chose H-hours from 0630 to 0755 to meet the tidal conditions for each beach.

The Allies planned to land on five beaches located between the Cotentin Peninsula and the Orne River mouth, near the city of Caen. The Americans were to land at Omaha and Utah beaches on the right flank and the British were to hit Gold, Juno, and Sword on the left flank. The principal objective of the landings, beyond establishing the beachhead itself, was to capture the port city of Cherbourg so the enormous flow of supplies could be handled quickly.

In the meantime the Allies planned to use artificial harbors, called by the codewords "mulberries" and "gooseberries." The mulberries were concrete caissons towed across the English Channel and sunk off the beachheads to form a breakwater, enclosing pontoon piers. The gooseberries were old merchant ships sunk nearer to shore to provide sheltered harbors for small craft. Mulberry "A" off Omaha Beach was receiving ships by 16 June. Three days later it was destroyed by the worst storm in 50 years. Mulberry "B" off Gold Beach held because it was protected by reefs; it was used for several months after the D-Day landings.

The landings went according to plan on 6 June—a day later than planned because of bad weather, which would have limited air

Tugs push the components of a mulberry harbor into position off a Normandy beach. The mulberry off Omaha Beach served only three days before a terrible Channel storm destroyed it.

support. Minor opposition was encountered on four of the five beaches, but at Omaha Beach the crack German troops were well dug in, and opposed the landing fiercely, causing heavy casualties. Many of the Germans assigned to the other beaches had been lured inland to counter Allied paratroops—dropped there for just that reason. The bad weather of the 5th had in fact led the Germans to think that a landing would not occur under such conditions. But the hole in the clouds on 6 June proved to be their undoing.

The Allied troops consolidated their beachhead while expanding south and west to cut off Cherbourg on the Cotentin Peninsula. By the 24th the 40,000 Germans in Cherbourg were surrounded. A U. S. naval force of battleships, cruisers, and destroyers was called in to pound the heavily fortified Cherbourg into submission. The Germans put up a determined counterbattery action. The battleships prevailed, but not until three destroyers and the battleship USS *Texas* were hit. On 25 June the Germans surrendered Cherbourg, and the Allies began the salvage of the wrecked harbor. It was back in commission and receiving cargo within two weeks.

With the storm destruction of Mulberry A the Navy came to the conclusion that it could meet the demands of the forces ashore by beaching the LSTs shortly after high tide and

American and British ships were scuttled to make breakwaters for ships and boats to bring in much-needed supplies at Normandy. These breakwaters were called gooseberries.

unloading them while the tide receded. This worked well, and by the end of June, 15,000 tons of supplies and 15,000 troops were being landed each day on Omaha Beach. All told, in the first 30 days 929,000 troops, 586,000 tons of supplies, and 177,000 vehicles were landed by the Allied navies onto the Normandy beachheads. Ten thousand aircraft kept the skies secure and kept German reinforcements away from the beaches.

The mine was the single most dangerous weapon of defense used by the Germans along the Normandy beaches. Nearly 400 minesweepers were used to clear the sea lanes in the English Channel approaches to Normandy. The Germans had planted every kind of mine: contact mines which exploded when struck by

a ship; magnetic mines set off by disturbance of the surrounding magnetic field by the steel hulls of ships; and pressure mines which went off when the hull of a ship passed over the mine. More than 30 ships were sunk during the invasion and more merchant ships were sunk in the succeeding weeks while ferrying supplies across the Channel.

Despite the resistance and the mines, however, by the Fourth of July the millionth Allied soldier had arrived on French soil. The time for the main Allied push had come. Taking advantage of a weak spot in the German lines found by General Omar Bradley's First Army, General Patton drove through with the U. S. Third Army, creating a major breakout and trapping 50,000 German troops. On 24 August

Paris fell and General Eisenhower assumed command of the Allied ground forces on the continent. The Germans were in full retreat.

OPERATION ANVIL:
INVASION OF SOUTHERN FRANCE

Only one more invasion remained to be staged in the European theater. Operation Anvil was to take place on the French Riviera near Marseille. The operation had two objectives: to gain another port for supplies flowing into France, and to serve as a diversion drawing German forces away from the primary beaches in Normandy. The landing was delayed until 15 August, however, because of a shortage of landing craft.

Admiral Hewitt was given the opportunity to conduct the first daylight landing in the Mediterranean. The assault was preceded by 1,300 bombers which pounded the German defenses for nearly 1½ hours, and by over a half-hour of heavy naval shore bombardment. The landing craft moved in under a canopy of missile-firing amphibious ships. The missiles, naval gunfire, and bombing eliminated German resistance, and Free French and American forces quickly took the offensive. Within two weeks they had captured the port of Marseille, the naval base at Toulon, and the Riviera cities of Nice and Cannes. The Allies then surged northward through the Rhone Valley, joining with Patton's forces near Dijon on 12 September. Most of France, Belgium, and Luxembourg had been liberated and the Germans were settling in behind their West Wall, the Siegfried Line.

Following the storm which broke up Mulberry A at Omaha Beach, U. S. Navy LSTs were used to carry their cargo directly up to the beach. The amphibious ships were beached during high tide and unloaded when the tide receded. This enabled faster unloading than ever, and by the end of June, 15,000 tons of cargo and 15,000 troops were being offloaded daily at Omaha Beach alone.

GERMANY IS DEFEATED

The rapid movement of Allied forces through France was possible mainly because of the complete control of the air. When winter weather arrived, however, air cover was reduced because of poor flying conditions. On 16 December von Rundstedt launched a major counteroffensive, named the Battle of the Bulge, in the Ardennes area of Belgium. The Nazis made quick advances through a break in the U. S. lines before being stopped by massive attacks on their flanks by Allied armies. The Germans then surrounded elements of the U. S. 101st Airborne Division at the Belgian town of Bastogne. The terrible seige was broken on 27 December when the U. S. Third Army broke through the German lines. It was the last German offensive.

In early 1945 the Allies resumed their attacks on the German Reich—Americans, British, French, and Canadians on the Western and Italian Fronts, and the Russians on the Eastern Front. In March the Allied forces reached the Rhine River, and the U. S. Navy was called on to make its last direct contribution in the fight against Germany. Navy landing craft which had been carried across Belgium by trucks and trains helped ferry elements of Bradley's armies over the river in most of their initial crossings.

Then, on 7 March, the First Army captured the Ludendorff Bridge at Remagen and established a major bridgehead across the Rhine. The bridge held up for ten days under intensive German artillery fire. This was sufficient time for major forces to cross and to assist boat and airborne crossings. The final push was now on from the west, while the Russians surged toward Berlin from the east. On 25 April U. S. and Russian forces met at the Elbe River. They had cut Germany in half from west to east.

On 28 April Mussolini was captured and killed by Italian anti-fascist guerrillas while trying to escape to Switzerland. Two days later, Hitler, beseiged in his bunker in Berlin by Soviet forces, committed suicide after naming Admiral Dönitz as his successor. On 7 May 1945, hostilities ceased in Europe. The representatives of the German Army, Navy, and government signed the unconditional surrender document at Eisenhower's headquarters in a little red schoolhouse in Reims, France. World War II was over in Europe after 5 years, 8 months, and 6 days of death and destruction.

Chapter 4. Study Guide Questions

1. What was the strategy behind the Allied invasion of North Africa? How did naval power make this the only successful attack against the Axis possible at that time?

2. Who was the "Desert Fox?"

3. What were the objectives of the three-pronged invasion of French North Africa?

4. What was the big political question confronting Operation Torch? How was it resolved?

5. What battle turned the tide of war against the Germans on the Russian Front?

6. What decision was made at the Casablanca conference regarding the surrender terms which would be demanded of the Axis?

7. Where was the second Allied invasion in the Mediterranean? How did naval forces contribute to its success?

8. What was the major political outcome of the Sicily campaign?

9. Where was the major Allied invasion beach in Italy? How did naval power succeed in making the invasion a success?

10. What port city was a major objective of the Allies in southern Italy? Following its capture, what had to be done there?

11. What was the situation which occurred at Anzio? How did the Navy help sustain the beachhead? Following the breakout at Monte Casino and the relief of Anzio, what major Axis city fell to the Allies?

12. What was Operation Overlord? When and where did it occur?

13. What were the main objectives of the strategic air attacks against Germany prior to D-Day? Why were these attacks so important?

14. How did oceanographic and tidal conditions influence the date and time selected for D-Day and H-Hour at Normandy?

15. What were "mulberries" and "gooseberries" and what were their purposes?

16. What was the first principal geographic objective of the invasion forces in Normandy?

17. How did the Navy meet logistic demands after the storm destroyed Mulberry A off Omaha Beach?

18. What was the most dangerous defensive weapon employed by the Germans along the Normandy beaches?

19. Where was the last invasion operation in the European theater? What was its purpose?

20. Where was the last German offensive against the Allies?

21. What was the last direct contribution of the Navy in the war against Hitler?

22. When and where did Germany surrender to Allied forces?

Vocabulary

consolidation
campaign
Casablanca, Morocco
Vichy France
El Alamein, Egypt
Stalingrad
unconditional surrender
determination
speculative
retrospect
Sicily
naval gunfire support
evacuation
rehearsal
depose
protective custody
armistice
Salerno
"zero in"
precarious
beachhead
scuttle

booby-trapped
Anzio
seaborne supply
battle fatigue
artillery
"Fortress Europe"
static defenses
railroad marshaling yard
D-Day
Normandy
crucial
underwater demolition team
caisson
pontoon pier
Cherbourg
submission
French Riviera
canopy
liberate
counteroffensive
bridgehead

Chapter 5. World War II in the Pacific: On the Defensive

The fires had not even been extinguished at Pearl Harbor before the U. S. Navy began to make both short- and long-term plans for the future conduct of the war against the Japanese. The Pacific War was going to be primarily a naval war, and planning had already been done concerning the conduct of such a war. Given the orders to hold the line of defense across the mid-Pacific and to protect the sea lanes to Australia, Admiral Nimitz knew his task would be a grim one for the first months while small Allied naval forces fought a delaying action in the Dutch East Indies. But after that, there was no question in his mind that the U. S. Navy would have to start on the offensive.

The Japanese moved quickly following their attack on Pearl Harbor. Within days they were making landings in the Philippines to guard communications lines to their principal objective, the oil of the Dutch East Indies. By mid-December they made the first landings near the oil fields in Borneo. They then began their amphibious hops southward through the other islands toward Java, the main island of the archipelago. Java was especially rich in the natural resources that Japan needed.

In January of 1942, the ABDA (American, British, Dutch, and Australian) defense command was formed, with headquarters in Java. It was never very effective because of the small forces at its disposal and the disagreements over what it should do. The Dutch considered defense of Java the principal goal; the British and Americans believed that successful

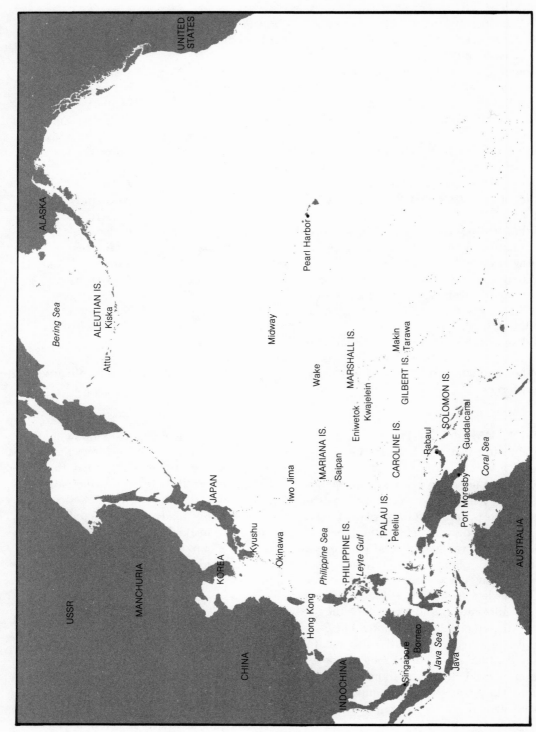

UNITED
STATES

ALASKA

Bering Sea

ALEUTIAN IS.
Kiska
Attu

Pearl Harbor

Midway

Wake

MARSHALL IS.
Eniwetok
Kwajelein

Makin
Tarawa
GILBERT IS.

MARIANA IS.
Saipan

CAROLINE IS.

SOLOMON IS.
Rabaul
Guadalcanal

Coral Sea

Iwo Jima

JAPAN

Kyushu

Okinawa

Philippine Sea

PHILIPPINE IS.

Leyte Gulf

PALAU IS.
Peleliu

Port Moresby

AUSTRALIA

KOREA

Hong Kong

MANCHURIA

USSR

CHINA

INDOCHINA

Singapore

Borneo

Java Sea

Java

The Pacific Theater

defense of Java was impossible, and that the best ABDA could do was delay the Japanese so they could not move their forces further into the Southwest Pacific and isolate Australia. The Japanese methodically moved through the Indies, setting up airfields for land-based air support at each succeeding location they conquered. In mid-February Admiral Nagumo's carrier striking force arrived in the area. It raided Darwin, Australia's northernmost port, and supported an invasion of Portuguese Timor, thus effectively isolating Java from any major reinforcement.

The ABDA naval force under command of Dutch Admiral Karel Doorman made several attempts to stop the Japanese advance, but was defeated at almost every encounter. The Battle of the Java Sea on 29 February all but eliminated the Allied force, the majority of ABDA ships being sunk by aircraft and destroyer-fired torpedoes. The Allies did fight gallantly, but inflicted only minor losses on the Japanese before Nagumo's naval aircraft mopped up the opposition. Surviving Allied destroyers made it to Australia to fight another day.

The Japanese began landing on Java on 28 February, and by 9 March the island was forced into unconditional surrender. Before the end of March all of the Dutch East Indies were in Japanese hands and the rich oil wells of Java, Borneo, and Sumatra were providing an inexhaustible supply of fuel. Additionally the Japanese had obtained rich resources of tin, rubber, rice, and quinine. They had attained all of their objectives in the south, and at the same time had conquered Burma and the Andaman Islands in the Indian Ocean. They had driven the battered British Indian Ocean Fleet into East African ports. They had accomplished all of their primary objectives in less than half the time they had planned, and with insignificant losses.

On 11 March, two days after the fall of Java, General Douglas MacArthur was ordered out of the Philippines by President Roosevelt. He slipped away from his command post on Corregidor in Manila Bay on a PT boat and made his way to the southern Philippines. From there he flew to Australia to take command of the defense of that nation. As he departed the Philippines he promised the Filipinos, "I shall return." In April and May, the last Filipino and American defenders of the Philippines were overrun on Bataan Peninsula and Corregidor. They suffered every form of human brutality as they were forced on a "Death March" from Bataan to their prison camps.

JAPANESE DEFENSE PERIMETER

The Japanese had now established their defense perimeter. Anchored by Rangoon in the Indian Ocean area, it included all of the Dutch East Indies and northern New Guinea on the south, extended to include Rabaul on New Britain and Kavieng on nearby New Ireland in the southwest. It then crossed the Pacific northward to newly acquired Wake, Guam, and the British Gilbert Islands. On the northern flank she was protected by her own bases in the Kurile Islands. She had also improved her many bases in the islands acquired from Germany during World War I—the Carolines, Marshalls, and Marianas. She made Truk in the Carolines into her "Pearl Harbor" of the central Pacific and developed Rabaul into her major forward base for further expansion southwestward. Only on the central perimeter, near Midway Island, did a gap exist. Admiral Yamamoto wanted to seal this gap, but the Japanese General Staff felt it was not necessary.

The Japanese hoped that their string of well-defended bases and their fine navy would be sufficient to keep the growing American strength at bay. They hoped to be able to inflict losses on newly arriving American units so that the American people would eventually become disheartened and force Congress to accept a compromise peace which would let Japan keep her conquests in Southeast Asia and the Indies. But Admiral Nimitz, the U. S. Navy, and the American people would not let the Japanese realize their hopes.

LIMITED OFFENSE CHOSEN AS BEST DEFENSE

Admiral Nimitz knew that the Japanese were planning additional moves into the southwest. The Japanese naval code had been broken by U. S. intelligence, and on crucial occasions Japanese intentions could be estimated with considerable accuracy. Nimitz felt that he could best defend the sea lanes to Australia by attacking Japanese bases in the Central Pacific with carrier task forces in a series of hit-and-run raids. This would cause confusion in the Japanese high command. Yamamoto himself was afraid that the Americans might even attempt a raid on Tokyo and endanger the Emperor's life.

Vice Admiral William Halsey was selected as the man to strike the Japanese bases. He was to hit bases at widely separated geographic extremes so as to cause the Japanese most anxiety. Halsey even hoped to make them believe that there were more U. S. naval task forces running around than they thought existed. The press exaggerated the effects of the raids and greatly boosted American public morale, and so the raids achieved part of their purpose.

Then came the electrifying attack that the Japanese had dreaded. Halsey's carrier striking force moved into Japanese home waters with 16 long-range Army B-25s lashed to the flight deck of USS *Hornet*. On 18 April 1942, the all-volunteer pilots led by Colonel James Doolittle successfully took off and made an air raid on Tokyo, Nagoya, and Kobe. None of the B-25s were lost over Japan. They continued on into China, since they couldn't return to the carrier. In Asia the pilots crash-landed or parachuted to the ground. Most escaped in friendly Chinese territory, though some were captured and executed in Japanese-controlled areas.

The Japanese armed forces were humiliated. Their boast that the sacred territory of the Land of the Rising Sun would never be attacked was proven wrong. Yamamoto's plans to attack Midway in June in order to close the gap in the Japanese defense perimeter were now revived. Another Japanese move into the Coral Sea area to cut the sea lanes to Australia was put into action for early May. A third Japanese move, a two-pronged thrust into the Solomon Islands and toward Port Moresby in New Guinea, also was started. Nimitz, aware of these intentions through decoding of Japanese messages, planned his own actions carefully.

BATTLE OF THE CORAL SEA

Nimitz directed his carrier task groups to converge on the Coral Sea to stop the Japanese moves toward the Solomons. The *Lexington* and her group were sent to reinforce Rear Admiral Frank Jack Fletcher's *Yorktown* group. Fletcher first struck the Japanese Solomons Invasion Force off the island of Tulagi on 3 May. For the next two days Fletcher and Japanese Vice Admiral Takeo Takagi's groups maneuvered south of the Solomons without locating each other. Then on 7 May U. S. fliers sighted the Port Moresby Invasion Force coming down from Rabaul. Fletcher attacked, sinking a Japanese light carrier and causing the force to turn back. In the meantime Takagi's fliers sank an American destroyer and an oiler which were detached from the main U. S. group.

On 8 May the Battle of the Coral Sea was fought. It was the first great combat between carrier forces, with neither fleet ever coming into sight of the other. Both groups launched their attack waves about the same time. The Japanese had several advantages: fliers with more combat experience, better torpedoes, and of particular note, protection from a foul-weather front which partly concealed their movements. The opposing waves hit the two

Doolittle raid on Tokyo on 18 April 1942. B-25s on the deck of the USS *Hornet*. The raid humiliated the Japanese armed forces, which had pledged that their homeland would never be attacked. When asked where the planes had come from, President Roosevelt said, "From Shangri-La," a mythical land of eternal youth in Tibet. Later in the war, a new U. S. carrier was named the USS *Shangri-La*.

task groups almost simultaneously; the Japanese carrier *Shokaku* was severely damaged and both the *Yorktown* and *Lexington* were hit. The *Lexington*, hit by two torpedoes which ruptured her fuel lines, began to release gasoline fumes into the hold, where the vapors finally exploded. The ship had to be abandoned and was later sunk by one of her own escorting destroyers.

The Battle of the Coral Sea turned back the Japanese advance for the first time in the Pacific War. Even though the American losses were somewhat greater, the strategic victory was clearly on the side of the United States. While only one Japanese carrier was sunk, another was damaged, and the third lost so many aviators it was kept out of the Midway operation. Nagumo's Midway Force would be short three carriers for the major action of Yamamoto's grand plan.

THE BATTLE OF MIDWAY

Yamamoto had immense superiority with the entire Combined Fleet under his com-

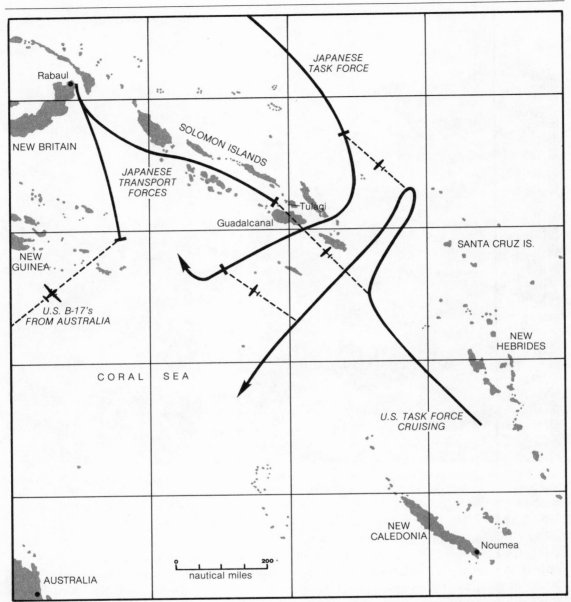

Battle of the Coral Sea. This was the world's first all-carrier air and sea battle, and turned back the Japanese advance into the South Pacific. The supply route to Australia was kept open.

mand. But he devised a curious battle plan which split his forces into ten separate groups, spread all the way from the Aleutian Islands Invasion Force to the four groups concentrating on Midway itself. The Japanese Combined Fleet was an immense armada of 11 battleships, 8 carriers, 23 cruisers, and 65 destroyers. They were pitted against Nimitz's tiny force of 3 carriers, 8 cruisers, and 14 destroyers. The key to the impending action, however, was

U. S. intelligence. Nimitz had deduced all the major movements in the Japanese plan through radio intercepts and code-breaking. The Americans were not going to be surprised—much to the surprise of the Japanese.

The first action occurred on 3 June, with a diversionary attack on Dutch Harbor in the Aleutians. A scout plane ranging 700 miles to sea from Midway alerted the Midway defenders. Fletcher drew his two task forces in to within 200 miles of Midway and waited. Nagumo launched his first attack of 108 planes on Midway at dawn on the 4th. Fletcher located the Japanese force with patrol bombers and then ordered Rear Admiral Raymond Spruance in the *Enterprise* to attack while the *Yorktown* recovered the search planes.

At the same time all aircraft on Midway took off to attack the Japanese force. The American planes proved to be no match for the maneuverable Zero fighters, and were quickly shot down. Nagumo now was faced with four hours of fast action and perplexing decisions. His carriers were successively attacked by torpedo planes and bombers, none of which scored a hit and almost all of which were shot down. Then an American submarine showed up in his formation and fired torpedoes, all of which missed. Finally, the aircraft returning from the first Midway attack reported that another attack was needed to destroy the runways there.

At almost the same time, Nagumo received word of the American carrier task force. He changed course to close them, directing that the bombs which had been loaded on aircraft for the second Midway attack be replaced with torpedoes for an attack on the U. S. carrier force. The bombs were left lying on the deck. At the same time, the first Midway attack wave returned and he ordered that they be recovered before launching the second wave.

The Nagumo force was now attacked by three waves of carrier torpedo planes, all of which failed to score a hit and were shot down

in flames. Nagumo had now turned back eight attacks in three hours without a scratch. But his luck had run out. About to launch his counterattack, the four Japanese carriers turned into the wind. At that moment another American wave from the *Enterprise* and *Yorktown* came in on a high-altitude dive-bombing attack. They met almost no resistance from the Japanese combat air patrol, which had been pulled down to meet the previous American torpedo attack.

The Americans caught the Japanese carriers with planes on their flight decks about to take off, other planes refueling, and the off-loaded bombs lying around waiting to be returned to the magazines. American bombs hit the carriers *Soryu*, *Kaga*, and *Akagi* and turned them into burning torches in minutes. Only the carrier *Hiryu*, further to the north, escaped this attack. Her dive bombers followed the *Yorktown's* planes back and stopped the U. S. carrier with three hits. Further hits by torpedo planes caused Fletcher to abandon his flagship and turn tactical command over to Admiral Spruance.

About the time the *Yorktown* was being abandoned, her search planes discovered the *Hiryu*, reporting her location and course. A short time later a wave of dive bombers from the *Enterprise* set the *Hiryu* on fire with four

The sinking USS *Yorktown* at the Battle of Midway.

direct bomb hits. Yamamoto was now without aircraft carriers to protect his Main Body of heavy warships. Though he ordered a counterattack during the night with four cruisers of his bombardment force, he cancelled the Midway operation in the early hours of the morning, rather than have his surface force exposed to a daylight dive-bombing attack. He ordered his entire force to retire to the west.

The cruiser bombardment force now came

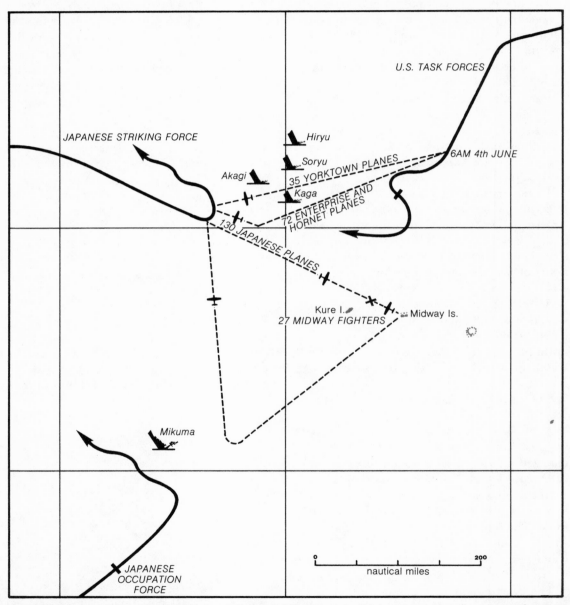

U.S. TASK FORCES

JAPANESE STRIKING FORCE

Hiryu

Soryu

Akagi

35 YORKTOWN PLANES

6AM 4th JUNE

Kaga

72 ENTERPRISE AND HORNET PLANES

130 JAPANESE PLANES

Kure I.
27 MIDWAY FIGHTERS

Midway Is.

Mikuma

0   200

nautical miles

JAPANESE
OCCUPATION
FORCE

The Battle of Midway was the turning point in the Pacific War. Not only did the Japanese lose four carriers, but more importantly, they lost the best of their carrier pilots.

under attack by a U. S. submarine, and in the process of dodging torpedoes, two of the cruisers, the *Mogami* and *Mikuma,* collided. On 6 June Spruance located the damaged ships and sank the *Mikuma.* The final action came when the *Yorktown,* which was under tow after being abandoned, was sunk by a Japanese submarine. The spread of torpedoes also sank an escorting U. S. destroyer.

The Battle of Midway was the turning point in the Pacific War. The Japanese loss of four carriers and a cruiser was compounded by the loss of the best Japanese carrier pilots. This loss of pilots was one of the chief causes of Japan's ultimate defeat at sea. After Midway, Japanese carrier flight training programs began to suffer. New aviators sent to the fleet were less prepared to face the growing number of well-trained American pilots.

Only the Japanese northern forces had achieved success in Yamamoto's grand plan. They had succeeded in occupying Kiska and Attu in the Aleutian Islands, this done without resistance. But from then on, the Japanese would never again be able to launch another major offensive.

Chapter 5. Study Guide Questions

1. What were Nimitz's orders upon taking over command?

2. What was the principal Japanese objective in the Dutch Indies?

3. What was the ABDA Command? Why was there some confusion as to the organization's principal objective?

4. What island was the main objective of the Japanese in the Indies?

5. Where were the last U. S. strong points in the Philippines? Who was ordered to escape from there to Australia? What command did he assume there?

6. What major island groups comprised the Japanese Pacific territorial holdings? Where was the gap in the Japanese defense perimeter?

7. Where was the Japanese "Pearl Harbor" located? In which group of islands is this?

8. What did the Japanese hope the United States would do in the Pacific?

9. What enabled Admiral Nimitz to go on a limited offensive to counter the major Japanese moves, even though his forces were far outnumbered at this early stage of the war?

10. How did the Doolittle raid on Japan operate? What was the principal effect of the raid?

11. What three major Japanese moves were planned following the Doolittle raid?

12. Where did the first major setback occur for the Japanese? What made this battle a "first" in naval history? What was the result of this battle?

13. What was the key to U. S. naval actions in the Battle of Midway?

14. Who were the carrier admirals opposing each other in the Battle of Midway?

15. How did the Japanese do during the first eight American attacks on their carriers? When did their luck run out?

16. What were the major Japanese losses in the Battle of Midway?

17. Where had the only successful Japanese portion of the grand Midway Plan occurred?

18. Why is the Battle of Midway regarded as the "turning point of the Pacific War?"

Vocabulary

extinguish	compromise
Pearl Harbor	geographic extremes
Hawaii	exaggerate
Java	humiliate
methodically	Solomon Islands
torpedo	Rabaul
survivor	abandon
inexhaustible	superiority
Philippine Islands	impending
Corregidor	diversion
Bataan Peninsula	maneuverable
brutality	bombardment
defense perimeter	turning point

Chapter 6. World War II in the Pacific: On the Offensive

Midway had turned the tide. The war was by no means over; the end wasn't even in sight. But the apparent Japanese "invincibility" had been proven false in the crucible of battle. Americans, even when outnumbered, were not to be outfought. Proper command use of intelligence would be the great equalizer until American industry rebuilt the Pacific Fleet. The general plan to accomplish the victory had been worked out. The details and the timetable had yet to be formulated, but time was now on the American side.

Solomon Islands Operations

After the defeat of the Japanese at Midway both Admiral Nimitz and General MacArthur believed that an Allied counteroffensive should be started while the enemy was still off-balance. To the Japanese, the defeat indicated that they had to consolidate their earlier victories, reinforce their advanced bases, and bring ships and troops down to the southwestern perimeter of their defense line. The Solomon Islands became the objective of both sides.

For the Japanese, this meant building an airfield on the island of Guadalcanal and developing the base so it could be used to cover their flank while they completed the conquest of New Guinea. For the Allies it meant launching an operation to blunt the Japanese threat to the Australian sea lanes, protect Port Moresby on New Guinea, and establish an advanced base from which to strike the Japanese base at Rabaul.

When an American scout plane discovered the Japanese building the Guadalcanal airstrip, that island became the focal point of a series of naval battles, and a prolonged struggle between U. S. Marines and Japanese forces, for the next six months of the Pacific War. The Marines landed on 7 August at Guadalcanal

and nearby Tulagi. By nightfall on the first day, 1,000 Marines were ashore. Things did not go as smoothly on Tulagi where the Japanese were well dug in, but the Marines prevailed.

The Marines landed from the amphibious task force anchorages off the northern coast of the island. This seaway area became known as Ironbottom Sound, because of the many ships sunk there during the forthcoming campaign.

Within a few hours the task force was under bombing attack from the Japanese base at Rabaul. After repelling the air attack, the U. S. carriers *Saratoga, Wasp,* and *Enterprise* retired because of heavy fighter-plane losses and the need for refueling. What the Allied force didn't know was that a major Japanese naval force of cruisers was heading for the amphibi-

A night battle in the Solomon Islands. The battle for Guadalcanal raged day and night on the island, and in the seas surrounding the island, for six months. Losses for both sides were heavy, but in the end American arms were triumphant and the Japanese had to pull back their defense perimeter and try to consolidate.

The mud of the jungles of the Solomon Islands made the fighting a terrible ordeal. Not only was there the enemy to fight, but the disease and discomfort of the jungle as well.

ous ships. They were coming down "The Slot," the passage between the major Solomon Islands from Rabaul.

It was soon discovered that the Japanese surface training in night operations would pay off for them. Catching the U. S. and Australian surface force completely unaware off Savo Island, Vice Admiral Gunichi Mikawa's cruisers gave the U. S. Navy the worst defeat it has ever suffered in battle: the cruisers *Astoria, Vincennes,* and *Quincy* plus the Australian cruiser *Canberra* were sunk; the cruiser *Chicago* and two destroyers were heavily damaged; and 1,000 Allied sailors were killed.

With the Allied surface force shattered, and the carriers away from the scene, the amphibious task force was forced to withdraw, leaving 16,000 Marines on Guadalcanal, without support and supplies. Only because the Japanese had no significant force ashore were the Ma-

rines able to capture Henderson Field and set up a defense perimeter. By 20 August the Seabees had the field in operation and the first planes were flying sorties and bringing in supplies.

BATTLES FOR GUADALCANAL

When the Japanese learned that the Americans were setting up an airfield on Guadalcanal, they realized that they had to recapture that field. They began pouring troops into the island at night, bringing them in by fast transports and destroyers with such regularity that the Marines called the enemy ships the "Tokyo Express."

Japanese submarines were stationed on the approaches to Guadalcanal and by early September had sunk the USS *Wasp,* damaged the USS *Saratoga,* and torpedoed the new battleship *North Carolina.* Japanese forces continued

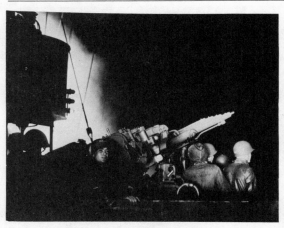
Night action in the Solomons. A gun crew is illuminated by the flash of another ship's guns during the height of the battle.

to be heavily reinforced despite terrible casualties and by 15 October 22,000 men were ashore.

Night naval battles and attacks by the Japanese Combined Fleet caused havoc in American forces. The Marines held, however, inflicting ten casualties for each one of their own men lost. Then, in the Battle of the Santa Cruz Islands on 24 October, Admiral Halsey gambled his carriers—and came out the loser. The *Hornet* was sunk and the *Enterprise* heavily damaged, leaving no operational U. S. carrier in the Pacific. In the process, however, two Japanese carriers and a cruiser were badly damaged and a hundred Japanese planes were shot down.

The naval Battle of Guadalcanal was now about to begin. On 12 November the Japanese started down the Slot with 11,000 troops jammed into 11 transports. Escorted by two battleships as well as many cruisers and destroyers, this was to be the last major attempt by the Japanese to relieve their army on Guadalcanal. In a cruiser night action the American and Japanese naval forces clashed head-on in the darkness. Heavy losses were suffered on both sides, the United States losing 2 cruisers and 4 destroyers, the Japanese 2 battle-

ships, a cruiser, 2 destroyers, and 7 transports with 9,000 troops.

Another night naval battle off Guadalcanal was fought in late November—again resulting in severe damage to U. S. cruisers by Japanese "long lance" torpedoes. But the Tokyo Express was slowly fading and resupply of Japanese troops on the island was becoming more difficult. Extremely heavy casualties were inflicted on troop reinforcements by destroyers and PT boats.

The Marines ashore continued their hard-fought advance, pushing the Japanese into the jungle interior. Finally, on 9 February 1943, the Japanese slipped out of the jungle and 12,000 half-starved survivors made their escape on fast destroyers. Guadalcanal was at last secured.

New Guinea

While Americans were securing Guadalcanal, the Allies took to the offensive on the ground in New Guinea. Australians and Americans pursued the Japanese over the mountains from Port Moresby and flew troops across to unoccupied airstrips in a drive toward the Japanese base at Buna on the north coast. Neither side put major naval vessels into the action because of the uncharted waters, the number of hostile airfields held by the other side, and the heavy naval involvement near Guadalcanal.

At any stage of the New Guinea operations, introduction of major naval forces by either side could have made the difference between victory and defeat for that side. As it was, the steady Allied pressure, continuously reinforced from Australia, eventually overwhelmed the Japanese—but at a cost nearly twice that on Guadalcanal. When the smoke of battle had cleared, the Allies had Papua, New Guinea to the west of Rabaul, and Guadalcanal was a secure base to the east. Allied forces were closing in on the major Japanese base in the southwest Pacific.

THE STRATEGY OF 1943: CONTINUOUS PRESSURE

A consolidation and planning period took place following the successes on New Guinea and Guadalcanal. Both sides paused to lick their wounds and to reinforce their front-line bases. The Allied leaders met in Casablanca and decided to allocate more military resources to the Pacific in order to keep the offensive there rolling.

Originally Roosevelt and Churchill had planned to make Hong Kong the focal point of the future Allied actions. This strategy called for major British and Chinese efforts in Southeast Asia through Burma and the Straits of Malacca. Meanwhile, MacArthur's forces would come up from Australia to the Philippines, and Nimitz's Central Pacific forces would come across Micronesia and Formosa. This plan did not get into operation because the British could not take forces from the Mediterranean to do their part. The Chinese were eliminated by a new Japanese offensive in southern China. It was up to the United States forces, assisted wherever possible by Australian and New Zealand (ANZAC) forces, to take care of the Japanese in the Pacific War.

The program finally put into effect called for:

1) elimination of the Japanese outposts in the Aleutian Islands.

2) intensified submarine attacks on the Japanese lines of communication from the Indies.

3) isolation of Rabaul with MacArthur's forces assisted by the South Pacific naval forces; and upon completion of this, westward movement along the northern coast of New Guinea.

4) an advance westward through the Micronesian island bases held by Japan, using Central Pacific naval forces under Nimitz.

RECONQUEST OF ATTU AND KISKA

The Japanese had occupied Attu and Kiska for nearly a year since the defeat at Midway.

From time to time the Japanese garrisons were harrassed by U. S. planes from Dutch Harbor. American cruisers and destroyers had bombarded the bases in late summer of 1942 and again in February 1943. In the winter of 1942–43 American forces occupied Adak and Amchitka islands and constructed airfields on them to support further operations against the Japanese-held islands.

The U. S. North Pacific Fleet turned back a Japanese attempt to resupply their garrisons in March 1943, in a surface action south of the Russian Komandorski Islands. The Japanese proved to be ineffective against a much smaller American force here and retired to the Kuriles in disgrace. This was their last surface attempt to resupply the freezing, starving garrisons in the Aleutians. Despite their ineffectiveness, however, the idea of Japanese soldiers occupying American territory was unacceptable to the American people, so plans to recover the islands were made.

On 11 May a strong assault force headed by three old battleships landed 3,000 troops on Attu. The Japanese garrison fought stubbornly in the mountains until 29 May. Then the 1,000 survivors came down the hills during the night and threw away their lives in a last fanatical *banzai* charge at the American lines. The remnants of the charge committed suicide; only 28 were captured alive. American casualties were high: 600 dead, 1,200 wounded, and 1,500 incapacitated because of poor winter clothing and footwear.

The Japanese garrison on Kiska was known to consist of about 5,000 men. After the expensive experience on Attu, no stone was left unturned to train, equip, and clothe the attacking force. Kiska was bombed for six weeks with 1,200 tons of bombs and heavily bombarded by naval surface forces.

The wily Japanese and the weather combined to provide one of the strangest experiences of the war, however. Under cover of heavy Aleutian fog, a relieving Japanese force of cruisers and destroyers slipped in and evacuated the entire garrison while the blockading American fleet had temporarily withdrawn to refuel. Three of the six weeks of bombing and shelling had been directed at empty barracks! The Aleutians returned to American control on 15 August and the North Pacific Fleet lapsed into patrol operations for the remainder of the war.

Submarine Operations in the Pacific

The submarine war in the Pacific was fundamentally different from that of the Atlantic. The shoe was on the other foot, so to speak. Whereas the Germans were striving to halt Allied shipping from reaching Europe, in the Pacific it was the Americans who sought to keep the Japanese merchant fleet from arriving in the home islands with cargos from the Indies.

The Japanese had tended to shortchange their submarine force. In general they underestimated the threat of the submarine. This philosophy had been reinforced by the poor showing of the submarines at Pearl Harbor and during the early months of the war. The lack of appreciation for their own submarines trans-

lated itself to less emphasis on training their own antisubmarine forces as well. There was no elaborate training system, either for individuals or of antisubmarine crews, comparable to those in Britain and America.

Also, there were technical shortcomings in the Japanese antisubmarine forces. They did not have radar, while American submarines did. Though Japanese antisubmarine ships had good sonar, they seemed to be unable to follow through on destroying a submarine once it was discovered. In fact, Japanese naval and air forces sank only 52 American submarines during the entire war—compared to the 781 lost by the Germans in the Atlantic.

Geography also was a very important factor in Pacific submarine warfare. The Atlantic is an open ocean in which convoys can follow any number of transoceanic routes. But this is not so in the Western Pacific. There, the routes from the supply sources in Malaya, Borneo, Sumatra, and Java to Japan are often narrow straits between islands. Routes through the Philippines are constrained, as are the channels of safe water in the Formosa Straits. All of these routes are further constricted by reefs and chains of shoals, which provide hiding places for submarines. Many shallow shipping lanes could also be mined by American aircraft and submarines. This further channelled ships into sea lanes where U. S. submarines could lie in wait, sure that sooner or later a Japanese merchantman would show up.

In the Atlantic the convoy proved to be the principal answer to the U-boat threat. But the Japanese use of convoys was not effective. Their escorts were too few in number, poorly equipped, and with ill-trained crews. The convoys themselves were improperly organized, often with only one escort which, by itself, could rarely outsmart the sub.

For most of the first year and a half of the war, U. S. submarines were hampered by ineffective torpedoes. Some Japanese ships were sunk, but many escaped after being hit by duds

Japanese merchant ship heads for the bottom after being torpedoed by a U. S. submarine. This photograph was taken through the periscope of the successful attackers.

or missed by torpedoes which had improper depth controls. The defective torpedoes meant the loss of many opportunities to destroy enemy shipping and to delay the initial Japanese moves in the war. It was not until mid-1943 that corrections were made on American torpedoes to eliminate the deficiencies. About the same time, electric torpedoes were developed to further enhance submarines' capability.

American submarines were built on a mass-production basis, just as DEs and merchant ships were. For the Pacific, very big submarines, nearly twice the size of German U-boats, were developed because of the need for greater fuel and torpedo-carrying capacity in the long-distance patrols against the Japanese.

Admiral Charles A. Lockwood, Commander of Submarines, Pacific, worked out a full strategy on the employment of his boats, which fitted into the grand strategy of interdicting the shipping from the Indies. As U. S. submarines became more effective and Japanese merchant losses leaped, the enemy's potential to build new merchant ships also declined, since the raw materials to support their ship-building program were not getting home. By May of 1943, Japanese cargo tonnage afloat was already a million tons below the pre-war figure. Her Southern Resources Area could not deliver the essential raw materials to support her war industry or military forces.

Certainly one vital factor in the success of American submarines, however, was the men in them. American submariners were all volunteers; they served in submarines because they *wanted* to serve in them. Physical and mental requirements were strict, and training was extremely demanding. Every man aboard was cross-trained to be able to operate other equipment aboard. The camaraderie between officers and enlisted men was strong, since the usual distinctions of rank and rate could not be observed in the close quarters of a submarine. Every man aboard depended on every other

man, and respect had to be mutual to get the job done.

The story of the decline of the Japanese merchant marine is really the story of the defeat of the Japanese Empire in World War II. U. S. submarines sank 1,113 merchant vessels, for a total of 5,320,000 registered tons. In addition, they sank at least 200 naval ships for a total of nearly 580,000 tons. The submarine, then, was the naval weapon which won the war for the United States in the Pacific. When surrender came, the Japanese no longer had any industrial capability or any fuel to run their war machine.

RINGS AROUND RABAUL

The Casablanca Conference decided on a movement through the remaining Solomon Islands toward the giant Japanese base at Rabaul. Admiral Yamamoto realized the importance of defending the Melanesian and Australasian approaches to Rabaul, so he reinforced his airfields with fleet carrier air wings and launched major raids on Ironbottom Sound. Heavy losses were inflicted on American ships; but in the process, the Japanese carrier air wings suffered further severe losses.

In an effort to boost morale, Yamamoto and his staff set out on an inspection trip to Japanese bases in the Solomons. Breaking the coded messages which outlined his itinerary, American long-range fighters from Henderson Field intercepted his plane over Bougainville Island and shot it down. This was a major defeat for the Japanese for it deprived them of their most able commander.

For the next 20 months, into March of 1944, the campaign against Rabaul progressed on two fronts—through the Solomons and on New Guinea. During that time the U. S. Fleet fought in no less than 15 major naval battles and 17 invasions in the Solomons and Southwest Pacific area. These fierce battles have come to be known as the Melanesian Nightmare.

The Melanesian Nightmare is a story of fantastic experiences and incredible hardships in the island jungles. The Japanese were aggressive, persistent, and often fanatical, fighting against the growing strength and well-trained might of the U. S. and ANZAC forces. The constant attrition of Japanese forces was to take from them their finest naval aviators and over 2,500 naval aircraft, reducing their air power to the point where carriers had to retire to Japan to retrain whole new air crews.

The successful campaigns by MacArthur on eastern New Guinea were made possible by the Solomons operations, which tied up the Japanese Navy. Since the Japanese could not concentrate on all fronts at the same time, the Allied advance toward the Philippines moved steadily onward.

In mid-March 1944 the U. S. Marines landed on Emirau Island northwest of Rabaul. At the same time MacArthur's forces secured Manus, main island of the Admiralty group. Rabaul was now encircled, and 125,000 Japanese troops—90,000 in Rabaul itself—were bypassed, surrounded by the advancing Americans without hope of relief or escape. There was now no need for the Americans to look back at Rabaul. It became a backwater as the war progressed westward along the northern New Guinea coast and northward toward the Philippines.

The final major benefit of the Rabaul campaign was the fact that it gained time for the United States to build up its naval striking forces, weapons, and trained manpower to advance across the Central Pacific in 1943 and 1944.

THE CENTRAL PACIFIC

While the South and Southwest Forces were concentrating on the isolation of Rabaul, the Central Force, comprising the new U. S. Fifth Fleet, began its moves toward the Philippines across the line of Japanese bases in Micronesia. The objective was for the Central Pacific

Force to meet with MacArthur's forces in dual support of the reconquest of the Philippines.

The Fifth Fleet was composed of the new carrier task forces organized for the purpose of projecting power at a distance. Placed under the command of Vice Admiral Raymond Spruance, a brilliant tactician, the Fifth Fleet had two purposes: fight and destroy Japanese naval forces wherever encountered and support amphibious forces which were organized to wrest control of selected island bases from their Japanese defenders.

The amphibious force had two components—the Fifth Amphibious Force commanded by Admiral Richmond Kelly Turner, comprising the naval transports, cargo ships, landing craft, and close-support bombardment ships; and the Fifth Amphibious Corps commanded by Major General Holland "Howling Mad" Smith, USMC, comprising the Marine and Army invasion troops.

The Service Force's mobile service squadrons kept these carrier and amphibious forces replenished, repaired, fueled, and fed, both at sea and from advanced bases near the operating area. The underway replenishment group kept the fleet and forces on the line, and was certainly a major factor enabling the U. S. Navy to drive from Pearl Harbor to the Philippines in less than a year.

The Central Pacific campaign was designed to advance across the Pacific—from Hawaii, through the U. S. bases in Samoa, Canton Island, and the Ellice Islands, to the Japanese bases in the Gilberts, Marshalls, and Marianas. The Japanese had made Tarawa in the Gilberts the most highly fortified spot in the Pacific at this time. They had also added defenses to Makin Atoll. These were to be the first targets of the Central Forces.

Just prior to the attack on the Gilberts, U. S. forces in the Solomons had defeated the Japanese in the Battle of Empress Augusta Bay and in devastating raids on Rabaul during the first two weeks of November 1943. These victories prevented the Japanese Combined Fleet from aiding the Japanese defenders in the Gilberts and the Marshalls. Most of the cruisers, two-thirds of the planes, and more than half of the flight crews had been lost by the Japanese in these two actions.

Makin was taken after three days of hard fighting, from 20–23 November. Costs were high despite American superiority, and especially high for the Navy. A turret explosion aboard the battleship *Mississippi* killed 43 men; and a Japanese submarine torpedoed the escort carrier *Liscome Bay*, hitting the bomb magazine. The ship blew up, taking with her 650 of the 900-man crew.

Tarawa, with 2,500 elite Japanese naval infantry and another thousand construction troops, plus 1,200 Korean laborers, proved to be extremely costly to the Marines. American casualties were grim: of 18,300 naval and Marine forces committed to the island, 3,000 were casualties, more than a thousand of which were killed. Of the nearly 4,000 Japanese defenders only one officer, 28 enlisted men, and 100 Koreans survived.

The American people were shocked at the cost. They began to realize that there is no cheap shortcut to winning a war. It showed that an enemy—well-trained, well-entrenched, and determined to fight—can be overcome only by other men with greater determination and firepower.

Many lessons were learned because of serious errors. This saved many lives in subsequent invasions; but the errors made Tarawa a bloodbath. Poor beach intelligence did not reveal that there was a reef in the lagoon which required at least four feet of tide to cross. Naval gunfire and bombing of the defenses, though spectacular, lifted too soon and enabled the defenders to reposition themselves and place direct fire on the boats stranded on the reef and their troops struggling through the water with heavy packs. Japanese machine gunners, hidden on a pier jutting into the la-goon all the way to the reef, held their fire until the Marines were stranded and most vulnerable.

The three-day battle on the tiny two-mile-long island was a battle of precedents: the first American assault on a fortified atoll; the first reef impassible to landing craft to be crossed under fire; the first operation to use amphibious tractors as troop carriers. It set the pattern for future amphibious operations in the Central Pacific.

THE MARSHALL ISLANDS OPERATIONS

Tarawa and Makin paved the way to the Marshalls. The Japanese had five strongpoints in the eastern Marshalls: Maloelap, Wotje, Mili, Jaluit, and Kwajalein. After the losses at Tarawa, Admirals Spruance and Turner recommended that Maloelap and Wotje be captured first and made into bases to support an assault on Kwajalein, the Japanese headquarters in the Marshalls. Nimitz, however, proposed a direct assault on Kwajalein after neutralizing the air strength on the other atolls. Their garrisons would be bypassed. The Japanese High Command had also figured that the Americans would strike first at the outer island defenses and so gave these atolls priority in defense materials and personnel.

Nimitz counted on this, believing that they would leave Kwajalein with lighter defenses; he was right. Though there were over 8,000 Japanese on Kwajalein, only 2,200 were combat troops, the others being technicians, laborers, and office personnel.

In January 1944, the attack on the Marshalls began with heavy carrier air raids on all the fortified islands. The raids were devastating; virtually all the Japanese planes were destroyed. Shore bombardment ships moved in and tore up the airfields, so that reinforcements could not be flown in from Eniwetok in the western Marshalls. Then the atoll defenses were softened by aerial and ship bombardment. On 1 February, the Marines landed on

Roi and Namur islands on the northern perimeter of Kwajalein Atoll, and the Army landed on Kwajalein Island on the south. Many of the defenders had been killed and many of their fortifications had been blown away. It was all over within four days. Only one hundred Japanese POWs were taken; the rest chose to fight to the end. American casualties were 373 killed and 1,550 wounded.

Admiral Nimitz now ordered an immediate invasion of Eniwetok, the largest of the western Marshalls. This atoll was only 1000 miles from the major Japanese bases in the Marianas and less than 700 from Truk, the "impregnable" Japanese "Pearl Harbor." Nimitz sent Vice Admiral Marc Mitscher's Task Force 58 to destroy the air capability which had been building up on these islands.

On 17 and 18 February, while Mitscher's planes hit Truk repeatedly, the new battleships *Iowa* and *New Jersey* and other bombardment forces from Spruance's task force swept around the base to catch anything trying to escape. Nimitz positioned 10 submarines in the area too. In those two days, the Americans destroyed 200 enemy aircraft and damaged 70 more, while sinking 15 Japanese naval vessels, 19 cargo ships, and 5 tankers.

While Truk was being blasted, Admiral Hill's Expeditionary Force landed on Eniwetok Atoll, in three separate amphibious landings on the major islands around the deepwater lagoon. The atoll was secured in three days. In the next few weeks all the Marshalls were secured except the strongly fortified bypassed atolls in the eastern part of the group. These were kept neutralized by occasional air raids, but otherwise the war had moved ahead of them.

Leapfrog on New Guinea

The raid on Truk had completed the neutralization of Rabaul. The rapidly growing Fifth Fleet now was capable of supporting invasions far beyond the reach of land-based aircraft. The next move in the two-pronged attack leading to the Philippines would be by MacArthur's forces, leap-frogging along the northern New Guinea coast. Units of Task Force 58 were called on to assist in these amphibious landings.

The first major landing was at Hollandia, a 400-mile jump from Saidor, the last New Guinea base secured by the Southwest Command. This was the largest amphibious landing to date in the Southwest Pacific, bringing 52,000 troops into three assault landings from 113 ships of the combined Fifth and Seventh Fleets. The intention was to bypass the Japanese 20,000-man Eighteenth Army at Wewak by capturing the major enemy air bases near Hollandia. Massive bomber raids by the U. S. Fifth Army Air Force destroyed 500 enemy planes at Hollandia. At the same time another landing was made at Aitape, between Hollandia and Wewak, in order to prevent the Eighteenth Army from getting into the Hollandia fighting. This Melanesian operation was a brutal campaign against jungle, disease, and fanatical Japanese. But it succeeded in destroying the enemy, nearly all of whom perished in the jungles after being driven out of their bases near the coast in hard fighting.

The Japanese thought the New Guinea movement was the single line of advance toward the Philippines. When MacArthur moved further to Wakde and then to Biak in May, the Japanese decided that they had to stop this advance. Biak had three airfields which were essential to the Japanese defense plan. The new Japanese Combined Fleet commander, Admiral Soemu Toyoda, decided to make an all-out attempt to hold Biak.

The Japanese first took much of their Central Pacific air strength and sent it to New Guinea to attack the newly won Allied air bases there. Then they made three reinforcement attempts by sea toward Biak, where MacArthur's forces had become stalemated by the strong Japanese defenses.

The two first attempts turned back after being sighted by Rear Admiral Thomas Kinkaid's Seventh Fleet. The third attempt was to be supported by the finest ships in the Japanese Navy, including the superbattleships *Yamato* and *Musashi*.

On 11 June, however, just as they were about to make their run on Biak, a thousand miles to the northeast the U. S. Fifth Fleet attacked the Marianas, preparatory to an invasion of Saipan.

Toyoda suspended the Biak operation and ordered Vice Admiral Jisaburo Ozawa northward to join the Main Body of the Mobile Fleet, east of the Philippines. MacArthur was now able to proceed unmolested by Japanese reinforcements. He proceeded to wrap up the New Guinea operation by the end of July.

The Marianas Operation: Saipan

June 1944 found United States forces engaged in the greatest military effort in history. At the very time the huge Normandy landings were taking place in Europe, the United States was about to place a huge amphibious force on Saipan in the Central Pacific. The mammoth task of projecting 127,000 troops on 535 ships some three thousand miles from Pearl Harbor, and providing them with fast carrier task force support against the entire Japanese Fleet, was just as complex as the D-Day invasion in Europe.

As the amphibious task force proceeded toward its objective, Army planes from the newly won bases in the Marshalls and Navy carrier planes from Task Force 58 struck Japanese bases in the Marianas and in the Carolines. The bombardment by U. S. battleships began on 13 June. It continued until the 15th when two Marine divisions crossed the coral reef, through passages blasted by the underwater demolition teams, and hit the beaches.

Heavy casualties were sustained; but by the end of the day 20,000 Marines were ashore. Reinforcements were put ashore and by 17 June the American offensive began to push the Japanese back after capturing the main airfield. By this time the Japanese Combined Fleet was approaching the operating area and Admiral Mitscher had to steam out to place himself between them and the forces on Saipan.

The Battle of the Philippine Sea

Maneuvering went on for two days as the two forces searched for each other, Mitscher always mindful of his primary orders: "capture, occupy, and defend Saipan, Tinian, and Guam." On the afternoon of 18 June, Admiral Ozawa's scout planes discovered Task Force 58.

Ozawa's Main Body had six carriers surrounded by cruisers and destroyers in the two circular formations. One hundred miles ahead of the Main Body was Vice Admiral Takeo Kurita with the main Japanese surface force of battleships, cruisers, and three carriers.

Facing the Japanese Mobile Force of 9 carriers, 5 battleships, 13 cruisers, 28 destroyers, and 430 carrier aircraft was Task Force 58—with 15 carriers, 7 battleships, 21 cruisers, 69 destroyers, and 891 carrier aircraft. From Japan, Admiral Toyoda radioed Ozawa that "the fate of the Empire depends on the issue of this battle; let every man do his utmost!"

Ozawa had counted heavily on getting air support from the Marianas bases. He felt that this land-based air support would more than equalize the opposing task forces. He did not know that only 30 operational planes remained after the devastating American raids made earlier. Nor did he realize that many of his carrier pilots returned from the Biak operations were sick with malaria and in poor fighting condition. Not aware that the odds were against him because of these factors, he moved to close Task Force 58.

Alerted to the impending attack, Mitscher and Spruance put more than 450 planes in the air to meet the challenge. New combat infor-

Battle of the Philippine Sea. Sometimes called the Marianas "Turkey Shoot," the Japanese naval air arm was destroyed in this battle. Photo shows a Japanese bomber plunging into the sea after being hit by heavy antiaircraft fire.

mation centers with the latest radar equipment guided TF-58's Hellcats to approaching enemy planes from advantageous altitudes and directions. The superbly trained American pilots, at peak efficiency from a year of successful combat experience, were ready for the battle.

In eight hours of furious air warfare, 330 Japanese planes were shot down in what historians now call the "Marianas Turkey Shoot." At the same time, the American submarine *Albacore* torpedoed Ozawa's new carrier flagship, the *Taiho,* and the submarine *Cavalla* put three torpedoes into the carrier *Shokaku.* Both carriers exploded a few hours later with great loss of life. But Ozawa and his staff survived and transferred to the carrier *Zuikaku.*

Ozawa ordered a general retirement to refuel, intending to resume battle the next day—even though he only had 100 carrier planes left. He believed the erroneous reports from his surviving pilots that TF-58 had been badly crippled.

Mitscher, in the meantime, had received no information on Ozawa's movements and chose a course which separated the forces well beyond his optimum operating radius. It was late the next day when a scout plane located the Japanese formation. Mitscher launched 216 planes on the Japanese when they were close to maximum operating range; it was a calculated risk. Then came the shock; the Japanese were 60 miles further away than originally reported. Mitscher decided to let his planes continue, while steaming full speed toward the Japanese in order to reduce the return flight distance.

Just before sunset the Americans found the Japanese force and attacked it, sinking two oilers and a carrier, and damaging two other carriers, a battleship, and a cruiser. Ozawa managed to get 75 of his fighters into the air; only 10 survived, and the crippled Mobile Fleet sailed away with only 35 planes left. Japanese naval air capability had been destroyed, and the Marianas invasion was able to continue with resistance only by the Japanese garrisons on the islands.

During the night after the final engagement, Admiral Mitscher daringly turned on the carrier lights to guide back the returning pilots. Many planes were lost, having to ditch in the sea when out of fuel. But of 209 aviators who had engaged the enemy that day, all but 49 were rescued either on the flight decks or from the water by destroyers and float planes.

CONQUEST OF THE MARIANAS

With the Mobile Force defeated and out of the area, TF-58 was able to concentrate on providing full assistance to the invading forces on Saipan and succeeding invasions of Tinian and Guam. Now sustained shore bombardment could be brought to bear before the troops landed, greatly reducing casualties. Both Saipan and Tinian were secured by the end of July and organized resistance ceased on Guam by 10 August.

Japan had lost her direct air route into the Carolines. The United States had acquired logistic bases for additional steps toward the Philippines, advance submarine bases for attacks on Japanese communications and sea lanes to the Indies, and air bases from which the new long-range B-29s would soon be bombing the industrial cities of Japan.

This was the beginning of the end for Japan. The Emperor and other high officials now knew that they would have to surrender. The Tojo government fell and was succeeded by a cabinet to whom the Emperor made known his desire for early peace negotiations. But the Japanese military code was still so strong that no official would initiate steps to end the war for yet another year.

Chapter 6. Study Guide Questions

1. What were the objectives of the opposing forces in the Solomon Islands?

2. On what particular island did the two forces converge to determine the outcome in the southwestern Pacific?

3. Where were Ironbottom Sound and "The Slot" located? How did they get these names?

4. What was the outcome of the Battle of Savo Island? What factor proved decisive for the Japanese?

5. What specially trained force developed Henderson Field on Guadalcanal, and many, many subsequent bases on the islands captured in the Pacific?

6. What name was given to the Japanese operations which attempted to reinforce their forces on Guadalcanal?

7. Which naval battle tipped the scales in favor of the U. S. Navy in the Solomons?

8. How did the Allied actions in New Guinea and Guadalcanal mutually assist each other?

9. Following the successes in Guadalcanal and New Guinea, what were the next offensive actions planned by Nimitz and MacArthur?

10. Why were the Japanese-held Aleutians chosen as objectives of our advancing forces?

11. What happened at Kiska?

12. What was the fundamental difference between the submarine war in the Atlantic and the Pacific?

13. What were the two principal shortcomings of the Japanese submarine and antisubmarine forces?

14. How did geography of the Western Pacific influence submarine warfare there?

15. What hindered U. S. submarine success in the first year and a half of the war?

16. What were the unique characteristics of American submarines built for Pacific duty?

17. What was the principal objective of U. S. submarines in the Pacific? Why?

18. What factors made American submariners successful?

19. Which naval weapon or force should probably be given the major credit for defeating the Japanese?

20. What was the significance of the death of Yamamoto?

21. What major Japanese base was the objective of the many battles in Melanesia? How was this base eventually handled?

22. What was the effect of "bypassing" in the American strategy?

23. How did the Rabaul and Southwest Pacific campaign benefit the naval forces in the Central Pacific?

24. What was the principal objective of the Allied moves from the Southwestern Pacific

(northward) and the Central Pacific (westward)?

25. What were the components of the U. S. Fifth Fleet?

26. What important lessons were learned on Tarawa in the Gilbert Islands?

27. What was Nimitz's plan to take the Marshalls? What was his first objective?

28. Why was Truk the specific object of American attack prior to the invasion of Eniwetok?

29. What did the Japanese consider the New Guinea leapfrog invasions to be for? How did they plan to stop the American advance? What caused the Japanese to halt their reinforcement and attack operations against American forces at Biak? What happened when the Japanese forces withdrew from the area with their major naval forces?

30. Name the three major Mariana Islands. Which island was the first U. S. objective?

31. What was the principal effect of the Japanese defeat in the Battle of the Philippine Sea?

32. What name has been given to the successful naval air battles fought in the Battle of the Philippine Sea?

33. What three particular assets had the U. S. gained by the conquest of the Marianas?

34. What major political change occurred in Japan as the result of their defeat in the Marianas?

Vocabulary

crucible	ANZAC
timetable	reconquest
consolidate	encounter
Guadalcanal	mobile service
New Guinea	squadron
anchorage	underway replenish-
repel	ment
inflict	formidable
skipper	atoll
Australia	Tarawa
Australasia	turret
Melanesia	entrenched
Micronesia	category
Polynesia	Marshall Islands
Aleutian Islands	Kwajalein
garrison	bypass
Attu, Kiska	devastating
fanatical	impregnable
incapacitate	lagoon
underestimate	expeditionary force
transoceanic	Mariana Islands
archipelago	Truk, Caroline Is-
constricted	lands
deficiency	circular formation
camaraderie	Saipan, Tinian,
distinction	Guam, Rota

Chapter 7. World War II in the Pacific: The Last Battles

RETURN TO THE PHILIPPINES

The next series of invasion plans had yet to be decided when Spruance, Turner, and "Howling Mad" Smith returned to Pearl Harbor to rest and plan their own future operations. The Fifth Fleet was redesignated the U. S. Third Fleet under Admiral Halsey, with Vice Admiral Mitscher remaining in command of the Fast Carrier Task Force, now called Task Force 38.

Knowing that the Palau Islands, Yap, and Morotai were the next probable objectives, Halsey joined TF-38 in his flagship, the USS *New Jersey,* and carried out air strikes against the central Philippines. The results were astounding. TF-38 destroyed 200 enemy airplanes and sank a dozen freighters and a tanker. Convinced that the central Philippines were weakly defended, Halsey sent Nimitz an urgent message recommending that the Palaus and Yap be bypassed and that ground forces for these operations be turned over to MacArthur for an invasion of Leyte Island in the central

Philippines. MacArthur agreed. The Joint Chiefs directed Nimitz and MacArthur to combine forces for the invasion of Leyte on 20 October 1944, after securing Morotai and Peleliu in the Palaus.

Morotai was captured in one of the easiest conquests of the war, but overcoming Peleliu cost the Marines the highest combat casualty rate (40 percent) of any amphibious assault in American history. A new Japanese strategy was put into effect following the series of Central Pacific defeats. The old strategy called for the defenders to meet the invasion on the beaches; this obviously had not worked in the face of devastating shore bombardment. The new strategy called for a "defense in depth." The defenders were to have prepared positions well behind the beaches, taking full advantage of the natural terrain. Impregnable fortifications were to be constructed and there were to be no useless *banzai* charges.

More than 10,000 Japanese had carefully prepared Peleliu in accordance with the new strategy. A series of natural ridges crossed the island, affording excellent concealment for artillery and caves for personnel. Many of these caves were interconnected. After three days of naval bombardment the Marines landed on Peleliu on 17 September, and quickly made good their beachhead and captured the airfield. Then, however, they ran into the ridge defenses and from then on it was costly and slow. It was not until February 1945 that the island was cleared of Japanese defenders. By that time the Marines had suffered 10,000 casualties, including nearly 2,000 dead.

Long before February, however, the airfields and the anchorages in the Palaus were in American use. Had they remained in Japanese hands, they would have been a threat to the Leyte invasion and subsequent Philippine operations.

In preparing for the Leyte invasion, the Third Fleet conducted heavy attacks on Formosa and Okinawa to destroy potential land-based air support for the Japanese forces in the Philippines. Just before the landings took place, they attacked Formosa again, destroying most of the torpedo bombers which had been sent from the home islands. Over 350 Japanese land-based aircraft had been destroyed between 11–15 October. This ensured control of the air over the Leyte beaches.

More than 60,000 assault troops were ashore on Leyte by sunset on D-Day, 20 October. From then on it was a tough fight in the interior of the island. General MacArthur waded ashore a few hours after the first landing, accompanied by President Sergio Osmeña of the Philippines. In a radio broadcast he announced his return to the islands and called for Filipinos to rise and strike the Japanese at every opportunity.

THE BATTLES FOR LEYTE GULF

Between 23–26 October the Japanese made their greatest challenge to the Leyte landings. Admiral Toyoda knew that if the Japanese lost the Philippines they would lose everything. The lifeline between Japan and the Indies would be cut and the Mobile Fleet would be divided, without fuel and ammunition. The Fleet would then be defeated piecemeal and Japan would be blockaded. Toyoda knew he was outnumbered, but this would be the last chance for the Imperial Navy to stop the American advance.

In the four-day action there were four major battles: the Battle of the Sibuyan Sea on 24 October; and the Battle of Surigao Strait, the Battle off Cape Engaño, and the Battle off Samar on 25 October. These battles were the largest and most complex naval engagements in history. When the battles were over, the Imperial Japanese Navy no longer existed as an effective fighting force and the United States Navy was in command of the Pacific Ocean.

The Japanese objective was to destroy the huge amphibious armada in Leyte Gulf. They had three forces to do this with: Ozawa's

Northern Carrier Force which the Japanese intended as a decoy; Admiral Shoji Nishimura's Southern Force of battleships and heavy cruisers in the Sulu Sea; and Admiral Kurita's Central Force of battleships and heavy cruisers coming in from the South China Sea through the Sibuyan Sea and San Bernadino Straits.

Kurita's force was struck first by submarines off Palawan Island, losing three cruisers. But it continued onward into the Philippine Archipelago, crossing into the Sibuyan Sea south of Mindoro. There U. S. carrier planes sank the giant battleship *Musashi,* another cruiser, and a destroyer. Despite this the Central Force continued on toward Leyte Gulf through the San Bernadino Strait.

The Southern Force entered Surigao Strait and headed into Leyte Gulf where it was intercepted by Kinkaid's Seventh Fleet of old battleships and other ships of the amphibious fire-support group. Rear Admiral Jesse Oldendorf set up an ambush designed to have the Japanese in the stem of a "T" crossed by American cruisers and battleships and flanked by light forces of destroyers and PT boats. In naval terminology, to be the stem of a "T" is to be caught in a hopeless position. The Japanese force of 2 battleships, 4 cruisers, and 10 destroyers was utterly destroyed; only one destroyer made it out of the trap, while only one American destroyer sustained any damage.

Ozawa's Northern Force, meanwhile, was sighted coming south, as the Japanese intended. Halsey steamed at full speed northward, thinking that Kurita's damaged Central Force was no longer capable of proceeding toward Leyte Gulf. The ruse worked; when Halsey went north he left the escort carriers and support forces off Samar without protection.

Against extreme odds, the baby flat-tops fought against Kurita's battleships with everything at their disposal, their reconnaissance, scout, and support forces hopelessly outgunned. Destroyers escorting the small carriers laid smoke screens and charged into certain destruction in order to drive Kurita back. They succeeded, sinking two cruisers and a destroyer, while losing an escort carrier, 2 destroyers, and 105 airplanes. The next day additional damage was inflicted on the Kurita force as it retired in defeat.

Halsey, in the meantime, engaged the Northern Force off Cape Engaño on the island of Luzon, sinking all four Japanese carriers. Ozawa, however, had achieved his goal of enticing Halsey away from Leyte Gulf so Kurita could get in to destroy the Amphibious Task Force and the invasion.

It was because of poor communications that Kurita had turned back from his mission in Leyte Gulf. He never received Ozawa's message telling that the main U. S. force was attacking him. If Kurita had received that message, and concluded that no major surface or air forces were in the Leyte Gulf area to stop him, there could have been a terrible disaster for the American forces.

With the Japanese surface navy ruined, its carriers sunk and pilots lost, the United States proceeded with the reconquest of the Philippines. Eighteen amphibious assaults were conducted between the landings on Leyte and the final landings in March 1945 on the islands of Mindanao and Panay. It was at Leyte Gulf, however, that another new threat appeared for the first time in the Pacific War—the kamikaze. From then on until the Philippine Islands were secured, U. S. naval forces suffered increasing damage and sinkings from these suicide planes. The worst from this type of attack was yet to come, however.

Iwo Jima

The conquest of the Marianas provided the bases for the giant B-29 bombers to make their devastating air raids on the Japanese industrial cities. But between the Marianas and Japan was the volcanic island of Iwo Jima. As long as the Japanese held the island, the home islands' defenses were alerted when bombers were en-route and fighters were scrambled to intercept them.

The 3,000-mile round trip was much too far for our fighters to accompany and defend the bombers. Damaged bombers were generally lost in the sea on the return trip because they would not hold up for that distance. The Americans determined to put an end to this dangerous problem. In U. S. hands the island's airfields could be improved to manage emergency landings for the big bombers, and to provide a base for fighter planes to escort them over Tokyo.

The Japanese, fully aware of the importance of the island to their defenses, expected an assault. They removed the civilians and reinforced the garrison to 23,000 troops. They proceeded to transform the island into the strongest fortress in the Pacific. Though only about 8 square miles in area, Iwo was a plateau of lava cut into hills and ravines overlooked by 550-foot Mt. Suribachi, an extinct volcano. The Japanese tunneled into the volcanic rock and made interconnecting passageways between 400 concealed pillboxes and concrete block-houses. Their artillery was placed in caves on Mt. Suribachi where it could sweep the beaches.

Some of the more than 500 amphibious craft enroute to the assault beaches at Iwo Jima. Mt. Suribachi looms in the background.

Heavy naval bombardment rained on the island for only three days of the ten requested by the Marines because of the speeded-up timetable decreed by the Joint Chiefs of Staff. This was to prove grossly inadequate.

D-Day was 19 February. Five hundred landing craft carrying eight battalions of Marines moved to the line of departure. Meanwhile more than a hundred of TF-58's planes attacked the island with rockets, machine guns, and general purpose and napalm bombs. Naval guns shifted from slow destructive fire to fast neutralizing fire to drive the defenders underground. When the assault waves approached the beach, the support ships shifted fire again to provide a barrage fire ahead and on the flanks of the advancing Marines. More than 50 rocket-firing amphibious ships advanced to give the Marines close support.

Despite all this preparatory fire, the assault waves quickly piled up on the beach, the amphibian tractors unable to climb the crumbling volcanic ash. Many landing craft broached or ran into earlier boat waves. The Marines, stranded on the steep beach, soon were hit by withering machine gun, mortar, and heavy gun fire from weapons which had withheld their fire earlier so as not to reveal their positions. Through this holocaust the Marines inched forward, isolating Mt. Suribachi and reaching the edge of the nearest airfield. Of 30,000 Marines who hit the beach that first day, 2,400 became casualties.

The fighting continued through the night and the next day the airfield was captured. The assault on Mt. Suribachi then began. After three days of blasting and burning out pillboxes and sealing up caves with grenades, flame throwers, rockets, and demolition charges, the mountain was surrounded and a patrol reached the summit and raised the American flag.

While the vicious fighting was in progress on Iwo Jima, the supporting naval forces of TF-58 and the Amphibious Support Force were subjected to repeated kamikaze attacks.

The carrier *Saratoga* was badly damaged and the escort carrier *Bismarck Sea* sank after a tremendous explosion which blew off her stern. Over 650 men were lost from the crews of these two carriers alone.

Instead of taking five days as originally planned, the conquest of Iwo Jima took over a month. It wasn't until 25 March that the last hidden Japanese troops made their final attack. Only 200 Japanese were captured; all the rest were killed. For the first time casualties among the assault forces exceeded that of the Japanese defenders. Over 19,000 American Marines and sailors were wounded and nearly 7,000 were killed. Of the American Marines on Iwo Jima, Admiral Nimitz said they made "uncommon valor a common virtue."

In the long run, Iwo proved to be a worthwhile objective. More than 2,000 heavy bombers landed there, too crippled or too low on fuel to make it back to the Marianas. Each B-29 carried 11 men, so at least 22,000 members of the Air Force probably owed their lives to the Marines who took Iwo.

Operation Iceberg: Okinawa

The war was now closing in on the home islands of Japan. From the middle of February, carrier aircraft began striking the Japanese cities with high explosives and incendiaries. On 25 February, even before Iwo was secured, fighters from TF-58 supported 200 B-29s in a massive raid on Tokyo, burning out two square miles of the enemy capital and destroying 150 Japanese aircraft. From there, TF-58 steamed past Okinawa, bombing the island's airfields and taking intelligence photography. The final gigantic amphibious assault and battle of the Pacific War was about to begin.

Weeks of heavy raids and softening up attacks on Japanese bases on Kyushu and Okinawa preceded the assault landings on Okinawa. On 1 April a force of 1,300 ships carrying 182,000 assault troops arrived off the island, having come from bases all over the Pacific. About 100,000 Japanese defenders awaited their attack from well-prepared positions, as on Iwo and Peleliu.

Almost from the beginning, elements of the invasion fleet were subjected to kamikaze attacks. On the morning of 6 April, however, the Japanese began their last major counterattack of the war. Over 350 Japanese kamikazes came out of Kyushu to strike the Fleet. Meanwhile, the last surviving surface force made up of the huge battleship *Yamato*, the light cruiser *Yahagi*, and eight destroyers sailed south from the Inland Sea, propelled by the last 2,500 tons of fuel oil in Japan. It was to be a one-way trip, both for aircraft and ships. Since the ships did not have enough fuel to return, their mission was to drive through the invasion fleet, causing as much damage as possible. They would beach themselves at the invasion site, firing until all their ammunition was expended or until they were destroyed.

The kamikazes sank the U. S. picket destroyers, but not before their approach had been

Kamikaze attack! A Japanese suicide plane comes in to attack the USS *Missouri* during the Okinawa invasion. The plane caused minor damage; it can be seen coming in over the port antiaircraft batteries.

An invasion beach on Okinawa. In the background, part of the huge invasion armada is busy offloading supplies to support the forces ashore.

radioed by the sinking ships. Met by an alert combat air patrol from TF-58, 150 planes were shot down; the remaining 200 made it to the Okinawa area. There they were destroyed by fighter planes and intense antiaircraft fire. They sank a few ships, and damaged others.

Meanwhile the *Yamato* force was allowed to proceed far enough southward so it would not be able to retreat to safety. Then Admiral Mitscher struck with the full force of his carrier aircraft. Only two destroyers survived the attack and made it back to base.

For the next three months the carrier task forces and other ships of the U. S. Fifth and Third Fleets sustained hundreds of kamikaze attacks as they supported the Okinawa action and thrust their power into the Japanese home islands. On 21 June Okinawa was declared secure after the defending Japanese general

and his chief of staff acknowledged defeat by committing suicide. By this time the Navy had lost 68 ships sunk and 368 damaged, and 4,097 Navy men killed—more than either the Marines or Army suffered in the hard going on the island.

But the U. S. Navy stayed, and Okinawa was secured. The battle had cost the Japanese 100,000 men and 7,000 airplanes. Okinawa was the end of the fighting for the Japanese. Emperor Hirohito told his Supreme War Council on 22 June 1945 that they must find a way to end the war. Japanese cities were being turned into ashes by fire-bombing raids; the navy and air force were gone. The Soviet Union had informed the Japanese that they would not renew their Neutrality Pact in April, and since Germany had surrendered on 7 May, entrance of Russia into the Asiatic War was imminent.

THE SURRENDER OF JAPAN

Ending the war was not simple. There were still powerful factions in Japan and in the military forces in Asia who favored a fight to the bitter end. Neither would the government or the people accept a surrender which would not preserve the Emperor and imperial system. The Japanese made peace feelers to the Russians during their negotiations for extension of the neutrality pact. But the Russians remained silent—so silent that Stalin didn't even tell the United States or Britain about the peace move during their meeting then going on in Potsdam, Germany!

But the United States knew about the peace feelers because U. S. intelligence was reading the messages going between the Foreign Ministry in Tokyo and the Japanese ambassador in Moscow. On 26 July the Potsdam Declaration spelled out the terms of surrender for Japan, specifying that unconditional surrender would pertain only to the military forces and that possessions except the four home islands—Hokkaido, Honshu, Shikoku, and Kyushu—would have to be given up. No provisions concerning the Emperor were made, since the Allies had not yet decided on this question.

As the Russians stalled and the Japanese procrastinated, the Americans and British were actively planning an invasion of Kyushu in November and an assault on Honshu the following March. Events were moving faster than governments, however. On 16 July the United States successfully exploded the first atomic bomb at Alamogordo, New Mexico; within hours atomic weapons were enroute to the Marianas bomber bases. And during the next three weeks the combined American and British fleets, the most powerful ever assembled in history, ranged freely up and down the Japanese coast shelling and bombing the cities with virtual impunity.

But on 6 August a B-29 carrying an atomic bomb departed Tinian and headed for Hiroshima, an industrial city on the Inland Sea. The weapon utterly destroyed the city. The Russians now realized that the end had arrived and they had to get into the Pacific War immediately if they were to get in on the victory. On 8 August the Soviet Union declared war on Japan and moved her forces into Manchuria and Korea, sweeping the Japanese before them. On 9 August the second atomic bomb was dropped on the industrial port of Nagasaki, flattening that city.

Emperor Hirohito now advised his Supreme Council to accept the Potsdam Declaration. The Cabinet agreed, but only on the condition that the imperial system remain. The U. S. Secretary of State, speaking on behalf of the Allied governments, accepted the condition subject to two stipulations: (1) the Emperor must submit to the authority of the Supreme Allied Commander during the occupation of Japan, and (2) the Japanese people should decide on the Emperor's ultimate status through free elections at a later date. The Cabinet, on the advice of the Emperor, agreed to these stipulations on 14 August. On 15 August, with one carrier raid already flying over Tokyo, the Third Fleet received the order to "cease fire." World War II was over.

In the next two weeks the Allies converged on Tokyo Bay. On 2 September, the Japanese foreign minister and representatives of the Imperial General Staff boarded the USS *Missouri* and signed the surrender document on behalf of the Emperor, the Government, and the Imperial General Headquarters. General Douglas MacArthur signed the acceptance as Supreme Allied Commander for the Allied Powers. Fleet Admiral Chester Nimitz signed as Representative for the United States. Following him were representatives for the United Kingdom, China, the Soviet Union, Australia, Canada, France, the Netherlands, and New Zealand. Shortly thereafter, General MacArthur moved into his Tokyo headquarters to direct the occupation of Japan.

The destruction of the city of Nagasaki, Japan, by an atomic bomb. Only a few steel and concrete buildings remain standing. Dropping the bombs on the two Japanese cities brought the war to an abrupt conclusion, thus saving the agony of invasion of the Japanese home islands where untold casualties would have been suffered by both sides.

THE U. S. NAVY AT WAR'S END

The U. S. Navy ended the war with the largest naval force ever assembled in world history. The Navy had grown from 330,000 men on 7 December 1941, to 3,408,347 at war's end. This number included 93,074 uniformed Navy women called WAVES. The Navy had more than 50,000 vessels, 1,200 major fighting ships, and 40,000 airplanes.

After this war, the United States could not retreat to a position of isolation and pre-war conditions. It had acquired responsibilities around the world, and the only way it could meet those responsibilities was with a power-ful Navy. The nation had worldwide duties to perform, and these duties could be discharged only if it continued to be a great sea power.

Chapter 7. Study Guide Questions

1. What were the two numbered fleets which conducted most carrier task force operations in the Pacific War? Who were the commanders of each of these fleets?

2. What was Admiral Halsey's recommendation after his raid on the central Philippines?

3. What was the new Japanese defense strategy first encountered on Peleliu in the Palau group? Why was this group of islands invaded by U. S. forces?

The Japanese "Surrender Delegation" boards USS *Missouri* for the final ceremony of the war. This was the first time the Japanese had surrendered to a foe in more than 2,000 years.

4. What was the purpose of the American naval air attacks on Formosa and Okinawa prior to invading the Philippines?

5. On what island did the American forces return to the Philippines?

6. Why were the Philippines so important to Japan?

7. What were the four major sea battles which comprised the Battles for Leyte Gulf?

8. What was the objective of the Japanese Combined Fleet in the Battles for Leyte Gulf?

9. What is the concept of "crossing the T" in naval tactics? In which battle for Leyte Gulf was it used effectively?

10. What was the purpose of Admiral Ozawa's Northern Force? How did it succeed? What caused Admiral Kurita to turn back when he had an opportunity to destroy the U. S. Amphibious Force at Leyte?

11. What was the result of the Battles for Leyte Gulf as regards the Japanese Navy?

12. What were the kamikazes? Where did they first appear?

13. Why did the American military leadership feel it was necessary to secure Iwo Jima?

14. What natural obstacle on the beach caused a buildup of amphibious craft and Marine tractors? How does this tragic experience point out the necessity for accurate beach intelligence?

15. What is the name of the famous mountain on Iwo Jima?

16. Where was the last major amphibious assault conducted in the Pacific theater?

17. What was the prinicpal Japanese weapon against the fleet off Okinawa?

18. To whom did the Japanese make their initial "peace feelers" to end the war? What happened? How did the United States know about the peace feelers?

19. What was the Potsdam Declaration? What important point was not included in the Potsdam surrender terms?

20. What are the four main islands of Japan?

21. What three major events occurred in early August which prompted the Japanese to accept the Potsdam Declaration as a basis for their surrender? What condition did they request be granted by the Allies? How did the Allies respond to this request?

22. When did the cease-fire take effect?

23. Where and when did the Japanese sign the surrender document? Who were the top two U. S. signers and who did each represent?

24. What was the position of the United States at the end of the war? Why was the Navy so important to the United States as the result of the victory in World War II?

Vocabulary

redesignate	batallion
Fast Carrier Task	napalm
Force	barrage
Peleliu, Palau Islands	broach
banzai charge	valor
"defense in depth"	virtue
Leyte Gulf	incendiary
San Bernadino Strait	Okinawa
naval terminology	Emperor Hirohito
ruse	Potsdam Declaration
entice	procrastinate
kamikaze	impunity
Iwo Jima	Hiroshima
scramble (aircraft)	Nagasaki
Mt. Suribachi	Tokyo
pillbox	confrontation

4

Naval Leadership and Discipline

Chapter 1: The Challenge of Leadership

Officers and petty officers are required to assume the responsibilities of leadership, by the very nature of their offices. Although weapons, ships, aircraft, and people have changed, the challenge of leadership remains the same: to get people to do the Navy's job effectively.

Leadership and discipline are indispensible qualities of a military organization. However, the same qualities which make a fine leader in the military services are equally helpful to the active civilian or citizen leader.

BASIS FOR EFFECTIVE LEADERSHIP

Naval leadership stresses the development of those qualities of intellect, human understanding, and moral character that enable a person to inspire and manage a group of people successfully. Effective leadership, therefore, is based on personal example, good organization and administration, and personal moral responsibility. The second of these, organization and administration, deals with a leader's personal attention and supervision of subordinates. Because the Navy is comprised of people, naval leaders must learn to understand and appreciate the many individuals with whom they must work during their career. An officer must be fully aware of the demands which he makes on his subordinates, as individuals.

The naval officer must have a philosophy of leadership based on firmly held moral values and integrity of character. Each officer must understand his responsibilities in relations with seniors, contemporaries, and juniors.

A naval officer will be ineffective in any working or shipboard environment if he does not understand good naval leadership and administration and is not able to promote the teamwork necessary for a ship to carry out its mission. Constant study and application of sound principles of leadership are necessary for a naval officer to become truly proficient.

Leadership concerns human relations—specifically those between a leader and a group. There must be the motivation for an individual to impose, either through command or persuasion, his will upon that group. Also required is a willingness on the part of the leader to sacrifice personal time and material gain to achieve this personal "power." Still, before a person can become a truly successful naval leader, he must first of all have learned the principles of good "followership."

PHILOSOPHIES OF LEADERSHIP

Philosophies of leadership differ widely. One extreme view holds that leaders are born, not made. The opposite view contends that anyone who can master a certain set of leadership principles can lead effectively. Other viewpoints stress leadership as a managerial process or as a matter of character and moral development. Still another holds that leadership can best be learned by studying the lives of great men and women. Each of these philosophies

The naval officer is expected to have the knowledge of the professional mariner. In addition, he must practice the good naval leadership necessary to promote teamwork, if the ship is to carry out its mission.

has merit, but none, by itself, answers the problem of how effective naval leadership can be developed.

There is no denying that some persons are much more favorably endowed with physical and mental qualities that make them natural leaders. However, history provides examples of persons who reached great heights of leadership as the result of arduous study, discipline, and hard work—in spite of small stature, physical handicaps, or a lowly family background.

Also, different naval activities, because of their varied missions, require different kinds of leadership. Shore activities, often industrial in nature, are often best served by managerial concepts of leadership. Such concepts, however, could be quite inappropriate aboard a combatant ship which must be a more rigidly disciplined environment. In a typical career the average naval officer and petty officer will have assignments to duty of both a military and an industrial character.

Leadership is an art, gift, or science by which a person is allowed to direct the thoughts, plans, and actions of others in order to command their obedience, respect, confidence, and loyal cooperation. Each of these attitudes is essential; lack of any one probably

will be sufficient to cause disaster in any situation where leadership is needed.

OBEDIENCE

Obedience is the most important of the attitudes which good leaders should strive to instill in personnel. Obedience is necessarily the first lesson which must be learned by any military person.

Comparing the military with civilian life with regard to obedience is relatively simple. There are both similarities and differences, however, in the results of obedience or disobedience in the two environments. The first lessons learned by children from their parents involve obedience: come here, go there, sit down, eat, don't touch, be careful, pick it up, etc. Obedience becomes the teaching tool to train the child in fundamental activities and to protect him from dangers. In adult life, however, obedience is of more immediate concern in military life than it might be in most civilian environments.

While disobeying the law will result in punishment of one sort or another in either environment, the loss of their jobs is probably the most significant result when civilians disobey their boss. Since business and industry generally measure their success on the basis of production output and sales, removal of the disobedient or uncooperative employee might be expected to solve the immediate problem.

The military "product," however, is defense of our country and our way of life. Service people, therefore, must be more idealistic than the average civilian, since they are serving, protecting, and defending America and her allies—even to the extent of giving up their lives in peace or war. Thus there is a greater need for obedience from persons in uniform. Protection of our way of life is the basic purpose of our military services, and all uniformed personnel are expected to contribute to this end by giving intelligent, devoted, and creative service. Truly disciplined service men or

Truly disciplined service men and women are constantly learning, and applying their knowledge.

women are willing to make the necessary sacrifices to defend our heritage, even in the most adverse conditions.

Obedience in the Military Services

Obedience has two forms in the military, each with its own time and place. *Blind obedience* might be regarded as automatic reaction to command, such as the response to commands during close order drill or positive actions by the helmsman following emergency steering commands. There is no time for questioning or determining the reason for the command. *Reasoned obedience,* on the other hand, is positive action based on an order which allows for personal initiative in carrying it out.

Reasoned obedience is the type most often desired in the Navy. Navy work means constant learning, and it is known that people work and learn best when allowed to use their own ideas. The "order" gives the receiver some freedom in deciding exactly how to carry it out in a responsible manner.

The best kind of discipline is self-discipline. To discipline one's self brings the reasoned kind of obedience the Navy desires of all its people. The more easily a person can work and learn on his own, the more self-disciplined he becomes. It stands to reason, then, that the leader must discipline himself first, because only by demanding the best from himself can he expect to get the best from his subordinates.

Self-discipline lessens the need for specific rules and regulations. Traffic laws, the Uniform Code of Military Justice, Civil Rights laws, alcohol and drug laws, and even school dress codes would be unnecessary if we all were perfectly self-disciplined individuals. Self-disciplined people need little or no supervision; however, you can expect the majority of any group of subordinates, military or civilian, to require some supervision.

Supervision of personnel under orders implies many things. Fundamentally it involves the leader's responsibility to periodically check on the progress of the assigned task. This serves not only to assure that progress is indeed being made and that proper methods are being used. It also indicates that the leader has a personal interest in having the task well done.

Orders may be given in various ways. Polite phrases such as "please" or "would you" and other common courtesies may be used by a senior when giving orders, but even if the order has the sound of a request, it is still an order. Because self-discipline is not always apparent, a more specific form of order called the command may be appropriate.

A command relies upon immediate obedience. Courteous terms normally are not used in commands. When orders are given, and time permits, the leader may explain the reasons for the task. The juniors may be encouraged to ask reasonable questions about the job; but this does not imply that subordinates may decide whether or not they will obey such orders.

People will obey the orders of lawful authorities either because of the hope of reward or the threat of punishment. Reasoned obedience to an order is usually given because of the hope of some kind of reward. Reward may be in the form of a simple verbal approval (such as "Well done!"), public recognition and praise, the privilege of greater responsibility, or improvement of status in the organization. The immediacy of a command response seldom lends itself to particular reward at the moment, and is more often associated with the threat of punishment should it be disobeyed. The good leader should strive to have the respect, confidence, and loyal cooperation of his personnel, but it is impossible for him to function without first obtaining their obedience.

THE OFFICER'S COMMISSION: A LEGAL AND MORAL OBLIGATION

Civilian executives hold their positions by virtue of superior knowledge and strong character or personality. The executive probably is not legally responsible for the persons otherwise employed, and any concern for the well-being of subordinates is primarily a moral one.

Military officers, by virtue of their commissions, have both a legal and a moral obligation to do all in their power to make themselves fully capable of leading men and women in war. The President, as representative of the people of the United States, has granted each officer extensive authority based on a legal contract. An officer represents our government's responsibility to enforce the law of the land; all officers are charged with the well-being of their assigned subordinates.

The military leader must depend upon his subordinates to accomplish assigned missions. Consequently, he has to be aware of their capabilities and their limitations. He must personally be concerned with their health, welfare, and any of the many problems—such as family illness, debts, and other difficulties—which may work to destroy peace of mind and efficiency on the job. Officers must gain the confidence of their personnel so that their people will feel free to consult with them about any problems. They must know that the officer will give all assistance possible, and may refer them to the chaplain or other skilled counselors.

THE OFFICER'S TASK

The officer has an especially difficult task in trying to motivate the disinterested persons or troublemakers who seem to exist in most groups of people. Hopefully, the leader will be able to guide and assist the majority of such individuals in gaining a sense of moral responsibility so they too can become assets to the organization. After all, everyone must live by rules and regulations, whether they are in the Navy or in civilian life. These rules, if followed by all, make life more pleasant and easier for all.

Personnel must be taught that the more they discipline themselves, the less they will have to be disciplined by others. They must be fully aware of their importance to the team. Their shipmates must be able to depend on them day-to-day, as well as in battle. All should be led to understand that increasing knowledge, advancing in rate, and assuming more responsibilities are duties of every contributive sailor and citizen, not just the choice of a select few.

Chapter 1. Study Guide Questions

1. What is the challenge of naval leadership?
2. Why are leadership and discipline important in civilian life?
3. Management of people is dependent upon what naval leadership qualities?
4. Upon what is effective naval leadership based?
5. Why is teamwork necessary for a naval vessel to carry out its mission?
6. What does good followership mean to you?
7. Which philosophy of leadership do you believe has most merit today?
8. Why are character and moral development aspects of leadership that are important today?
9. Why is it a privilege to be in a position of leadership?
10. What is the first lesson which military personnel must learn?
11. Why must military personnel have a more idealistic outlook on the importance of obedience?
12. What are the two forms of military obedience? Why is there a necessity for each in the Navy?
13. What is self-discipline?
14. If persons were perfectly self-disciplined, would there be any need for supervisors?
15. What is the difference between a senior's request-order and a command?
16. What motives generally control the actions of men and women?
17. Why does his commission make the military officer essentially different from the civilian executive?
18. Why is motivation an especially difficult task for a leader of a group of people? What makes this situation so different for the civilian leader as compared to the military leader?
19. What are considered to be fundamental duties of every sailor? Why?

Vocabulary

naval leadership	self-discipline
discipline	order
personal example	command
moral responsibility	representative
proficiency	executive
managerial concept	commission
delinquency	efficiency
reasoned obedience	motivation

Chapter 2. Qualities of a Leader

No two leaders are exactly alike. They do not possess the same qualities in equal proportions; neither do they accomplish their goals in the same ways. All great leaders, however, have certain characteristics and abilities which they develop to the greatest advantage. Not every leader will possess every quality dis-cussed here, but all will have a substantial number of them. It stands to reason that the less natural ability a leader has, the more important it is for him to work on those qualities he needs to become more effective.

MORAL RESPONSIBILITY

A high sense of moral responsibility is one of the most important leadership characteristics.

All truly great leaders have been bound by personal codes of conduct which would not permit them to exploit their abilities and positions at the expense of their fellow citizens or subjects.

Most of us understand the written and unwritten laws which guide our actions, and are aware that suitable punishments will result if we break them. It is more difficult, however, to define moral laws since most have no legal standing under law-enforcing branches of government. Each person must establish these laws for himself, basing them on his own principles. Depending upon the person's character, the sense of moral responsibility may be extensive or almost nonexistent. The only enforcer is the individual's own conscience.

The Navy provides training and guidance for all its personnel to encourage high standards of moral responsibility. The Navy expects its officers to set such standards at all times. Commanding officers and others in authority are directed by *Navy Regulations* and the *Marine Corps Manual* to "show in themselves a good example of virtue, honor, patriotism, and subordination; to be vigilant in inspecting the conduct of all persons who are placed under their command; to guard against and suppress all dissolute and immoral practices, and to correct all persons who are guilty of them; and to take all necessary and proper measures to promote and safeguard the morale, the physical well-being, and general welfare of the officers and enlisted persons under their command. . . ."

LOYALTY

Loyalty means faithful and enthusiastic devotion to one's country, organization, and associates. In the military this must be broadened to include one's superiors and subordinates. While human nature is such that the ordinary person willingly extends loyalty to others in the organization, everyone must earn the right to that loyalty.

Loyalty is a two-way street. Subordinates are particularly sensitive about loyalty extending downward to them and are quick to notice when it's absent. The loyalty of a senior toward his personnel has direct bearing on the morale within the organization, and this may translate into that extra effort which is so often necessary to accomplish a mission well.

DEVOTION TO DUTY

Devotion to duty may be defined as loyalty to the position or job one now holds. In general, devotion to duty is shown by the person who exerts a maximum effort on his present job, and then spends his extra energy and talents in learning about tasks and billets demanding increased levels of responsibility. This person not only fulfills his present obligations well, but inspires his men to greater efforts and earns the respect of all concerned. Recommendations, advancements, and promotions are likely to result from such performance of duty.

A young person showing ambitious traits on the job in a civilian firm would normally be considered a valuable asset; such a person might eventually be trained for a management role. Mere ambition does not suffice in the military service, however. All officers and enlisted persons are expected to place duty above self. Everyone must do his duty to the best of his ability at all times—not because of the personal gain which might occur, but because that is the best way to accomplish the mission. Anyone who refuses to do his share causes hardship and extra workload for others in the unit. Indeed, lives may be lost needlessly and the unit might fail in its mission if some individuals fail to do their part.

PROFESSIONAL KNOWLEDGE

The person who knows his job thoroughly is far better qualified to lead than one who does not. Mere schoolbook knowledge is not sufficient to attain professionalism; experience is

Professional knowledge includes both academic proficiency and experience. A First Class Hull Technician provides guidance to subordinates in his unit so they may do their part in the operation.

also essential. The new leader, therefore, must also call upon experienced individuals to assist him in assuming his leadership role.

The person being relieved by the new leader normally provides instruction concerning the duties and difficulties of the job, and the abilities and personalities of the assigned personnel. Senior officers are ready to assist the new officer, and petty officers will be eager to help, if their new leader wants to gain from their experiences. It pays to be willing to listen to advice and suggestions, for most people will lose the desire to help as soon as a person shows lack of interest or curiosity.

SELF-CONFIDENCE

Self-confidence is one of the most important qualities of leadership. As a leader's knowledge grows, self-confidence should also grow. In fact, knowledge is meaningless without confidence and ability. Past accomplishments and educational degrees by themselves will not suffice; proven ability on the job is the most fundamental requirement. Arrogance on the part of an untried, inexperienced junior officer or new leading petty officer will result in the loss of subordinates' respect, which will greatly diminish the leader's control over them.

INITIATIVE AND INGENUITY

The Navy has so many regulations, instructions, and policies that a new officer or petty officer might believe there is little room for personal initiative and ingenuity in the Navy today—but this simply is not so. Actually, with new ships, new equipment, new weapons systems, and new concepts of naval warfare, the demand for officers and petty officers with these qualities is greater now than ever before in the history of our Navy. All of these new developments require leaders with the imagination, skills, and daring to find the best uses for new systems and ideas.

Few days will pass without some opportunity to exercise initiative and ingenuity. The new leader must take advantage of small everyday opportunities in order to gain the self-confidence necessary to tackle bigger problems when they arise.

Before tackling any problem, though, it is necessary to have a solid background knowledge of that problem. You can be sure that problems which exist today did not suddenly materialize out of thin air; problems grow over a period of time, as do new ideas and new equipment. Consequently, when problems need to be solved, it is wise to be aware of what has been tried before. To try again with a method which has failed before is merely an exercise in wheel-spinning. The new Navy and the modern community need truly innovative and constructive ideas which will improve both the Navy and the nation. Modern youth is capable of meeting this challenge.

COURAGE

It would be difficult to imagine a true leader who did not possess courage. Courage is that quality which enables us to accept our responsibilities and to carry them out, regardless of the consequences. The courageous person can meet dangers and difficulties with firmness. A courageous person is not necessarily fearless, but one who has learned to conquer his inner fears and concentrate on the tasks demanded of him in the heat of battle. Courage is a quality of the mind and may be developed and strengthened with use. Each time a person meets an obstacle—whether it is a tough examination, or a football opponent, or a broken machine part—and successfully overcomes it, the courage of that individual will be strengthened.

We should be careful to add, however, that continual success with every problem, while encouraging and satisfying to a person at the time, may not necessarily prepare that individual for the disappointment of failure. Courage is developed on firmer foundations when a person learns to strive again for success, after an initial setback.

It is normal for a young man going into combat to doubt his ability to conduct himself with honor. He is sure to experience fear; his main question will be whether or not he has what it takes to overcome that fear. Military services have recognized this fact since the beginning of organized conflict, and so have attempted to train their warriors under the most realistic conditions. In the Navy the men are trained and drilled at battle stations under conditions closely resembling actual combat, until their actions become almost automatic. From this training and development of a true sense of duty, the inspiration of good leaders, and the teamwork of his shipmates, any man can muster enough courage to endure the comparatively short, but trying, periods of actual battle.

Ability to Organize and Make Decisions

A junior officer's primary job is to coordinate the efforts of his personnel to achieve a common purpose. An officer must be able to organize his subordinates so that their labors and training will be used to gain best results. A first requirement for effective organization is a full awareness of the skills and physical capabilities of assigned personnel.

While it is entirely proper to call upon senior experienced petty officers to assist in the fulfillment of a mission, young officers must eventually decide on their own organization and make decisions concerning it. Without the power of decision-making, an officer is useless as a leader.

Subordinates expect clear-cut decisions from their leaders when they bring personal problems to them for discussion or when professional problems require solutions. If complicated problems arise, especially those which are clearly beyond a junior officer's authority, he or she will want to discuss them with a superior. Those which are within immediate purview should be disposed of quickly after taking all factors into consideration. Honest mistakes will occasionally occur, but from mistakes comes experience, and from experience comes wisdom.

Personal Example

Every young person has a strong need for examples to live by until determining a set of personal principles of conduct. By following the example of someone admired—father,

Officers must be able to organize, plan, and coordinate the efforts of their personnel, so that the common purpose can be successfully attained. Pilots go over plans for an upcoming cruise with squadron maintenance personnel.

Rank has its privileges—but it has its responsibilities, too. Here the navigator of the aircraft carrier *Enterprise* and his assistants plot the ship's course.

mother, brother, teacher, officer, or national leader—the young adult will acquire those fine qualities. When officers' conduct is outstanding, those around them are often inspired to pattern their own actions after them, to the good of the whole Navy. No leader, then, can live by the rule of "Don't do as I do—do as I say." It will not work. Elected, appointed, and commissioned leaders are particularly vulnerable to personal disaster if they are not honest.

No officer can expect subordinates to adhere to regulations if he ignores them himself. He will at once be regarded with suspicion and distrust, and will lose control of his people. Regaining respect and control once they are lost is exceptionally difficult.

Rank has its privileges, but that does not excuse deviations from proper conduct. Rather, when it comes to conduct, it should be stressed that rank also has its responsibilities. "Conduct" in the Navy means conduct ashore, as well as aboard ship or station. No good citizen and certainly no service person would do anything to dishonor the uniform, for such conduct can bring dishonor upon the United States and its armed forces.

Chapter 2. Study Guide Questions

1. What are the nine qualities of a good leader which are discussed in this chapter?

2. What unique code of conduct have all truly great leaders possessed?

3. Why are moral laws apparently more difficult to define than written "legal" laws?

4. How does *Navy Regulations* regard moral responsibility?

5. Why must loyalty be a two-way street?

6. Why is good morale so important within an organization?

7. What is devotion to duty? How does it relate to healthy personal ambition? How does it relate to the ability to take orders?

8. What must be the military person's outlook concerning duty and self?

9. What two principal background qualifications are necessary for a person to be regarded as professionally knowledgeable?

10. What leadership quality will enable a person to use his knowledge effectively and meaningfully?

11. Do you believe there is ample room for initiative and ingenuity in the Navy and in civilian life today? Why?

12. What is *your* definition of courage? How can courage be strengthened?

13. Why is training important to the development of courage?

14. What is the first requirement for having an effective military organization?

15. Why is decision-making important for a young officer? How can the young leader obtain help when confronted with problems beyond his experience to solve?

16. Why is the leader's personal example so important in leading subordinates?

Vocabulary

dignity	arrogance
character	initiative
vigilance	innovative ideas
loyalty	courage
devotion	honor
self-analysis	vulnerable
professionalism	suspicion
self-confidence	privilege

Chapter 3. Leadership and the Code of Conduct

The "Code of Conduct for Members of the Armed Forces of the United States" was put into effect by President Eisenhower in 1955. The Code was developed for the purpose of giving members of our fighting forces specific guidelines for behavior in the event of any future conflict with an enemy. While relatively new in a formal written sense, the provisions of the Code actually have been followed by American men-at-arms throughout our history and in all our wars.

The Code in its written form grew out of the Korean War. In this conflict the Chinese and North Korean Communists added a new dimension to warfare by extending it into prisoner-of-war (POW) camps. Hardships beyond those normally imposed upon POWs were inflicted upon captured Americans with the intent of progressively weakening their physical and moral strength. Persistent interrogation called "brainwashing" was aimed at undermining the Americans' loyalty to their country and faith in the democratic way of life.

The Communist goals would be achieved when a POW, no longer able to withstand the threats, torture, bribes, and fear, would inform on other prisoners, sign statements unfavorable to the United States, or broadcast propaganda messages to the world by radio. A few Americans succumbed to this type of personal assault and, perhaps, either willingly or unknowingly, did cooperate with the enemy.

Such conduct is contrary to American tradition and honor. Over 1.6 million American servicemen fought with distinction in the Korean War. Of some 4,460 who endured capture, only a tiny minority wavered under Communist pressures; 23 chose not to return to the United States during the POW exchanges at the time of the armistice.

The President issued the Code as an Executive Order and the services reissued it as a General Order. Following are the articles which make up the Code:

ARTICLE I

I am an American fighting man. I serve in the forces which guard my country and our way of life. I am prepared to give my life in their defense.

ARTICLE II

I will never surrender of my own free will. If in command I will never surrender my men while they still have the means to resist.

ARTICLE III

If I am captured I will continue to resist by all means available. I will make every effort to escape and aid others to escape. I will accept neither parole nor special favors from the enemy.

ARTICLE IV

If I become a prisoner of war, I will keep faith with my fellow prisoners. I will give no information nor take part in any action which might be harmful to my comrades. If I am senior, I will take command. If not, I will obey the lawful orders of those appointed over me and will back them up in every way.

ARTICLE V

When questioned, should I become a prisoner of war, I am bound to give only name, rank, service number, and date of birth. I will evade answering further questions to the utmost of my ability. I will make no oral or written statements disloyal to my country and its allies or harmful to their cause.

ARTICLE VI

I will never forget that I am an American fighting man, responsible for my actions, and dedicated to the principles which made my country free. I will trust in my God and in the United States of America.

Articles I and VI together form a creed which affirms dedication to national security and devotion to American principles. Article II emphasizes resistance as the keynote to behavior in battle. The remaining articles explain what is expected of an American fighting man who has the misfortune of being captured by an enemy. Few men who enter combat become prisoners of war, but all who go into combat must be prepared for that possibility. Articles III, IV, and V provide the captive with basic knowledge concerning disclosure of information and the treatment of prisoners of war under the Geneva Convention. These provisions are internationally accepted.

In a POW camp, unity of purpose and staunch discipline are essential. Strong leadership is necessary to maintain discipline, and without is, survival may be impossible. Normal military requirements of personal hygiene, sanitation, and care of the sick must continue. Officers and petty officers must continue to carry out their responsibilities and exercise their authority after capture. Those who are senior assume command according to grade or rate, without regard to service. The responsibility for camp leadership cannot be refused or evaded.

Subsequent tests of the Code of Conduct—the *Pueblo* incident in 1968 and the Vietnam War—established the worth of the document. Varying legal interpretations arose with these differing situations, however, and improvements in the teaching of the Code were found to be necessary.

The most significant result of these legal "tests" was a determination that the Code is not a "law" and was never intended to stand alone as such. It is a moral code designed to provide men and women in the armed services with a standard of conduct in any confrontation with a foe of our nation. It also serves in part to implement the provisions of the 1949 Geneva Convention Relative to the Treatment of Prisoners of War.

There is, of course, no direct civilian counterpart for the military Code of Conduct other than society's mores, the accepted standards of conduct within law, and common decency. It is again clear, then, that the requirements for leadership, conduct, and discipline shouldered by the person in uniform are unique in American society. The burden of protecting the nation requires that this be so.

Chapter 3. Study Guide Questions

1. What is the purpose for having the Code of Conduct?
2. Why did the Code in its written form come into being?
3. What was the intent of the exceptional hardships imposed upon American POWs by their captors during the Korean War?
4. How successful were the Communists in achieving their goals in the Korean POW camps? Why?
5. What do you think of the Code of Conduct as a guide for military behavior? Do you believe the Code is realistic today? Why?
6. Why is leadership so essential in a POW camp? Who must assume leadership? Can this duty be refused?
7. What do you believe the difference between "law" and "moral code" implies in regard to the Code of Conduct?
8. How does the Code of Conduct illustrate the special responsibility of the American service man or woman?

Vocabulary

behavioral guidelines	national security
provisions of law	Geneva Convention
prisoner-of-war	keynote
interrogation	hygiene
democratic way	sanitation
propaganda	legal interpretation
repatriation	confrontation
surrender	legality
parole	mores
principles	unique

Chapter 4. Discipline: The Key

Now these are the laws of the Navy
  Unwritten and varied they be;
And he that is wise will observe them,
  Going down in his ship to the sea.
As the wave rises clear to the hawse pipe,
  Washes aft, and is lost in the wake,
So shall ye drop astern, all unheeded,
  Such times as the law ye forsake.
Now these are the laws of the Navy,
  And many and mighty are they.
But the hull and deck and the keel
  And the truck of the law is—OBEY.
    —Admiral Ronald Hopwood, Royal Navy

Discipline is the basis of true democracy. It requires adherence to rules of conduct that man, through experience, has found desirable for governing relations among members of civilized society. Such rules of conduct do not deprive an individual of his fundamental rights; in fact, they protect everyone's equal rights.

Rules which are written by duly constituted authority, such as a city council or state legislature, are called *laws*. Other rules which have become a part of our culture by custom and usage are called *conventions*.

Discipline is not peculiar to military organizations. It is the training that develops self-control, character, or efficiency. Discipline does not imply severity, unreasonable curtailment of freedom, or unnecessary restrictions. Rightly viewed, it is a character builder which develops mature individuality. Discipline means control of conduct so there can be a coordination of effort for the good of all.

A dictionary defines discipline as "control gained by enforcing obedience," or "that state of orderliness gained through self-control and orderly conduct." A description of discipline in military terms would be "that degree of control which moves an organized group to appropriate action upon receipt of an order, or in anticipation of that order when circumstances prevent its being given."

A military organization could not function properly without orderliness and orderly conduct. Admiral Arleigh Burke, USN, a former Chief of Naval Operations, stated: "A well-disciplined organization is one whose members work with enthusiasm, willingness, and zest as individuals and as a group, to fulfill the mission of the organization with expectation of success." The signs of discipline can be seen in smart salutes, proper wearing of the uniform, prompt and correct action in any emergency, and battle efficiency that brings victory.

The purpose of discipline in the military services is to develop an efficient organization of personnel trained to attain a common goal. Each person should know where he or she fits into the organization, each should understand that all in the group are unified in purpose and interest, and that all are to follow and obey their leader. Such a group is so well organized and trained that it can handle any emergency, as well as its normally assigned tasks. A well-disciplined naval unit responds automatically to an emergency and will not panic.

SELF-DISCIPLINE

True discipline demands habitual but reasoned obedience to command. Such obedience preserves the sense of initiative, and functions even in the absence of the leader. Self-discipline, therefore, is essential before true discipline can be developed. The self-disciplined person will always be dependable, and will fulfill his responsibilities under all circumstances without need of direct supervision. He will develop the habit of immediate and controlled response. We need such disciplined sailors to ensure success in battle.

Self-discipline must begin with the realization that there is a need for self-control. Development of self-discipline comes only through repeated practice of self-control. The person who has developed self-control in day-

In every organization, each person should know where he or she fits in. Here, the leading signalman talks with his signal-bridge personnel.

to-day tasks is also the one who can hold up in the face of hardship and danger. *Navy Regulations* provides the framework and rules by which the Navy operates. But it is the self-discipline of each individual that determines how well the regulations are followed.

When the Navy's regulations are observed, good order and efficient operations will result; moreover, there will be high morale and esprit de corps, because all members of the crew know that their well-disciplined shipmates will not break under pressure. Good order and discipline are inseparable and are essential to combat readiness.

AN INCIDENT OF SHIP DISCIPLINE

An actual incident illustrates the difference between a well-disciplined ship and one which is not.

Two sister ships lay in adjoining anchorages. One was known as a "taut" ship. Her commanding officer recognized the value of proper organization, discipline, and training. The other ship was an example of the opposite condition. Her decks were dirty, her crew was slovenly and careless in observing military courtesies, and her records showed many cases of courts-martial and shore patrol reports.

It was nearly midnight and the tide was running out strongly against the wind, making a nasty chop. A motor launch from the "slack" ship was returning from the beach with her liberty party huddled in the stern under a tarpaulin to avoid the cold spray from the bucking sea. The coxswain had ordered the men to distribute their weight farther forward so he could better see over the bow. In keeping with the lax discipline of their ship, however, most

The beginning of discipline is self-discipline; it is the foundation upon which good order is built.

had not moved. In the blackness the launch struck a channel buoy, capsized, and sank almost immediately.

On the "taut" ship the cries of the victims were heard coming from the dark waters. Though her boats were hoisted and most of the crew turned in, her anchor watch was on lookout as provided in the ship's organization. At the first cries for help, the words "Man overboard!" rang through the ship. Officers and men responded promptly wearing whatever clothing was within reach. Three boats reached the water almost simultaneously, and by the time they were away the searchlights had been manned and were scanning the water. Before the tide could sweep them away, sixteen men from the liberty boat had been saved.

Meanwhile, what was happening on the second ship? No one knows exactly. Perhaps the officer of the deck was engaged in some duty on the far side of the ship; perhaps he had stepped below for a moment. There was no man stationed topside for their anchor watch. At any rate, the second ship did nothing until a lifeboat from the first one hailed it in passing, while searching for survivors. At this point the officer of the deck asked about the cause of the

excitement. (Official records of the incident do not reveal the reply of the lifeboat officer!) The record does show, however, that sixteen men owed their lives to the hard-earned discipline and training of the crew in their sister ship—rather than their own shipmates.

NAVY DISCIPLINE: AN AMERICAN IDEAL

Present-day Navy discipline is based on what is normally considered the American ideal of discipline: willing allegiance to a cause in which there is sincere belief, and cheerful acceptance of subordination to leaders who have earned their charges' respect and confidence.

As mentioned earlier, people are motivated largely by one of two things: fear of punishment and hope of reward. Hope of reward is a better motivating device, for it results in greater efficiency and harmony. Words of John Paul Jones are applicable here: "No meritorious act of a subordinate should escape attention or be left to pass without reward, even if the reward be only one word of approval." He went on to say that an officer should be just as universal, impartial, and judicial in giving out punishment or reproof for negligence or misconduct. Jones stressed the use of rewards *first*. Then if reward fails, disciplinary action is warranted. In other words, fear of punishment has its place, but to use punishment as a club is often a sign of failure as a leader.

The Navy wholeheartedly accepts the "preventive theory of discipline"; according to this principle, preventing disciplinary problems is more important than trying to cure them after they have occurred.

To support this theory, the Navy has an extensive welfare and recreation program to develop healthy interest among naval personnel during off-duty hours. These programs include sports and athletic activities; hobby carpentry and machinery repair facilities; advanced and professional educational opportunities; travel tours; theater and movie programs; and religious and counseling programs, to name some. Many activities in support of dependents' requirements also fall into this category, for it is very important for Navy men and women to know that their families are receiving necessary assistance and services.

Such programs are usually administered by line officers, usually division officers in direct contact with their men. Often these programs are assisted by officers of the Chaplain Corps on shore stations and larger ships.

It is just as important to notice and give praise for a job well done as it is to give censure for one poorly done. A word of friendly counsel to the new men and women, a little encouragement to the easily discouraged, a look of approval to a smart turnout at quarters, a nod of recognition to a particular group of men after an exceptionally good drill, and a willing ear to the fellow with a suggestion— these will do much to keep men loyal to their officers.

When people put forth extra effort to obtain superior results, recognition should be given publicly, and, if warranted, officially. It is wise to officially commend and to give out awards and medals for those actions which are clearly above and beyond the regularly expected good performance of duty or required standard. But it is poor judgement to administer praise too liberally. It will discredit the higher awards if you give them to those who do only what is normally expected of any well-trained, effective person.

Know Your Personnel

The business of dealing with juniors or subordinates is a complete subject in itself. It is of vital importance for the young officer to develop a level of communication with his personnel which will foster mutual respect. The key to this is learning the personality and character of every one of those juniors— understanding what makes them tick.

It is the duty of the officer to study his people, watch them, learn their approach to problems, work with them, and guide them. Honest concern is the watchword. To maintain discipline, the officer must be continually concerned about his personnel; he should not wait until they get into difficulties. This means ensuring that they are comfortable and as well cared for as circumstances permit; seeing that they receive their fair share of earned privileges; and showing that their personal and family lives are of real interest to the officer, the ship, and the Navy as well. It is not enough to see to it that the necessary actions are being done; the officer should also let personnel *know* what is being done, so they are fully aware of the Navy's and the officers' efforts on their behalf.

An officer should bear in mind that everyone wants, needs, and responds to recognition. Thus, a division officer should know the names of personnel and call them by their last names or title with last name—not by first names or nicknames. Honest pride makes each individual naturally feel that he or she is important in the scheme of things.

If the best in people is to be brought out, they must be made to feel important in their own eyes, they must feel respect from their associates, and they must definitely feel competent in the eyes of their superiors. When a person is given a task to perform, he should have the self-confidence to believe that he is being given that job because he has the ability to do it.

An officer will need to use all the understanding of human nature that he can gain through experience and study. The acquisition of this knowledge can be gained only by working at the job of human relations. The better his insight into human nature, and the better he understands his own personnel and their intelligence, education, and backgrounds, the more effective he'll be in handling those people.

Mutual respect, trust, and understanding are necessary for the mission to be successfully accomplished. The flight leader gives out the details of the mission and the squadron's pilots listen intently. Both senior and subordinate must be confident in his leader, his flightmates, and in himself.

Friendship and Familiarity

The relationship between officers and their subordinates influences discipline. Officers shouldn't fraternize with enlisted persons or attempt to be "one of the boys." Discipline is undermined quickly by this type of familiarity. If subordinates become familiar, and fail to keep the proper distance between senior and subordinate, it is usually the officer's fault.

There is a great difference between familiarity and friendship. The officer who talks to his men in a friendly manner, taking a personal interest in them and being concerned with their problems, quickly gains their confidence and respect. Young men and women want to be able to look to their seniors for guidance; they want to be proud of their senior petty officer and officers. Such leaders, because they

are friendly and approachable, will be the first ones turned to for advice. The division officer, as the first officer most personnel are associated with in the administrative chain of command, should have earned a degree of respect and confidence which cause subordinates to seek him out for counseling. If he is lacking in those qualities, they won't come to him and could very well grow dissatisfied or get into the trouble which such counsel might otherwise have prevented.

Being friendly with subordinates does not mean being easy with them. An officer may be as exacting as the situation requires, so long as he is fair.

Consistency in Disciplinary Action

Breaches of discipline must be handled immediately, justly, and consistently; severe reactions to breaches one day cannot be passed off as insignificant the next. Such an approach can only result in confusion, poor morale, and distrust of the leader.

If personnel are allowed to defy a regulation openly, they'll develop an indifferent attitude toward other regulations. Two fundamental rules apply: (1) never make a regulation that you cannot or will not enforce, and (2) take immediate fair action which leaves no doubt in the mind of the offender as to why he is being reprimanded or punished.

Delay in taking disciplinary action which is warranted brings resentment toward the entire system—especially if the offender "gets off" because of a time lapse which dulls memories or makes it seem as though the offense has been overtaken by subsequent events. Wrong acts or poor performance require immediate guidance and correction in order to bring about the necessary changes.

Junior officers and new petty officers may have a tendency to be too lenient with minor infractions of discipline, thereby penalizing good men while favoring bad ones. When this error is pointed out to some junior leaders, they may become uncertain of themselves, and in trying to compensate for the fault, they overreact, becoming too arbitrary. In either

Officers should be especially careful to steer a steady course in disciplinary matters—giving praise as well as criticism.

case the leader will lose the confidence of his men because of such inconsistency in action. It is best to chart a steady course when dealing with disciplinary matters. An area of human relationships such as this will tolerate few errors without having an impact on morale.

LOSS OF TEMPER = LOSS OF CONTROL

An officer cannot afford to lose his temper. Losing one's temper usually brings out a personality weakness and does not always improve the individual and his work within the crew. To be sure, it is not always easy to refrain from anger, but a conscious effort to do so must be made.

When a person loses control of himself, he usually loses control of the situation. Rare indeed is the case when proper action or desired results come from an expression of anger. In admonishing error or administering punishment the officer must remain calm, impersonal, and dignified. If extremely incensed, he will find it constructive to pace the deck for a few minutes rather than take unwise precipitous action. The calmer the officer is in his usual performance of duty, the more action he can get when the occasion demands. The officer who is inconsistent, quick-tempered, or constantly shouting only creates confusion and

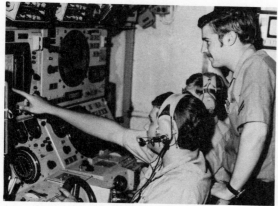

There's a big difference between friendliness and familiarity. A leader should be friendly with subordinates, but should not try to be "one of the boys."

soon ceases to be effective, since he eventually will get little or no response from his subordinates.

Chapter 4. Study Guide Questions

1. What is meant by the statement in Hopwood's poem, "So shall ye drop astern, all unheeded, such times as the law ye forsake?"

2. What is the basis of true democracy? Explain.

3. What is the difference between laws and conventions?

4. Why have discipline and laws or rules developed?

5. Compare the dictionary and military definitions of discipline. How do they differ? How are they similar?

6. Is it true that the desirable and happy citizen obeys the laws and conventions? Why?

7. What is Admiral Burke's definition of a well-disciplined organization?

8. What is the purpose of military discipline?

9. How is a well-disciplined ship expected to respond in an emergency?

10. What does true discipline require?

11. How does a person acquire self-control?

12. Why will morale be good aboard a ship with a well-disciplined crew?

13. What is a "taut ship?"

14. What are some of the examples of good training and discipline revealed in the true story about the boat accident?

15. What is considered to be the American ideal of discipline?

16. What was John Paul Jones' approach to discipline? Do you think his approach would be the correct approach today? Why?

17. What is the "preventive" theory of discipline? What Navy programs assist this concept of discipline?

18. What is a fundamental rule about giving praise or censure?

19. Under what general circumstances are praise or awards earned?

20. What is the key to establishing the necessary degree of communication with subordinates?

21. Why must an officer be concerned about his personnel? How should an officer show this concern and interest?

22. Do you believe that personal recognition is important in order to build honest pride? Why?

23. How well should a division officer know his personnel?

24. How should the division officer address his personnel?

25. Why is an understanding of human nature important in dealing with people?

26. Why is fraternization or familiarity between officers and enlisted personnel unwise?

27. What is the difference between friendship and familiarity?

28. Why is consistency in disciplinary action essential?

29. What is a common cause for junior officers to lose the confidence of their men when dealing with minor infractions of discipline?

30. Why is it important not to make rules which are unenforceable?

31. What is the usual result if a leader loses his temper?

32. Why do you think that calmness in usual performance of duty makes possible a more active response when emergencies arise?

Vocabulary

severity	preventive theory
enthusiasm	recognition
zest	acquisition
tedious	familiarity
controlled response	fraternization
morale	consistency
esprit de corps	leniency
taut ship	infraction
deteriorate	arbitrary
lax discipline	personality
impartial	precipitous action
negligence	resentment

Chapter 5. Character, Conduct, and Command

We have discussed many aspects of leadership and the importance of the training function in any leadership program. It is time to reemphasize two key requirements for effective leadership specified in General Order 21: personal example and moral responsibility. We shall talk of these requirements from the standpoint of moral character. In the leadership role, self-evaluation can assist in molding the type of character which best approximates the ideal example of leadership.

BEHAVIOR AND PERFORMANCE

Personal example is directed to the behavior and performance of officers and petty officers in their positions as leaders of men and women. Personal qualities of leadership imply that there is a chain of respect as well as a chain of command. The good leader retains support and respect because he lives up to certain high ideals which he undertakes along with his commission or his certificate of advancement in rate. High ideals are inherent in Navy life: integrity, bravery, self-discipline.

Good example must show itself not only in personal behavior and dedication to others, but in the everyday performance of duty. By the way he acts every day, the good leader inspires subordinates to act with sincerity, enthusiasm, smart appearance, military behavior, technical competence, and courage.

SELF-EVALUATION

Each person who is in a leadership capacity, wants to advance on the ladder of success, and wants to determine where he or she stands *now*, should submit to an honest self-evaluation test. This is not an easy task, for it can put one on the spot. Self-evaluation is a method used to clarify the individual naval officer's or petty officer's personal responsibilities in leading others.

The first step in solving any problem—military or civilian—is to estimate and evaluate the situation. Self-evaluation checklists, if properly used, can help an individual to visualize his strengths and weaknesses and to plan specific steps toward improvement. Improvement of self as a leader will enhance one's personal stature and increase one's sense of self-respect and satisfaction with a job well done. This will win the respect of others.

The *Armed Forces Officer* has stated: "The man who is concerned most of all with his responsibilities will be fretted least about the matter of his privileges and . . . his exercise of any rightful privilege will not be resented by his subordinates, because they are conscious of his merit."

The Navy has prepared a number of self-evaluation leadership checklists for officers and petty officers. These can easily be modified for NJROTC cadets, or, for that matter, for anyone who wishes to compare his or her mental outlook with that of others. The Navy suggests that a self-evaluation checklist might best be used by each person on a quarterly basis so that any deficiencies can be quickly corrected.

The *Petty Officer's Guide* states: "Because men know that the conquest of one's own

Anyone in a leadership role should submit to periodic self-examination. Here junior officers and chief petty officers discuss leadership qualities in a Fleet Training School.

weaknesses is a far more difficult task than any other, they know that he who can conquer himself can also conquer whatever problem is at hand. Your first job, then, is to learn your own weaknesses and conquer them."

MORAL COURAGE

Moral courage means a show of firmness in difficulties where the danger of death is not an immediate concern. It is a form of courage less glamorous than physical courage—risking life to save another, being fearless in the face of enemy fire; or braving the unknown dangers of the deep seas or outer space. Situations requiring moral courage, however, affect each person far more often than the more glamorous experiences.

The pressures of our daily lives can be formidable obstacles indeed, and this is where moral courage comes in. It may be easier to allow the wrong thing to be done and to say nothing, to observe incorrect procedures or damaged equipment and to let it go unreported. Sometimes it is easy to disagree with a senior—or worse, to agree with a senior when you are certain that he is wrong. Fear of reprisal from seniors, fear of ostracism by peers, and lack of confidence due to immaturity or ignorance are the pressures that make the exercise of moral courage difficult.

Moral courage is necessary to ensure that seniors get the information they need to make prudent decisions—even if such information upsets them. It is necessary to make sure that the rights of others, particularly subordinates, are protected when they become endangered through oversight, inattention, or malice. A person needs moral courage to bring forth his own new ideas for improving operations, especially if he is going against hard precedent or well-laid plans. The person who says nothing or agrees with the senior and then criticizes him behind his back to juniors loses both the respect of the juniors and the trust of the seniors. The leader who takes care of his personnel is admired and respected because of his moral courage.

It takes moral courage to admit one's mistakes. It takes moral courage to be honest, just, and truthful at all times. It takes moral courage to insist on adherence to regulations and laws when they are being disregarded by many others. It takes a very special moral courage to stick to one's high principles in the face of ridicule by peers and so-called friends, because everyone wants to feel like "one of the boys."

MUTUAL TRUST AND CONFIDENCE

Officers and petty officers must set a proper example by letting subordinates know that they are trusted. If leaders fail to show trust in their subordinates, they will soon find themselves constantly checking up on their people, doubting the records and reports prepared by them, and consequently performing their own duties less efficiently.

It would be naive to suggest that all leaders in the Navy, the government, business, or anywhere else, are continuously efficient, invariably honest, and always perform their duties responsibly and with honor. We know that our leaders should do things that way, of course, and we have a perfect right to expect that they do. When leaders fail in fulfilling their responsibilities, society has the right to demand corrective action, and if sufficient cause is evident, punishment under the law may be warranted.

In any event, when an officer or petty officer fails to back his men, refuses to pay his debts, condones dishonest activities, allows sloppy work, or evades legitimate regulations, he jeopardizes the reputation of all naval leaders and the Navy itself—not just himself. Mutual respect, trust, and understanding can prompt all hands to exercise a greater degree of personal responsibility. Then morale will be higher, efficiency will be improved, and administrative burdens will be lighter.

The word of an officer or petty officer should be dependable. Consequently, if the leader

A leader must present an image of integrity and honor. It is his example that the younger sailors will follow.

cannot make good on his word or his promises, he should not make commitments. Keeping one's word is important evidence of personal honor. If one does not make a special effort to uphold his word, he can be sure that he will lose the respect of his subordinates and all of his associates, and the attitudes of all in his company will be adversely affected. A sense of honesty and mutual trust must be present if a command is to operate efficiently.

Conduct Ashore

The naval leader, because of his command responsibilites, must do all in his power to prevent improper actions by naval personnel ashore. Often the stimulus for such actions is dissatisfaction with conditions on board the ship or station. If a person does not like his work assignment or living conditions, if he feels that command policies are unfair, or if he has troubles at home, the weak or uncounseled may resort to unauthorized absence, to alcohol, or to other forms of escape. Uncounseled and unwarned, such personnel may lose their sense of moral responsibility.

The Navy's goal is for every uniformed person to develop a sense of personal moral responsibility toward family, the Navy, and the nation so that he or she will drive carefully, control drinking, retain moral perspective, and resolve dissatisfactions in constructive ways. An officer or petty officer has the responsibility to know the needs of subordinates and to know their anxieties. It is his duty to remind them of their responsibility to conduct themselves properly on liberty, to reflect credit on their families, their Navy, and their nation, and to be ready to perform their duties when they return on board.

Irresponsible conduct ashore can involve any infraction of the law, but the most common fall into five principal areas. They are: unauthorized absence, hospitalization from accidents or disease, deaths from accidents or disease, inefficiency as the result of various personal indiscretions, and confinement for disciplinary reasons either in civil or military jails. The typical causes for these losses are dissatisfaction with conditions on board, drinking to excess, poor automobile driving habits, or the lack of a proper sense of personal moral responsibility. It can safely be stated that these same causes result in similar losses in civilian business and industry.

The big difference between civilian and naval environments in this regard, however, comes in the corrective actions expected of the leadership. In civilian institutions a certain degree of concern is generally expected: some insurance coverage, reasonable minimums established for health and welfare conditions on the job, mostly to increase the productivity of the workers or to satisfy union agreements. But there is little concern for, or involvement in, the employee's home life, recreation, financial involvements, moral outlook and practices, or living conditions. The worker punches in, does his job, punches out, and goes his own way. If he doesn't do the job satisfactorily he may be warned, but the supreme threat is the loss of his job by firing. On the other hand, if the worker is sufficiently dissatisfied with his job, he may quit.

In the Navy, corrective actions are a primary responsibility of the leadership. The officers must know their personnel and take care of their needs, and must insist on the acceptance and exercise of personal moral responsibility. The naval leader must accept this responsibility by regulation; but he must also do so for the simple practical reason that he has to do all in his power to make his crew a working team which can respond properly to emergency situations.

The Enlistment and Commission

When any man or woman first enters the Navy, that person is administered an oath by which he swears to uphold and defend the Constitution of the United States against all enemies, to bear true faith and allegiance, and to faithfully discharge all assigned duties. There is little doubt as to what is demanded of an individual who takes such an oath. It establishes a contractual obligation between the individual and the government, which the enlistee cannot quit whenever it suits his fancy.

When an especially well-qualified individual is commissioned as an officer, he or she reaffirms the basic oath—but there is a good deal more involved. The President, as a representative of the people of the United States, having "special trust and confidence" in the abilities of the officer, has granted that officer authority. The officer has become party to a contract with the nation. The nation will keep its bond; it expects no less from the officer.

The officer acquires a strict moral obligation

A naval officer enjoys the special trust and confidence of the United States government.

to make himself fully capable of leading men in war. A career officer must be aware of this tremendous responsibility, and it must constitute a significant part of his justification for choosing the naval profession. These are the irreducible terms of the commission.

This nation should finally have learned that military strength is a necessary part of ensuring security. We never seek war; but, by staying prepared and vigilant, we offer any aggressor the prospect of defeat and destruction. In the uneasy peace in which we live, the officer's responsibility is just as important. He is charged with doing everything in his power to maintain and increase national strength. He accomplishes this by the exercise of professional skills, proper training and guidance of his subordinates, development of improved devices and methods, and by looking after the personnel and materials placed in his trust. It must be noted here that the charge of the commission is exactly the same for both male and female officers, though at the present time, United States law prohibits the direct participation of women in a combat role.

COMMAND AUTHORITY

Navy Regulations outlines the responsibility and authority of the commander of a principal organization of the operating forces of the Navy, the commanding officer of a ship or unit, the officer of the deck, and so forth. The "level" of responsibility, of course, increases with rank and position, but responsibility and authority are present to the appropriate degree with each officer and each position.

A commander shall be responsible for the satisfactory accomplishment of the mission and duties assigned to his command. The responsibility of the commanding officer for his command is absolute except when properly relieved by senior competent authority. In either case, this authority is commensurate with his responsibility. At times the officer may delegate authority to his subordinates for the execution of details, but delegation will in no way relieve him of his continued responsibility for his command's well-being and efficiency.

COMMAND AT SEA:
THE ULTIMATE RESPONSIBILITY

Command at sea, with all its responsibilities and all its opportunities, is the goal of every

The ultimate goal of every line officer is command at sea. This entails enormous responsibility, especially in complex and demanding situations—such as an underway replenishment in heavy seas.

line officer in the United States Navy. Each level of responsibility leading to command should be looked upon as a new challenge, preparing the officer for the ultimate command position. Having attained command of a large ship or a small one, the commanding officer is the "captain," regardless of the number of stripes worn. On the captain rests the entire responsibility for that ship, whether the mission ends in success or failure. The captain's discipline, training, and orders will have shaped the actions of the ship's personnel, and the captain will be held accountable for those actions and their results. There is no way to evade this accountability, and it is this important fact which makes the naval officer's profession so unique.

Admiral John S. McCain, Jr., USN, stated that the naval commanding officer's "ever-present cloak of responsibility . . . is never light; and, once accepted, can never be cast off. The commanding officer is mindful of this responsibility in his every challenge and decision every moment of the day and night."

On the subject of command and accountability, the *Wall Street Journal* of 14 May 1952, when referring to the collision of a United States destroyer and carrier resulting in the loss of the smaller ship and 170 men, printed the following comment: "On the sea there is a tradition older even than the traditions of the country itself—it is the tradition that with responsibility goes authority and with them both goes accountability. It is cruel, this accountability of good and well-intentioned men. But the choice is that or an end to responsibility and finally, as the cruel sea has taught, an end to the confidence and trust in the men who lead, for men will not long trust leaders who feel themselves beyond accountability for what they do."

At sea, the burdens of accountability and responsibility for lives and equipment are secure only when entrusted to those who have qualified for command at sea, by virtue of their performance. The responsibilities are great, and leadership is the single most important responsibility in the Navy. Advanced computer technology aids in operating and fighting a ship, but the men who man Navy ships do not lend themselves to computerized control. The bluejacket is the single most important element in the fleet. A sailor always has and always will respond to good leadership, a leadership which applies to all echelons, from top to bottom.

Chapter 5. Study Guide Questions

1. How does a good leader retain support and respect?

2. How must good personal example be shown to subordinates?

3. Why is honest self-evaluation important for everyone? How can it help an individual?

4. What does this statement mean: "A leader concerned most with his responsibilities will fret least about his privileges"?

5. What does this statement mean: "He who can conquer himself can also conquer whatever problem is at hand"?

6. What is moral courage? What are the principal factors which make moral courage difficult?

7. How can a lack of moral courage lead to the loss of both the respect of juniors and the trust of seniors?

8. Why would it be especially dangerous to neglect reporting a disagreeable fact to an operational commander?

9. Why is mutual trust and confidence so important in dealing with people?

10. What will be the result of an atmosphere of mutual respect, trust, and understanding in an organization?

11. How can good leadership help resolve dissatisfactions aboard ship or troubles at home?

12. What are the most common personnel losses to the Navy as the result of irresponsible conduct?

13. What is the big difference between the corrective actions of the leadership of the Navy and civilian institutions, regarding personnel conduct?

14. What is the meaning of the contractual obligation of the Navy enlistment and the officer's commission?

15. What is the officer's moral obligation by virtue of his commissioning contract?

16. What is an officer's responsibility concerning the readiness of the armed forces in peacetime?

17. What does it mean to say that "the responsibility of the commanding officer for his command is absolute?" Can he delegate this responsibility to subordinates?

18. What should be the goal of every line officer in the Navy? What do you think aspiring to such a goal actually means for each individual concerned?

19. What does command accountability mean?

20. What is the single most important responsibility in the Navy? Why?

Vocabulary

dedication	mutual trust
suppress	violation
self-evaluation	echelon
merit	unauthorized absence
moral courage	personal indiscretion
formidable obstacle	contractual obligation
reprisal	
prudent decision	oath
criticism	command accountability
naive	

5

The U. S. Navy in American Democracy

Chapter 1. Fundamentals of American Democracy

If you were to be asked for your definition of democracy—as you surely have been in one of your social studies classes—you would probably reply that democracy means "government by the people." That is true, but our democracy is actually more complex than that. In American democracy, we elect representatives to organize and conduct the affairs of our government. America, therefore, is a *representative* democracy. But American democracy has other facets that go beyond even this definition.

Democracy in America is founded on the principles stated in the Declaration of Independence. These basic ideals say that all men are created equal; that all people have certain unalienable rights, among which are life, liberty, and the pursuit of happiness; and that all powers of the government come from the consent of the governed.

American democracy, then, is not merely a form of government. It is a way of life, in which all human relations and activities are based on a belief in human dignity. Everyone is free to live as he or she pleases, as long they act within the law and don't interfere with the rights of others.

No nation is "democratic" unless it protects human liberties. Freedom of expression, movement, and association are essential to a democratic society. The people must be able to say, write, and do what they believe, if the best ideas are to come to the fore. For a democracy to work, its citizens must speak out and participate. Good citizens need to be able to act without fear of interference, without arbitrary and unlawful controls, and with the assurance that they will be treated as equals before the law. Moreover, race, religion, or wealth should have no direct bearing on their rights.

Constitutions are the documents which guarantee the liberties of citizens in democracies. The Constitution of the United States, drawn up in 1787, is the basic law of our land. Our Constitution is designed to protect the rights of all American citizens, wherever they may be. The Bill of Rights—the first ten amendments to the Constitution—guarantees citizens many of their essential freedoms. These include: freedom of religion, speech, and press; protection against unreasonable search or seizure of property or person; the right to a fair trial by jury; protection against deprivation of life, liberty, or property without due process of law; and protection against double jeopardy (being tried twice for the same crime).

A government of the people, however, cannot exist solely by the words of a document.

The U. S. Fleet is our first line of defense, and serves on behalf of democratic governments all over the world.

Americans must participate in the work of their government in order to improve themselves and their nation. From participation they will gain a sense of dignity and worth that can only come from pride in self-government.

Each generation must rededicate itself to the values of self-government; no generation can take for granted the accomplishments of preceding generations. Any nation which chooses to do so will soon lose its democratic form of government—either from forces within, or from foreign dangers. When democracy no longer exists in a nation, men and women become the tools of unprincipled persons or nations, which will deprive them of their freedoms.

EQUALITY OF MAN

An important part of democracy is a belief in social equality. No real democracy can exist if people do not have equal opportunity within their society. This equality must extend to all aspects of life: housing, health care, recreational opportunities, education, and employment opportunities.

Equality of opportunity does not mean that all persons are identical in every respect. In fact, democracy recognizes the fact that there are differences. Some persons are smarter or more able than others. Some people are born into better economic circumstances and more comfortable environments than others. Their equality lies in what they have in common—the possession of certain rights. It should be understood that these rights give them "legal opportunity to seek happiness,"—not a guarantee that they will attain it.

A democratic society neither attempts nor desires to make everyone equal. Equality cannot be legislated. The law, however, can serve to minimize differences in opportunity among people of differing social and economic backgrounds.

In a democracy the value of the individual is emphasized. This is perhaps the greatest strength of the democratic form of government, because each of us has a natural desire to excel. We want to own our home and the piece of ground upon which it is located. We want to work and enjoy the benefits of our toil by living comfortably, purchasing the things we need, enjoying the recreation of our choice, raising a family, and socializing with our friends within an atmosphere of security, prosperity, and well-being. Given an equal opportunity to learn, earn, and participate we can each proceed on our own route toward our goals and objectives, without interference either from government or others.

It is this independence of the individual spirit in each person that makes democracy so natural and so sought after—but, at the same time, so difficult to attain in many places on earth.

For many years the official policy of the

Department of the Navy has been one of equal treatment and opportunity for all personnel, regardless of race, color, creed, or national origin. Promotions and advancements are determined on the basis of a person's merit, ability, experience, performance, and potential.

People come into the Navy from all walks of life and from all parts of the country. Some of these people bring with them prejudices common to their environment—racial, economic, and social. In the Navy, however, where every

The Navy has a firm policy of offering equal opportunity to all. These Naval Academy midshipmen are rendering honors.

person is a shipmate, and the effectiveness of a ship as a fighting unit depends on teamwork, such feelings must be overcome. The Navy has training programs emphasizing equal opportunity and positive evaluation. All personnel are evaluated regarding their performance in that important area of leadership and supervision.

Any person with a legitimate claim of discrimination can file a complaint without fear of retaliation. But the complaint must be valid, not merely an attempt to get back at someone for an imagined wrong. Falsely accusing a person of discrimination is as wrong as discrimination itself.

Economic Equality and Democracy

It is in the area of economic equality that the world has experienced great conflict in the twentieth century. In the capitalistic Western democracies, economic democracy is generally interpreted to mean that the individual has the right and opportunity to pursue his livelihood fully, free from government oppression and undue regulation. There are those, however, who almost traditionally have opposed this concept. They believe that in order for there to be equality, society should not have classes or differences in wealth. To ensure this, there must be government control over most aspects of life.

Socialism

Socialist doctrine holds that if self-government can work in political democracy, it ought to work in economic matters as well. This socialist approach to government has many interpretations, which vary from country to country. Basically, socialists want the government to control and regulate essential goods and services, such as railroads, tools, machinery, factories, and raw materials. They also advocate some degree of government control over distribution of these goods and services. At the same time, however, people have a broad range of opportunities to pursue their daily life as they want. They are permitted to own property and to gain wealth by investment and careful personal management. This form of government, employed by most Western European governments, is called *democratic socialism*. Most of the countries in our NATO alliance have governments and economies which fall in this category.

Fascism

The fascist concept of government and economy emphasizes strong central control. This form of economy is government-controlled, and is strongly nationalistic. It allows privately owned business to flourish, but all such industry and business is strictly regulated.

Under this type of government, the national state and predominant race assume primary importance. While profits can be made by owners of business, the government will control the owner and his business in whatever way it deems necessary for the good of the state.

The rights of individuals are not considered important; individuals are of value only in relation to the state. Freedoms like those guaranteed by our Constitution are denied to citizens of the fascist state. The public media become propaganda organs of the state. The object of education is to train children to revere the state above all else, and to believe that working and fighting for the state is their only goal in life. While Italy and Germany were the classic fascist-type countries of World War II, there are today many nations with a fascist regime—including many of the underdeveloped nations which gained their independence by helping to fight the fascist Axis powers. These governments usually have a single ruler, a president-dictator for life, who refuses to grant citizens the human rights normally enjoyed in a representative democracy. Some of them have "rubber-stamp" legislatures, which provide a facade democracy, but are actually under the dictator's control.

COMMUNISM

Communism is a political and economic theory in which the government has total ownership and control of the production and distribution of goods. There is no privately owned real estate. All manner of things—press, radio, television, education, art, athletics, recreation, food production, and business—are run (and therefore controlled) by the government. People are actively discouraged from practicing any form of religion—other than loyalty to the state and its leaders. People do not have the right to work where they wish; they may not travel when or where they wish; they may not write or even discuss what they wish concerning the government. Elections are held, but only approved candidates of the Communist Party are on the ticket.

Karl Marx, the founder of the basic theory of communism, contended that capitalism, and in particular, the private ownership of property, was the root of all evil. He believed that capitalists exploited the laboring people, who only would become poorer as the rich became richer. He called for the workers—the proletariat—to rise up and overthrow the capitalists in violent revolution. In fact, Marx believed a major war between capitalism and communism was inevitable. Lenin, the first leader of the Soviet Union, echoed the words of Marx, as did Stalin, his immediate successor.

According to Marx, when true communism, called the dictatorship of the proletariat, was achieved, the state would wither away. There would no longer be any need for government, because all persons would be working according to their abilities, and drawing their needs from a central storehouse. Since the exploitation of the masses would no longer be going on, there would no longer be crime, injustice, poverty, or discrimination of any kind.

Needless to say, this utopia has not yet arrived in the USSR. In fact, Stalin modified Marx's theory by stating that before the state could wither away, there first would have to be an absolute dictatorship in which the Communist Party was supreme over all aspects of life in the Soviet Union. He, as dictator, would be supreme over the Party. Not until that absolute control was attained, and capitalism elsewhere in the world exterminated, would the Soviet Union or any other socialist country be able to proceed to utopian communism. Stalin thus brought into being a totalitarian communism with an all-powerful, oppressive government. It attained mastery over the Russian people, and began aggressively exporting its philosophy of economics and government.

COEXISTENCE AND DETENTE

It was not until the 1960s, during Nikita Khrushchev's leadership, that the USSR developed a new policy concerning relationships with the Western democracies. This was called the policy of coexistence. However encouraging this word sounded to the West, however, to the Russians it only meant a less violent approach to their ultimate objective—domination of the entire world. Since relative equality had been achieved in military and economic strength, a lessening of world tensions would allow the Russians to win their objective by means short of all-out war. The objective remained the same, but the means to attain it would be more subtle and less violent. Meanwhile, material assistance to communist political and military insurgents in underdeveloped countries would be stepped up.

In the 1970s, diplomats of the West began to use the term "détente," a French word meaning "a lessening of tension." The policy of détente assumes that neither side would do anything to change the balance of military power—because neither side would want to cause a nuclear holocaust. In this atmosphere, the Strategic Arms Limitation Talks (SALT) between the United States and the USSR took place. They resulted in a treaty which was intended to further clarify the policy of détente. The United States made a number of concessions in this treaty, concerning numbers and types of missiles, in the apparent hope that the Soviet Union would interpret this as a genuine attempt to relax tensions and further the "spirit of détente." But it was not very long before U. S. intelligence determined that the Soviets were violating key provisions of the treaty. With that discovery, President Gerald Ford publicly disavowed the policy of détente. He left the door open, however, for further SALT talks which would slow down the arms race.

There is nothing wrong with the concept of SALT, or any other discussions with the Soviets concerning arms limitations. But it must never be forgotten that the Soviet Union and each of its leaders, regardless of the current words they may use, are continually striving to expand the USSR's sphere of influence.

The danger, then, of SALT or other talks is not the written agreements which may result from such negotiations. The danger is that such agreements may tend to lull the Western democracies into believing that the objective of the Soviet Union and militant communism has changed. It hasn't. Such interpretation should not cause the West to lower its defenses, reduce its research and development programs, decrease its training of adequate numbers of highly qualified military personnel, or otherwise make itself unprepared to withstand Soviet diplomatic or military advances. Then we are only asking for an aggressive move by them. Once our own deterrent strength no longer has credibility, the Soviet Union will move into that vacuum.

Americans must never forget that communist and fascist governments—which now control a significant portion of the peoples of the world—are dictatorships. There is no way that we can reconcile or eliminate our fundamental differences with them. Such governments, in their refusal to grant human rights, show themselves to be the enemies of democracy and our way of life. On this issue there can be no compromise.

GOVERNMENT AND THE PEOPLE

The basic idea of a democratic government is that it is the servant of the people, not their master. It maintains peace and order so they can go about their daily lives unhindered. The people, not the government, decide what is best for them as individuals and what is best for all.

Sometimes the mass of society may change its views on moral, business, social, or political concepts. Then laws are changed accordingly or new laws are written to conform to existing standards and conditions. Laws should not be changed on the basis of temporary whim, however. Nor are modifications required when cyclical trends in conduct appear to be changing for the moment. Thomas Jefferson wrote in the Declaration of Independence: "Prudence, indeed, will dictate that Governments long established should not be changed for light and transient causes; and accordingly all experience hath shown, that mankind are more disposed to suffer, while evils are sufferable, than to right themselves by abolishing the forms to which they are accustomed."

A democratic government interferes as little as possible with the lives of its people, but it always must be ready to defend the rights of each individual. A democratic government believes that people can handle their own problems, for the most part. But for conditions beyond the control of individuals or groups of citizens—such as disaster relief, regulation of pollution, widespread unemployment, conservation of natural resources, or raising forces for the national defense—then government must be ready and able to lend guidance, provide expertise, and organize the necessary programs and assistance.

Whenever possible, private rather than government agencies should take necessary actions. The government, through its Social Se-

A democratic government depends for its survival on the participation of its citizens.

curity program, ensures old age benefits such as financial and medical assistance. But at the same time, private organizations have established pension systems, medical insurance plans, and other ways to help those in need in their respective communities.

Everyone, including those in government, must operate within the framework of the Constitution. Sometimes this means that the Federal government gets involved in local affairs because of financial or legal assistance regulations. An example of this is public education. While the Federal government does not control education, as in communist or fascist states, it must ensure that all people have the same educational opportunities guaranteed them under the Constitution. This is normally accomplished through local governmental agencies, rather than by the Federal government directly. Today, however, Federal grants of financial aid, and professional assistance in solving local problems, are coming to be more and more common.

DEMOCRATIC PROCESSES

In America and other democratic countries, there are two or more political parties. This is a political feature of democracies which is not present in fascist or communist nations. It would be rare indeed if all persons believed that only one man was capable of government leadership, that one person's idea was the best idea available, or that only one political or economic solution to a national problem existed. Consequently, political parties have naturally evolved so groups of persons with similar political ideas have an organization to present their views to the people. This way the voters can elect a leader who represents the political party of their choice.

In a democracy, the majority rules. Once the voting is over, the minority must abide by the wishes of the majority. However, the majority must respect the rights of the minority too, for the new leaders are now the representatives of the entire population. In fact, in most elections, the outcome is relatively close, indicating that the minority party has to be considered in the future decisions of the government. Better government can be achieved in such a representative system because the minority party can be counted on to keep a close watch on public affairs and inform the people. After all, one day there will be another election!

The importance of using democratic means to achieve national goals cannot be overemphasized. American citizens enjoy the privilege of having a voice in achieving these goals. They also are protected from undue interference in achieving their personal goals by the "due process of law" provision of the Constitution. Such a privilege is not afforded citizens of a totalitarian state, where at any time, without warning or trial, they may be arrested, jailed, or persecuted in other ways.

In time of war or national emergency the two major political parties in the United States have traditionally joined together in an expression of national will. In World War II the Republican minority in Congress worked closely with the Democratic administration of Franklin Roosevelt, so the nation was able to present a united front. This policy of cooperation was called the bipartisan foreign policy. This did not mean that the two parties agreed on everything in conference, but it did mean that the minority views were positively considered and used wherever possible. Then, when the decision was made, both parties voiced their support of the President in his conduct of foreign policy.

In peacetime, even in the absence of a formal bipartisan agreement, the minority party in Congress is closely consulted on foreign-policy matters. On domestic issues, there is probably less bipartisanship; but in general, when the Congress has approved a bill and the President signs it into law, the whole Congress and American people try to give the bill the necessary support to benefit the nation. A similar logical arrangement exists in the British Parliament where the minority party and its allies are called the Loyal Opposition. This sort of healthy relationship exists only in functioning representative democracies with informed electorates.

Human Rights and the Rule of Law

The Congress of the American Colonies solemnly declared on 4 July 1776, that the 13 original colonies were free and independent states. It is more properly part of the study of American history to go into the background of this vital document. It is impossible, however, not to talk about the Declaration as a part of American heritage, tradition, and fundamental concepts of law. Further, the idea behind the Declaration is a part of the American democratic process and underlines the importance of the United States military forces in preserving that process.

The Declaration states that "all men are created equal, that they are endowed with certain unalienable Rights, that among these are Life, Liberty and the pursuit of Happiness; that to secure these rights, Governments are instituted among Men, deriving their just powers from the consent of the governed."

Our democracy in America is therefore founded on the belief that the rights of human beings are granted by a "higher law," that the individual's life, liberty, and happiness are sacred. This was why the Declaration was made: to break away from a rule which was oppressing the right of the people to live free and independent lives. The Declaration expressed this right; the Constitution and the laws of our land uphold and reinforce this belief.

Our military forces have only one purpose: to defend the people and their rights as proclaimed by the Declaration and defined by the Constitution. The President, members of his Cabinet, all members of Congress, and the personnel of the United States Armed Forces are committed by their oaths to support and defend the Constitution against all enemies, foreign or domestic.

Under our "government of law," officials may do only what the law allows them to do.

Personnel of the U. S. Armed Forces are committed to support and defend the Constitution against all enemies, foreign and domestic. Here new Marine officers take their oath of office.

Escort frigate USS *Brewton* makes a sharp turn to starboard while keeping in fighting trim off Pearl Harbor, Hawaii.

They should be no more immune from the law than any other good citizen. In fact, the government is composed of citizens elected by their peers for the sole purpose of serving the American people as a whole. In the American democracy a citizen may do anything not prohibited by law; under a totalitarian government a citizen may do only what the government permits him to do. This latter concept gives great powers to officials, enabling them, legally, to punish citizens for such vaguely defined acts as "crimes against the state."

The widespread abuses of human rights in totalitarian states are difficult for a free people to understand. Such abuses are abhorrent to the fundamental beliefs which we in America have long regarded as simple guaranteed facts of life. In fact, we as a people are often complacent with our well-being, our abundance, our freedoms. Sometimes we have become indifferent to the tremendous responsibility each of us has to maintain these rights. This is the worst threat to our continued independence and prosperity.

Chapter 1. Study Guide Questions

1. What is the real meaning of American democracy?

2. What is the essential characteristic of democratic government?

3. Why are freedoms of expression, movement, and association so important in a free society?

4. What is the purpose of our U. S. Constitution?

5. What is necessary for free democratic government to endure?

6. What does "equality of opportunity" mean?

7. What is often regarded as the greatest strength of the democratic form of government?

8. What is the intent of equal opportunity in the U. S. Navy? Why is equal opportunity so important in the Navy, and especially so aboard ship?

9. Why is there a growing problem in the world regarding economic equality? What are the two opposing interpretations for solving the problem?

10. What is socialism and where is it the common form of politics in government?

11. What are the key features of fascism? Where is fascism most common today?

12. What is communism? What are some of its distinctive features?

13. Who are the "proletariat?" What did Marx believe would be the result of worker exploitation?

14. Has "utopian" communism arrived in the USSR? Explain.

15. What does coexistence really mean? Who started this policy?

16. What was the policy of détente? Why has it largely been abandoned as an official U. S. policy?

17. What is the real danger of negotiations with the Soviet Union?

18. Why is reconciliation of fundamental differences between democracy and communism or fascism not possible?

19. How should laws be changed in a democratic society? Why?

20. What is the proper relationship between government and individuals in a democracy?

21. What is the relationship of the Federal government to education in America? . . . in fascist and communist countries?

22. What is the basic political feature which differentiates democratic and fascist or communist nations?

23. What should be the relationship between majority and minority political parties in a democracy?

24. What is bipartisan foreign policy and why did it come into being in the United States?

25. How do the Declaration of Independence and Constitution deal with human rights in America?

26. What is the fundamental difference between democratic and totalitarian governments in their interpretation of "government of law?"

27. What is probably the worst threat to American independence and prosperity?

Vocabulary

representative democracy	propaganda
	communism
Bill of Rights	self-criticism
U. S. Constitution	exploitation
equal opportunity	proletariat
non-preferential treatment	dictatorship of proletariat
prejudice	capitalism
minority, majority	coexistence
discrimination	ideology
economic equality	détente
socialism	reconciliation
fascism	cyclical trend
"rubber-stamp" legislature	bipartisan
	electorate

Chapter 2. The Navy and the Nation

The Continental Congress passed legislation on 13 October 1775, to form a committee to purchase and arm two ships. They thereby created the Continental Navy. This is regarded, historically, as the "birthday" of the U. S. Navy. The Continental Navy fought gallantly in the Revolutionary War, contributing substantially to the independence of the new nation. They successfully established a heritage and tradition of victory which is still the watchword of our modern Navy.

The new United States Constitution provided for the establishment of the Navy. Article I, Section 8, Clause 13 states that "The Congress shall have Power to provide and maintain a Navy." Clause 14 states that "The Congress shall have Power to make Rules for the Government and Regulation of the land and naval Forces." Article II, Section 2, Clause 1 says that "The President shall be Commander in Chief of the Army and Navy of the United States. . ."

These three short entries are the only specific reference to the Navy in the Constitution. From these few lines, however, Congress authorized the establishment of the Navy, directed that a set of regulations be developed to run the organization, and appointed the President as Commander in Chief.

ACTIONS OF PRESIDENTS
AS COMMANDERS IN CHIEF

The power of the President in his capacity as Commander in Chief of the armed forces is extensive. History is full of examples of actions taken by the armed forces, under the President's instructions. Often he has referred the matter to the Congress as a *fait accompli* (an act already done and no longer worth opposing). Here are some examples:

1) In 1801 President Jefferson informed Congress that he had sent a naval squadron to the Mediterranean to protect United States ocean commerce against threatened attack by Tripoli's pirates.

2) In 1811 President Madison announced

The battleship USS *New Jersey* enters one of the locks of the Panama Canal. It was through the actions of President Theodore Roosevelt that the United States gained control over the Canal Zone. The Canal Zone is to be returned to the Panamanians, however, by the terms of a treaty ratified by the U. S. Senate in 1978.

that he had been employing a naval force to guard the United States coast in the interest of national security and to protect U. S. commercial shipping. Seven months later he recommended a declaration of war against Great Britain for her unwarranted actions against the American merchant marine.

3) In 1845 President Polk announced that he had deployed military and naval forces on the coasts of Mexico and the western frontier of Texas to prevent any trouble due to the annexation of Texas by the United States. Five

months later he asked Congress to declare war on Mexico.

4) In 1861 President Lincoln effected the blockade of the Confederacy by proclamation; the President's authority to institute a blockade was tested and upheld by the Supreme Court in 1863.

5) In May 1862, President Lincoln assumed actual military and naval command of successful operations against Norfolk, Virginia.

6) On 22 April 1898, by proclamation and without statutory authority, President McKin-

ley declared a blockade of Cuba. Three days later Congress declared war on Spain and authorized the President to take necessary action.

7) In 1903, as the United States Government was negotiating with Colombia for rights to build the Panama Canal, a long-standing dispute between Colombia and their Panamanian province erupted into revolution. President Theodore Roosevelt ordered the United States Navy to guard the Panama area and prevent Colombian troops from being landing in Panama to suppress the insurrection. On 3 November Panama declared its independence; the United States recognized the new republic three days later. The United States and the Republic of Panama then promptly signed a treaty authorizing the construction of the Panama Canal and granting the United States exclusive control of the Canal Zone.

8) In 1908 President Theodore Roosevelt sent the United States Fleet on a trip around the world—even though Congress had not appropriated enough funds for the trip. Congress was forced to make a supplemental appropriation to allow the fleet to complete the trip back to the United States.

9) On 21 April 1914, by order of President Wilson, a force of sailors and Marines was landed at Vera Cruz, Mexico, to capture the city because of an insult to the U. S. flag. The city was occupied militarily for 7 months. The action was taken without Congressional authorization.

10) In April 1941 President Franklin Roosevelt ordered the Navy to patrol ship lanes to Europe, and to report movements of German vessels in American defensive waters. In May the President issued a proclamation declaring an unlimited national emergency, and ordering American naval craft to "sink on sight" foreign submarines found in our "defensive waters." In July he ordered the Navy to perform convoy duty for supplies being sent to Great Britain under the Lend-Lease agreement.

11) President Truman issued a statement, following the invasion on 25 June 1950 of South Korea by communist North Korea, that pursuant to a decision made by the United Nations Security Council, he had "ordered the United States air and sea forces to give the Korean Government troops cover and support." He also ordered the Seventh Fleet to guard Formosa (Taiwan).

12) In 1958 President Eisenhower, responding to a call for assistance from the president of Lebanon, directed the Navy and Marine Amphibious Ready Group of the Sixth Fleet to invade Lebanon and come to the support of the Lebanese Government.

13) On 22 October 1962 President Kennedy addressed the nation on television and announced that he was issuing orders for the establishment of a naval "quarantine" of Cuba on the basis of proof obtained of the presence of Soviet ballistic missiles and air bases on that island.

14) In April 1965, President Johnson sent U. S. military forces into the Dominican Republic to restore order when a revolution threatened to overthrow the government.

15) On 2 August 1965, following North Vietnamese PT-boat attacks against U. S. destroyers in the Gulf of Tonkin, President Johnson ordered U. S. naval forces to respond to any attack. After a second North Vietnamese attack on 4 August, the President announced to the American people that "(naval) air action is now in execution against gunboats and certain support facilities in North Vietnam."

The Office of Commander in Chief

This office is a source of considerable (and undefined) power. The Supreme Court has evaded making a precise description of the powers of the office; the Court traditionally has avoided entanglement in contests between the President and Congress for the direction of military policy.

In the absence of authoritative judicial ruling, therefore, the responsibility for the making of military policy has been determined largely by competition between Congress and the President. The Constitution directs Congress to "raise, support, and discipline" armies and navies. But it also designates the President as "commander in chief" of these forces, and it gives neither branch—executive or legislative—any suggestion of what actual power it has in carrying out its constitutional responsibility.

The greater share of power has, over the years, been acquired by the Presidency. Historically, the greatest steps in support of presidential power were made by Lincoln. Relying upon his constitutional commission as commander in chief, he determined the existence of the "rebellion" which became the Civil War; he called out the militia to suppress this rebellion and increased the Army beyond its authorized strength. He proclaimed martial law, emancipated the slaves, established a blockade, and spent money from the Treasury without a Congressional appropriation, deeming these actions indispensable to the successful prosecution of the war.

Lincoln undertook many of these measures when Congress was not in session. When Congress finally assembled, it was faced with the *fait accompli,* and its only practical course was to pass legislation which affirmed the President's actions. This lent legal support to many of Lincoln's moves, and has provided legal precedent for other Presidents in times of military and political crisis.

MAHAN AND FDR

The other President who notably advanced the power of the Presidency in this competition with Congress was Franklin D. Roosevelt. Before the U. S. entry into World War II, Roosevelt was blocked from supplying arms to the Allies by the Neutrality Act of 1937. Thus he had to call Congress into session to implement his plans and actions against the growing Axis menace to America, her democratic ideals, and her potential allies. Since the dangers were becoming apparent, the Congress dutifully authorized the President's recommendations.

Mr. Roosevelt believed in the teachings of Alfred Thayer Mahan—that the enemy must be halted long before he reaches American shores. This meant that the European coast of the Atlantic must be controlled by friendly nations. It became U. S. business to assure that the proper control was maintained.

In Roosevelt's estimation, the doctrine of Mahan was underscored by the war of movement and technology then taking place in Europe. He saw how rapidly armies and their air and naval counterparts could be moved. This mobility greatly reduced the significance of distance as a measure of defense. He believed that those who thought there was safety in the broad waters of the Atlantic were the victims of a dangerous illusion.

Therefore, he believed that American defenses had to stretch to the outermost points from which the nation might be threatened. Naval and air bases far from the home shores provided this outer periphery of defense. Consequently the U. S. Navy was called upon to convoy, patrol, and fight German submarines months before the actual declaration of war. U. S. military forces were placed in Greenland and Iceland by Presidential order. They were to act as obstacles for the German forces then threatening the approaches to the United States.

MODERN WARFARE: QUICK REACTION

President Roosevelt wrote: "Modern warfare has given us a new definition for that word 'attack.' There was a time when we could afford to say that we would not fight unless attacked, and then wait until the physical attack came upon us before starting to shoot. Modern techniques of warfare have changed all that. An attack today is a very different

Modern weapons systems such as the fleet ballistic missile submarine make extension of the nation's defense lines and early warning system necessary for survival. To guard against that menace, the nuclear-powered attack submarine USS *Finback* is deployed to the far reaches of the oceans.

thing. An attack today begins as soon as any base has been occupied from which our security is threatened. That base may be thousands of miles away from our own shores. The American government must, of necessity, decide at which point any threat of attack against this hemisphere has begun; and to make their stand when that point has been reached."

This philosophy bears the unmistakable mark of Mahan. It does not espouse the idea of "preventive war," occasionally voiced by irresponsible persons. Preventive war means striking first, on the assumption that some other nation might be planning an attack on the United States. This is contrary to any sensible policy, for it merely provides an excuse for bold aggression. This has never been an American policy anywhere, and certainly cannot be

justified in this day of potential nuclear holocaust.

When an attack is made against the United States, its armed forces may strike back without awaiting a formal declaration of war. That principle is established by dictates of practical necessity which defy any other considerations of Constitutional theory. If the Commander in Chief could not call out his forces until Congress formally declared war, enemy forces might make great advances against U. S. territory and interests. All issues of this nature might not be as clear-cut as when the Japanese attacked Pearl Harbor, however. The issue was clear when missiles and missile sites were discovered on Cuba only 90 miles from America, even though the Soviets and Cubans protested that their purpose was only "defensive." The extent of danger to the United States when the North Vietnamese unsuccessfully attacked our destroyers in the Tonkin Gulf is much less clear, even if that hostile action itself was abundantly clear.

Today, surveillance, patrol, and intelligence operations are the means which can give warning that an enemy attack is imminent or underway. The military forces alone are in a position to make the important determination whether an attack has been made or is about to be made, and if the situation requires immediate reprisal. The President, in his military leadership role, must be able to make a quick operational decision to retaliate. The consequences of judgement of the President with his chief military advisors at this time are drastic, for if force is used, the nation is then committed to fight.

But the Roosevelt–Mahan philosophy of preparedness and power far from home is the only practical defense posture today. Modern weaponry, such as intercontinental ballistic missiles and ballistic missile submarines, extend the nation's mobile defense lines and early warning system. These are absolutely indispensable to survival. The authority and capability of the President as Commander in Chief to employ the nation's armed forces in instantaneous response to hostile enemy action must be available today as never before.

CONSTITUTIONAL TRADITION

Created by congressional action, the Navy and its personnel have sworn to defend the Constitution. The Constitution, with its complex system of checks and balances, stresses the worth of the individual. Preservation of the Constitution and its traditional ideals has, under the American system, required that the armed forces operate under civilian authority. Thus, there is a balance between the legally dominant civilian authority and extreme militarism—because the Constitution was written to prevent such militarism. Since the task of

every officer and enlisted person is to serve the nation, the Navy has a fundamental role in defending the rights of all citizens under the Constitution.

At times the complexities of civilian–military relations and the problems of administration of the armed forces make the system appear cumbersome. But it has saved our country from the abuses of dictatorship and the excesses of militarism. The constitutional system of checks and balances is involved in administration of the armed forces and helps prevent long-range mistakes.

ROLE OF THE NAVY IN WORLD AFFAIRS

The operational responsibilities of the Navy are in direct proportion to the international roles of the United States. The nation has as-

The constitutional system of checks and balances was created by the founding fathers to prevent excesses of militarism. The civilian authority remains supreme in the United States, and all military personnel swear to defend the Constitution, thereby defending the rights of all citizens. Marching in front of their barracks are these midshipman candidates at the Naval Academy Preparatory School, Newport, Rhode Island.

sumed a position of world leadership since World War II, and in this position has striven to keep peace and order. We have committed ourselves to economic and military support of friendly nations around the world. Unless the United States shows that its determination is backed by strength, in ensuring that these commitments are carried out, our very survival as a nation is threatened.

The United States is the leader because of its natural resources, industrial and military strength, and because of its deep allegiance to the principles of human dignity, self-government, and personal freedom.

Millions throughout the world look to us for leadership. We have given our pledge of support to the entire free world. Carrying out this pledge means a heavy operating schedule for the U. S. Navy. In response to the determinations of the President and Congress, the Navy assists in protecting the sovereignty of free nations in all parts of the world. The survival of the United States is at stake whenever the Navy and its sister services are called upon to defend these free states. Such nations serve as the beacon lights on the edge of America's own defense lines. Defeat of freedom and independence in a remote corner of the world creates a gap in that defense, allowing hostile forces and bases to move that much closer to our own homeland.

The Navy has fleets deployed—the Sixth in the Mediterranean and the Seventh in the Western Pacific—to guard our outer bastions. The First and Second fleets protect the Atlantic and Pacific Ocean approaches to the North American continent. These fleets are ready to aid those nations who need them. In so doing, they protect our own shores. These fleets are the major deterrents to totalitarian aggression around the world today.

THE NAVY AND FOREIGN POLICY

A foreign policy is an expression of a state's attitude or posture toward other nations. All

Each person in the Navy should understand the nation's basic foreign policy, as should all citizens. In a democracy, the public must support the policy or else it will be weakened and national security endangered. Naval Academy Brigade Staff officers discuss problems in a seminar.

nations have some sort of foreign policy. It is the role of each person in the Navy to assist in the implementation of our nation's foreign policy.

Many necessary actions of government are based on complex reasons. Often they are misunderstood by the people or even misinterpreted by the other nations whom the actions affect. Dealings with foreign policy are almost always essential to national security. It stands to reason, then, that the public in a democracy must understand its government's policy. Otherwise, support for the policy may be weakened and national security seriously degraded.

The President sets the tone for the foreign policy of his government. The Secretary of State, guided by the President and his Cabinet, initiates the actions between the United States and foreign countries. This is done either directly, or through ambassadors stationed in those countries, who have official access to the host government.

The Congress controls enabling legislation and appropriations, and the Senate must approve all foreign commitments, such as treaties. Thus, support from the public is essential. In the long run, taking everything into account, the public is in control. That may seem difficult to believe, especially in fast-moving diplomatic negotiations, but in the American democracy this is basically true. Through periodic elections, the citizens control both foreign and domestic policies. This factor again makes it imperative that the American public remain educated and concerned with foreign-policy matters so they can make intelligent decisions at the polls. The future welfare of the nation in its relations with other countries is dependent on this.

Background of U. S. Foreign Policy

Traditionally, American foreign policy has tended toward neutrality and isolation. Washington, in his famous Farewell Address, advised against entangling alliances and involvements in foreign wars. Changing events and times, however, would not let the United States adhere to this comfortable sounding policy. As the nation grew, so did its commercial and political relationships with other countries.

A notable exception to this policy was the Monroe Doctrine of 1823. In this declaration, the United States expressed a strong responsibility for the Western Hemisphere. It was designed to prevent further European interference in South America and the Caribbean. Then, war with Spain in 1898 gave the United States overseas territories and obligations. This made us a factor in international affairs, regardless of our natural desire to remain aloof.

After World War I the United States was offered world leadership—but refused it. Congress refused to let us join the League of Nations, even though it was President Wilson's idea. Rather, the nation retreated into isolationism, reemphasizing neutrality. Meanwhile the world became entrapped by economic depression and the rise of the fascist dictators. President Roosevelt did develop the "Good Neighbor" policy with Latin American nations and gradually edged toward support of Britain and France, as Germany and Italy dragged Europe toward World War II.

Finally, drawn into the world conflict, the traditional position of the United States was reversed. The United States now had world leadership thrust upon it—many alliances, strong foreign commitments, and a role as the champion of the democratic cause around the world. Following the war we sponsored the Marshall Plan to rebuild the democracies of devastated Europe into viable allies, able to stand up against external threat. The North Atlantic Treaty was signed to give the alliance a credible military capability. Wars were fought against communist aggression in Korea and Vietnam. Threats against established friendly governments in Greece, Turkey, Lebanon, and the Dominican Republic were countered by military and economic aid.

The United States became a leader in the United Nations Organization, the mediator and spokesman in countless disputes between friendly nations, allies, and newly formed nations. Reports of negotiations, telling of deep involvement with foreign nations, became daily headlines in every American newspaper: "summit" conference, "shuttle" diplomacy, mutual defense treaty, strategic arms talks, Middle East diplomacy, Geneva conferences, base renewal agreements, foreign-aid bills, and so forth. President Washington would have been amazed at our involvement in world affairs—military alliances with over 60 nations, military forces stationed in Europe and Asia, and naval forces deployed in every ocean.

Characteristics of Strong Foreign Policy

A strong foreign policy must be carefully coordinated with all elements of the nation and must be consistent in its objectives. The people and the government must be unified in seeking the national goals. These goals must be reached by common agreement, and need to be clearly defined.

The policy must be long-range in scope,

American foreign policy must be respected by the nations of the world. To ensure that respect, our foes must know that an attack on American military units will bring a swift and strong response.

with common purpose, durable under any changing conditions. The most common purposes of national policy are national survival, prosperity for all citizens, and a better life for all. Peace is a common objective, and certainly one which American foreign policy seeks for all peoples.

Foreign policy must also be flexible, alert to changing conditions which make it necessary to adapt a course of action. Flexibility, however, does not imply changing fundamental goals. Rather, it means being able to modify actions to take advantage of changed conditions.

Finally, foreign policy should be respected. It develops prestige through integrity, by keeping commitments and agreements, and by expressing goals that are widely understood and admired both at home and abroad.

There must be a careful coordination between the various agencies of government in foreign-policy matters. The two agencies in which this coordination is most readily seen are the State and Defense Departments. In time of peace, State normally takes the initiative in foreign relations and is supported by Defense. In time of war, military strategy should be developed by Defense and supported by State. Both agencies, however, must work together on the long-term objectives and the planning which will determine the roles of each.

Some typical examples of coordination are these: State negotiates for foreign bases; Defense builds the base and assigns personnel and equipment to it. State arranges for treaties calling for mutual assistance; Defense administers and distributes the military aid. State warns the Soviet Union not to invade Turkey; Defense shortens the alert time and sends the Sixth Fleet to the Eastern Mediterranean.

Unified foreign actions of this type require

complete and quick coordination of activities within our government. This coordination goes down the line to the officers and seamen on each of the ships involved in an action. They must be unified by a common purpose and common understanding. Because of the fluid world situation, each person in the Navy plays an active role in the implementation of the nation's foreign policy. The policy is made in Washington, but the Navy and other armed forces are its field representatives.

Chapter 2. *Study Guide Questions*

1. When is the historical birthday of the U. S. Navy? When was the establishment of the U. S. Navy officially authorized? How?

2. What is the general impression one gains from reviewing the actions of the President as Commander in Chief?

3. What was the significance of Theodore Roosevelt's use of the Navy in Panama in 1903?

4. How has the power of the office of the Commander in Chief of the U. S. Armed Forces evolved?

5. Which two presidents made the largest steps in acquiring power as commanders in chief?

6. How did Mahan's concept of national defense compare with that of Franklin D. Roosevelt's as concerns the Navy?

7. Why did Roosevelt regard an extension of the periphery of defense as so important to American security?

8. Why is "preventive" war contrary to American policy?

9. What would be the reaction of any U. S. military unit if subjected to an armed attack by a hostile force?

10. How does the United States hope to gain early warning of an attack, or impending attack, by enemy forces?

11. Why is preparedness and extended defense the only practical defense posture the United States can have today?

12. What has effectively prevented the rise of militarism in the U. S. system of government?

13. Why must the United States show that its determination is backed by strength when playing its role in international affairs?

14. Why has the United States become the natural leader of the world's democracies?

15. How does the Navy assist the U. S. Government in playing its role as the leader of the democracies?

16. What is foreign policy? Who sets the tone for U. S. foreign policy? Who, in the long run, controls U. S. foreign policy?

17. What was the U. S. foreign policy most of the time prior to World War II? What has it been since then?

18. What are the four characteristics of a strong foreign policy?

19. Why must foreign policy be carefully coordinated between the State and Defense Departments? Which department should take the initiative in foreign relations during peacetime? . . . in wartime?

20. What is the role in the nation's foreign policy of the officers and crews of naval ships?

Vocabulary

legislation
Commander in Chief
fait accompli
employment (of
  naval forces)
unwarranted actions
proclamation
statutory authority
insurrection
supplemental appro-
  priation
entanglement
prosecute war
periphery of defense
"preventive" war
surveillance
preparedness

militarism
Constitutional checks
  and balances
mutual assistance
deterrent strength
outer bastions (of de-
  fense)
foreign policy
Monroe Doctrine
Good Neighbor
  Policy
summit conference
shuttle diplomacy
SALT
flexibility (in foreign
  policy).
alliance

Meteorology and Weather

Chapter 1. The Weather: An Introduction

The men who "go down to the sea in ships" fight a continuous close action with the elements. Situations still arise in which the safety of a ship and the lives of her crew depend on evasive action taken to avoid the full fury of a storm. Extra security measures are taken well in advance of an approaching storm, to minimize damage to the ship, her gear, and her cargo.

We've all heard the statement "Everybody talks about the weather but nobody does anything about it." In the past, this statement may have been true; but it isn't today. Meteorology—the science of weather—is helping to make our lives safer and easier. Storm forecasts and weather warnings are much more accurate than they have ever been before. A network of weather stations provides information for safe commercial and military flights. Naval weather services give mariners routing information, so they can avoid storms and heavy seas. Satellites provide worldwide weather services and meteorological information used in weather prediction and scientific research. Agricultural weather services help farmers plan for planting, harvesting, and marketing. Applied meteorology enables aircraft to take advantage of air currents, thus improving fuel conservation and flight time. There have even been successful experiments in *causing* rain. In addition, meteorologists are exploring ways to

break up dangerous tropical cyclones before they can reach populated areas. Indeed, something *is* being done about the weather!

METEOROLOGY AND HISTORY

The importance of weather in history cannot be overemphasized. Weather has influenced the struggles of humanity, in peace and war, since earliest times.

Most people are well aware of the damage weather can do to the economy, transportation, and housing. The study of any war will show that the weather has been critical in major battles and campaigns, on both land and sea. Some examples of the influence of weather on warfare are listed below; many more could be given.

1) The defeat of the Spanish Armada in 1588 by Sir Francis Drake's small fleet was helped greatly by a bad storm in the English Channel.

2) The brutal Russian winter was instrumental in defeating Napoleon's invasion of that country in 1812, and Hitler's invasion during World War II.

3) In 1941, gales and poor visibility in the North Pacific helped the Japanese fleet move unobserved to within striking distance of Pearl Harbor.

4) The D-Day landings on Normandy's coast in June 1944 were delayed due to storm warnings. Whole artificial harbors were created to protect ships which were offloading supplies from the fury of storms expected during the early phases of the invasion.

Sailors fight a continuous close battle with the weather. A U. S. destroyer noses into a heavy sea in the central Pacific.

5) The wet and dry monsoons of Southeast Asia determined, to a large extent, the active military operational areas during the Vietnam War.

The first meteorological instrument, developed by a Frenchman in the 15th century, was a crude hygrometer which measured moisture in the air. Galileo Galilei, an Italian scientist, invented the first simple thermometer in the late 15th century. This invention may be regarded as the first step in the development of meteorology as a science. During the 17th century barometers, wind-measuring devices, and improved thermometers were developed.

A major advance in meteorology occurred in 1854–56. During this time a French astronomer named U. J. Leverrier developed a system for organizing weather observations in the Black Sea area. He found that he could locate and trace various storms from one map to an-other, predict their future positions, and thus make a weather forecast. This was the forerunner of *synoptic meteorology,* our present-day system of observing and collecting weather data. Synoptic meteorology means a general view of the weather.

Significant advances in the science of meteorology were made during the two world wars. A Norwegian meteorologist, Vilhelm Bjerknes, developed the air-mass and polar-front theories of weather. These theories are the basis for many of the forecasting rules used today. A network of reporting stations were established and means of collecting data were thus greatly improved. As aviation advanced, frontal forecasting became highly developed. This increased knowledge became critical for safe commercial, passenger, and military flights.

Great progress has been made in meteorology during recent years, but much remains to be learned. Considerable amounts of money and a great deal of research time are spent annually on the weather. Study of the world's weather was a significant part of the International Geophysical Year studies in the late 1950s. Today, the satellite is an observational tool of meteorologists. Circling the earth many times daily, it sends back accurate photographs of cloud cover and storm fronts, and records temperature, humidity, and other weather phenomena.

Chapter 1. Study Guide Questions

1. What is the science of weather?
2. What are some things that man is doing in the field of weather science?
3. What are some examples of how the weather has affected the outcome of battles in military history?
4. What meteorological instruments had already been invented by 1700?
5. What was the significance of Leverrier's weather observation stations?
6. Why has frontal forecasting become so important?
7. What is synoptic meteorology?
8. What are the newest observation tools of meteorologists?

Vocabulary

meteorology	synoptic meteorology
applied meteorology	International
hygrometer	Geophysical Year
thermometer	weather satellite
barometer	frontal forecasting

Chapter 2. Our Atmosphere

It is not possible to understand much about weather without having a fundamental knowledge of the atmosphere around us. Actually we live at the bottom of a vast ocean of air which completely covers the earth. This atmosphere exists in major layers up to about 1,000 miles above the earth's surface, though it is believed that minute gaseous elements, such as helium, are present as far out as 18,000 miles.

Our atmosphere is a mixture of different gases. Near the surface of the earth the air is made up of approximately 78 percent nitrogen, 21 percent oxygen, and 1 percent argon and other gases such as carbon dioxide, hydrogen, and neon. Within these figures is scattered about 1 percent water vapor, called *humidity*. The amount of water vapor is greater in equatorial regions and less in the polar regions.

It is rather interesting to compare the "water" ocean with the "air" ocean. Water, for instance, is nearly incompressible; a cubic foot of surface water weighs about the same as a cubic foot taken from the bottom of the Marianas Trench. But this is not the case with a cubic foot of air taken from different altitudes. The higher one goes, the lighter the air becomes, and consequently the more compressible it is.

The atmosphere thins so rapidly that over half of the total atmosphere by weight is in the first 3½ miles of atmosphere. It is within that 3½-mile envelope that virtually all of the earth's weather occurs. By the time a balloon has ascended to 20 miles, 99 percent of the atmospheric weight and gases lie below. Beyond 45 miles, only helium and hydrogen exist, in minute amounts. Within the air envelope, then, lies the tempestuous air ocean, constantly churning and mixing the gases we breathe. Here are all the winds, clouds, rains, and storms which make the weather.

The atmosphere consists of five principal layers. From the earth's surface outward into space, they are the troposphere, stratosphere, mesosphere, thermosphere, and exosphere. There are also transition zones of vital importance between some of these layers. The tropopause lies between the troposphere and the

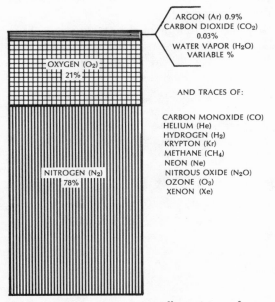

ARGON (Ar) 0.9%
CARBON DIOXIDE (CO₂)
0.03%
WATER VAPOR (H₂O)
VARIABLE %

AND TRACES OF:

CARBON MONOXIDE (CO)
HELIUM (He)
HYDROGEN (H₂)
KRYPTON (Kr)
METHANE (CH₄)
NEON (Ne)
NITROUS OXIDE (N₂O)
OZONE (O₃)
XENON (Xe)

What we call the air ocean is really a mixture of gases. By volume it is composed of about 21 percent oxygen and 78 percent nitrogen, with the remaining 1 percent made up of carbon dioxide, hydrogen, helium and traces of the rare gases such as neon, argon, krypton, and xenon. Because of the air circulation, the proportions of these gases remains remarkably uniform up to levels of about 50 miles. Water vapor is not mentioned in this list because, while it is abundant in the atmosphere, it varies widely in volume—from over 5 percent in the air overlying a tropical ocean, to a fractional percent in cold, dry polar air.

stratosphere; the chemosphere or ozone layer lies mainly between the stratosphere and mesosphere. The ionosphere is the whole area encompassing the mesosphere and the thermosphere. We will talk about each of these important layers and transition zones.

The Troposphere

The *troposphere* is the ocean of air immediately above the earth's surface. It extends to a height of about 11 miles above the equator, some 7½ miles in the temperate zones, and only 5 miles above the poles. Currents, storms, and waves occur in this air ocean, much as in

the seas. Air in the troposphere is constantly turning over; in fact, "tropos" is a Greek word meaning "changing" or "turning." In the troposphere, the temperature and composition of gases change rapidly.

Nearly all clouds are in the troposphere, so it is here that weather occurs. Air heated by the earth rises, in a process called *convection*, and is replaced by cooler air descending from higher altitudes. As the hot air rises, the pressure lessens, and the air expands to become less dense. When it rises, if it cools sufficiently, it will condense into clouds and then perhaps into rain or snow. The whole process is deter-

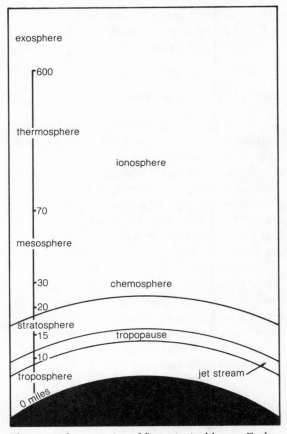

The atmosphere consists of five principal layers. Each layer has unique characteristics. The boundaries are not sharp and are illustrated here only in average heights.

mined by the simplest of the laws of gases: expansion is a cooling process, while compression causes heat.

The average temperature of the air at sea level is about 56°F. At the top of the troposphere the temperature is about −85°F. The air automatically cools about 5½° for each 1,000 feet it travels upward; the reverse occurs in descent. This automatic temperature change in rising or falling air is called *adiabatic* warming or cooling.

Air circulation in the troposphere is of great concern to us, for the circulation of air masses determines our weather. Consequently, accurate weather prediction is dependent upon a thorough understanding of air movement in the troposphere. Intense study of the atmosphere during the International Geophysical Year proved that the swift movement of cold air masses about the vast Antarctic continent were a major factor in determining the world's weather. This is one of the main reasons that both the United States and the Soviet Union have a continuing interest in Antarctic research.

THE TROPOPAUSE

The *tropopause* is that transitional zone between the troposphere and the near void of the stratosphere. It starts just above the troposphere, at altitudes of from 5 to 11 miles, and is divided into three overlapping areas—tropical, extra-tropical, and Arctic tropopauses. The area between 20,000–40,000 feet is of importance to air navigation. This is the jet stream, a current of air which moves swiftly from west to east around the earth. The jet stream is most prominent above the extratropical and Arctic tropopause overlaps.

The jet stream was discovered in World War II when B-29 bombers flying at about 4 miles altitude found great assistance from westerly winds of up to 300 mph. Planes were able to get into this stream and increase speed, shorten air time, and conserve fuel. Staying out of these currents on the return trip also saved both time and fuel.

The jet streams have now been charted seasonally as well as geographically. It has been found that these winds are strongest over Japan and the New England states. Three major jet streams move over the North American continent in winter. One of them nearly blankets the United States. Information on the jet streams is especially significant to commercial fliers, who invariably use the information in plotting their flight paths.

There is a direct relationship between the jet streams and lower atmospheric air masses. Meteorologists have found that the jet streams move with the cool air masses near the earth's surface. Thus in winter the streams are over the temperate zones, where U. S. and Eurasian pilots can take advantage of them. However in summer the jet streams move much further north, out of most of the main commercial lanes.

THE STRATOSPHERE

The *stratosphere* lies just above the tropopause and extends to an altitude of about 30 miles. There is almost no weather here, because the air is too thin to create clouds. The temperature in the stratosphere drops much more slowly than in the lower layer. In fact, the temperature averages a fairly constant −40°F to −50°F, and actually begins to get warmer in the upper limits. Modern commercial aircraft seek to fly in the stratosphere when not using the jet streams because there is so much less air resistance. This makes much better fuel mileage possible. Pilots also favor this flying level because there is no turbulence and they can fly at top speeds.

TRANSITION AREAS AND SPECIAL LAYERS

By the time a pilot has reached the stratosphere, about three-fourths of the weight of the air is below his aircraft. Above the stratosphere lies an area of electrically charged particles

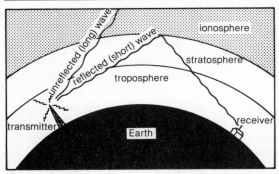

The ionosphere is a radio mirror. Short radio waves rebound from it and make intercontinental broadcasts possible. The longer waves of standard radio communication are not reflected by the ionosphere.

called ions. This *ionosphere* begins perhaps as low as 30 or 40 miles up, and extends to about 500 miles. Disturbances on the sun, such as sunspots, change the ionosphere's form, and it is turbulent with magnetic and electrical storms. It is in the ionosphere that the Northern Lights create their colorful display.

It is possible to send ordinary radio waves around the world by bouncing them off ionospheric layers. In other words, the ionosphere will reflect radio waves. By determining the best frequencies and times of day to do transmitting, communications are greatly enhanced. This phenomenon is one every Navy radio operator is well acquainted with.

The *mesosphere,* the lowest layer of the ionosphere, extends from about 30–50 miles above the earth. This layer is one of extreme temperature changes. At the lowest part of the layer the temperature may be as high as 32°F. But it will drop again to below −100°F at the mesosphere's upper limits. It will then start to rise again above 70 miles, as one moves into the thermosphere.

Another very important layer within the broad ionospheric region, but actually starting well below it, is the *chemosphere* or ozone layer. Beginning at an altitude of about 15 miles, this layer shields the earth from the harmful ultraviolet rays of the sun. Ozone, a

gas composed of three atoms of oxygen per molecule (rather than the usual two) converts the ultraviolet rays into harmless heat waves.

THE THERMOSPHERE

The *thermosphere* is the highest layer of the ionosphere. The air is extremely thin and the particles are ionized, or electrified, by loss of their electrons. This ionization is caused by the constant bombardment of cosmic rays from outer space. It is in the thermosphere that the principal radio-reflecting layers of the ionosphere exist.

Extremely high temperatures exist in this layer. Recent information shows that temperatures in the thermosphere can become 1700°F at a 300-mile altitude.

THE EXOSPHERE

The topmost layer, or outer fringe, of the atmosphere is called the *exosphere*. It begins about 500 miles above the earth's surface, and continues out to about 18,000 miles. Only the lightest hydrogen and helium atoms exist in the area, in atomic form because of the intense cosmic radiation. The temperature may be as high as 4500°F in daylight, and will then drop to near absolute zero (−460°F) at night.

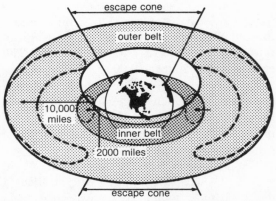

The Van Allen radiation belts encircle the earth, somewhat like a doughnut. Van Allen radiation is very intense everywhere in the exosphere, except in the "escape cones" over the poles.

Within the exosphere are the intense radiation areas called the Van Allen radiation belts. These belts are in two segments; one is 1,400–3,400 miles above the earth, while the outer belt is from 8,000–12,000 miles away. The belts are very weak above the earth's magnetic poles, and it is through these "escape cones" that manned spaceships must travel to avoid the deadly radiation. The exosphere is the end of our air ocean; beyond it is outer space.

Atmospheric Pressure

The layer of atmosphere that surrounds us exerts a pressure of nearly 15 pounds per square inch (14.696 psi) at sea level. The weight of the atmosphere varies with the amount of water vapor present, the temperature, and the height above the earth's surface. Variations in atmospheric pressure are measured by a *barometer*.

The aneroid barometer has a cell which expands or contracts with the decrease or increase of air pressure.

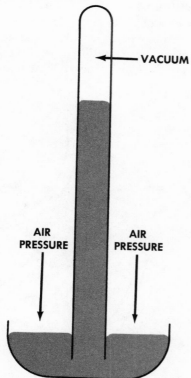

Principle of the mercurial barometer.

The Navy uses two types of barometers: mercurial and aneroid. Usually the latter is employed aboard ship. The mercurial type consists of an accurately calibrated glass tube, filled with mercury. It is used at shore activities to check aneroid barometers for accuracy.

The aneroid, or dry, barometer contains a small metallic cell which contracts when atmospheric pressure increases, and expands when pressure decreases. The cell is connected to a needle, which points to a graduated scale around the face of the barometer. As the cell expands or contracts, the needle indicates the atmospheric pressure on that scale.

Barometers may be graduated in either inches of mercury or millibars. Both inches and millibars are measurements of the height of the mercury column supported at a given time. One "atmosphere" equals 14.696 psi, the pressure at sea level; a bar equals about 0.98 atmosphere, and a millibar equals $\frac{1}{1000}$ of a bar. The average atmospheric pressure at the

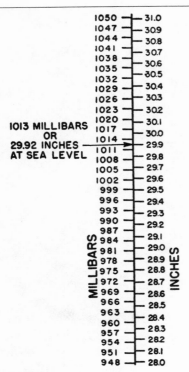

MILLIBARS	INCHES
1050	31.0
1047	30.9
1044	30.8
1041	30.7
1038	
1035	30.6
1032	30.5
1029	30.4
1026	30.3
1023	30.2
1020	30.1
1017	30.0
1014	
1011	29.9
1008	29.8
1005	29.7
1002	29.6
999	29.5
996	29.4
993	29.3
990	29.2
987	29.1
984	29.0
981	
978	28.9
975	28.8
972	28.7
969	28.6
966	28.5
963	28.4
960	
957	28.3
954	28.2
951	28.1
948	28.0

1013 MILLIBARS OR 29.92 INCHES AT SEA LEVEL

Inches and millibars.

inches of soil will absorb radiation. This means that oceans are slower to warm up, and slower to cool down, than are land or continental surfaces. Maritime air, therefore, will tend to bring moderate temperatures, neither too hot nor too cold, as it moves over land areas.

In the winter, the United States is swept by continental air masses from the cold Arctic. In the summer, it is swept by warm, moist maritime air masses from the Gulf of Mexico, Caribbean Sea, and the Pacific Ocean off the Mexican coast.

When warm and cold air masses touch, the boundary between them is called a *front*. There will usually be cloudiness and precipitation in a frontal area. A *warm front* is formed when a warm air mass moves over a cold air mass; when the reverse occurs, it is called a *cold front*. When neither mass advances on the other, a *stationary front* is said to exist.

Violent frontal weather systems can be predicted from a chart showing atmospheric pressures. Weather charts usually illustrate barometric pressures as *millibar reading points*. The lines in the figure, drawn through points of

earth's surface is 29.92 inches or 1013.2 millibars. You will often hear the barometric pressure readings given in inches on the TV weather forecast. Millibars, however, are normally used on weather charts.

An *air mass* is a large body of air with the same temperature and humidity. An air mass takes on the characteristics of the surface over which it forms. Thus, cold air masses originate in the cold polar regions, and warm air masses originate in the tropics.

The tropical or polar air masses can develop over either continental or maritime surfaces. These two surfaces give their names to the different kinds of air masses. Since land and sea reflect the sun's radiation differently, the two kinds of air masses have different characteristics.

More heat is needed to raise water temperature, for that heat is absorbed to depths in excess of 80 feet. However, only a few top

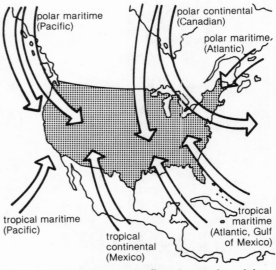

The primary air masses that affect the weather of the United States.

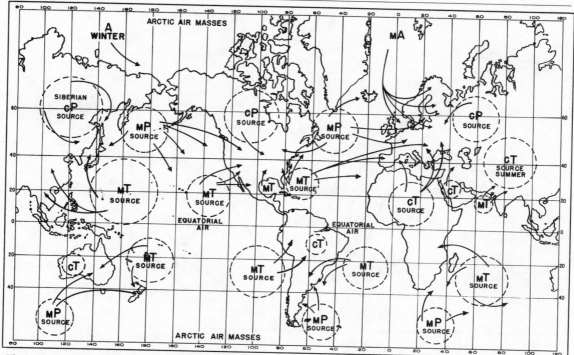

This map shows the world's principal air masses. The arrows indicate the direction in which the masses generally move. There are four types of air masses: Arctic (A), Polar (P), Tropical (T), and Equatorial (E). Each of the four types is referred to as Continental (c) or Maritime (m), depending on whether the source region for the air was a land or ocean area. Thus, mP is Maritime Polar, cP is Continental Polar, mT is Maritime Tropical, and cT is Continental Tropical.

equal pressure, are called *isobars*. Isobars never join or cross. Some may run off the chart, but others may close, forming irregular ovals. Reporting stations send in their barometric readings to a central weather bureau, where weather charts are made.

Isobars also give a rough indication of the amount of wind in an area. The closer that the isobars are to one another, the stronger the wind in that area.

What Makes the Weather?

Weather is the condition of the atmosphere. Changes in weather are caused by changes in the air's temperature, pressure, and water-vapor content; wind causes the weather to move. It can be said, therefore, that weather is the condition of the atmosphere, expressed in terms of its heat, pressure, wind, and moisture.

It is heat, and the transfer of heat, however, which make weather. This heat, of course, comes from the sun. Heat causes the weather changes, and without it there would be no winds, varying air pressures, storms, rain, or snow. All weather changes, then, are caused by temperature changes in different parts of the atmosphere.

There are some very fundamental natural laws which determine these changes. Warm air is lighter in weight and can hold more water vapor than cold air. Cold air is heavier and has a tendency to flow toward the rising warm air, replacing it on the earth's surface. As this air moves, wind is created, thus beginning the complex forces which cause the changing weather.

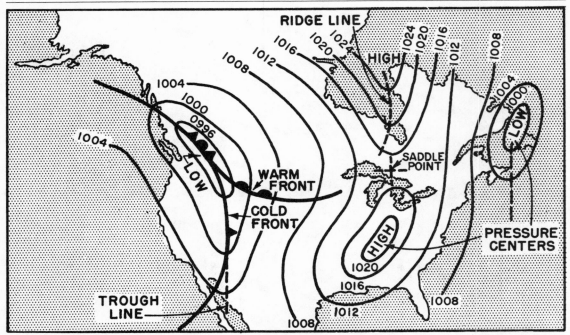

A sample weather map showing frontal systems outlined by lines drawn through points of equal pressure called isobars. Isobars never join or cross. Some may run off the chart, and others will close, forming irregular ovals that define the areas of highest and lowest pressure. Such a map makes it possible to gauge wind intensity, since wind flows from high-pressure areas to low-pressure areas.

Our principal source of energy, the sun, bombards the earth with 126 trillion horsepower each second. The sun's energy is transmitted as waves, or radiation, travelling at 186,300 miles per second. The solar radiant energy is referred to as insolation (INcoming SOLar radiATION). About 43 percent of the radiation reaching our planet hits the earth's surface and is changed into heat; the rest stays in the atmosphere or is reflected into space.

Clouds and other atmospheric influences absorb some of the incoming radiation, but reflect much of it. A typical cloud reflects back 75 percent of the sunlight striking it. Since the earth's average cloudiness is 52 percent, about 36 percent of the total insolation never reaches the earth. Dense forests absorb up to 95 percent and water reflects from 60–96 percent, depending upon the angle at which the light hits the surface.

Over a long period of time the earth's temperature remains fairly constant, in spite of the constant inflow of solar radiation. This tells us that the earth is also giving off its heat. In effect, the earth's cloud cover acts like the glass on a greenhouse. It lets the short solar rays pass through, the earth absorbs those which enter, and then re-radiates long heat waves. These long heat waves cannot get through the atmosphere because they are absorbed by the water vapor, so they stay within the "greenhouse" in a continual cycle. You will notice this especially on hot, overcast, summer nights when the humidity is high.

The atmosphere, then, acts almost like an automatic thermostat in controlling the earth's heat. It screens out the dangerous solar radiation, and acts as an insulating reflector to keep most of the heat from escaping at night. Without the atmosphere, the earth would be like

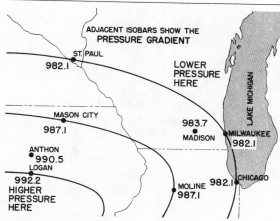

ADJACENT ISOBARS SHOW THE
PRESSURE GRADIENT

ST. PAUL
982.1

LOWER
PRESSURE
HERE

LAKE MICHIGAN

MASON CITY
987.1

983.7
MADISON

MILWAUKEE
982.1

ANTHON
990.5
LOGAN

992.2
HIGHER
PRESSURE
HERE

MOLINE 982.1
987.1

CHICAGO

A weather chart for a section of the Midwest. Note the similar barometric readings in millibars for Chicago, Milwaukee, and St. Paul. An isobar is drawn through these points of equal pressure. Even though you only see the upper right portion of the air mass shown, you can see that the area of greatest pressure is near Logan, Iowa, at the system center. This high-pressure area may also be called a high or anticyclone. If millibar readings were reversed, then Logan would be near the area of lowest pressure—the low or cyclone.

the moon—with boiling temperatures during the day and freezing temperatures during the night.

MEASURING TEMPERATURE

A thermometer is an instrument for measuring temperature. It is a glass tube of small bore filled with alcohol or mercury. The liquid expands and contracts with the rise and fall of the temperature of the surrounding medium. A temperature scale is marked on the tube.

The Navy usually uses mercurial (mercury-filled) thermometers with a Fahrenheit (F) scale. On that scale, the freezing point of water is 32° and the boiling point is 212°. Temperatures in meteorology are often expressed according to the Celsius (C) scale, in which the freezing point of water is 0° and its boiling point is 100°.

The Celsius scale is in the metric system which one day will be the principal measurement system used in the United States, as well

as the rest of the world. It is likely, however, that for a good many years conversion of temperatures from one scale to the other will be a common problem.

There are 5° of Celsius temperature for every 9° of Fahrenheit. Since 32°F is equivalent to 0°C, to change a Fahrenheit reading to Celsius you just subtract 32° and then multiply the remainder by $\frac{5}{9}$. Formula: $C = \frac{5}{9}(F - 32)$. Let's say you want to change 59°F to Celsius. Subtracting 32° from 59° leaves 27°. Multiply 27° by $\frac{5}{9}$ and you get 15°C.

To change a Celsius reading to Fahrenheit, the process is reversed. Simply multiply the Celsius temperature by $\frac{9}{5}$, and add 32°. Formula: $F = \frac{9}{5}C + 32°$. Using the same figures from the previous example, to change 15°C back to Fahrenheit, first multiply it by $\frac{9}{5}$, which gives you 27°; and then add 32°. You are now back to the original 59°F.

Most inexpensive house thermometers are filled with red-dyed alcohol. If you compare a

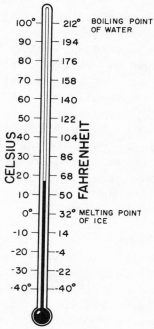

100°	212° BOILING POINT OF WATER
90	194
80	176
70	158
60	140
50	122
40	104
30	86
20	68
10	50
0°	32° MELTING POINT OF ICE
-10	14
-20	-4
-30	-22
-40°	-40°

CELSIUS   FAHRENHEIT

Celsius and Fahrenheit scales.

mercurial thermometer with a red-alcohol one you will note that the top of the column of liquid is in the shape of a curve, called a meniscus. Because of the different characteristics of the liquids involved, the accurate reading for an alcohol thermometer is at the *bottom* of this curve; for a mercury thermometer it is at the *top*.

MEASURING RELATIVE HUMIDITY AND DEWPOINT

The atmosphere always contains water in the form of vapor. Nearly 71 percent of the earth's surface is covered by water. Heat causes the evaporation of millions of tons of water from these surfaces daily. In a process called *transpiration,* additional huge amounts of water enter the air from the green leaves of plants. As this warm, moist air rises, it expands and cools, eventually reaching its saturation level—100 percent relative humidity. Then the vapor condenses into a liquid. The water droplets form into clouds, and precipitation (usually rain or snow) will occur. This water cycle of evaporation, condensation, and precipitation is continually in process.

We already have mentioned that the amount of water vapor the atmosphere can hold varies with the atmosphere's temperature. The *relative humidity* is the amount of water vapor the air is holding, expressed as a percentage of the amount that air, at that temperature, can hold. When the air contains all the water it can hold at a given temperature, humidity is at the 100 percent saturation point. If it contains half of what it could hold at that temperature, the relative humidity is 50 percent. Since warm air can hold more water than cold air, the relative humidity goes up when air with a given amount of water vapor cools, and it drops when that air is heated. It follows, then, that as air rises, it cools and condenses, eventually falling as some form of moisture.

The *dewpoint* is the temperature to which air must be cooled—at constant pressure and

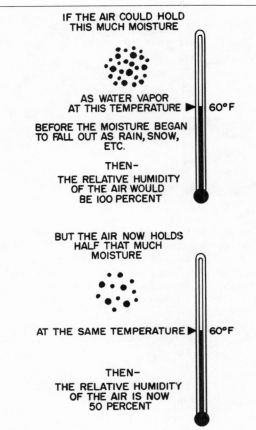

Relative humidity.

constant water vapor content—to reach saturation (100 percent relative humidity). When air is cooled to its dewpoint temperature, small water droplets condense on objects on the ground; dew is formed. At higher altitudes, this simply means that the air has been cooled sufficiently to cause a cloud to begin losing water vapor. If conditions are right, these cloud droplets will fall as rain or snow.

Relative humidity and dewpoint are measured by using a *psychrometer*. A psychrometer is simply two ordinary thermometers mounted together on a single strip of material. The bulb of one is covered by a water-soaked wick, from which the moisture is allowed to evaporate. The moisture will evaporate until the amount of water in the wick equals the amount of water vapor in the surrounding atmosphere. Since evaporation is a cooling process, the reading on the wet bulb will be lower than on the dry bulb—unless the humidity is 100 percent, at which time both readings are the same. The difference between the wet-bulb and dry-bulb readings is applied to tables developed for that purpose. From the table, the relative humidity and dewpoint can be read easily.

Aboard ship, sling psychrometers are often used to speed up the process of getting accurate wet- and dry-bulb readings. A handle and chain are attached to a psychrometer and the apparatus is whirled around in order to rapidly bring the wet bulb into contact with a greater volume of air. Using a steady, slow swing, the whirling is continued until no further change can be detected in the wet-bulb reading. Then the table is referred to.

Chapter 2. Study Guide Questions

1. What are the two main components of our atmosphere and the approximate percentages of each of these elements?

2. What happens to the air as one ascends into the atmosphere?

3. Where does the earth's weather occur? What is the "air envelope"?

4. What are the five principal layers of the earth's atmosphere?

5. In what layer are most clouds found? What are the laws of gases which apply to the development of clouds?

6. What is adiabatic temperature change?

7. Why have both the United States and USSR continued stressing their studies of Antarctic air masses?

8. What is the tropopause? Why is it so important to commercial aviation?

9. What are some of the current studies concerning the jet stream and why are these studies important?

10. When and why do aircraft seek to use the stratosphere for flight paths?

11. What visual phenomenon occurs in the ionosphere over the polar regions?

12. What is the particular importance of the ionosphere to communications?

13. Of what is the chemosphere composed and why is it important to us on earth?

14. Where does man seek to depart the earth's atmosphere when enroute to the moon? Why?

15. What is the average air pressure at sea level? What instrument measures air pressure?

16. What are the two types of barometers used by the Navy? How does each work?

17. Upon what three things does the weight of the atmosphere depend?

18. What are air masses? What are the names given to air masses which move over land and sea?

19. What is the main reason for the two kinds of air masses to be of different temperatures?

20. What are millibars and isobars? How can they help to interpret a weather map?

21. What is weather? What three things cause the changes in weather?

22. What are the fundamental characteristics of warm and cold air?

23. What is insolation? What happens to most of it?

24. What is the "greenhouse effect" on earth?

25. What are the two types of thermometer scales? What are the freezing and boiling points of each?

26. What is the meniscus?

27. What is the water cycle?

28. Work out the following conversion problems:

122°F _____	60°C _____
86°F _____	20°C _____
−4°F _____	−10°C _____
104°F _____	35°C _____

29. What do we call the amount of water vapor the atmosphere holds at a given temperature?

30. What is dewpoint?

31. What instrument measures relative humidity and dewpoint?

Vocabulary

atmosphere	ionosphere
humidity	chemosphere
troposphere	mesosphere
stratosphere	thermosphere
tropopause	exosphere

ozone layer	isobar
convection	continental air mass
dewpoint	maritime air mass
adiabatic change	precipitation
jet stream	insolation
air turbulence	Celsius, Fahrenheit
ionization	meniscus
atmospheric pressure	relative humidity
aneroid barometer	saturation
millibar	psychrometer

Chapter 3. Clouds and Fog

Water is always present in the air, in greater or smaller amounts. It can be found in three states: solid, liquid, and vapor. We have just discussed water vapor in the air and called it humidity. We have also defined relative humidity as a percentage of the amount of vapor the air can hold at a given temperature. We shall now discuss the formation of water vapor into clouds, find out the names given to the different classes of clouds, and what kind of weather they may foretell. This information is vital to a Navy or civilian meteorologist, a staff aerographer's mate, or a ship's quartermaster; but it can be both helpful and interesting to the average person.

DEFINITION OF A CLOUD

Tiny particles of dust, sand, pollen from plants, factory smoke, and salt particles from oceans are always present in the air. These fragments of matter are called *hygroscopic nuclei,* a term meaning "particles that readily absorb moisture." A cloud is a mass of hygroscopic nuclei that have soaked up moisture from the water vapor in the air.

The heat generated by the sun's energy causes earth-bound moisture to evaporate into the sky in the form of water vapor. This water vapor rises, since it is lighter than air. If the air it passes into is cold enough, the vapor condenses—that is, turns back into moisture. The water droplets that result from this process cling to the hygroscopic nuclei. Bunched together, these water-soaked nuclei form a cloud. Fog is formed the same way; it is a cloud very close to the ground.

As these droplets ride air currents, one of three things can happen, depending upon the temperature and wind. They may re-evaporate and rise further into the atmosphere; they may rise and freeze into ice crystals, sometimes in sufficient amounts to form ice crystalline clouds; or, they may collide with other nuclei and form larger drops that become heavy enough to fall as rain, snow, or sleet.

Changes in atmospheric conditions account for the many different shapes of clouds, and for their presence at various altitudes. Cloud formations give a clue concerning the forces at work in the atmosphere. Naval personnel who deal with meteorology must keep accurate records of clouds in the deck log, and must account for cloud cover in weather reports. Such information is important in forecasting.

CLOUD CLASSIFICATIONS

There are three basic guidelines in determining what kind of clouds are in the sky, and how they may affect weather prediction. You must decide what type the clouds are, how high they are, and how fast they are changing.

There are three basic cloud types: *cirrus* (wispy), *cumulus* (heaped-up), and *stratus* (layered). In addition to the three basic types,

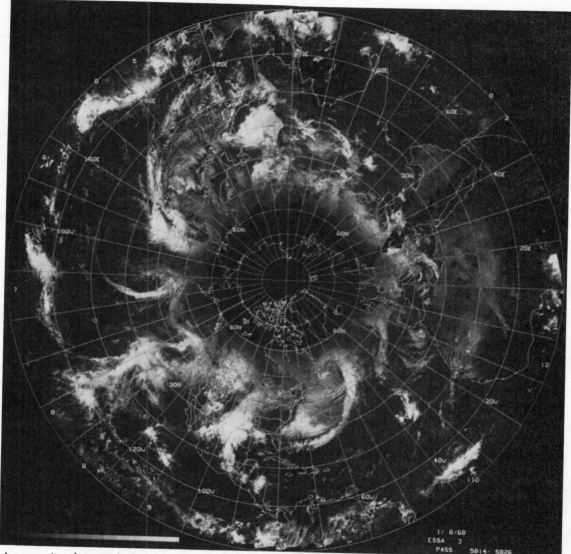

A composite photograph showing all of the cloud formations in the northern hemisphere.

there are other types having names that are combinations of these with the word *nimbus* (meaning rain) or the prefix *alto-* (meaning high), identifying clouds in the middle altitudes. Another prefix, *fracto-*, is often used to describe fragmented or wind-blown clouds.

Clouds are often classified in accordance with the altitudes in which they most frequently occur. The altitude classes are *high*, *middle*, or *low*. Sometimes a fourth class, *towering*, is used to identify an exceptionally high cloud with its base in the low-altitude area. Altitudes associated with each of these classes are as follows:

1) Low: surface to 7,000 feet
2) Middle: 7,000 to 20,000 feet
3) High: above 20,000 feet

Middle clouds seldom attain heights greater

than 13,000 feet in the polar regions, though they may reach 23,000–25,000 feet in the temperate and tropical zones.

Clouds are usually named according to their appearance. Appearance, though, is largely dependent upon the altitude in which they are found. Grouped by appearance and altitude, there are ten general cloud types.

Low Clouds

Low clouds are of three main types:

1) *Stratus* clouds, the lowest cloud type, are often like a gray layer with a uniform base. They may cause drizzle, but never rain. Fog becomes stratus when it lifts.

2) *Nimbostratus* are dark, shapeless, rain-layered clouds, often blanketing the sky. They are true rain clouds and "look wet" because they often have streaks of rain extending to the ground beneath them. They are often seen in the summer at the base of thunderheads. In the winter they bring steady, heavy snow.

3) *Stratocumulus* are irregular rounded masses of clouds spread out in puffy or rolling layers. These large clouds are usually gray with darker spots or shading. They do not produce

Nimbostratus clouds.

Stratocumulus clouds.

rain, but sometimes fuse at the base and change into nimbostratus. They usually bring bad weather.

Thunderheads start at almost any altitude and sometimes extend to heights of as much as 75,000 feet. *Cumulonimbus* is the name given to these clouds. They are very dense clouds of the towering variety. The base of the cloud is the dark nimbus rain cloud. Severe thunderstorms and destructive tornadoes may come from these clouds, which normally are seen only in the summer.

Cumulus clouds are dense puffy clouds with a beautiful, cauliflower-like appearance. On

Stratus clouds.

Cumulonimbus clouds.

Cumulus clouds.

summer days they appear like giant cotton balls in the sky. They rise by day in warm air and usually disappear at night. Fleecy cumulus clouds usually mean fair weather ahead—unless the puffs begin to pile up and the dark edge of a nimbus rain cloud starts to form at the base.

MIDDLE CLOUDS

Middle clouds are basically stratus or cumulus, but with bases beginning about 10,000 feet. They are therefore denoted by the prefix "alto-."

1) *Altocumulus* are gray or whitish layers of puffy, fleecy clouds. These roll-like clouds are made of water droplets, sometimes laid out in parallel bands. The sun will sometimes produce a pale blue or yellow corona through altocumulus clouds. The presence of these clouds means that rain probably will occur within 24 hours.

2) *Altostratus* clouds are dense sheets of gray or blue, sometimes looking like ridges of

Altocumulus clouds.

Altostratus clouds.

frosted glass, or flattened vapor trails. The sun or moon will glow dimly through altostratus, but without a halo or corona. Light rain will probably occur within 24 hours.

High Clouds

High clouds are composed almost entirely of tiny ice crystals. Three basic types exist:

1) *Cirrus* clouds are thin, wispy clouds, composed primarily of ice crystals. They are often called "mare's tails." In scattered patches, they normally indicate clear, cold weather. But if they are in parallel lines across the high sky, it usually signals a violent change in the weather within 36 hours. Spring ice storms, hurricanes, typhoons, or other severe storm conditions are generally in the offing—even if the day when you see the parallel cirrus is beautiful and sunny.

2) *Cirrostratus* clouds may nearly cover the sky with a filmy cloud. They often have a curly appearance at their edges. Because they are made of ice crystals, these clouds form large halos around the sun and moon. They indicate that clear and cold weather can be forecast.

3) *Cirrocumulus* clouds are thin, patchy clouds often in wavelike patterns. These clouds do not leave shadows on the earth. Precipitation will usually follow them, within 24 hours.

Cirrostratus clouds.

Cirrocumulus clouds.

Clouds at Sea

Clouds have been leading lost seamen, navigators, and explorers to land since the days of the earliest hardy sea voyagers. Fleecy white clouds on the horizon which are seemingly stationary usually indicate that an island is close by. Clouds form above islands for the same reason that they do above any land: moisture rises from vegetation, meets cooler air aloft, and condenses into clouds. In the tropics, these clouds often reflect the colors of sandy beaches or coral reefs below. Overhanging clouds may also warn seamen of rocks, reefs, or shoals surrounding islands.

Cirrus clouds.

Rain

Rain, snow, sleet, and hail cannot occur without clouds. The fact that there are clouds, however, does not necessarily mean that the moisture in them will fall as some form of precipitation. Temperature, and the presence of hygroscopic nuclei or ice crystals will determine whether or not there will be precipitation and what form it will take.

Raindrops are formed when moist air is cooled, to the point where the moisture condenses into heavy drops. Normally, droplets move about in the cloud somewhat like dust blowing. Cloud moisture droplets are very tiny—only $1/2,500$ of an inch in diameter—and too light to fall to the earth. Only if the droplet grows to a diameter of $1/125$ of an inch or larger will it fall from the cloud. The average raindrop, then is a million times larger than a cloud droplet. Cloud droplets grow to a size large enough to fall as rain or snow by combining with one another—a process called *coalescence*.

Coalescence occurs in two known ways: (1) Bigger droplets move about slowly in the clouds, eventually bumping into other droplets and combining with them. This is usually the case when rain falls from a nimbostratus or other low cloud. (2) The more important kind of coalescence occurs when, in higher-altitude clouds (such as the middle layer of cumulonimbus), ice crystals and water droplets form near each other. The droplets evaporate, and the resulting vapor collides with the ice crystals and condenses into snow or ice pellets which fall toward earth, melting into rain as they pass through warmer air at lower altitudes.

Rainmaking

Rainmaking has been a concern of man since the most ancient times. Rain dances, sacrifices, drums, cannons, and smoke have all been used to try to make rain, especially when the land was parched with drought. None of these methods worked, of course. But modern rainmaking techniques, based upon the known facts of coalescence, have been quite successful in causing rainfall.

In modern rainmaking techniques, an aircraft drops dry-ice crystals or silver-iodide crystals into potential rain clouds. This process is called *seeding* the cloud with artificial nuclei. It has been found that one pound of frozen carbon-dioxide (dry-ice) crystals spread by airplane can start a shower from a large cumulus cloud. Silver iodide can also, using special generators, be sent up from the ground in the form of a gas—a somewhat less expensive method. Both methods cause water droplets to form around the foreign substance, and then to fall as rain.

Seeding, however, is not successful unless conditions are nearly right for natural rainfall. Seeding can make rain come a bit earlier, and may cause more rain to fall than might have occurred naturally. It might also cause rain to fall from a cloud which, under natural conditions, would never have produced raindrops. But seeding cannot cause rain to fall from fair skies or from fair-weather cumulus clouds; nor is it possible to cause rain to fall over a large area.

Snow, Sleet, Hail, and Frost

Sleet occurs when rain which has formed in relatively warm air falls through a layer of freezing air. The air is not quite cold enough to cause the falling rain to freeze—until that rain comes into contact with a bit of dust. The dust will cause the raindrops to freeze, at least partially, into a supercooled mush, which freezes when it hits the ground, trees, or telephone wires. Such a sleet or ice storm can cause power-lines to collapse, or tree branches to break and fall on power and telephone lines, roofs, and roads.

Hail usually occurs in the summertime, beginning as frozen raindrops in high levels of cumulonimbus thunderheads. The ice pellet may grow if updrafts of air push the pellet upward one or more times, after it is coated with water from lower cloud layers. It will eventually fall when it is too heavy to be lifted by an updraft. It may grow still more during its descent, picking up moisture which then freezes. Most hailstones are smaller than marbles; but people and animals have been killed or severely injured by hailstones as large as baseballs. Hail can utterly destroy a growing crop in minutes.

In wintertime, when the upper air is very cold, water vapor will condense into ice crystals. What we call *snow* is the result. Water vapor will also crystallize around hygroscopic nuclei floating in the air, when the cloud's temperature ranges from $-4°F$ to $+10°F$.

Dew and frost do not fall from the skies as do rain, sleet, and snow. *Dew* is water vapor that condenses on objects that have cooled below the condensation point of the air around them. *Frost* is similar to dew, but it forms at temperatures below freezing. The water vapor changes directly into ice crystals on contact with the object, without first changing into dew.

Fog

What we call *fog* is really a low-lying cloud, near or touching the surface of the earth. It is formed when cool air moves in and mixes with warm air having a high relative humidity. When the temperature falls below the dew-point, fog is formed. Each water droplet has a particle of dust or smoke as its central nucleus.

Fog formation thus requires the presence of moisture, a gentle breeze, and a combination of warm and cold temperatures. A cool breeze passing over warm waters will create fog, and so will warm air passing over a stretch of sea. The breeze will spread the fog out over the surface, and it will lie in lower areas such as valleys and swamps.

Fog is hazardous to aviation because it limits both "ceiling" and visibility. Similarly, fog at sea—along coasts, in bays and inlets, harbors, river mouths, and near offshore islands—is a continual hazard to safe navigation. Although aircraft and ships have radar to assist them in foggy conditions, the eyes of alert pilots and ship lookouts are necessary for safe navigation. Indeed, the nautical "Rules of the Road" explicitly require that lookouts be stationed aboard ship. And many an airplane flight has been delayed, either in landing or taking off, because of poor visibility—even though their GCA (Ground Controlled Approach) radar is working perfectly.

Fog at Sea

Fog at sea is frequently formed through a process known as *advection* (moving forward). When warm air which has passed over warm water moves to an area of colder water, fog is likely to develop. Because seawater temperatures are fairly uniform within a large area, fog often lasts for many days and nights once it develops in a given area.

The great fog banks of the North Atlantic and those of the northern Pacific around the Aleutian Islands of Alaska demonstrate what happens when two adjacent bodies of water have greatly different temperatures. In the vicinity of the Grand Banks of Newfoundland, warm air that has passed over the warm Gulf Stream quickly turns to fog when it strikes the current of very cold water that flows southward from the Arctic. Off Alaska, the same situation exists; the air over the warm Japanese Current comes in contact with the cold, southward-flowing waters of the Bering Sea.

Advection Coastal Fogs

Advection fog is the name given to air-mass fog produced by air in motion, or to fog which is formed in one place and transported by wind to another. These fogs occur when the wind moves warm, moist air from a warm ocean surface to a colder land surface—or vice-versa.

These fogs will normally dissipate each day, since the winds carrying the air will change direction when the sun rises.

Every sailor is fully aware of the fogs which blanket the harbors and coastlines near Newport, Norfolk, New York, San Diego, Los Angeles, San Francisco, and Puget Sound. Many a ship has spent hours listening to fog signals when faced with "pea soup" in harbor. It is even more difficult, however, to listen *for* fog signals when underway. Lookouts covering all quarters peer into gray nothingness, while the Junior Officer of the Deck never takes his eyes off the radar repeater on the bridge.

STEAM FOG

This is a type of advection fog, formed by air saturation. It occurs when cold air moves over warm water. When this happens, water evaporating from the warm surface easily saturates the cold air, thus producing the steam fog. You can produce this same effect by setting a pan of warm water out in freezing cold air. This type of fog occurs often in the far north, where it is called "sea smoke." It can often be seen in the late fall or winter, when the river or pond "steams," as frigid air cools the water until it begins to form a coating of ice.

RADIATION FOG

This fog is caused by the heat that the earth radiates. It forms only at night, over a land surface. This is a common type of fog, and it may cover a large area; but it usually lifts before noon, having been "burned" away by the sun's rays. After sunset, the earth receives

Arctic sea fog or "sea smoke" caused by cold air of about 35° over water with a temperature of 74°.

no more heat from the sun, but continues to radiate heat. The surface begins to cool and layers of air close to the surface are cooled by conduction. If the air is sufficiently moist, it will chill to its dewpoint and form fog. This type of fog can be extremely hazardous for drivers. Fog patches may suddenly develop in low areas, drastically reducing visibility.

FRONTAL FOGS

Although weather fronts are discussed in Chapter 5 of this unit, *frontal fog* should also be mentioned here. This fog is caused by the movement of cold air masses. It most commonly occurs under the frontal surface of the cold air mass, and is caused by the evaporation of falling precipitation. Such a circumstance is common in December or January when a warm front (the mid-winter thaw) is caught between the normal cold weather of winter and a new cold front which pushes the warm air ahead of it over cold ground. In the upper Midwest this results in "case weather" with very heavy, wet fog dampening the air, melting snow, and causing extremely dreary days.

Chapter 3. Study Guide Questions

1. What is a cloud made of?
2. What causes earth-bound moisture to evaporate?
3. What are the three basic guidelines used to determine which kind of clouds are in the sky and how they may affect weather prediction?
4. What are the names of the three basic cloud types? What additional types combine with these basic ones?
5. What are the two means of classifying clouds?
6. What are the ranges of altitude for low, middle, and high clouds?
7. What type of weather is associated with:
   A. stratus   D. cumulus
   B. nimbostratus   E. cirrus
   C. cumulonimbus   F. altocumulus

8. How were early navigators often able to find previously uncharted islands at sea?
9. What is precipitation?
10. How do raindrops form? What is coalescence and how does it happen?
11. What two techniques are used in modern rainmaking?
12. Under what conditions can rainmaking succeed? When will rainmaking techniques be unsuccessful?
13. What is sleet? What causes it to occur?
14. What is hail and how are hailstones formed?
15. When does snow form and fall?
16. What is fog and how is it formed?
17. Why is fog so dangerous to air and sea navigation? Does radar eliminate the danger? Explain.
18. What is advection? When does advection create sea fog?
19. Where are the two most famous natural sea-fog areas located? Why do they have such frequent fog?
20. How are advection coastal fogs created? In what "Navy towns" are these fogs common?
21. What is "sea smoke"?
22. How can radiation fog present a danger for automobile drivers?

Vocabulary

hygroscopic nuclei	silver-iodide crystals
cloud	cloud "seeding"
fog	thunderhead
ice crystalline cloud	hailstone
cirrus	"ceiling"
cumulus	visibility
stratus	advection fog
nimbus	Grand Banks,
alto-	Newfoundland
cumulonimbus	Aleutian Islands,
nimbostratus	Alaska
coalescence	"sea smoke"
rainmaking	weather phenomenon
drought	frontal fog

Chapter 4. Wind and Weather

Air in motion is called *wind*. Winds blow because they are attempting to achieve a balance in atmospheric pressure. The unequal distribution of atmospheric pressure is caused by the unequal heating of the earth's surface. Winds blow from high-pressure areas to low-pressure areas. The strength of these winds depends on the distance of the high from the low, and the difference in pressure (the gradient) between the two areas. Since various places on the earth's surface receive more heat than others, temperatures and densities of winds differ from one area to another.

There is a continual flow of wind over the face of the earth as the result of this uneven heating. From about 2½ to 3 miles above the surface to the tropopause, winds are westerly in direction at all degrees of latitude, from the equator to the poles. At the surface, a band of easterly winds called the *trade winds* extends from the equator to 30°, both north and south. Between 30° and 60°, in both the northern and southern hemisphere, there are the *prevailing westerlies*. Finally, between 60° and both poles there are winds called the *polar easterlies*.

Why are there so many different wind directions, and why are there differences in wind circulations in the northern and southern hemispheres? The answers to these questions come from our knowledge of the motions of the earth itself.

WIND AND THE EARTH'S ROTATION

Two motions of the earth affect the weather. The movement of the earth around the sun accounts for the seasonal changes on the earth; we will talk briefly about this a bit later. The other motion is the rotation of the earth on its axis. This rotation causes night and day, with the consequent heating and cooling effects on the atmosphere. It also produces the major wind belts of the earth.

If the earth did not rotate, the warmer air over the equator would rise and move north and south toward the poles, high above the earth's surface. The air would then cool and sink as it moved toward the poles. Later, it would move back toward the equator at a steady speed and direction.

The force of the earth's rotation causes the

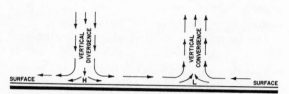

Convergence and divergence. Unequal distribution in pressure is the result of unequal heating near the earth's surface. Warm air rises, or converges, and the colder surrounding air diverges, moving toward the low which has been created, and thus causing winds.

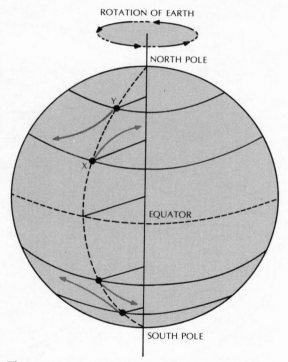

The apparent force of the earth's rotation causes the wind to curve to the right in the northern hemisphere and to the left in the southern hemisphere. This wind deflection is called the Coriolis Effect.

direction of the wind to curve to the right in the northern hemisphere and to the left in the southern hemisphere. This deflection of winds is called the Coriolis Effect. This curving or defection effect continues until a balance with other forces is reached.

At this point, we must again bring in the factor of atmospheric pressures in order to explain why there are different belts of prevailing primary winds on earth.

We know that air rises at the equator and begins moving northward at high altitudes. It eventually sinks and accumulates near the surface, forming a high-pressure area. This sinking and accumulating takes place in the area of 30° north and south latitudes. These areas are called the Horse Latitudes.

Air must always flow outward from the cen-ter of a high-pressure area; this is a basic law of science. The air flowing inward from the Horse Latitudes toward the equator is deflected to the right by the Coriolis Effect to become the easterly trade winds. The wind moving outward from these highs to the poles become the prevailing westerlies. Similar rising, sinking, and pressure factors combine in the regions of the polar highs at about 60° north and south latitudes where there is a convergence of the warmer westerlies and the cold polar easterlies.

PREVAILING WINDS

1) *The Doldrums.* The equatorial belt of light and variable converging winds is called the doldrums. They vary in position and tend to move north and south of the geographic equa-

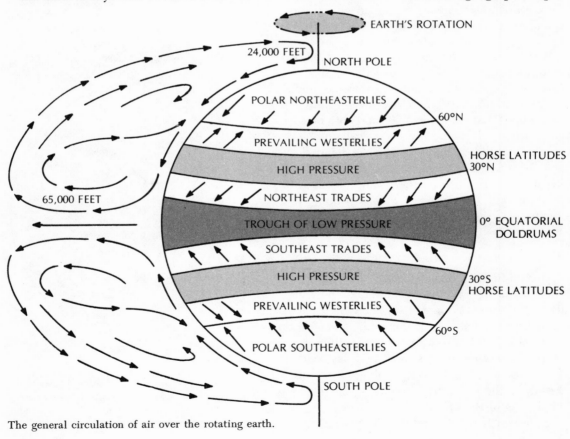

The general circulation of air over the rotating earth.

tor with the sun. In the doldrums the temperatures are high and excessive precipitation occurs. Days go by without a breath of wind; thus, in the days of sail, ships avoided this area, if possible. Severe tropical storms begin here.

2) *Trade Winds.* At the surface and on the poleward sides of the doldrums there are bands of easterly winds called the trade winds. The northeast trades were a popular route for sailing vessels, and aircraft traveling west are favored with a tail wind and clear skies if they fly near 30° N. The winds come from the southeast in the southern hemisphere, and thus are called the southeast trades.

3) *Sub-Tropical High-Pressure Belt.* These are the Horse Latitudes. Because of sinking wind from aloft and diverging winds at the surface, these areas generally have fair weather. The diverging winds cause the trade winds found on the equatorial side of this high-pressure belt. The Horse Latitudes tend to be cloudless and calm, with weak undependable winds. The term "Horse Latitudes" comes from the fact that, in the days of sail, ships carrying horses from Europe often were becalmed here. When this happened, the horses died for lack of food and water, so the dead animals were thrown overboard to prevent the spread of disease.

4) *Prevailing Westerlies.* These winds are found on the poleward side of the sub-tropical highs and are created by the diverging winds of these highs. They blow from the southwest in the northern hemisphere and from the northwest in the southern hemisphere. The prevailing westerlies provide most of the air flow over the United States.

5) *Polar Front Zone.* The belt of low pressure known as the polar front zone lies in the area of 60° north and south latitudes. In the north it is called the Arctic Semipermanent Low, and in the south it is called the Antarctic Permanent Low. These two areas are noted for their bad weather because the westerlies and the polar easterlies converge in them.

6) *Polar Easterlies.* This is a zone of poorly developed surface winds created by outflow from the high pressure at the poles. They have a northeasterly direction in the northern hemisphere and a southeasterly direction in the southern hemisphere.

Wind and the Earth's Revolution

We have discussed in some detail the effects of the rotational movement of the earth on weather, and particularly its effect on winds. Another important movement is the revolution of the earth around the sun. This movement, combined with the earth's inclination, causes our seasons.

The earth is inclined at an angle of $23\frac{1}{2}°$ from the perpendicular to the plane of the orbit of revolution. This simply means that the earth, somewhat like a top as it begins to slow down, tips at this angle all the time. Because of this fact, the sun's most direct rays will strike the earth's surface between $23\frac{1}{2}°$ North (Tropic of Cancer) and $23\frac{1}{2}°$ South (Tropic of Capricorn), depending upon the earth's position in its orbit.

The revolution of the earth directly causes major seasonal weather. This weather is the result of the directness with which the sun's rays strike the earth, not the nearness of the earth to the sun. In summer the rays are more direct, even though we are further away. Thus, its rays are more concentrated and there is more time for the rays to warm the earth. In winter the earth is actually closer to the sun; but sunlight hits our planet at a greater slant, so the same amount of sunlight spreads over a larger area. Because of the slanted path, the rays must pass through more atmosphere than they would in a straight path; therefore more energy is diffused away from the earth.

Secondary Wind Circulation

We have discussed the primary circulation of winds on the earth. It is the unequal heating of the earth between the equator and the poles

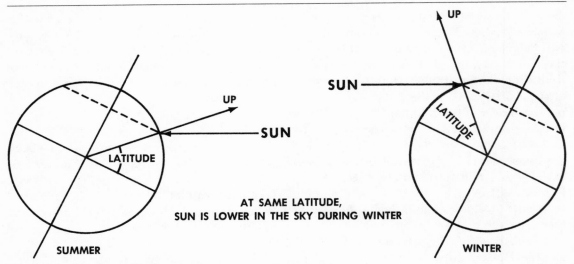

AT SAME LATITUDE,
SUN IS LOWER IN THE SKY DURING WINTER

The inclination of the earth in relation to the sun, in summer and winter.

which causes north–south winds. The rotation of the earth turns these winds east or west depending upon the hemisphere in which they occur. But winds are also affected by the topography of the land and the currents of the seas.

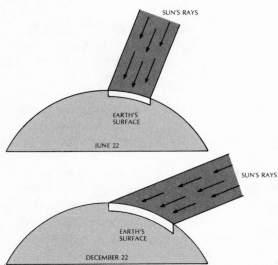

The seasonal weather of the earth is a direct result of the angle at which the sun's rays strike the earth's surface. Note the difference in the surface area covered by same amount of sunshine in summer and winter. The area is much larger in winter.

We know that nearly three-fourths of the earth's surface is water. But did you know that three-fourths of the world's land surfaces are in the northern hemisphere? In the summer these land surfaces heat very rapidly, while the water areas heat very slowly. In winter, the land cools rapidly and the water cools comparatively slowly, because the water retains part of the heat it gained during the previous summer. For this reason, water areas are cooler than land areas during the summer, and warmer during the winter. The daily variation of temperature over open water is seldom more than two or three degrees; but 300 miles inland, it is rarely less than fifteen degrees.

The difference between the land and sea temperatures causes the pressure belts of the primary wind circulation to be broken up into enclosed high- and low-pressure areas, called *centers of action*. We see, therefore, that the geography of the continents and seas can also influence the wind and weather.

HIGHS (ANTICYCLONES)

In the northern hemisphere, air flows in a clockwise manner around high-pressure centers of action (also called anticyclones). Air subsides (sinks) in the center and diverges (blows outward) from the center of the high-pressure area. Subsiding currents are warmed adiabatically, so few clouds are formed. Generally fair weather prevails, either warm or cold, depending upon the season.

Local high-pressure areas will develop any place where air cools, compresses, and subsides. The Horse Latitudes and the polar highs are good examples of this. But high-pressure areas can develop anywhere. When a high develops, the clockwise anticyclonic spiral of air develops and air begins flowing to surrounding lower-pressure areas.

Major high-pressure areas exist near the poles. They produce very cold air, dependent on the seasons. A high-pressure area exists over Greenland all the time, because of the vast icecap there. Sub-tropical highs can usually be found southwest of California and near the Azores in the Atlantic. The high associated with the north polar zone repeatedly creates icy polar fronts which every winter sweep over most of North America east of the Rockies. This area is called the North American High. A similar high-pressure area exists in Siberia, where the temperate zone's coldest temperatures have been recorded. The North American and Siberian highs are continental highs.

Lows

The only "permanent" low-pressure area on earth is the Doldrum Belt. The Aleutian Low off Alaska is a low-pressure cell associated with the Polar Front and influenced by the Japanese Current. It is intense during winter but is very ill-defined in summer. Another low-pressure area lying near Iceland is called the Icelandic Low; the Gulf Stream influences this low.

Traveling low-pressure cells are frequently found in the area of the Polar Front. These are formed by the interaction of the polar air to the north and the maritime tropical air to the south. These lows are called *migratory lows*. Migratory storms may also move into lower

latitudes from the Polar Front. Such storms often occur in the south-central United States and on the U. S. east coast near Cape Hatteras.

Local lows often form directly below large thunderhead clouds. Heat lows form over deserts and other intensely hot areas; a low-pressure area lasts most of the summer over the Arizona and California deserts. Lows sometimes form on the leeward side of mountain ranges and cause rushing winds to "pour" down from the nearby mountains. These lows are common just east of the Rocky Mountains in Colorado.

Mountain Winds

We have just mentioned the lows which sometimes form on the lee side of mountain ranges. These winds are so persistent and predictable in some areas that they have earned their own names. The topography of the earth is a major factor in the formation of such winds, but temperature differences and the rotation of the earth also contribute.

As warm air rises on one side of the mountains, it cools and loses its moisture as rain or snow. The dry, cooler air then rushes down the opposite side, heating the air and pushing it into the low. Famous mountain winds are the Chinook Winds of the Rockies, the Santa Anas of southern California, and the foehns of the Swiss and French Alps. These winds sometimes reach gale force and, in the western United States, often become dust storms.

Valley Winds

Probably the most famous valley-wind system is the mistral of southern France. This is a cold, dry wind which rushes down the Rhone Valley toward the low-pressure system which often develops over the Mediterranean Sea. Reaching whole gale and storm force over 60 miles per hour, this wind is one the U. S. Sixth Fleet must be on the alert for, when involved in western Mediterranean operations.

MONSOONS

Monsoons are seasonal winds characteristic of South and Southeast Asia, though they occur elsewhere with less intensity and regularity. The monsoon is a very persistent wind that blows on predictable seasonal paths and with definite seasonal characteristics.

Summer (Southwest) Monsoon. As continental Asia begins to warm in the spring, the water area over the Indian Ocean remains relatively cool. The warming effect gradually creates a continental low over the central Asian plateaus and desert. This low draws cooler air from the south. As the moisture-laden Indian Ocean air pushes northeastward over the land, it begins to cool and condense. The rains begin to fall in southern India in mid-May, and continue to build up in intensity as the continent warms. The wet air rushes into the southern slopes of the Himalaya Mountains and dumps astounding amounts of rain on the southern Asian countries. It is common for the southeast Burmese coast to have two hundred inches of rainfall during the period between mid-May and late September. At the foothills of the Himalayas, 500 inches of rain in the same period have been recorded almost every year. The greatest rainfall ever recorded occurred at Cherrapunji, India, during the monsoon: 1041.78 inches. Squalls and typhoons occur over the Bay of Bengal during this time.

Winter (Northeast) Monsoon. As the cold season of the northern hemisphere approaches, the continental high over Siberia regenerates and begins to dominate the air circulation over South and Southeast Asia. The wind now re-

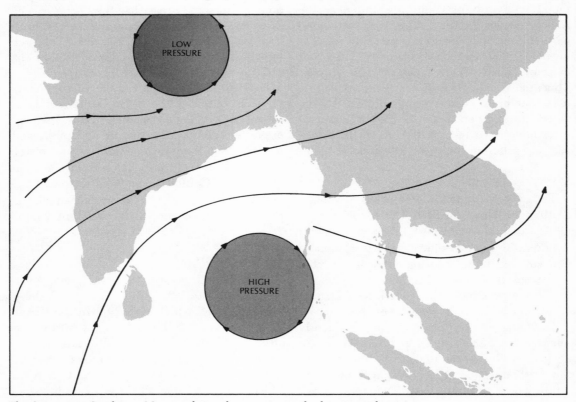

The Summer or Southwest Monsoon brings heavy rains to the low in southern Asia.

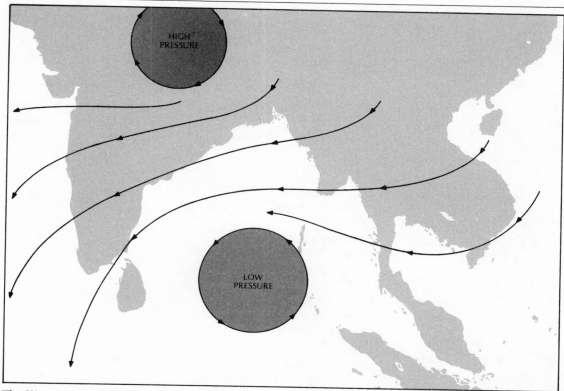

The Winter or Northeast Monsoon brings dry air from Central Asia toward the Indian Ocean low.

verses itself and blows from the northeast. The rains of the summer season cease. A warm, low-pressure area now exists over the Indian Ocean. The cooler, dry air from central Asia now blows southwestward across the continent over the Himalayas and into the southern countries. The northeast wind persists from late September until April, when the humidity begins to rise for the next summer monsoon.

During the winter monsoon there is little rain, and by the time January and February arrive, the soil is parched and cracked, leaves have curled and died, and dust lies thick over much of the countryside. Dust in Upper Burma around Mandalay will be four to six inches thick along roads and in villages.

"Reverse" Monsoon. Monsoon effects in Ceylon, Indonesia, and the Philippines are different, because of the island geography of these countries. Here, the heaviest rains fall in the summer as in the rest of Southeast Asia. But after a transitional break between seasons, rains also fall in the winter monsoon. This happens because the northeast wind has already picked up moisture north of the islands. This moisture falls in the form of heavy showers as the northeast wind passes on the way back toward the Indian Ocean low.

In Vietnam, the northern half of the country has "reversed" wet and dry monsoons because the Annam Mountain Range blocks the flow of moisture-laden air from the southwest, but serves as the barrier forcing humid northeast wind to rise after crossing the Gulf of Tonkin and the China Seas. This "reverse" monsoon phenomenon in Vietnam was a significant factor affecting military operations in that country during the Vietnam War of 1964–73.

Beaufort Wind Scale and Correlative Sea Disturbance Scale

Beaufort No.	Knots	Descriptive terms	Sea criterion	Approximate equivalent Sea Disturbance Scale in open sea		
				Code Fig.	Description	Mean height of waves (in feet)
0	Less than 1	Calm	Sea like a mirror	0	Calm (glassy)	. . . . . .
1	1–3	Light air	Ripples with the appearance of scales are formed, but without foam crests.	1	Calm (rippled)	½
2	4–6	Light breeze	Small wavelets, still short but more pronounced. Crests have a glassy appearance and do not break.	1	. . . . . .	1
3	7–10	Gentle breeze	Large wavelets. Crests begin to break. Foam has glassy appearance. Perhaps scattered whitecaps.	2	Smooth (wavelets)	2½
4	11–16	Moderate breeze	Small waves, becoming longer. Fairly frequent whitecaps.	3	Slight	5
5	17–21	Fresh breeze	Moderate waves, taking a more pronounced long form. Many whitecaps are formed (chance of some spray).	4	Moderate	9
6	22–27	Strong breeze	Large waves begin to form. The white foam crests are more extensive everywhere (probably some spray).	5	Rough	14
7	28–33	Moderate gale	Sea heaps up and white foam from breaking waves begins to be blown in streaks along the direction of the wind. (Spray begins to be seen).	6	Very rough	19
8	34–40	Fresh gale	Moderately high waves of greater length. Edges of crests break into spray. The foam is blown in well-marked streaks along the direction of the wind.	7	High	25
9	41–47	Strong gale	High waves. Dense streaks of foam along the direction of the wind. Sea begins to roll. Spray may affect visibility.	7	. . . . . .	31

Beaufort No.	Knots	Descriptive terms	Sea criterion	Approximate equivalent Sea Disturbance Scale in open sea		
				Code Fig.	Description	Mean height of waves (in feet)
10	48–55	Whole gale	Very high waves with long overhanging crests. The resulting foam in great patches is blown in dense white streaks along the direction of the wind. On the whole the surface of the sea takes a white appearance. The rolling of the sea becomes heavy and shocklike. Visibility is affected.	8	Very high	37
11	56–63	Storm	Exceptionally high waves. (Small- and medium-sized ships might for a long time be lost to view behind the waves.) The sea is completely covered with long white patches of foam lying along the direction of the wind. Everywhere the edges of the wave crests are blown into froth. Visibility affected.	9	Phenomenal	45 or more
12	Above 64	Hurricane and Typhoon	The air is filled with foam and spray. Sea completely white with driving spray. Visibility very seriously affected.	9	. . . . . .	. . . . . .

WINDS AND THE BEAUFORT WIND SCALE

Navy weather observers must always be aware of wind velocity and wind direction. Wind speed is always given in knots, according to international agreement. The instrument used to measure wind speed is called an *anemometer*. The anemometer is afixed atop the masthead. Wind blows into metal cups, which are attached to arms. The whirling cups turn a spindle, which is linked to a synchro-repeater near the bridge. A dial will indicate the apparent wind velocity and direction.

Though there normally is wind-measuring

A Marine aerographer tracking a weather balloon; behind him are an anemometer and a wind vane.

equipment aboard a commissioned vessel, the Beaufort Wind Scale with Correlative Sea Disturbance Scale can also be used to estimate wind speed. This scale is based on careful observation of sea conditions. Admiral Sir Francis Beaufort of the British Royal Navy developed the scale in 1805 to estimate wind speeds from their effect on sails. His table numbered the winds from 1–12, in order of increasing severity, and compared them to the Sea Disturbance Scale, which describes sea state and mean height of waves on a scale of 1–9. Descriptive terms identify the winds and their counterpart waves. The Beaufort Wind Scale enables the shipboard weatherman or sailor to visually estimate wind speeds by merely looking at the sea state and then comparing the two scales.

Chapter 4. Study Guide Questions

1. What is a simple definition of wind? Why do winds blow? Upon what does the strength of wind depend?

2. What are the three primary wind belts in the northern hemisphere?

3. What two motions of the earth affect the weather? Which of these motions causes the major wind belts?

4. How does the Coriolis Effect cause wind deflection?

5. How does atmospheric pressure affect the primary wind belts? What are the principal high-pressure belts on the earth's surface named?

6. What determines the directional name of a wind?

7. Explain each of the world's prevailing wind and pressure belts.

8. What movement of the earth causes the seasons? What is meant by the earth's "inclination?"

9. What names are given to the 23.5°N and 23.5°S latitude lines around the earth?

10. What are the principal causes of secondary wind circulation?

11. What is the effect of the continents and seas on the primary wind belts in the northern hemisphere? Why are these effects so important?

12. How does air "act" in a high-pressure area?

13. Over what countries in the northern hemisphere do "permanent" high-pressure areas exist?

14. Where do the principal low-pressure areas exist on the earth? Where do seasonal lows usually develop in the United States?

15. What are the most famous mountain winds and where do they blow? What type of weather do these winds bring?

16. What valley wind is of particular concern to the Sixth Fleet?

17. What are monsoon winds and where are they most common? Describe the generation of the Southwest and Northeast Monsoons.

18. How did the "reverse" monsoon affect military operations in the Vietnam War?

19. What instrument is used to measure wind velocity? What dialed instrument indicates wind speed and direction to the ship's bridge watch and navigator?

20. What is the Beaufort Wind Scale? How is the Correlative Sea Disturbance Scale used with the Beaufort Wind Scale?

Vocabulary

wind	Tropic of Cancer
gradient	Tropic of Capricorn
Coriolis Effect	subsiding air currents
wind deflection	wind divergence
prevailing winds	migratory lows
anticyclone	Chinook Winds
cyclone	Santa Anas (winds)
doldrums	foehn winds
wind convergence	mistral
trade winds	monsoon
high-pressure belt	Beaufort Wind Scale
low-pressure belt	anemometer
Horse Latitudes	synchro-repeater
prevailing westerlies	Correlative Sea
inclination (of earth)	Disturbance Scale

Chapter 5. Fronts and Storms

Even large ships have much to fear when they are engulfed by a severe storm. A North Atlantic gale can strain rigging, spring seams, bend plates, smash equipment, and tear loose topside equipment, even on aircraft carriers or bulk petroleum tankers. Winds of 100 knots and waves of 60 feet or more are respected by an experienced seaman. The prudent mariner will maneuver to stay clear of storms whenever possible.

A good navigator should be able to see when weather disturbances are coming. One should observe the sky and sea, and carefully assess readings of the meteorological instruments aboard. In addition, today's radio communications provide regular weather summaries. The captain and navigator, along with the quartermasters, aerographer's mates, or staff meteorologists, will carefully plot such weather information, relative to the ship's position and her proposed track.

DEVELOPMENT OF FRONTS

Fronts develop when air masses of different temperatures collide; air masses rarely fuse unless they are very similar in temperature and moisture content. Fronts are weather systems that are sometimes called *waves*, as in the term "cold wave."

Along the meeting edge or boundary of two dissimilar air masses, a battle for supremacy is fought. Usually the colder of the two masses, being heavier, predominates and forces the warmer air upward. A *cold front* displaces the warm air ahead of it upward, while a *warm front* moves upward over a retreating cold air mass.

When a cold front moves faster than a warm front, it overtakes the warm front, forcing the warmest part of the air mass upward but leaving the cooler air below. By the time the cold front meets or converges with the cool mass, the warm air has been pushed above both

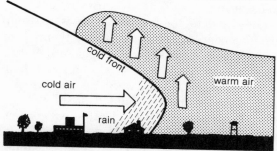

A cold front occurs when a cold air mass moves into a warm air mass, causing the warm air to rise.

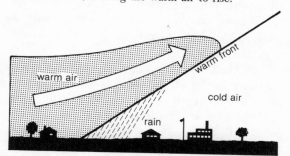

A warm front occurs when a warm air mass rises over a cold air mass.

masses. The convergent frontal mass which remains is called an *occluded front.* Regardless of the type of front—cold, warm, or occluded—the frontal weather is either unsettled or stormy. Fronts always bring bad weather.

A cold front or warm front may extend for hundreds of miles. But the area in which frontal weather disturbances take place is usually a band 15–50 miles wide for a cold front, and up to 300 miles for a warm front. The point where the cold and warm fronts converge is frequently the center of a low-pressure area.

FRONTAL ZONES

The world's primary frontal zones are the Intertropical Convergence Zone, Arctic Frontal Zone, and Polar Frontal Zone. The convergence of the northeast trade winds of the northern hemisphere and the southeast trade winds of the southern hemisphere causes a band of unstable weather encircling the earth in the doldrums. This is called the Intertropical Convergence Zone. It varies in position, largely due to the seasons. This is a storm development area, but the storms themselves have usually moved poleward before they become severe. Brief violent windstorms called *squalls* occur when the warm air rises, resulting in sudden, intense rainfall of short duration. There normally is good visibility between these independent squalls. In tropical seas it is often possible to see three to seven separate rain squalls in progress, and several rainbows, all within horizon distance of the ship. The Deck Department can be quite busy indeed "covering all hatches and gun covers" to avoid a quick deluge in such a squall zone.

The Arctic Frontal Zone develops between the true arctic air of the far north and the polar maritime air of the North Atlantic and Pacific Oceans. This frontal zone may disappear as it moves northward during the summer, when it meets similar cold air.

The Polar Frontal Zone is formed by the convergence of the air which flows toward the equator from the Polar Easterlies and the Prevailing Westerlies—in other words, the temperate zones. This polar front is very significant, since it greatly influences the weather in the temperate zones. The polar fronts move toward the poles during the summer and toward the tropics in the winter. This is why we in the temperate zones often experience a series of cold waves or snaps—because the colder polar easterlies often break through the warmer band of westerlies.

COLD FRONT

When a cold front is coming your way, the first change you notice is a darkening of the horizon to the west and to the north. Very soon thereafter, the cloud ceiling lowers, and rain begins.

A fast-moving cold front, which may move as much as 700 miles in a day, with cumulonimbus clouds preceding it, brings sudden violent showers or thunderstorms. Rainfall proba-

bly will be steady if cumulonimbus clouds are not in the vanguard of the front. Passage of the cold front is usually marked by a wind shift, a drop in temperature, a rise in pressure, and a rapid clearing of the sky and visibility. Squall lines often precede the cold front; these are often violent, causing flash floods from downpours, cloudbursts, and extremely turbulent winds.

WARM FRONT

A warm front will be heralded in advance by cirrus clouds in parallel; then, in order, will follow cirrostratus, altostratus, nimbostratus, and finally stratus. Visibility is poor in advance of a warm front. Frequently fog forms, and steady rain or drizzle prevails. Thunderstorms may develop ahead of this front.

When the frontal line is passing, a marked shift occurs in the wind direction, and the temperature rises sharply. Gradual clearing will take place and pressure remains steady or falls slowly. A warm front moves much more slowly than a cold front, normally less than 15 mph. Cloud sequences will begin as much as 48 hours in advance, often with rain. Cloud sequences may occur 1,000 miles in advance of the front itself.

OCCLUDED FRONT

This is an unstable frontal cyclone with a rapidly moving cold front. It will overtake warmer air masses. The cold front in this cyclone will always move so rapidly that it will force the whole overtaken warm front aloft. This type of occlusion is called the cold-front type.

The cold front which remains on the surface is called the *occluded front* and the warm front which is raised aloft is called the *upper front*. Most occlusions of this type occur on the eastern portions of continents. Extensive frontal precipitation with thunderstorms occurs, though of less intensity than with a regular cold front.

A warm-front type of occlusion occurs when the air ahead of the warm front is colder than the air behind the cold front. When this occurs, the cold front rides up over the warm frontal surface. The warm front, in this case, remains on the surface and is called the occluded front, while the cold front lifted aloft is called the upper front. This type of occlusion occurs chiefly in the Pacific Northwest. Severe icing and precipitation may be found in the area just behind where the cold front starts to rise.

THUNDERSTORM

The thunderstorm occurs within clouds with vertical development, such as cumulus and cumulonimbus. They are characterized by loud thunder, flashes of lightning, very heavy precipitation, strong gusts of wind, and occasional hail or tornadoes. Because the thunderstorm is local in nature and relatively short in duration, it is difficult to forecast.

A thunderstorm develops in three rapid stages. The first stage is an updraft of warm, moist air into the atmosphere. The water vapor cools and condenses into clouds, and the clouds grow taller and taller as the updrafts continue. This first stage of development is called the *cumulus stage*.

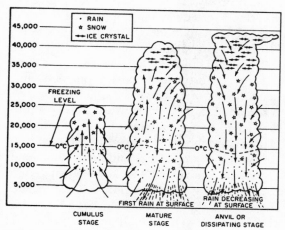

Life cycle of a thunderstorm cell.

The *mature stage* of thunderstorm development is characterized by both updrafts and downdrafts within the storm-producing cloud. The cooler the upper part becomes, as it towers into the atmosphere, the faster raindrops and even hail will begin to form and fall. Downdrafts are caused by the raindrops falling. There is frictional drag between the raindrops and the surrounding air, so that the air is pulled down with the raindrops. The mature cell usually extends above 25,000 feet. The downdrafts do not extend that high, however, because there is insufficient moisture at the higher altitudes.

The final stage is called the *dissipating* or *anvil stage*. As more and more air is brought down by raindrop friction, these downdrafts take the place of updrafts, and spread out. The entire lower portion of the cloud becomes downdraft, and the high winds in the upper altitudes flatten the top of the cloud into an anvil shape. Rain is now falling heavily on the ground and the storm will dissipate in a short time.

WEATHER PHENOMENA WITHIN THE THUNDERSTORM

Rain is found in every thunderstorm. Some of this rain will be below freezing level. Hail will form if the updrafts carry melted or partially melted raindrops into the higher, colder altitudes. Snow and ice crystals also may be in any thunderstorm, winter or summer, though in summer they will melt into rain when nearing the earth.

A thunderstorm is most turbulent in the area of heaviest precipitation. Icing will often occur just above the freezing level, making this a very hazardous area for aircraft. Temperatures between 34° and 26°F produce maximum icing conditions.

The first gust of wind is one of a thunderstorm's hazards. This gust occurs just prior to the passage of the storm. The strong winds at the surface are the result of the horizontal spreading-out of the storm's downdraft currents, as they approach the surface of the earth. The speed of the first gust usually is the highest recorded during any thunderstorm, and can blow in any direction—even in opposition to the surface wind that is "pushing" the storm.

Surging air currents in the thunderhead cloud create static electricity, the source of *lightning*. This process is not completely understood yet, but it is generally believed that lightning is caused by the breaking-up of large water droplets into positively and negatively charged particles. Positive charges develop near the top of the cloud and negative particles accumulate in the lower reaches. There is an electrical discharge when the positive charges are attracted, beyond resistance, to the negative field below. The lightning, then, is nature's way of equalizing the charges between the two electrical zones.

The buildup of electricity in a thunderhead may reach millions of volts. The lightning may flash within the cloud, jump to other clouds, from the clouds to the ground, or even from the ground up to the cloud.

Lightning occurs in two steps. First, a leader of electrified air runs from the cloud toward the ground. This establishes the "circuit" for the second stroke which leaps up from the ground to complete that circuit. This second stroke is the one you see, and consequently, the one which causes the thunder you hear. The lightning generates terrific heat, causing an explosive expansion of glowing hot air and producing the audible thunder.

Lightning follows the shortest route between a cloud and the earth. Thus, high points of ground, trees, telephone poles, TV antennas, and the like are the places most apt to be struck by lightning.

Lightning also follows the easiest route after striking, so it will follow electrical wires, plumbing pipes, and even drafts of air in its attempt to reach the ground. It is very unwise to be on or near bodies of water during a thunderstorm, and never be out in a boat. Mountainous areas are also good to stay away from during an electrical thunderstorm, especially crevices or rushing mountain streams.

A fundamental rule for airplane pilots is to never fly under a thunderstorm. It is safest to fly around the storm. When frontal thunderstorms occur, the pilot should try to fly between the independent cells of the individual storm clouds.

TORNADO

The most intense and violent storm is the *tornado*. It is usually associated with violent thunderstorm activity and heavy rain. They are whirlpools of such violence that houses in their path will disintegrate like matchsticks, brick buildings will be destroyed or deroofed, and trains will be lifted from their tracks and derailed. Feathers and straws may be carried by the swirling wind with the force of power-driven nails.

Tornadoes are of very small diameter, usually 300–400 feet; but they may continue on an erratic path for more than 100 miles. Winds in the *vortex*—the whirlwind causing the funnel—often exceed 300 mph. But the speed of the storm moving over the earth's surface is comparatively slow, usually 25–40 mph. The duration over any given spot may be only seconds—but in that short time the devastation can be almost total.

Tornadoes build up only during severe thunderstorms. Fortunately, only about one thunderstorm out of a thousand develops a tornado. A tornado forms on the forward edge of a fully developed cumulonimbus cloud. Rising air causes a swirling at the base of the cloud. As the swirl increases in size and speed, the funnel drops out of the cloud, like an elephant's trunk dangling toward the ground. As it approaches the ground, the disturbance raises a huge dust cloud and it soon has all manner of debris traveling in it.

The ominous funnel of a tornado meets the ground and creates a destructive whirlwind. This is a local weather phenomenon, often difficult to forecast. Whenever severe thunderstorms are present, a tornado is a possibility. Most tornadoes occur in the summer.

Tornadoes are most common in the temperate zone, probably because of the greater atmospheric-temperature contrasts there. The midwestern United States is the most tornado-ravaged area of the world. Usually these storms hit in the late spring or early summer. But they can occur at almost any time.

The extreme low pressure in the vortex causes closed homes and barns to explode from the normal pressure of air trapped inside. There is a 100–200 mph updraft in the center of the funnel, which can suck up houses, animals, and even people.

Over a lake or the ocean, such a funnel may lift water into the air, creating a *waterspout*.

There are two types of waterspouts. The tornadic or "stormspout" is usually a land-born tornado that goes out over the water, picking up water in its funnel as it goes. This is a true waterspout, in which the vortex forms in the clouds, just as a tornado does. These waterspouts are most common in tropical regions, but they can also occur in higher latitudes.

The second kind of waterspout originates just above the water surface and builds upward, frequently in clear skies. It has the same wind characteristics as the whirling pillars of sand and dust called "dust devils," often seen in the desert or on a plowed field in the hot days of August. This fair-weather spout is usually small, of short duration, and interesting to watch, but not destructive.

There have been some spectacular waterspouts observed and photographed over the years. Perhaps the most notable was a tornadic spout near Martha's Vineyard off Massachusetts in 1896. During a period of about an hour, three separate gigantic waterspouts came from the same cloud system, each causing the sea to react violently, lighting up the sky with weird hues, and making a huge roaring sound. Wild thunderstorm activity hit the area shortly after the third waterspout. The diameter of this waterspout was about 240 feet at the water, and 840 feet at the base of the cloud; it was about 3,600 feet in height. The highest waterspout on record is one of 5,014 feet, seen in New South Wales, Australia.

TROPICAL CYCLONE

A *cyclone* is a circular area of low atmospheric pressure around which winds in excess

The famous tornadic waterspout near Martha's Vineyard off Massachusetts, in 1896. This huge waterspout was calculated to be 3,600 feet in height and 240 wide at the base. The spout recurred three times and brought severe thunderstorms to the area.

of 74 mph blow. These winds are counterclockwise in the northern hemisphere and clockwise in the southern hemisphere. The so-called "tropical cyclone" is subdivided into three categories as follows:

1) Tropical depression—maximum wind less than 34 knots.

2) Tropical storm—maximum wind 34–63 knots.

3) Hurricane or typhoon—maximum wind 64 knots and up.

Tropical cyclones occur in many places throughout the world, and are called by various names. They form over all tropical oceans except the South Atlantic, but do not form over continents. They are common in the West Indies, ranging up the east coast of the United States and the Gulf of Mexico, where they are called *hurricanes*. Tropical cyclones occurring east of the International Date Line in the Pacific have also become known as hurricanes. In the Western Pacific, off the coast of China, they are called *typhoons*. Off the west coast of Australia they are called *willy-willies,* and off the Philippines they are called *baguios.*

Although the velocities associated with these tropical cyclones are less than those of a tornado, they cover hundreds of times the area and last much longer. The tropical cyclone is the most destructive of all weather phenomena, and the one which is of greatest concern to the oceangoing sailor.

LIFE OF A HURRICANE

The birth of a hurricane often occurs in that region near the equator where trade winds meet to form the Intertropical Convergence Zone (ITCZ). Tropical cyclones, however, never occur on the equator because they require the twisting forces of the earth's rotation to start them spinning.

A hurricane is born in a hot moist air mass over the ocean. The rotating low at the ITCZ pushes air toward its center, forcing the hot moist air to lift. The lifting causes the moisture

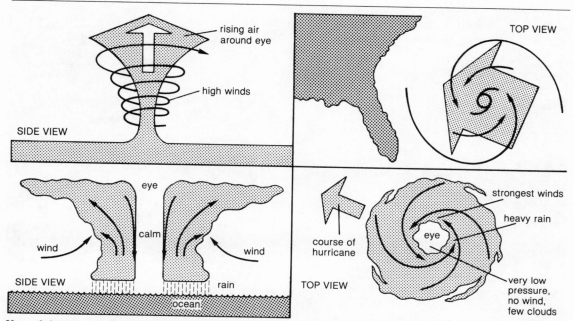

Upper left: Hurricane winds rise in a counterclockwise spiral around an eye of calm air. Lower left: A cross section shows the shape of the hurricane cloud layers. Upper right: The whole hurricane system moves toward the southeast coast of the United States. Lower right: Seen from above, the hurricane has a circular shape with a central eye.

to condense. As this moisture condenses, it heats the rotating air more, causing it to rise even more swiftly. As more moist tropical sea air sweeps in to replace this rising air, more condensation takes place, and the cycle seems never-ending. That is why hurricanes are so violent—because of the tremendous energy released by the continuous condensation and an inexhaustible source of moisture. All the while, the Coriolis Effect keeps the air turning more and more rapidly, until it is a giant wheel of swirling winds.

In the northern hemisphere, hurricanes move westward from their point of origin, then recurve to the northeast. In the southern hemisphere they start out westward and then curve southeastward. They vary in diameter from 60 to 1,000 miles. They have moderate winds at their outer edges, increasing toward the center, where velocities higher than 175 knots (200 mph) have been recorded. At the center is an area called the *eye* of the storm,

which averages about 14 miles in diameter. This area is relatively calm, with light winds and clear or moderately clear skies, and some drizzle.

An Atlantic hurricane, then, starts as a tropical low, grows into a storm, and eventually matures into a hurricane when its winds exceed 75 mph. While it is moving along its track, it is growing in intensity. By the time it begins to curve to the northeast, it comes over cooler waters and into cooler air. Cooling reduces its internal action, until it finally dissipates into an extratropical low, ending as a gale or storm over the North Atlantic or North Sea.

The elements of wind, temperature, pressure, humidity, and rain vary little in the different quadrants of a tropical cyclone. Winds increase from the outer limits to the edge of the eye. The temperature rises and the humidity falls at the center. Precipitation is in the form of showers at the outer limits. It becomes

The eye of Hurricane Gracie, September 1959. The picture was taken from a "hurricane hunter" aircraft which was tracking the storm.

heavier toward the center, and is heaviest in the right front quadrant.

Hurricanes are usually associated with great wind-caused tides that inundate the surrounding land areas and cause more damage than do the wind and rain of the storm itself. The doldrums, with their baffling winds and rains in frequent squalls and thunderstorms is the breeding place of most tropical cyclones.

Hurricanes, Typhoons, and their Tracks

Hurricanes occur most frequently in September and October, but they can happen any time from June to December. The track of a typical hurricane, originating in the doldrums east of the West Indies, curves northeastward from the Greater Antilles. It then hits the east coast of Florida, spreading destruction along the eastern seaboard of the United States, sometimes as far north as New York.

With somewhat less frequency, but often with greater violence, a hurricane originating from the same area will move south of Cuba and swing into the Gulf of Mexico, where, like a captured tempest in a bathtub, it will wreak havoc up and down the Gulf coast. A Gulf Coast hurricane often will dissipate in the Mississippi Valley, with heavy rainfalls extending as far north as Tennessee, Kentucky, and

Illinois. The east coast hurricane will usually cause heavy rains, from Philadelphia northward into New York, Connecticut, Rhode Island, and Massachusetts. It will also cause tidal flooding from Georgia to Virginia, even if the main brunt of the storm never actually hits the coast.

Any sailor who has been assigned to a ship in the Seventh Fleet will probably experience a Western Pacific typhoon. The southwestern part of the North Pacific has more tropical cyclones than any other place on earth. These are born between the Marshall Islands and the Philippines, and move toward the east coast of China, then northeastward over the Philippines, Taiwan, Okinawa, and Japan. The typhoon may veer into the Asian continent almost anywhere along its east coast. When it does, it is usually accompanied by terrible tidal waves. These sweep deep inland along the low-lying coastal plains and up the numerous rivers, causing widespread destruction and loss of life. And, just as a hurricane may move into the Gulf of Mexico, a typhoon may sweep south of the East Indies (Indonesia) into the Bay of Bengal. It then hits the coast of southern Asia.

Typhoons and hurricanes often produce massive floods, uproot trees, and cause giant waves which make naval and merchant shipping extremely hazardous. Waves up to 40 feet or more damage or sink ships, and sweep away coastal villages, towns, and cities.

During World War II, Admiral Halsey's Third Fleet was caught in a typhoon east of the Philippines. Even the largest ships were tossed about like corks. Not one ship escaped heavy damage, and three destroyers were sunk with few survivors.

A terrible hurricane struck New England in 1938, causing 600 deaths and property damage exceeding $250 million. The entire boardwalk at Atlantic City, New Jersey, has been swept away on several occasions. The entire city of Belize, British Honduras, was destroyed in the late 1960s, causing the survivors to rebuild on a new site further inland on higher ground. A hurricane which hit Galveston, Texas in 1900 killed 6,000 people. In probably the greatest natural catastrophe of history, a typhoon swept over the Bay of Bengal in 1737. The storm pushed a 40-foot wave inland, killing 300,000 people.

Cyclonic winds in the northern hemisphere circulate in a counterclockwise direction; those in the southern hemisphere circulate clockwise. Ship captains must know this when it becomes necessary to maneuver out of a hurricane's path.

If you face in the same direction the storm is moving, winds in the right semicircle are circulating so as to draw a ship in that area into the path of the storm center. This is called the *dangerous semicircle*. The wind also will tend to carry the ship along with the storm as it moves along its track. On the other hand, winds in the left semicircle, called the *navigable semicircle,* tend to drive the ship out of the path of the storm and help her to get behind it.

Maneuvering a ship in a hurricane consists mainly of determining whether she is in, or approaching, the dangerous semicircle; and if she is, finding the best method of working out of that undesirable position.

SIGNS OF AN APPROACHING TROPICAL CYCLONE

Even though weather forecasting is much improved today, tropical cyclones can develop very rapidly and can move faster than a ship. Navigators should know the signs of an approaching tropical storm so as to avoid the dangers of having to "ride it out" while trying to maneuver out of its grip.

During the typhoon or hurricane season, any major variation in the regular diurnal movement of the barometer should be considered as a warning of an approaching weather change. Once a storm begins, the barometer indicates with considerable accuracy its speed of approach and the ship's distance from the storm center. At storm center, the barometer will read less than 28 inches of mercury.

A long, low swell rises well in advance of the violent winds. The direction of swell origin will normally indicate the bearing of the storm center. Light, feathery plumes of cirrus cloud appear shortly after the swell begins, fanning out from a whitish arc on the horizon. Then the sky becomes more and more overcast, until the dark hurricane cloud appears on the horizon.

The barometer begins a steady fall, the air becomes heavy, hot, and moist, and the wind begins to pick up. A faint humming sound, caused by an increase in wind velocity, can be detected. Fine, misty squalls of rain break off the main cloud bank; these increase to heavy showers, and finally to torrents as the center approaches. The sea begins to roll in mountainous waves which can completely engulf a large ship.

Storm Warning Signals

Flags and pennants hoisted at the National Weather Service and other shore stations, indicate the presence or forecast presence of unfavorable winds. These signals are now flown over most major marinas on the Great Lakes, other major recreational lakes in the nation, ocean beaches, coastal harbor marinas, and Coast Guard stations.

Small craft warning: One red pennant displayed by day, and a red light over a white light at night, indicate that winds of up to 38 mph (33 knots) and sea conditions dangerous to small craft are forecast in the area.

Gale warning: Two red pennants displayed

TYPE OF WARNING	DAYTIME SIGNALS	NIGHT SIGNALS	EQUIVALENT WIND SPEEDS	
			KNOTS	MPH
SMALL CRAFT			UP TO 33	UP TO 38
GALE			34–47	39–54
STORM			48–63	55–73
HURRICANE			64 OR GREATER	74 OR GREATER

Warning displays.

by day, and a white light above a red light at night, indicate that winds ranging from 39 to 54 miles an hour (34–47 knots) are forecast.

Storm warning: A single square red flag with a black center displayed during daytime, and two red lights at night, indicate that winds of 55 mph (48 knots) and above are forecast.

Hurricane warning: Two square red flags with black centers displayed by day, and a white light between two red lights at night, indicate that winds 74 mph (64 knots) and above are forecast for the area.

HURRICANE WARNING SYSTEM

The U. S. Hurricane Warning System was set up in 1938 as a cooperative effort of the National Weather Service, Navy, and the Army Air Force. Up to that point, hurricanes struck with almost no previous warning. Reconnaissance airplanes fully equipped with radar scopes and weather instruments were sent to scout suspected storm areas.

In recent years, weather satellites have largely replaced reconnaissance aircraft. Bulletins are issued every few hours, forecasting the latest information on the storm, its intensity, its probable path, and giving timely warning to all who may be in danger. Ships and aircraft can change course to avoid the storm; people have time to evacuate low areas, and can secure their property to reduce damages.

Chapter 5. *Study Guide Questions*

1. When do weather fronts develop? What usually happens when a cold front meets a warm air mass?

2. What kind of weather do fronts usually bring?

3. What are the three types of frontal systems?

4. What are the names of the world's primary frontal zones? Where is the Intertropical Convergence Zone and why is it of particular importance?

5. What are squalls and what are their characteristics?

6. Why is the Polar Frontal Zone important to those who live in the temperate zones?

7. What are the first signs of an approaching cold front?

8. What are the signs of an approaching warm front?

9. What weather is associated with occluded fronts?

10. What are the three stages of a thunderstorm? What happens in each stage?

11. What weather phenomena occur within a thunderstorm?

12. Why should aircraft avoid flying through a thunderstorm?

13. What is lightning and what causes it to happen?

14. What is meant by the statement, "Lightning follows the easiest route?" What causes thunder?

15. What storm type is the most severe?

16. Where do most tornadoes occur?

17. What name is given to a tornado over water?

18. What are the three categories of tropical cyclone? What is the established minimum wind velocity of a tropical cyclone?

19. Where do tropical cyclones occur? What are the local names given to tropical cyclones around the world?

20. How does a hurricane develop and why is it so violent? List five characteristics of a tropical cyclone.

21. What are the two tracks or paths of a North Atlantic hurricane? Where do North Atlantic hurricanes originate?

22. What is the "eye" of the hurricane and what is unusual about this part of the storm?

23. What aspect of a hurricane usually causes the most damage and casualties?

24. When is "hurricane season"?

25. What is the usual track of a West Pacific typhoon?

26. Explain the "dangerous" and "naviga-

ble" semicircles of a hurricane.

27. What meteorological signs will give hint of an approaching hurricane?

28. What are the four categories of signals for unfavorable winds in the vicinity of harbors and beaches in the United States?

29. Who participates in the hurricane warning effort in the United States? What means are now used to locate and track hurricanes?

Vocabulary

warm or cold front
occluded front
Intertropical Convergence Zone
squall
drizzle
thunderstorm
tornado
dissipating stage (of storm)
static electricity
lightning
vortex (of tornado)
waterspout
"dust devil"
tropical depression
tropical storm
tropical cyclone
hurricane
typhoon
willy-willy
baguio
storm quadrant
inundate
Greater Antilles
tidal wave
dangerous semicircle
navigable semicircle
condensation

Chapter 6. Weather Forecasting

Weather forecasting has developed into a full-time activity of the U. S. government, the armed services, and many commercial meteorological enterprises. This chapter will discuss some of the techniques used by the National Weather Service and the Navy Fleet Weather Central, to forecast the weather.

NATIONAL WEATHER SERVICE

The National Weather Service of the Department of Commerce is our government's weather agency. Because accurate weather forecasting depends on information from many areas, the NWS operates over 1,000 weather stations throughout the United States. These stations also cooperate with the armed forces, the Federal Aviation Administration, and the Canadian Weather Service.

Over 9,000 part-time weather stations also assist in reporting to the NWS. Accurate information on the meteorological situation at each station is transmitted daily to the regional forecasting centers. Reports are made more often if significant weather data is developing. Weather which will affect the United States in a week or more is now in its formative stage elsewhere in the world. A worldwide network of weather stations under the World Meteorological Organization, an agency of the United Nations, provides the NWS with regular exchanges of data. When in transit, U. S. naval and merchant ships and aircraft regularly report in to their headquarters and to the NWS. The NWS is able to achieve approximately 85 percent accuracy on its 24-hour and 36-hour

A Navy quartermaster plots the course of his ship, and storms which are in the area of operation. The quartermaster serves as aerographer on smaller ships.

forecasts, thanks to these worldwide reporting services.

NAVY WEATHER SERVICE

The Navy Weather Service is now organized as a part of the Navy Oceanography and Meteorology Command at Suitland, Maryland. It is organized to provide global forecast services to meet Navy requirements, as well as Department of Defense oceanographic needs. The Service embraces elements of the operating forces, shore establishment, and Navy Department. The Navy cooperates with all national, regional, and international weather agencies. Only in this way can it fulfill its mission. The U. S. Navy is an active participant in the World Meteorological Organization.

Navy weather units are maintained with all major aviation units, certain major combatant and auxiliary vessels, fleet flagships, and at most naval shore activities. Trained enlisted aerographer's mates and meteorological officers are assigned to these weather units. On ships which do not carry trained aerographers and meteorologists, weather observations and reporting are carried out by the ship's navigator, assisted by trained quartermasters.

Although the Navy has many different-sized weather units and detachments, we are most concerned with the U. S. Navy Fleet Weather Central. The Central uses the basic information acquired from various sources, compiles it into weather broadcasts, and transmits it to the operating forces of the fleet. A significant input to its weather predictions comes from individual ships at sea. Major Fleet Weather Centrals are located at Norfolk, San Francisco, and Guam where they can serve their respective major ocean basin areas.

FORECAST SERVICES

The National Weather Service publishes many kinds of weather forecasts. Among these are: 24-hour detailed forecasts, 5-day forecasts, 30-day general outlooks, 12-hour aviation forecasts, and a host of special bulletins, weather maps, and storm and frost warnings.

Newspapers, TV, and radio weather reports rely on many of these services. For air safety, complete weather reports are given to pilots by the Federal Aviation Agency, in cooperation with the NWS. Pilots also get frequent in-flight updates of weather information. It is common for commercial airline passengers to hear their captain, just a few minutes after the plane takes off, reporting the weather conditions expected at the destination of the flight.

The two kinds of weather reporting are local and long-range forecasting. The long-range study is more concerned with an overall view of the climate, and with predictions for a year or more in the future. An almanac provides a long-range weather prediction for the year ahead, and is based on average weather reported for years past.

Local weather is predicted up to a month or so in advance. The accuracy of these predictions is dependent upon timely readings taken at many reporting stations—on land and by weather ships, balloons, and satellites circling the earth. While forecasting is becoming much more accurate, it still is not an exact science, due to the wide variety of local atmospheric uncertainties.

Elements of the Navy Weather Service prepare several types of forecasts, each for a specific purpose and containing specific information.

Area forecasts are prepared by major units afloat, Fleet Weather Centrals and Facilities, and major units ashore. The area covered is either the "area of responsibility" of the Centrals or the "operating area" of the major units. Area forecasts will include a synopsis of weather conditions in the forecast area. They will report all pressure systems and their associated weather, including the system's position, intensity, and direction of movement. Intensity will include wind direction and velocity, visibility, and weather types. Position will always be reported by latitude and longitude.

Local forecasts are prepared by ships or stations and are used in planning local operations. These reports will include a brief summary of the synoptic pressure situation, fronts, severe weather, fog, etc. They normally cover a 36-hour prediction period. Specific details affecting operations (such as flying conditions, temperatures, precipitation, sea conditions, icing, ceilings, visibilities, and turbulence) are all included in the local forecasts.

Route, flight, and *terminal forecasts* are prepared for a flight operation and are issued by the station or ship involved in the operation. The *route forecast* refers to weather conditions along a specific route. The *flight forecast* pertains to the weather conditions on successive stages of a flight. The *terminal forecast* concerns itself with the landing and takeoff conditions at fields enroute.

Storm warnings are included in scheduled broadcasts to both the Fleet and Merchant Marine. Warnings are issued by the Fleet Weather Centrals responsible for the area in which the storm is located. Storms reported are thunderstorms, tornadoes, local wind storms, and major cyclonic storms. Special warnings are issued for tropical cyclones.

WEATHER SATELLITES

Weather satellites are the newest forecasting tool available to the meteorologist. Early weather satellites began with the TIROS (TV and Infrared Observation Satellite) in 1960. Since then, improved systems have been developed and placed in orbit.

The newest satellites are equipped with radiometers that transmit pictures of the cloud formations on the earth's surface, either by day or night. Other equipment sensors relate surface temperatures and fronts, storms, snow, sea ice, and cloud heights. Orbiting at a height of about 900 miles, these satellites circle the earth every 115 minutes and view the entire earth three times a day.

Geo-stationary satellites, hovering 22,300 miles above the equator, photograph an entire hemisphere every half-hour. Spectacular pictures of whole hurricane systems and frontal weather patterns are now a regular part of weather forecasting.

WEATHER MAPS AND CHARTS

Weather maps are printed and distributed each week by the National Weather Service. Each packet contains the weather maps for each day of the week, in pamphlet form. All symbols used on the maps are explained in map legends, so even the novice can obtain considerable information from them. Isobaric forecasting is possible by careful reading of the weather maps, since all frontal zones are carefully charted, along with wind direction.

Shipboard weather charts are plotted by the ship's navigator from data obtained from Fleet Weather Central synoptic weather bulletins. The navigator creates a weather chart for the area in which the ship is operating, and predicts the probable weather the ship will encounter. When a ship is beyond the areas covered by official weather forecasts, analysis of the weather chart usually is the only way of determining what conditions are likely in the near future.

FACSIMILE

The use of facsimile equipment often eliminates the need for the navigator to construct his own weather chart. *Facsimile* (FAX) is a process for transmitting pictorial and graphic information by wire or radio, and reproducing it in its original form at the receiving station.

Two forms of FAX are now available. One transmits photographs, the image being reproduced on photographic film or paper. This equipment is generally used for intelligence data and photos rather than for weather. Weather charts are usually received on a spe-

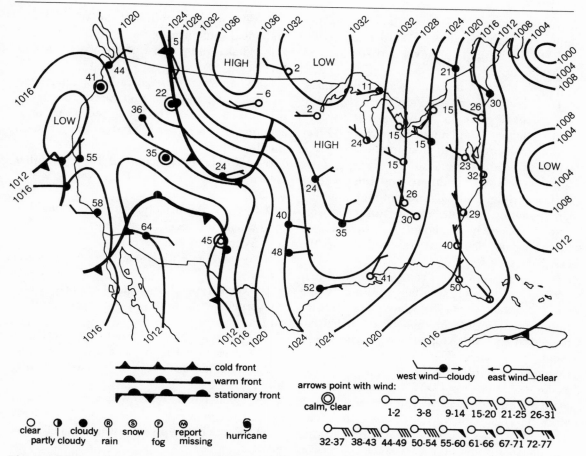

cold front
warm front
stationary front

west wind—cloudy   east wind—clear
arrows point with wind:
calm, clear
1-2 3-8 9-14 15-20 21-25 26-31
32-37 38-43 44-49 50-54 55-60 61-66 67-71 72-77

clear   cloudy   ®   ⑤   ⑤   ⑩   hurricane
partly cloudy rain snow fog report
missing

This simplified weather map is similar to those issued daily by the National Weather Service. Temperatures are in degrees Fahrenheit and pressure lines are labeled in millibars. 1000 millibars equal 14.5 pounds per square inch. Normal atmospheric pressure is 14.7 lbs./in.², or 1013 mb. Arrows indicate wind direction and velocity in mph.

cial electrographic paper, in less detail than is required for photo transmission. Facsimile has been used for many years in transmitting "radio photos" for newspapers over wire circuits. The Navy has been using it since World War II.

The most useful application of facsimile is in transmitting fully plotted weather charts. The National Meteorological Center Facsimile network (NMC FAX), sponsored by the National Weather Service, is devoted exclusively to this work. The NMC FAX network now covers the entire United States.

This network doesn't meet the Navy's worldwide need for weather data, however. The Fleet Weather Centrals, therefore, must prepare most of the Navy's current FAX traffic. They correlate weather observations from all over the world, and then transmit the finished charts to Navy ships and stations worldwide. Because facsimile eliminates the need for duplicate plotting aboard each ship, it has made weather service cheaper, quicker, and more accurate.

SHIP ROUTING

Fleet Weather Central can recommend the best navigational track to a ship making an ocean crossing. This service is known as Optimum Track Ship Routing (OTSR), and is available to the skippers of naval and commercial seagoing vessels.

A ship about to make a voyage will request OTSR services from the FWC in a *departure movement report*, sent by the ship at least 72 hours before a planned departure. Fleet Weather Central will recommend a track which takes into consideration the speed of the ship, its loading condition, and the weather and seas likely to be encountered enroute. Great savings in time, reduced ship damage, comfortable operating conditions, and reduced fuel consumption have resulted from the OTSR service.

A ship sailing under OTSR receives regular updates on changing weather conditions while on her voyage. The OTSR is not mandatory for the commanding officer, though—even if he has requested it. He is responsible for the movement of his ship, and can deviate from the recommended track if he sees fit to do so. Major deviations from OTSR are not generally made by a prudent skipper, however. OTSR is most beneficial for voyages over 1,500 miles long in the open sea. It is not practical for the Caribbean and coastal routes, since voyages on these routes are of short duration.

An individual route weather forecast, known as WEAX, is a Fleet Weather Central service which will provide a ship with a synoptic weather summary for the route, and a 24-hour forecast on the ship's projected track. These forecasts are updated every 12 hours. WEAX is requested along with OTSR, since OTSR does not provide daily forecasts.

Chapter 6. *Study Guide Questions*

1. What is the purpose of weather forecasts? Who uses them?

2. Which U. S. government agency is responsible for providing weather forecasts and accurate meteorological information? How does this agency obtain its data?

3. What is the function of the World Meteorological Organization?

4. What is the purpose of the Navy Weather Service?

5. What Navy enlisted rating specialty has weather interpretation and forecasting as its primary concern? Which enlisted rating must accomplish weather-related tasks aboard smaller ships?

6. What is the function of Fleet Weather Central? Where are the U. S. Navy's FWCs located?

7. What is the principal difference between long-range and local forecasting?

8. What is an area forecast?

9. What are local forecasts used for in the Navy?

10. What type of operations are principally concerned with route, flight, and terminal forecasts?

11. What weather information do satellites report back to earth weather stations?

12. What is facsimile (FAX)? What is it used for?

13. What is OTSR? How can a ship obtain OTSR services?

14. For what type of voyage is OTSR of greatest value?

15. What is the WEAX service? Who provides it to the fleet?

Vocabulary

weather forecasting
National Weather Service
Fleet Weather Central
World Meteorological Organization
aerographer's mate
quartermaster
area forecast
local forecast
geo-stationary satellite

terminal forecast
equipment sensor
isobaric forecasting
synoptic weather summary
facsimile (FAX equipment)
Optimum Track Ship Routing
departure movement report
route weather forecast (WEAX)

Chapter 7. Weather and Naval Operations

There is nothing that can compare with the fury of a storm at sea—and nothing that can make a man feel so small. Weather forecasting, however, has lessened the threat of foul weather—as long as the mariner takes adequate precautions. No naval operation of consequence can be planned or executed without taking the weather into careful consideration.

Meteorological Officer

The meteorological officer has a vital job to do. He is normally responsible for providing weather information to the units of an entire formation. This information may be for air, surface, antisubmarine, or amphibious operations. The meteorological officer usually serves on the staff of the commander of a major operational task force, group, division, or squadron. The success of the whole mission and the lives of the men involved depend to a large extent on his predictions.

The meteorological officer provides information about wave, surf, tide, and currents—information absolutely essential to a successful amphibious operation. He will provide a wide range of oceanographic information to support ASW operations. He will provide the weather information necessary to implement air operations. He can provide information about the effect of weather on radar, sonar, and radio communications.

Collection of Weather Information

Navy ships operating beyond territorial waters are normally required to make periodic weather reports. If several ships are steaming in formation, one ship will be designated to make the report for the whole formation.

These reports are sent to the area Fleet Weather Central by radio four times daily, in a special message format. The weather data supplied by all ships reporting from that area are analyzed by the FWC and sent back to the ships at sea as weather forecasts for their locality.

Heavy Weather Bill

All naval vessels have, as a part of their Ship's Organization Manual, a Heavy Weather Bill. This bill outlines the duties of officers and departments when there is a probability of heavy weather.

The operations officer keeps the captain and other key officers informed concerning the likelihood of bad weather in the operational area. He also advises officers and crew concerning storm indications and local conditions.

One of the key rules of any heavy weather bill is that there should be no loose gear or equipment in any part of the ship. Loose objects fly through the air with such force in a heavy sea that they are called "missile hazards," because of the injury and damage they cause. Once the ship is in heavy seas, the securing of heavy gear can be extremely dangerous. Loose gear can cause widespread damage to the ship and other nearby equipment. Heavy cargo loose in holds can punch holes in the hull of the ship, causing flooding and water damage.

Everyone aboard must help the ship secure for heavy weather. Each department head has to report to the executive officer that his assigned spaces have been inspected and found secure. All hatches, doors, portholes, gun covers, magazines, and mobile equipment have to be secured to prevent leakage or cargo shift.

The Engineering Department must pump bilges and transfer fuel and water to ensure maximum ballast and stability. The Supply Department must ensure that storerooms and cargo are secured, and that mess menus are suitable for preparation in rough weather; deep fat friers, for example, would be secured in heavy seas. The Medical Department must be prepared to minimize discomfort of bedridden patients. The Deck Department rigs heavy-weather lines topside. All departments must ensure that lifejackets are available for anyone who must go topside.

Special precautions and actions are also in the bill to satisfy requirements, should the ship receive storm warnings while anchored or alongside a pier. Anchor chain may be veered to a longer scope, or a second anchor may be dropped "underfoot." Engines may be prepared to get underway, in the event that anchors begin to drag. The quarterdeck watch may be shifted to the bridge. If ship's boats are in the water, they will be hoisted aboard and secured or sent to safe haven. If a hurricane is expected, the ships in harbor may put to sea or be sent to more protected hurricane anchorages.

In short, the approach of heavy weather involves the total preparation of the ship—much as is done for "general quarters" and "battle stations." Indeed, the battle with the elements of wind and sea can be every bit as demanding—and as disastrous, if the ship and crew are not prepared.

The Ship in Heavy Weather

"Heavy weather" refers to more than severe storms. It can also describe the relative effects of the wind and sea on a specific type of ship. A carrier, for instance, might not consider seas "heavy" until flight operations would have to be cancelled. But the same seas could be pounding a destroyer unmercifully. The officer in tactical command must view the situation as it affects all units, and ensure that courses and speeds are maintained to reduce the possibility of damage and injury.

With the approach of a storm or heavy weather, preparations are made for the expected conditions—low temperatures, rain, snow or ice, winds, and seas. Poor weather will require that members of the bridge watch and topside personnel have foul-weather gear. Topside traffic routes may have to be prohibited and re-routed below decks. Reduced visi-

A lookout on the bridge wing of an aircraft carrier during heavy weather. International Rules of the Road require the stationing of adequate lookouts, especially in poor visibility. The assistance of modern radar has not eliminated that requirement. This lookout wears the seaman's oilskin "slicker," his "foul-weather gear."

bility, slick and icy decks, or cold metal surfaces become additional hazards.

Watchstanders must be especially alert in bad weather because of the reduced visibility. The number of lookouts may have to be increased. Constant vigilance becomes the watchword for all hands—whether they are on watch or in the compartments, off duty. All hands must be alert to any sudden movement, pitch, or roll which could cause loss of balance and injury.

Tactical Planning and Weather

The planning of any large operation requires particular attention to the weather. Extensive research is made to ensure that every possibility is covered. Movement to an objective area can be planned to take advantage of poor visibility. The duration of an operation may be dictated by the forecast of a storm in the area. Use of air support may be curtailed by low ceilings. Heavy rains may preclude the movement of troops and vehicles. Availability of forces and reinforcements, logistic support, and political as well as military urgency may all be affected by the weather situation. Success of an operation can never be taken for granted; but if weather factors are disregarded, failure or limited success can be expected.

Forces at sea can use cloud cover to obscure the movement of ships and hinder air attack. Sophisticated electronic warfare devices, however, have reduced the effectiveness of cloud cover. In World War II the weather played a significant role in many sea battles and amphibious operations, and was a constant nightmare to North Atlantic convoys. In the Vietnam War, the monsoons hampered shore bombardment and logistic support; but at the same time, they hindered the enemy's defending radar when it was seeking out our attacking aircraft.

Weather and Amphibious Operations

More than any other type of operation, an amphibious landing requires accurate weather information. Every aspect of the amphibious operation—airborne, surface, and subsurface—is directly affected by the weather. The meteorologist on the staff of the amphibious task force commander must be knowledgeable about every phase of the operation so that he can advise of the possible weather impact on each. The following conditions may influence the day or hour of landing and the scheduling of offensive, defensive, and logistic support:

1) *Wind and sea.* Strong winds and heavy sea and swell significantly affect the approach of ships, and the offloading of boats, troops, and supplies. Heavy seas may make the running of assault boats and amphibious craft impossible.

2) *Surf.* Winds affect the state of the sea, tides, currents, and surf. The condition of the surf has direct impact on beaching operations. Swell and surf in excess of 4 feet make landing-craft operations dangerous, and cause boats to broach (turn sideways) on the beach. When surf is over 6 feet, beaching should not be attempted at all, for there are sure to be severe personnel and equipment losses. Heavy

Storm-twisted piers on Normandy beach, after the storm which nearly destroyed the Allied beachhead in World War II. Pontoon causeways and floating piers are particularly vulnerable to high surf and swell on an amphibious assault beach.

seas will delay scheduled boat waves and make troops seasick. Operations by underwater demolition teams (UDTs) and minesweeping procedures, part of a successful amphibious assault, are impossible in heavy surf and swell. Surf conditions are probably the most crucial factor an amphibious commander must face.

3) *Visibility.* Improved radars have reduced the impeding effect of poor visibility—as long as ships in an amphibious task force don't have to maintain electronic silence. Boat wave commanders and wave guides, however, are severely hindered by poor visibility. If radio or radar silence is imposed or caused by enemy action, poor visibility can cause the landing to fail. Delay of the attack could upset the entire operation.

4) *Flying conditions.* One of the fundamental rules of an amphibious assault is to gain control of the air over the assault beach and transport area. Today, with guided missiles in every potential adversary's inventory, that area must be extended to 60–100 miles around the assault area. Suitability of flying conditions is determined by cloud cover, ceiling, visibility, wind turbulence, and icing. Air observation in support of assault waves, and bombing of enemy defenses and beaches, may be restricted or eliminated by unfavorable flying conditions.

The modern amphibious assault normally

Visibility, both for aircraft and amphibious vessels, is essential in amphibious assault operations. Here an observation plane directs gunfire support for Marines heading to the beach in the Palau Islands in World War II.

involves one or more assault waves by troop-carrying helicopters. This assault technique is called vertical envelopment. These early waves secure key positions behind the enemy defenses, and prevent reinforcements from moving to the beach area. Poor visibility will make successful helicopter assault or resupply operations nearly impossible.

ICE AND COLD-WEATHER OPERATIONS

Polar operations were quite limited in World War II, though some notable actions did take place. The most significant naval operations in the north polar seas involved the convoys to the Soviet port of Murmansk. Since World War II, however, more attention has been paid to Arctic and cold-weather sea operations, because of our proximity to the Soviet Union via the north polar air and undersea routes. In addition, intensive research and exploration has been conducted on the Antarctic continent. All such operations demand special attention to navigation and ship handling, given the severe conditions imposed by cold weather.

Weather conditions encountered in these areas will require extensive shipboard polar training, covering: shiphandling in icepack areas, icebreaker operations, ice safety, ice seamanship, damage control procedures, low-temperature operating instructions for machinery, cold-weather effects on equipment and materials, cold-weather clothing, survival, ice reporting, and difficulties of polar communications and navigation, caused by the Aurora Borealis and the proximity of the magnetic north pole.

Ships scheduled for polar operations are specially fitted with piping which will not break when the water freezes. They also are fitted with special heaters and insulators, installed in equipment and machinery spaces. Polar weather, like other severe weather conditions, must be understood and planned for, if operations are to be successful.

The U. S. Coast Guard icebreaker *Northwind* rests momentarily during her mission in the Bering Sea.

Chapter 7. *Study Guide Questions*

1. What is evasive action?

2. Why must weather be considered in planning any significant naval operation?

3. What are the tasks of the meteorological officer? To what naval organization is he normally attached for duty?

4. Why is the meteorologist charged with providing his commander weather and oceanographic information? What must the commander do with this information if it is to be of value?

5. What is the purpose of a Heavy Weather Bill?

6. What are "missile hazards"?

7. What is the task of the Engineering Department when preparing for heavy weather? . . . the Supply Department?

8. What actions might an anchored ship be required to take upon receiving a hurricane warning?

9. What is the lookout requirement aboard a ship underway in reduced visibility? How does radar affect this requirement?

10. What are some foul-weather phenomena which would probably require modification of military operations?

11. What is the purpose of gathering and analyzing weather information for naval forces?

12. What are the three weather conditions which may have significant effect on an amphibious operation?

13. How can surf affect an amphibious landing?

14. How can poor visibility affect an amphibious assault, from the sea and air?

15. Where were the most significant Arctic naval actions fought in World War II?

16. Why have cold-weather operations taken on new importance since World War II?

Vocabulary

meteorological officer	pitch and roll
territorial sea	surf conditions
Heavy Weather Bill	broach (boats)
ballast	electronic silence
stability	vertical envelopment
safe haven	helicopter
anchor underfoot	polar operations
foul-weather gear	icebreaker operations

7 Astronomy

Chapter 1. The Study of the Universe

Astronomy is the study of the universe—in particular, of the stars and other heavenly bodies, and their composition, motion, position, and size. You might ask, "Why delve into the mysteries of the universe? What does an astronomer produce or achieve?"

The product of astronomy is a greater knowledge and understanding of the universe. True, most of this knowledge has not yet been used directly. However, the study of astronomy led to the discovery of the fundamental laws governing all modern technology. Astronomy is directly responsible for the scientific age, which has fundamentally altered our lives.

The universe is the most awesome concept in the human imagination. The size of the universe is utterly beyond our comprehension. The Hale Telescope on Mt. Palomar near Los Angeles, California, has found one million galaxies in the Big Dipper alone. It can see galaxies from which starlight departed five billion years ago!

There are many theories about the origin of the universe. Indeed, ever since the ancient Greeks first began to study the world around them, scientists have wondered how the earth and the universe came to be. Although we certainly know more than ancient thinkers did about the origin of things, many questions still remain unanswered.

The "Big Bang" or expanding-universe theory was first proposed in 1927 by the Belgian astronomer Georges Lemaitre. His theory has been supported by other scientists, including the American scientist George Gamow. In his book *The Creation of the Universe*, Gamow contends that all matter in the universe was originally concentrated into an incredibly dense glob or mass. Packed inside was all the material of today's universe, at a temperature exceeding 100 *trillion* degrees.

According to this theory, creation began about 16 billion years ago, when a huge explosion sent dust and gas hurtling through space in all directions. As this exploding fireball expanded, particles destroyed one another, releasing high-energy radiation. Gamow believes that this expanding motion will never cease. Indeed, studies of the movements of other star groups indicate that *all* are moving away from us at fantastic speeds.

All the matter in this early central core was separated into protons, neutrons, and electrons, because of the extremely high temperatures there. Just after the explosion, however, the temperature dropped enough that particles could combine. Elements with high atomic weight were created when protons captured large numbers of neutrons. But these elements were unstable and quickly decayed into atoms of lesser mass. Slow neutron capture produced more stable elements, with low atomic weight. This accounts for the high percentage of hydrogen and helium in the universe, and the small amounts of heavier elements.

Gamow believes most of this element formation took place in about 30 minutes. After that time, the temperature was too low to permit neutron capture. The clouds of matter then separated into balls of gas, and eventually condensed into stars and planets.

There are other theories of the creation of the universe, of course. The correct one has yet to be positively determined. Perhaps with bigger telescopes, observation posts on the moon, and satellites in outer space we can find out for sure.

The Spectrum

By gathering light rays from starlight, and analyzing their colors, astronomers can determine the amount of hydrogen, helium, and the other elements in the universe. These light rays, though sometimes very feeble, carry with them the complete story of their birth. This story is told by their *spectrum*, the rainbow of colors produced by a prism. The *spectrograph*, which is attached directly to a telescope, breaks up starlight into its component wavelengths or colors, to be photographed. It filters starlight through a prism, which divides light into the separate colors of the spectrum.

The radiation spectrum, arranged in order of increasing wavelength, ranges from gamma rays on the low end of the scale through X-rays, ultraviolet rays, visible light, infrared light, to radio waves. Visible light is only a small part of the total spectrum. Except for certain radio waves, most of the other types of radiation cannot penetrate the earth's atmospheric shield.

The photograph which records the color bands in the spectrum is called a *spectrogram*. When analyzed under a microscope, it tells scientists which elements exist in each star. Each chemical element, when it is vaporized and glowing in a star, gives off its own pattern of colors. Light from vaporized iron gives out one pattern, while hydrogen, helium, oxygen, and the others each emit different patterns. These color patterns are clearly visible in the spectrum of incoming starlight. This is one way the astronomer can tell that the sun and stars are made of the same elements that we find here on earth.

The atmospheric shield which protects our earth from radiation also distorts the light which gets through to our telescopes on earth. In order to gain more accurate knowledge of the universe, then, we have had to go beyond our atmosphere. For this purpose, we have sent up Orbiting Astronomical Observatories which are controlled by radio from earth. Astronomers have also made use of high-altitude balloon observatories which can go up to about 20 miles above the surface. In these balloons, they are above 99 percent of the atmosphere. Fitted with television cameras, the OAOs and balloons are opening up whole new horizons in astronomy.

Although quite new, balloon astronomy is playing a greater and greater part in man's

WAVELENGTH IN METERS

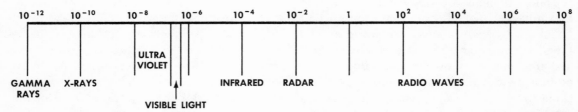

The radiation spectrum, arranged in order of increasing wavelength. Notice how small a portion is occupied by visible light. Certain radio waves can come through the "radio window," but most of the rest of the spectrum can't pierce our atmospheric shield.

Scientists of the Office of Naval Research launch plastic high-altitude balloon from a Coast Guard ship, to measure cosmic radiation near the northern geomagnetic pole.

study of the universe. Balloons are much cheaper than satellites and can easily carry men aloft in their gondolas. They also can carry up to two tons of telescopes, spectrographs, and other instruments. The pictures and other findings can be brought directly down to earth, rather than by radio transmission, as from satellites.

An even newer method of detecting matter in space is *radio astronomy*. Astronomers have discovered that reactions in the stars cause radiation which can be picked up by radio receivers set for certain frequencies. Called *radio telescopes,* these receivers have already added much to our knowledge of the makeup of stars.

The spectroscopes and radio telescopes have found that hydrogen and helium account for more than 99 percent of all matter in the universe. It is believed that 93 percent of all the atoms in the universe are hydrogen, accounting for 76 percent of its mass. Almost 7 percent are helium atoms, totaling 23 percent of the mass. Thus, all the rest of the elements add up to only a fraction of 1 percent of the total. Remember, however, that these figures pertain

to the *total* universe, not to the elements found only on the earth's crust. The figures should make us realize what a tiny and very special section of the universe the earth is.

No matter where astronomers have searched in space, the universe appears to be made up of the same elements. This is a very important fact. It tells us that if life exists elsewhere in the universe, such life certainly would consist of the same elements we have on earth.

Chapter 1. Study Guide Questions

1. What is astronomy and why does man study it?

2. Why do many people consider the study of astronomy responsible for the scientific age?

3. Explain the "Big Bang" theory.

4. What is a prism?

5. Relate the radiation spectrum in order of increasing wavelength. What is meant by the term "wavelength?"

6. What is the purpose of a spectrograph? Why is it important and how does it work?

7. How do scientists study the universe beyond our atmosphere? Why is it necessary to get beyond our atmosphere?

8. Why is balloon astronomy the most practical way to make some studies of the universe?

9. What is an OAO?

10. What are the two principal elements present in the universe?

11. What interesting fact have astronomers deduced concerning elements and life elsewhere within the universe?

Vocabulary

universe	mass
astronomy	infinity
radiation	spectrograph
element	spectrogram
proton	prism
neutron	wavelength
electron	spectrum
particle	ultraviolet
matter	infrared

Chapter 2. The Creation of the Solar System

The solar system is composed of the sun, the planets and moons, asteroids, occasional comets, and frequent meteors. There have been many attempts to account for the formation of the solar system, but none is completely satisfactory.

In 1755 a theory of the heavens was published by Immanuel Kant, a German philosopher. Kant suggested that in the beginning there was an immense whirling cloud of dust and gas, extending to where the farthest planets now orbit. First heavier elements began to separate from lighter ones. This caused the forces of repulsion and attraction to set the gaseous mass into rotation. Condensations gradually resulted: these became planets revolving in regular orbits around a central mass, which became the sun. Several other theories came into favor during the next 200 years, but today's theories are based on Kant's theories.

THE PROTO-PLANET THEORY

The present theory is called the *proto-planet* theory. It is the result of the combined efforts of astronomers, mathematicians, chemists, and geologists. It gives unity to many of the details known about the solar system. Most astronomers are convinced that it correctly accounts for at least the broad features of the solar system's evolution.

The proto-planet theory assumes that a large cloud of gas and dust once filled the space where our solar system now is. This gas consisted of the "cosmic mix" of molecules found everywhere in the universe—principally hydrogen and helium, with much smaller amounts of oxygen, carbon, iron, and others. Small eddies developed within the cloud, as the entire volume turned in space like a giant whirlpool. The large eddy at the center contracted more rapidly than the rest of the cloud and formed the "proto-sun." Scientists believe that our sun developed from this swirling mass of gas and dust some 4.6 billion years ago.

In the cold depths of the cloud surrounding the proto-sun, certain gases combined to form compounds such as water and ammonia. Solid dust and metallic crystals appeared. Gradually, forces in the spinning cloud flattened it into the shape of an enormous disk. At a great distance, this disk would have looked somewhat like a gigantic revolving phonograph record, with the proto-sun at the center.

Within this whirling disk, eddies and swirls continued to appear. Some were torn apart in collision, while others were broken up by the increasingly strong gravitational pull of the proto-sun. As this battle continued in the wheeling system, some local swirls might gain material, and others might lose it. Finally a number of these swirls became swirling disks, large enough to hold together under the strength of their own gravitational fields. Each was a proto-planet, moving through space around the sun and sweeping up material left over from the original cloud.

As the proto-sun's mass was pulled together, collisions, compression, and radioactivity heated the mass until temperatures at the center reached millions of degrees. In a process called *thermonuclear fusion,* hydrogen atoms fused to form helium. This process is the source of the energy that has kept the sun ablaze ever since.

The thermonuclear fusion at the core of the proto-sun released large amounts of energy and caused the proto-sun to shine. At first a dull red, in time it became the golden yellow star that we see today. Because it was about one hundred times larger in diameter than the proto-planets, it became a star instead of a planet. Its gravitational pull was strong enough to trap light hydrogen atoms in its interior. These atoms fueled the thermonuclear fusion process.

Proto-earth and the other proto-planets were born as whirling clouds of ice particles and solid fragments—each a cosmic dust storm. This process has given another name to the proto-planet theory: the *dust-cloud hypothesis*. Later this material collected into a ball, sticking together because of the cohesive attraction of water and ice molecules. Thus, the proto-planets were formed by the accumulation of cold dusts from the region of space near the sun. (Even today, planets continue to sweep up dust and meteorites.)

Gradually, radioactive elements within the cold earth began to give off heat. After millions of years the temperature became high enough to melt the materials at the earth's center. The iron, nickel, and other heavy metals spread throughout the ball then began to sink, forming the molten core of the planet. Later, the molten rock at the core broke through fissures to the surface. This allowed molecules of hydrogen, water vapor, and other gases to escape, creating an atmosphere above the planet's surface. The lighter gases, especially hydrogen, did not stay in the atmosphere long. They left behind a high concentration of the heavier, rare elements of the universe—

elements essential for the formation of rocks, plants, and our own bodies.

Chapter 2. Study Guide Questions

1. What are the principal types of bodies within our solar system?
2. According to Kant, how did the solar system originate? Does this theory agree with the proto-planet theory?
3. When do most astronomers believe our sun and solar system developed?
4. What forces caused the sun and planets to develop from the cloud of gases and dust?
5. Explain thermonuclear fusion as it exists in the sun. Why does it occur?
6. How did the earth retain a concentration of heavier elements during its evolution?

Vocabulary

solar system	thermonuclear fusion
philosopher	helium
cosmic evolution	hydrogen
proto-planet	dust-cloud hypothesis
gravitational force	cohesive attraction
eddy, eddies	atmosphere

Chapter 3. The Moon

The earth and moon were probably formed at the same time, in about the same way. Studies of rock samples brought back by the *Apollo 11* and *Apollo 12* moon explorations have shown that the moon is about the same age as earth—about 4.6 billion years. The moon is the only natural satellite of the earth.

The moon is about one-fourth the earth's diameter, but not as dense. The moon is so large in relation to its parent planet that earth and moon are sometimes called the "double planet."

The moon's diameter is 2,160 miles. The moon is generally said to be about 239,000 miles away from earth; this, however, is an average distance. The distance actually varies

from about 226,000 miles at the closest to 252,000 miles at the farthest.

The moon circles the earth every $27\frac{1}{3}$ days. This period of time coincides with its rotation about its own axis. This accounts for the fact that the moon always has the same side facing the earth. In other words, the moon rotates once on its axis, and revolves once around the earth, in the same length of time.

The moon has no atmosphere. Thus, there is no gradual daily temperature change from hot to cold, as on earth. On the moon, a person partially in the sunlight and partially in the shade would feel extreme heat and cold at the same time. The moon's surface temperature may get as high as 243°F; in the dark of the lunar night, it goes down to −261°F.

Because there is no atmosphere on the

moon, there is no sound either. Also, since there is no obscuring effect such as that made by the earth's atmosphere, a person on the moon can see twice as many stars in the sky.

Moon Geography

Erosion on the moon takes place very slowly, because there is no rain or wind. However, our astronauts learned that the spray of the *breccia*—broken rocks from crashing meteorites—causes extensive erosion. The constant stream of atomic particles coming from the sun also causes a steady wearing away of the moon's surface rocks.

Among the lunar rocks returned to earth was one which scientists labeled *igneous*. This means that the rock was once molten, but later became solidified. This indicates that the moon, like the earth, has (or once had) a hot interior and volcanoes.

Some scientists believe it possible that the moon is both hot *and* cold. They believe it has a cold exterior shell or crust, perhaps 250–625 miles deep, surrounding a warm belt of rock, and possibly even a molten core. This would make it much like earth—except that the earth's outer crust, called the *lithosphere*, is only about 15 miles thick.

The surface walked on by the astronauts was covered by breccia. There also is a layer of dust made up of tiny glass *tektites*. These little spheres are no bigger than sand granules, and some are microscopic in size. They are multicolored, with hues ranging from dark brown to yellow to clear. Tektites make up one-quarter to one-third of the lunar dust. Many scientists believe that the beads are congealed rock droplets, formed when meteorites blasted the moon and sent out a spray of fine molten particles.

This breccia layer is so deep over the moon that for millions of years meteorites have not penetrated it. It probably will be many years before man will be able to find the bedrock of the moon—if such a bedrock does exist.

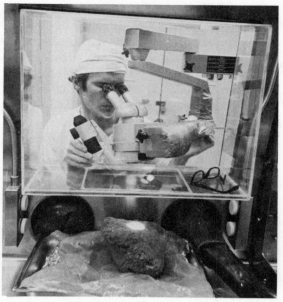

A test director at the Lunar Receiving Lab looks at basketball-sized moon rocks through a microscope.

The Lunar Receiving Laboratory of the National Aeronautics and Space Administration in Houston carefully examined all the lunar dust and rock samples brought back by the Apollo expeditions. Some rocks appeared to be rich in iron and magnesium; others sparkled with colorful crystals. When scientists burned a fragment of moon soil and studied its spectrograph, they found some 60 elements. The moon rocks appear to be rich in titanium, but with less than one-third of the sodium and potassium found in comparable igneous rocks on earth.

The Surface of the Moon

The surface of the moon is pockmarked with craters. The circular craters, easily seen through binoculars, have been visible for centuries. There are also smooth plains and mountain ranges on the moon's surface. Galileo mistook the plains for bodies of water and called each one a *mare* (plural, *maria*), the Latin word for "sea." The craters have been named in honor of scientists and philosophers. The mountain ranges are named after mountain ranges on earth.

The great black maria are younger than the rest of the moon. They cover up older craters and show less sign of meteorite bombardment. Radioactivity measurements of rocks from the Sea of Tranquillity show that they were made 3.6 billion years ago—a billion years later than the moon or the earth.

Some maria have definite magnetic fields. This was discovered when space exploration vehicles orbiting the moon experienced a higher pull of gravity over certain maria. Probably a massive body, such as an iron asteroid, lies under such maria. It is thought that the "seas" welled up when the lunar crust was punctured by a swarm of asteroids, some 2–3 billion years ago.

These buried super-heavy magnetic concentrations beneath the lunar surface have been named *mascons*. Mascons are much too heavy to remain on the surface of a molten body. But

This is a photo of the moon's dark side, taken by the *Apollo 10* Command and Service Module from an altitude of 60 nautical miles.

they are known to be near the moon's surface, because of the extra gravitational pull they exert on spaceships in lunar orbit. This lends strength to the belief that the moon's crust is strong and very thick. If this were not so, the mascons would have sunk into the deepest core of the moon—especially if the moon were a soft, molten body.

There are about 20 maria, and they cover about half of the moon's surface. Most are on the near side of the moon. The term "maria" has been retained, though now they are believed to be filled with lava or volcanic ash, not water. Through a telescope the maria look much darker than the craters or mountains. This is because the lunar plains have a lower *albedo*, a term used to define the percentage of light reflected from a surface. An object which reflected all light would have an albedo of 100 percent, while one which absorbed all light would have 0 percent. The moon is actually a rather poor reflector, with an albedo of only about 11 percent. The moon gives off no light of its own, but reflects the sun's light; moonlight, therefore, is reflected sunlight.

CRATERS

It is still not known how the moon's craters were formed. One theory says they were formed by the impact of huge meteorites. This theory is supported by the fact that craters on the moon look much like craters formed by meteorite collisions on the earth. Another theory states that craters were formed by volcanoes. If so, these volcanoes had to be far bigger than any known on earth. Another theory suggests that craters were formed by the bubbling action of the molten moon, as it cooled.

A seemingly infinite number of craters cover the moon's surface. The largest on the near side is Bailly, 183 miles in diameter; but several unnamed ones on the far side exceed 200 miles in diameter. The craters are the most striking formations on the moon, and they exist in all sizes. The typical crater has a surrounding ring, which is from 1,000 feet to 20,000 feet high.

Many smaller craters can quite positively be identified as the result of volcanic activity, probably the escape of gases and dusts from the moon's interior. Some of these can be compared to the earth's volcanic craters, which are formed when the earth's surface collapses into an underlying cavity from which lava has flowed. (Often a central peak remains in the center of such craters—for example, the island in Crater Lake, Oregon.) Though spectrographs have found eruptions of gas molecules leaving the moon's interior, these effects seem to be much less violent than those associated with volcanoes.

The most conspicuous crater is Tycho, in the moon's southern hemisphere. It is easily seen when the moon is full. Tycho has a great system of rays which radiate as far as 1,500 miles out from the edges of the crater. The crater Copernicus has a similar system. Rays are thought to be fine surface material, splattered out of the most recent craters. Some rays are chains of small craters, created by the explosive ejection of material during the formation of the main crater.

Moon Mountains and Rilles

The moon's mountain ranges lie in great arcs bordering the circular maria. Some of their peaks are as tall as the highest earth mountains. They are concentrated in the moon's southern hemisphere. With peaks sometimes rising more than 20,000 feet above the plains, lunar mountains are very rugged, since they are not eroded by wind, water, or ice.

A large telescope will also show that the moon's surface is covered with many cracks, called *rilles*. They are similar to shallow, flat-bottomed river beds on earth. There seems to be no connection between rilles and other surface features because they sometimes extend hundreds of miles, uninterrupted by mountains, valleys, or craters.

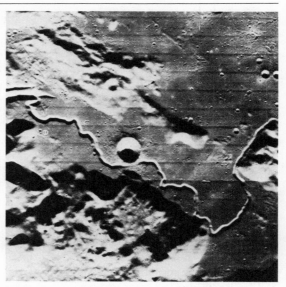

Rilles are cracks in the lunar surface similar to shallow, meandering river beds on the western deserts of the United States.

Moonquakes

The *Apollo 11* astronauts set up a moonquake detector at the Sea of Tranquillity. This detector was an instrument called a *passive seismometer,* a device which transmits reports of tremors on the moon's surface. Scientists had expected the moon to experience quakes similar to our earthquakes. But they found out that a moonquake causes the moon to vibrate in an entirely different way. Earth tremors are severe only for seconds; beyond the rather small area of the quake, only the finest instruments can record them. Moonquakes, however, cause the whole moon to vibrate for extended periods of time.

In only three weeks after its placement, the Tranquillity Base seismometer had registered 25 different tremors on the moon's surface. Fourteen of them were from avalanches of lunar rocks falling down the slopes of crater walls. When the *Apollo 12* lunar module was purposely crashed back on the surface of the moon in 1969, the shock set the whole moon vibrating for nearly an hour. It will take many years and many seismograph stations to explain this, and to find out how the interior of the moon is built.

PHASES OF THE MOON

The moon circles the earth in approximately one "moonth" or month. This movement takes 27⅓ days, in what is called the *sidereal month*. The moon's rotation about its own axis also takes 27⅓ days, which accounts for the same side always being toward the earth.

The interval between two successive conjunctions (alignments) of the moon with the sun is called the *synodical month*. This interval between new moons is about 29½ days.

The sidereal month is the true period of the moon's revolution, but the synodical month is better known to us, because it is the full cycle of the moon's phases. Calendars which picture the phases of the moon show the position of the moon with respect to the sun in the synodical month. The synodical month is often called a "lunation."

The moon's motion causes its phases. Since the moon shines only by reflected sunlight, the relative positions of the moon, earth, and sun determine how much of the moon we can see at a given time. At new moon, the moon is between the earth and the sun, with the dark side facing the earth. A day or so later the moon is seen as a thin, bow-shaped figure called a *crescent*. As the lighted part grows in size, the moon is said to *wax* to full moon. At full moon, the entire illuminated side is turned toward the earth, since it is exactly opposite the sun in the sky.

The full moon rises in the east as the sun sets in the west; thus, we can see it all night. When the moon is halfway between the new moon and the full moon, one-half of the moon is bright and it is in its first quarter; this means that the moon is a quarter of a circle (90°) away from the sun. After full moon, the lighted part gets smaller, and the moon is said to *wane*. It goes through its last quarter and back to new moon again. When more than half

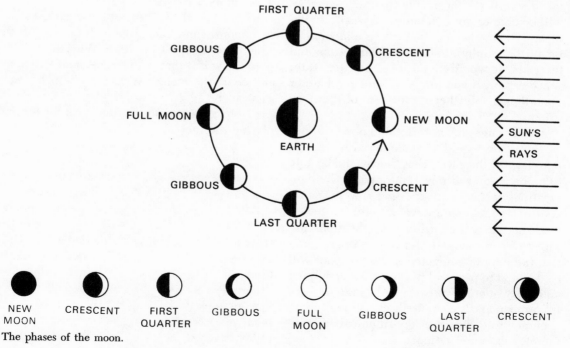

The phases of the moon.

of the moon is visible, between the first and last quarters, it is called *gibbous*.

Because the earth and moon are both solid bodies illuminated by the sun, they both cast cone-shaped shadows in space. Occasionally, the moon passes through the conical shadow of the earth. This event is known as a *lunar eclipse*. Such an eclipse can be either partial or total, depending upon how much of the moon enters the earth's shadow.

WHY EXPLORE THE MOON?

The moon has been mapped and charted with great precision. Telescopes and radio-telescopic photography enabled mappers to detail the lunar surface, years before the *Apollo 11* astronauts set foot on Tranquillity Base. In fact, maps of the moon are even more complete than those of some areas of the earth. This is because complete coverage of the moon's surface has been possible from observatories and satellites.

There are many practical reasons to explore our moon. It is conceivable that man someday will be able to mine the mineral wealth of the moon. The moon can also serve as a laboratory for further exploration of the solar system and the stars. It would be an ideal place to train space explorers and to provide them a base of operations for further exploration of the solar system.

Astronomical laboratories and observatories on the moon would be unhindered by the atmosphere of the earth; thus they would be able to probe greater distances into space. Communications relays or missile and transportation control stations could serve in a wide variety of constructive ways. Military applications are sure to be developed also, though one hopes that the steps of humanity into outer space will be devoted to peaceful purposes. The mapping and study of our own earth and its atmosphere from moon and space satellites will lend more accuracy to our current geographical and meteorological information.

Chapter 3. Study Guide Questions

1. How and when was the moon probably formed?
2. Why do we on earth always view the same side of the moon?
3. Why is there no gradual daily temperature change on the moon?
4. What causes erosion on the moon's surface?
5. What are breccia?
6. What are the "maria" and how did they get that name?
7. What are mascons? How were they discovered?
8. What is albedo? What is "moonlight?"
9. What caused most moon craters?
10. What is a volcanic caldera?
11. What are rays and rilles on the moon?
12. Explain the basic differences between a moonquake and an earthquake.
13. What is the purpose of a seismometer?
14. What are the phases of the moon? What does "gibbous" mean?
15. Explain the difference between the sidereal month and the synodical month. With which are we most familiar? Why?
16. How is it that man has been able to map and chart the moon's surface with such great accuracy?
17. What are some practical reasons for exploring the moon?

Vocabulary

astronaut	telescope
moonquake	lunar crater
Apollo 11	volcanic caldera
hazardous	seisomometer
inclination	sidereal month
erosion	synodical month
breccia	lunar eclipse
lithosphere	crescent
igneous rock	wax, wane
lunar mare, maria	irregularity
radioactivity	gibbous

Chapter 4. The Sun

The earth has been warmed by the light of the sun for 4.6 billion years. All life is maintained by the solar energy that is converted into chemical energy by plants. Moreover, the power from coal, petroleum, water, and winds can be also traced back to the sun. The sun, therefore, is the source of most of the world's energy. (The only exceptions are nuclear energy created by man, lunar tidal energy, and the heat produced in the interior of the earth by volcanoes and hot springs.)

The sun actually contains 99.86 percent of all the matter in our solar system. An "average" star, it is considered by astronomers to be medium-sized. It is composed of luminous gases. The sun's weight is about one million times that of earth. The sun's gravitational attraction is 270 times that of earth; consequently, a 100-pound keg of nails would weigh 27,000 pounds on the sun!

The average distance from the sun to the earth has been calculated to be 92,870,000 miles—nearly 93 million. This average distance is known as an *astronomical unit*, a huge unit of measure often used in describing distances within our solar system. The sun has a diameter of about 865,000 miles—about 109 times that of earth.

It is not possible for us to look directly at the sun without first protecting our eyes. Any attempt to do so will cause temporary blindness, unless some sort of filter or special fogged lens is used. The best way to see the sun is through a telescope—but *only* if using special precautions. Use this method: hold a white cardboard a foot or so behind the eyepiece, and focus the scope until the sun's edge appears sharp. *Never* look directly at the sun through a telescope or binoculars. The sun's rays will burn the retina of your eye, causing permanently impaired vision, or even blindness.

COMPOSITION OF THE SUN

Spectrographic evidence shows that the sun consists of gases at very high temperatures. The majority of these are concentrated under great pressures in the interior, possibly into a "core." Energy released by thermonuclear reactions in the core makes its way outward to the *photosphere*, the light-giving surface of the sun. The photosphere blends into the next layer, the *chromosphere*, which is the lowest layer of the sun's atmosphere.

Composed principally of hydrogen and gaseous calcium, the chromosphere has an average depth of 8,000–10,000 miles, with flame-like prominences often shooting far higher.

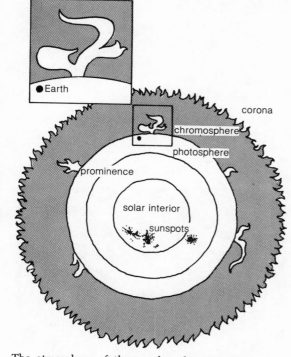

The atmosphere of the sun has three main layers. Innermost is the *photosphere*, the 200-mile thick layer from which visible light is emitted. Outward from this is the *chromosphere*, a layer of hydrogen and helium which extends from about 6,000 to 10,000 miles above the photosphere. Solar flares and prominences are often seen shooting from the chromosphere. Beyond the chromosphere is the sun's *corona*, a vast area of low-density gas, extending millions of miles into space.

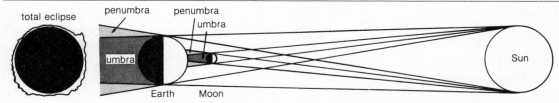

total eclipse — penumbra — penumbra — umbra — umbra — Earth — Moon — Sun

A solar eclipse. The umbra is the darkest part of the shadow of the moon on the earth's surface; the penumbra is the outer, or less dark part of the moon's shadow on the earth.

The chromosphere is visible only during eclipses of the sun, or by using a *coronagraph,* a telescope that uses a black disk to hide the sun's brightness.

It happens that the moon has almost the same visible size in the sky as the sun. Consequently, when the moon passes between the earth and the sun, the bright photosphere is sometimes completely covered, creating the glorious spectacle of a total eclipse of the sun, or *solar eclipse.*

From the chromosphere, shock waves carry the energy through a transition zone to the *corona,* the outermost layer of the sun's atmosphere. It is very large and very faint, and can be seen only in a total eclipse. The corona has been seen out to a distance of 7 million miles from the sun, and it is quite certain that the corona extends at least to the earth. Its low density, however, makes it invisible beyond the 7-million-mile limit.

Sunspots

Sunspots are whirling fountains of hot gas which have come out of the interior of the sun. Hotter than the surrounding gases of the photosphere, these fountains of gas rise through the chromosphere, expanding and then cooling. When cooling, they appear darker than the hotter and brighter environment behind them—thus earning the name "sunspots."

The sunspot may often be seen projecting well beyond the chromosphere as a *prominence.* An eruptive prominence extending more than 400,000 kilometers above the surface of the sun was photographed in 1973 by the Naval Research Laboratory's telescope

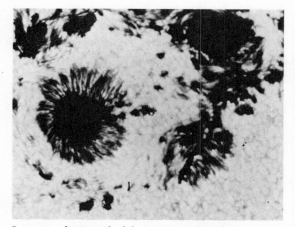

Sunspots photographed by a Navy balloonist from an altitude of 80,000 feet. The black spots are dark cores of relatively cool gases embedded in strong magnetic fields. Sunspots produce magnetic storms and major disturbances in radio broadcasts on earth.

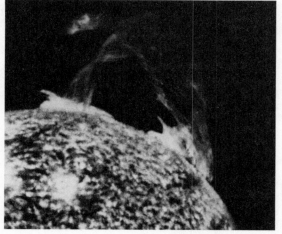

A photograph of the sun taken on 19 December 1973, from NASA's *Skylab 4.* This shows one of the most spectacular solar flares ever recorded, spanning more than 367,000 miles across the solar surface.

mounted on *Skylab.* Sunspots may last only a few minutes, or as long as a year and a half. There are times when few are seen, and other times when there are many. There does seem to be a sort of sunspot cycle, with the greatest number occurring about every eleven years.

It is believed that the sunspots are responsible for the beautiful and spectacular Aurora Borealis in the Arctic. Similar polar lights exist in the southern hemisphere, and are called Aurora Australis. Here is how these lights are created: The radiation pressure of the sun pushes some of the hot sunspot material completely away from the chromosphere. These gases are electrically charged since they came from the sun's interior, where atomic nuclei and electrons are separated. Some of these particles are drawn into the earth's atmosphere near the magnetic poles. There they form an electric field. When elements of oxygen and nitrogen collide with hydrogen, or re-form into complete atoms, radiation in the form of light is produced, causing an aurora.

Sunspots create electrical and electronic disturbances on earth. The great hydrogen flares erupting from the spots send x-rays and atomic particles racing thousands of miles beyond the planets of our solar system. This barrage is called the *solar wind.* This wind erodes the lunar surface, distorts comet tails, and even causes erratic changes in compass readings and the weather. It also affects the height of the ionosphere, causing fading and static in short-wave radio transmissions.

THE MAGNETOSPHERE

In Unit 6, Chapter 2, we named the levels of atmosphere above the surface of the earth. The outermost layer that we discussed is the exosphere, which extends to about 18,000 miles. But surrounding or overlapping the exosphere is the *magnetosphere.* The magnetosphere is formed by the sun's effect on the earth's magnetic field.

The metals within the earth make it act as a huge magnet, surrounded by a magnetic field. But this magnetic field does not dissipate into space. It is confined within the magnetosphere by the solar winds, which rush by at up to 900,000 miles per hour. The boundary of the magnetosphere is called the *magnetopause.* It is 40,000 miles from the earth's surface on the

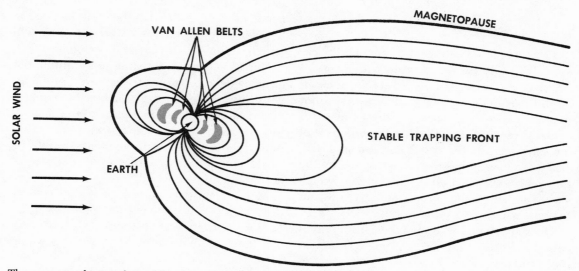

The magnetosphere is formed by the sun's effect on the earth's magnetic field. The outermost boundary of the magnetosphere is the magnetopause. Notice the location of the Van Allen radiation belts.

sunward side, and is drawn out into a huge comet-like tail, between three and four million miles long, on the side away from the sun. The magnetosphere changes its shape daily as the strength of the solar wind varies. This causes changes in the areas closer to the earth and affects radio transmission and the weather.

Inside the magnetosphere are huge numbers of charged particles which have been trapped by the earth's magnetic field. These particles circle the earth in 4 doughnut-shaped regions—1 man-made and 3 natural. The earth is in the doughnut hole and there are no trapped particles above or below the north and south poles. These rings are: the narrow *Starfish ring* caused by a U. S. hydrogen bomb exploded at a height of 250 miles in 1962; the *inner Van Allen radiation belt* containing high-energy protons; the *outer Van Allen belt* containing high-energy electrons; and the *stable trapping region,* containing lower-energy particles. This last region extends almost the whole length of the magnetosphere. The magnetosphere, then, is the region overlapping the exosphere, within which the magnetic field of the earth is confined by the solar wind. (For more on the Van Allen belts, see Unit 6, Chapter 2.)

The Sun's Energy

The sun produces gigantic amounts of energy. It can cause temperatures in excess of 100 degrees Fahrenheit, at a distance of about 93 million miles—as we well know on a hot summer's day. And consider this—the earth actually receives less than 1 two-*billionth* of the sun's energy, the rest being lost in space. The sun's energy passes through space by the process of radiation. It is this energy which warms us, grows our crops, and gives us our seasons, winds, and weather.

The sun actually is its own fuel. It literally is eating itself up at the rate of some 600 million tons of hydrogen each second. But it contains enough hydrogen to keep going at this rate for at least six billion more years!

We can take an imaginary journey to the center of the sun, as astronomers do, by means of mathematics. The 10,000-degree heat on the surface of the sun will melt, and then vaporize, any known substance. For every mile below the surface of the sun, the temperature rises 40°F. By the time we arrive at the core the temperature has risen to 15 *million* degrees. In that swirling cauldron, the hydrogen gases are being transformed into helium.

This process is called *nuclear fusion*. In the process, some of the hydrogen is destroyed; it reappears, with a tremendous burst of energy, as radiation. This "cooking" process takes millions of years, but the radiation eventually becomes visible sunlight, after escaping from the sun's surface. A process similar to the one going on in the sun was used to develop the hydrogen bomb.

Solar Energy: Answer to the World's Energy Problem?

The direct use of the sun's energy is of great and immediate importance. Most of the world's energy needs are still being met through the use of water power, coal, and petroleum. These sources, however, are not enough to keep pace with the rapid increase in the demand for energy. Moreover, we will someday run out of coal and petroleum.

Nuclear energy is assisting to a limited, but growing degree. There are, however, problems with this form of energy—such as the dangers of radioactive contamination, and the difficulties in disposing of radioactive wastes. Uranium fuel itself is not in abundant supply on earth. Thus, alternative sources of energy must be found and developed.

Many scientists in government and industry are looking for ways to use the sun's power. By harnessing even a small fraction of this virtually inexhaustible source of power, we would solve the world's energy problem. Solar furnaces, batteries, and motors, and solar heating of buildings and houses have been tried successfully. But these have been used only on a limited scale, because of the high costs. When the problems of solar energy are solved in a cheap and practical way, the standard of living of the entire world is certain to rise. The opportunities for astronomers and scientists in the area of solar power and energy development are unlimited. Along with the oceanographic development of the seas and the conservation of our natural and human resources, research in solar energy will determine the future of humanity.

Chapter 4. Study Guide Questions

1. What is the source of most of the earth's energy? What are the exceptions?
2. How far is the earth from the sun?
3. Why is it so dangerous to look at the sun through any kind of lens?
4. What is the composition of the sun? List and describe each succeeding major layer.
5. What is the corona? What is a coronagraph?
6. What is the importance of sunspots to the earth?

7. What is the magnetosphere? Explain the effect which the solar winds have on the magnetosphere.
8. How does the sun's energy get to the earth?
9. How is the sun its own fuel?
10. Is solar energy the answer to the world's shortage of fuels for energy?
11. What problems exist in the use of nuclear energy for power?
12. What three "sciences" may well determine the future of humanity?

Vocabulary

solar energy
luminous gas
astronomical unit
photosphere
chromosphere
corona
coronagraph
prominence
sunspot
auroras: Borealis,
    Australis

solar eclipse
transition zone
cauldron
magnetosphere
exosphere
magnetopause
uranium
fission process
radioactive
    contamination
ionosphere

Chapter 5. The Stars

The stars are distant suns in space. The closest star, of course, is the sun. But the universe contains literally billions upon billions of stars. The sun is 93 million miles away; the next closest star is Alpha Centauri—about 26.46 *trillion* miles distant. It readily becomes apparent that we are talking of distances which are mind-boggling. Miles or kilometers are useless in measuring such vast spaces. Thus, the *light-year* has been adopted as the common unit of astronomical distances.

A light-year is the distance that light travels in a year. This distance is, for practical purposes, nearly 6 trillion miles. Remember that a light year is a unit of *distance* and not a unit of *time*, even though the word "year" is used. It's

a bit like when you describe the distance to some location as "a 20-minute drive" or a "15-minute walk." When an astronomer says some star is "10 light-years away," he means that it takes light 10 years to travel from the star to his observatory.

Even when using light-years to measure cosmic distances, the numbers can become huge. Modern telescopes can see out to distances of several billion light-years. This means, in fact, that astronomers are looking back "into time." They see distant stars and galaxies as they were millions or billions of years ago, since it has taken their light that long to arrive on earth. The light which is leaving the stars tonight will not reach here for countless centuries. Since radio waves and light waves travel at the same speed, any "communication" directed at beings in distant galaxies would not be received for many years.

Because of the development of larger and better telescopes, astronomers have begun to use a special astronomical unit, called the *parsec*. To understand the fundamentals of such a measurement, it is necessary to first explain the term *parallax*.

Parallax And Parsecs

Parallax is the apparent change of position of an object when viewed from two different points which are not on the same straight line with that object. The parallax effect can be simply demonstrated: Hold your finger at arm's length and look at it, first with one eye, then with the other. The finger will appear to jump back and forth as you alternate eyes.

To measure the distance to a star, astronomers observe the star against a background of stars much farther away. The telescope takes the place of your eye and the star takes the place of your finger. To measure the distance to the moon by the parallax method, astronomers use the radius of the earth (4,000 miles) as a base line. The distance to a star, however, is much too great to use that base; there would be no measurable angle for our triangle. Therefore, astronomers use the diameter of the earth's orbit (186 million miles) as the base line. They can thereby measure the shift of certain stars with respect to the background stars.

Because the earth is on the opposite side of the sun every six months, photographs are taken at that interval to see how much the apparent position of the star has shifted due to the movement of the earth. One-half of the amount that the star has shifted is called the *stellar parallax*. The parallax shift of even "nearby" stars is extremely small; closer stars have a greater shift than do more distant ones.

If the parallax angle of a star is 1 second ($\frac{1}{3600}$th of a degree), its distance is called 1 *parsec*. This word is a combination of the first

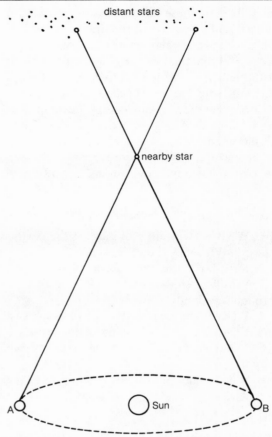

Parallax. To an observer at A, the nearby star appears to be in a slightly different position among the distant stars than it appears at B. The apparent shift tells us the distance from earth of the nearby star.

three letters of the words "parallax" and "second." The calculated value of 1 parsec is about 20 trillion miles, or 3.26 light-years.

Mentioned earlier, Alpha Centauri is 26,460,000,000 miles away; that translates to about 4.4 light-years, or 1.4 parsecs. Our sun is the only star which is nearer to us than 1 parsec.

Stars Classified

The nature of a star can best be determined from its spectrum, though other information is also necessary. Because of the stars' spectral differences, scientists classify them according to their temperature and color. This information, along with data on brightness and distance, has enabled astronomers to develop a *spectrum-luminosity diagram*. This diagram divides the stars into distinct groups according to their color (spectrum) and their magnitude or stellar brightness (luminosity). The term *luminosity* refers to the brightness of a star as compared to the brightness of the sun.

The spectrum-luminosity diagram, then, shows the relationship between the color and magnitude of a star. In general, blue stars are large and bright. Red stars are usually smaller and dimmer, though there are a number of well-known giant and super-giant red stars. Colors range from blue through white, yellow, orange, and red. The sun, a yellow star, is an average star in brightness and temperature.

The *apparent magnitude* of a star is its

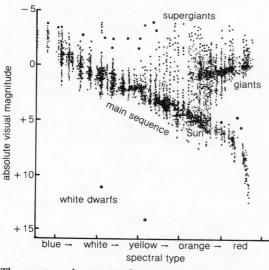

The spectrum-luminosity diagram shows the relationship between the color and magnitude of a star. Red dwarf stars are cooler and less bright than our own sun and are found below the "main sequence." The main sequence comprises 98 percent of all stars. As helium builds up the centers of stars, they get their hottest and most brilliant, and become blue giants. As they age, blue giants cool, and move off the main sequence to become red giants, supergiants, and finally white dwarfs.

brightness as it appears to an observer on earth. The *absolute magnitude* is its brightness as seen from a standard distance—10 parsecs, or 32.6 light-years. First-magnitude stars are about 100 times brighter than those of sixth magnitude. The ratio of 2.51 for a difference of one magnitude (2.51 multiplied by itself five times is approximately 100) is the base of the magnitude scale used in modern astronomy. Stars fainter than the sixth magnitude can only be seen through a telescope. The sun has a $+5$ absolute magnitude.

The giant stars are given an absolute magnitude of 0, which makes them 100 times brighter than the sun. There are even brighter stars called *supergiants* which are as much as one million times as bright.

The most interesting class, however, is the one called *white dwarfs*. These stars are at least 100 times fainter than the sun, but are much hotter. They have about the same mass as the sun, but are smaller in size. The white dwarfs have densities much greater than any substance known on earth. A cubic inch of material from one of these stars could weigh as much as a ton. An ordinary finger ring would weigh 75 pounds.

Of the more familiar stars, Rigel, Polaris (the North Star), and Antares are supergiants; Arcturus and Capella are giants. Vega, Altair, and the sun are medium-sized stars in the group called the *main sequence* on the spectrum-luminosity scale. The main sequence comprises 98 percent of all stars presently observed by astronomers.

CEPHEID STARS

One way astronomers can determine a star's brightness is by using Cepheid stars as reference. These bright stars expand and contract with a definite rhythm; thus they are called *cepheid variables*. They are sometimes called the "lighthouses of space." The cepheid variables are hottest when they are at maximum brightness and coolest when they are at minimum brightness. Their variations in brightness are usually about one magnitude. There also are changes in the spectrum radiations as the star's brightness varies.

When the star contracts, its internal pressure and temperature increase. The star must expand in a sort of explosion. Once the star has expanded, the balance is again upset—so the star contracts again, under its gravitational attraction. Another name for the cepheid variable, because of this alternating phenomenon, is *pulsating star.*

The discovery of the relationship between the period of variation and the brightness of pulsating stars has enabled astronomers to use them for measuring distances in space, where no other method works. By noting how many days it takes the star to grow bright and dim, they can deduce the real brightness of the star, and consequently how far away it is. When the parallax method is impossible, because of extreme distance, cepheid variables provide the only available method for calculating star distances.

THE LIFE CYCLE OF A STAR

A star begins as a huge, cold, dark sphere of gas and dust. Where or how this original star material was formed is not known. Some astronomers believe it came from the ashes of stars long gone; others say it had been present since the "beginning." No one knows when that was, of course; and there are those who think that the universe didn't have a beginning, but has always existed. Astronomers are still trying to find the answers to these questions.

But we do know that stars are being born today, out of the gas and dust of the Milky Way, our galaxy of stars. Because of advances in astronomy and nuclear physics, the major stages in the life of a star have been fairly well determined.

The main factor determining what kind of star will be born is how much gas and cosmic dust become locked together by gravity in that particular area. If there is a lot of material available there, the star will probably end up as a brilliant blue giant. If it is like most stars, it will become a yellow star like our sun, with a much longer "life" than a blue giant. With even less dust and gas, it will become an orange dwarf that will live on for billions of years.

It perhaps seems somewhat unusual that the brighter stars have a shorter life. Actually this is rather easily explained. The more fuel there is to burn, the greater the heat and the consumption rate; so, comparatively speaking, the brighter star is burning itself out faster. The rate of fuel consumption is set at the beginning, and doesn't vary. Once the hydrogen-to-helium fusion cycle begins, it will continue until the hydrogen is expended.

In Chapter 4, we described the birth of the sun. Thus we need not explain the entire cycle of the birth of a star again. By way of review, though, we know that the radiation pressure eventually builds up toward the center of the gas-dust ball. As the temperature and pressure increase, the ball begins to glow. When the nuclear furnace starts working full-time, the whole swirling gas ball glows, sending its nuclear radiation out into space in the form of sunlight.

Most astronomers believe there is a "normal" evolution of stars. As the helium content builds up in the center, leftover hydrogen accumulates, upsetting the internal balance of the star. To compensate, the star increases in size and luminosity, until about one-eighth of the original hydrogen has been transformed to helium. The star continues to increase in size, finally becoming a blue giant. As a giant, the star consumes fuel at a tremendous rate, until its hydrogen is exhausted.

The helium produced in thermonuclear fusion actually is the star's ashes. But the helium ashes also burn as the pile grows, gradually changing into heavier elements. Eventually the ashes themselves are gone, and after a final burst in size and brilliance, the star collapses or explodes, and disintegrates.

Most of the bright stars we can see in a clear evening are stars in the giant or supergiant stages, edging closer to their last burst of glory. A few are bright new ones, and others are ordinary ones that are close enough to appear very bright.

Novae: New Stars

Sometimes a star appears in the sky for the first time in recorded astronomical history. These stars have been called *novae* (plural form of *nova,* the Latin word for "new"). Even more rarely this new star is a *supernova* which blazes forth with a luminosity as much as a million times that of an ordinary star.

Records of these "new stars" appear in accounts as far back as 134 B.C. when the ancient Greek astronomer Hipparchus observed one in the constellation Scorpius. Chinese records tell of a brilliant star appearing in the daytime sky in 1054 A.D. Tycho Brahe, a German astronomer, found one in the constellation Cassiopeia in 1572 and observed it until it disappeared in 1574. Others have been found throughout history, including at least five in the 20th century.

Since these stars appear suddenly and disappear relatively quickly—after only a few days for supernovae, and a year or two for other novae—they are now more correctly called "temporary stars." Novae really are not new stars at all. This is proved by the fact that they last so short a time.

Actually, novae are in the very last stages of star life. Due to the instability which develops in their nuclear core in the end of their life as giants, their nuclear furnace finally explodes. After the explosion, it is thought that the star returns to about its original state, but with a loss of mass. It becomes a huge expanding gas and dust cloud, surrounding a small dense core. This atmosphere remains lighted by the core embers. After a year or two, it can be photo-graphed through a large telescope as a gaseous cloud, called a *planetary nebula.*

Nebulae

Some nebulae are easily visible through a telescope; thus they can be studied very minutely through the spectrograph. Nebulae are among the most beautiful of all astronomical bodies.

There are three kinds of nebulae. The *bright nebula* glows and is easily visible, because there is a bright star nearby which illuminates it. A *dark nebula* is composed of the same gas and dust as the bright nebula, but it is visible only because it is silhouetted against the stars behind it; there is no illuminating star in the region of a dark nebula.

The third kind is the *planetary nebula;* this is actually a nova or temporary star, with a large cloud of particles surrounding it as the result of the stellar explosion. These nebulae show considerable surface detail, even though they are much less dense than planets.

Binaries and Star Clusters

Stars have a tendency to cluster together due to gravitational attraction. Pairs of stars are called *binaries,* or *double stars.* Larger groups of stars are referred to as *star clusters.*

Clusters are classified both by their appearance and their "population." A *moving cluster*

The Whirlpool Nebula. This is a bright spiral nebula.

A globular cluster named Messier 3. Globular clusters contain thousands of stars. Clusters form a system nearly spherical in shape.

contains a few stars that travel in parallel lines. *Open clusters* are loosely grouped stars, often found in areas where there are glowing masses of dust and gas. Most open clusters are found in the Milky Way, so they often are called galactic clusters. *Globular clusters* contain thousands of stars—too many to count, even with the best photography. They may contain as many as 100,000 stars. *Star clouds* are clusters in which the stars are so thick that they look like glowing clouds.

THE GALAXIES

On a clear night you can see what appears to be a wispy cloud extending across the northern sky. It is in fact a vast band of stars called the Milky Way—our own *galaxy*. A galaxy is a huge collection of stars, star clusters, dust, and gas, all held together by gravitation.

When people refer to "the galaxy" they usually mean the Milky Way, since it is our own island universe. It is shaped like a giant disc or pinwheel, with more stars in the center than at the edges. It is estimated to be 80,000–100,000 light-years from one edge to the other; from top to bottom is 10,000–15,000 light-years. The Milky Way contains over 100 billion stars, revolving about a common center in the constellation Sagittarius. These stars revolve at fantastic speeds.

The sun is located about two-thirds of the distance from the center of the galaxy to its outer rim. The sun and the rest of our solar system revolve around the center of the galaxy, moving at a speed of about 150 miles per second. Still, it takes about 225 million years for us to complete one journey.

The galaxy looks much like a spiral nebula; in fact, earlier astronomers thought the Milky Way was a nebula. But modern telescopes clearly show that the galaxy is composed of billions of stars too far away to be distinguished as separate points of light. The Milky Way is best seen on a clear summer night, running across the sky from north to south.

As crowded as the stars in the Milky Way appear, we see only a fraction of the actual number because of the huge amount of gas and dust fogging up the space between the stars. Most of the stars in the center of the galactic swirl are thus blocked from view.

All the stars in our galaxy can be placed in two distinct groups. These groupings are called *Population I* and *Population II*. The basis of these classifications is their location in the galaxy. Population I stars are found in regions where there is a great deal of dust and gas. These are young stars which are still growing and adding mass. The stars in the neighborhood of our sun belong to Population I, as do the open clusters.

Population II stars are older stars, located in regions essentially free of dust and gas. They have used up the available supply of raw material from space and are near the end of their lives as luminous stars.

There are billions of other galaxies, each

containing billions of stars. Each galaxy is separated from neighboring galaxies by oceans of space. Many of the galaxies have cepheid variables in the outer regions of their formations, as well as temporary stars and some supernovae. Galaxies may be classified, according to their shapes, into three different groups: (1) *ellipsoidal galaxies,* which have rather clearly defined symmetrical shapes, ranging from spheres to ellipsoids; (2) *spiral galaxies,* which have a distinct nucleus with one or more spiral arms; (3) *irregular galaxies,* which have no regular shape.

Chapter 5. Study Guide Questions

1. What are the stars?
2. After the sun, what star is closest to the earth?
3. What is the most common unit of astronomical distance? In miles, what distance does it represent?
4. Why is communication with distant galaxies impractical at the present time?
5. What is a common method of determining cosmic distances to stars?
6. How are stars classified? What are the principal star colors?
7. What does "luminosity" mean?
8. What is the difference between apparent and absolute magnitude of stars?
9. What is the "main sequence" of stars? What is the spectrum-luminosity scale?
10. What is so unique about white dwarf stars?
11. What are Cepheid stars?
12. What is believed to be the sequence in the life cycle of a star?
13. What is the principal factor determining what kind of star will be "born?"
14. Why do brighter stars have shorter lives?
15. What is thought to be the normal evolution of stars?
16. What are novae?
17. What is a nebula? What are the three kinds of nebulae?
18. What are binaries?
19. How are star clusters classified?
20. What is a galaxy? To which galaxy does our solar system belong?
21. What is the shape of the Milky Way?
22. What is the difference between the two population groupings in our galaxy?
23. How are galaxies classified? What are the three classifications?

Vocabulary

light-year
parsec
parallax
stellar distance
luminosity
stellar magnitude
cepheid variable
main sequence
star evolution
constellation

nova, -ae
nebula, -ae
fluorescent
supernova
binaries
galaxy
Milky Way
spiral galaxy
ellipsoidal galaxy
irregular galaxy

Chapter 6. The Planets

There are nine known planets in our solar system. Named in order outward from the sun, they are: Mercury, Venus, the earth, Mars, Jupiter, Saturn, Uranus, Neptune, and Pluto. Planets circle the sun in regular orbits, and in that respect are similar to the earth. Venus and Mars have some additional similarities to the earth; but the other planets are quite different.

Mercury scorches under the intense rays of the sun. The outer planets are strange cold worlds, surrounded by poisonous atmospheric gases and chemicals uncommon on the earth.

The planets are wanderers in the sky; the word "planet" actually means "wanderer." They are called that because they are constantly moving about the sun in their orbits. Since they are moving, it is difficult to keep track of them without some sort of star chart.

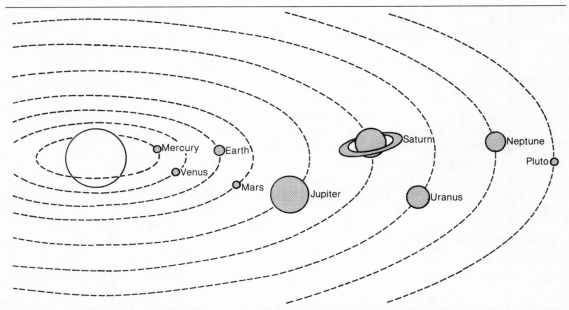

The planets of our solar system. The planets orbit the sun in the same direction and generally in the same plane. The usual reference to which the orbital planes of the planets are referred is the plane of the Earth's orbit about the sun, called the plane of the ecliptic. Each planet's heliocentric path is an ellipse which varies in most cases only slightly from a circle.

A chart which serves as a timetable for the movement and location of the planets is called a *daily star almanac* or an *ephemeris.*

The planets orbit the sun in the same direction and generally in the same plane. The earth's orbit about the sun, called *the plane of the ecliptic,* is the usual reference to which all the other orbital planes are compared. The planets' orbits around the sun are each in the shape of an ellipse—just a slight variation from a circle. The gravitational pull of the sun keeps the planets in their orbits; were it not for this gravity, the planets would continue moving in a straight line. You might compare the orbital plane to a phonograph record—the sun is at the center, and each planet's orbit falls into the proper groove outward from the center.

Although planets are much smaller than stars, they are also much closer to us, so that a telescope can magnify them. Five planets can be seen without a telescope—Mercury, Venus, Mars, Jupiter, and Saturn. Uranus is just at the

limit of visibility, and Neptune and Pluto can be seen only with a telescope.

The planets Venus, Mars, Jupiter, and Saturn are sometimes called the "Big Four," because they are so easily visible. Venus can only be seen just after sunset or before sunrise, because its orbit is between that of the earth and the sun. It is thus called the *evening star* or *morning star.* Mars, Jupiter, and Saturn have orbits which lie outside that of the earth. Thus they can be seen all night, even when the sun is on the opposite side of the earth from us. The Big Four are brighter than any of the stars and do not twinkle as stars do. They appear as discs instead of points of light, because of their relative nearness. The planets, like our moon, shine only by reflected sunlight.

On page 223 is a table comparing statistics concerning each of the planets with those of the earth. The time it takes a planet to go around the sun is called its *orbital period.* Also shown in the table are distances from the sun,

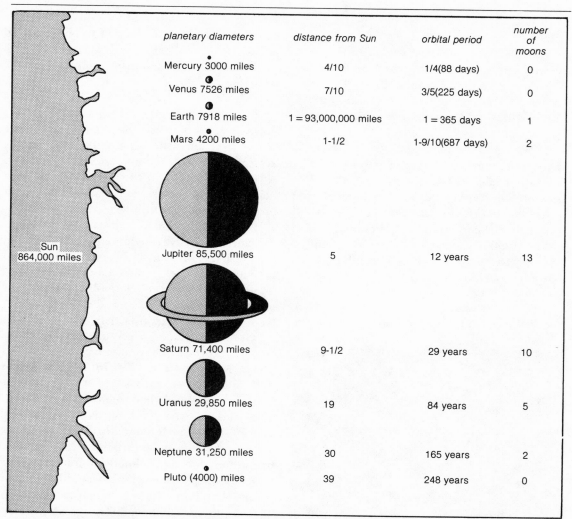

planetary diameters	distance from Sun	orbital period	number of moons
Mercury 3000 miles	4/10	1/4(88 days)	0
Venus 7526 miles	7/10	3/5(225 days)	0
Earth 7918 miles	1 = 93,000,000 miles	1 = 365 days	1
Mars 4200 miles	1-1/2	1-9/10(687 days)	2
Jupiter 85,500 miles	5	12 years	13
Saturn 71,400 miles	9-1/2	29 years	10
Uranus 29,850 miles	19	84 years	5
Neptune 31,250 miles	30	165 years	2
Pluto (4000) miles	39	248 years	0

Sun 864,000 miles

A planet table. Distances, diameters, and periods are all given in terms of the earth's distance from the sun, diameter, and period. The earth's distance from the sun (93,000,000 miles) is called the astronomical unit. It is an important "measuring stick" used by astronomers in measuring distances in our solar system.

structural diameters, and the number of moons each planet has.

Sometimes the planets seem to go backwards in their orbits, that is, east to west. This backing up, or *retrograde motion,* is easily explained. The best example of observable retrograde motion is with the planet Mars. Mars travels slower than the earth does, since it is farther from the sun. Thus, when the earth comes along on its orbit, it catches up to Mars and literally overtakes it—like a car passing another on a highway. Mars then seems to be moving backwards, or in retrograde motion, as viewed from earth.

Mercury, Venus, and Pluto do not have satellite moons. All others except earth have two or more; Saturn and Jupiter have 10 and 13, respectively. Galileo discovered the first four of Jupiter's moons in 1610 after he developed one of the first telescopes.

Mercury

Mercury is the smallest planet in the solar system. Its temperature is so high on the sunny side that it has no atmosphere. The temperature is 800°F on the lighted side, and −300°F on the dark side. Since there is no atmosphere, there is no erosion.

TV cameras mounted on the *Mariner 10* spacecraft observed Mercury in 1974 and 1975. It has a heavily cratered, dusty surface like that of the moon, and a large core of iron somewhat like earth. Mercury has a series of cliffs called *rupes,* up to two miles high, which cut across the surface for hundreds of miles. They probably formed about four billion years ago when cooling of the planet's core crumpled the crust.

Mercury was named for the speedy messenger of the gods in Greek mythology. It has the shortest period of revolution about the sun, 88 days. The planet is difficult to observe, but it is best seen just after sunset in March and April and just before sunrise in September and October.

A photograph of a densely cratered region of the planet Mercury, taken by a *Mariner 10* TV camera in 1974. The photo was taken from a range of about 47,000 miles above the planet's surface.

Venus

It was once believed that Venus was almost a twin sister of earth, because the two planets are so nearly alike in size, mass, and density. Astronomers of the 17th and 18th centuries believed Venus to be very warm, but with plentiful water and lush vegetation, and probably peopled by small dark-skinned people.

Since 1962, five Soviet and three United States spacecraft have observed Venus. Two unmanned Soviet craft have successfully landed on its surface. These observations plus extensive studies by radar and radio telescope have convinced scientists that the planet is a very unlikely place for life of any kind.

The most recent probe was the United States' *Mariner 10* in 1974–75, in conjunction with the Mercury flight. *Mariner 10* found that there is no water and no free oxygen on Venus. The surface temperature is a scorching 900°F—hot enough to melt lead and zinc. The atmosphere is even less friendly. A deep layer of carbon dioxide, a hundred times heavier than the earth's atmosphere, would bear down on an inhabitant with the weight of the ocean at a depth of 3,300 feet. The great heat on Venus is caused by what is commonly called the "greenhouse" effect, in which the heavy layer of carbon dioxide traps entering sunlight, preventing the escape of heat energy. The dense atmosphere keeps the intense heat evenly distributed around the planet, with little variation between day and night or from pole to pole. Vision in this atmosphere of carbon dioxide would be limited to a few hundred feet, since only 2 percent of the sun's light breaks through the cloud layers to the surface. The light which breaks through is further scattered by the carbon dioxide molecules.

The thick cloud cover makes it nearly impossible to observe any surface features. However, the area in which the Soviet *Venera 8* spacecraft landed appeared to be composed of loosely packed granite.

The earth turns once on its axis every day, but Venus turns only once in 225 days. A solar day on Venus is 117 days from one sunrise to the next, but because of the super-refractivity (extreme bending of light rays by the ultradense atmosphere), no one on the Venusian surface could tell the difference. Unlike most planets, Venus spins clockwise, opposite to its orbit around the sun.

Photographed by *Mariner 10,* the clouds above Venus race at more than 200 miles per hour from east to west. These clouds lie up to 40 miles above the huge shallow craters which have been detected on the surface. Above the clouds, a haze extends another 15 miles. Findings sent back so far do not reveal the composition of the inner cloud layers. The tops, however, seem to consist mainly of fine sulfuric-acid droplets—a mist which is thought to be more corrosive than automobile-battery acid.

Venus, named for the Roman goddess of beauty, is a grim and lifeless inferno hidden behind its clouds. But to us on earth, Venus is often the brightest object in the sky, besides the moon and sun. Venus can never be seen late at night because its orbit lies between the earth and the sun. Venus shines most brightly when it is between us and the sun, even though the sunlight falls on the side away from us, for the planet is closest to us at that time. It can be seen only shortly after sunset or before sunrise; thus it is always either an evening or morning "star."

MARS

Of all the planets in our solar system, Mars, the fourth from the sun and the next one beyond earth, has aroused the greatest interest. Named after the Roman god of war, it is often

A global mosaic of the planet Mars. It is made of more than 1,500 computer-corrected television pictures taken by *Mariner 9* in 1971–72. The residual north pole ice cap is at the top.

called the "red" planet. It is not as easily recognized as Venus or Jupiter because it is not as bright. But Mars's red color, and its rapid movement from west to east among the stars, make it stand out in the sky.

The best time for viewing Mars is when it is nearest to the earth in August and September. In those months it sometimes comes as close as 30 million miles. In February and March it is over 60 million miles distant, and much less easily viewed. It is best seen when in direct opposition—that is, when the earth is directly between the sun and Mars.

Many scientists of the past thought Mars capable of supporting some kind of life. Italian astronomer Giovanni Schiaparelli announced the discovery of straight lines on the Martian surface in 1877 and called them *canali*—channels or canals. Many people believed that the canali must have been man-made to be so straight. Or perhaps they were created by free-flowing water; this also would imply that Mars is capable of supporting some kind of life.

Extensive photography from the Mariner series of space probes have revealed nothing substantial concerning the canali; in fact, the canali have proven to be an illusion. It is possible that there are narrow regions or shadows of areas which change color with the seasons and provide some sort of symmetry, but the whole canal theory has largely faded into nothing.

In 1969 and 1970, *Mariner 6* and *Mariner 7* made a six-month-long journey to photograph Mars, looking specifically for life on the planet. But they found no sign of living things or an environment that could support them. The landscape appeared barren and there was no evidence of water.

Mariner 9, by extensive photography of the Martian surface, revealed that water in great torrents must have once washed over the planet to form great canyons, meandering hundreds of miles across the surface. There is a possibility that torrential rains, caused by variations in the planet's orbit around the sun, occur on a 50,000-year cycle. Today, however, Mars has a grim lunar-like landscape, pockmarked with craters.

The Martian atmosphere contains small amounts of oxygen and water vapor, but not enough to sustain animal life as we know it on earth. The atmosphere is only about 1 percent as dense as earth's—about the same as our atmosphere 20 miles up.

Thin white clouds appear in the Martian atmosphere each afternoon, and a veil of haze shrouds each polar region during the winter seasons. The polar regions grow and shrink during the winters, which appear to be similar to earth seasons. The Martian polar ice is a thin layer of frozen carbon dioxide with tiny amounts of frozen water vapor.

Fierce Martian winds whip up huge dust storms of the pinkish-colored iron oxide which covers about three-fourths of the Martian surface. The Martian wind storms may rage for months, at speeds of up to 300 miles per hour, covering much of the planet with swirling reddish and yellowish dust clouds. The dust of Mars is extremely fine, something like fine talcum powder. This dust sometimes is carried 35 miles above the Martian surface.

Huge inactive volcanoes exist on the Martian surface. Nix Olympica (Snow of Olympus) is the size of the state of Nebraska; it rises 15 miles above the surrounding terrain and has a main crater 40 miles in diameter. A volcano named South Spot has the largest volcanic crater on Mars, measuring 75 miles across!

Temperatures on Mars range from near 32°F in the early afternoon to more than −135°F just before sunrise. The surfaces of the darker areas may be 40 degrees warmer due to absorption of the sun's rays. But because of the thin atmosphere, the air a few feet above the ground may be as much as 80 degrees cooler than the surface itself. The daily temperature

Closeup of the great Martian volcano Nix Olympica. This volcanic mountain rises 15 miles above the flat plain and is more than 370 miles wide at its base.

range of 180 degrees would be extremely uncomfortable, if not fatal, to the earth's higher organisms. The polar regions seem to have fairly constant temperatures of about −190°F.

Mars is about twice the diameter of the moon and about half that of earth. While the earth has a surface area of 197 million square miles, Mars is only about one-quarter that size, 55½ million square miles. Mars's gravity is only about one-third (.38) of the earth's. That means a man weighing 150 pounds on earth would weigh only about 57 pounds on Mars.

A NASA Viking spacecraft landed safely on Mars in 1976. Carrying cameras, sensors, and radio-controlled arms, the Viking retrieved and analyzed samples of Martian soil and rocks. The analyses were sent back to earth. In what has been the most detailed search for life on Mars so far, the results have proven negative—as have all previous attempts.

JUPITER

Jupiter is the fifth planet from the sun. Larger than all the other planets put together, its diameter is more than 10 times that of earth. It orbits some 484 million miles from the sun and never comes closer to the earth than 367 million miles. Despite its great distance, it usually outshines everything in the night sky, except the moon and Venus.

Named after the king of the Roman gods, Jupiter remained an almost complete mystery until NASA's *Pioneer 10* passed within 82,000 miles of its cloud tops in December 1973. *Pioneer 11* moved to within 27,000 miles a year later to find out more.

Jupiter can easily retain all kinds of gases in its atmosphere, especially hydrogen and helium. The whirling planet rotates so swiftly that a day is only 10 hours long. The force of Jupiter's gravity is such that a 150-pound man would weigh 350 pounds at the equator and 425 pounds at either pole.

Travel to Jupiter by astronauts is beyond the most advanced space technology today. The

A view of the planet Jupiter from *Pioneer 10* shows the cloud tops and the famous red spot. The picture was taken in December 1973. The red spot is 25,000 miles long. It is possible that the spot is a "permanent hurricane."

21-month trip itself would be beyond the capability of present life-support systems. Also, communications would have a 45-minute lag because of the tremendous distance. Temperatures above the planet's cloud layer are about −200°F; and much higher temperatures, possibly in the thousands of degrees, exist closer in. The chief peril, however, comes from Jupiter's radiation belts. Lethal doses of radiation, 1,000 times more than a human being could stand, were sustained by *Pioneer 10* for several hours prior to its point of closest approach. It seems possible that Jupiter is surrounded by radiation belts similar to the earth's Van Allen belts.

The atmosphere of Jupiter is made up mostly of hydrogen and helium. There also are small but extremely important amounts of methane, ammonia, and water. Wide circling bands of white, yellow, brown, and gray make up much of Jupiter's face. Inside these belts of clouds there is much turbulence, and jet streams race through the area. Farther in, after an area of relatively clear atmosphere, there is a darker cloud deck. It consists of dark yellow, orange, and brown clouds, composed mainly of icy particles of ammonium hydrosulfide. The innermost layer of clouds is a massive thick stratum of liquid-water droplets suspended in the hydrogen-helium atmosphere, with ice-crystalline cirrus-like clouds on top.

Beneath this deep cloud deck, about 125 miles below the tops of the outermost cloud layer, pressures approach 100 times that of earth's atmospheric pressure at sea level (14.6 pounds per square inch). The temperature can reach 800°F here. Beyond this area, our present space vehicles cannot go.

We do not yet know what is within the cloud layers. But according to current theory, there is no solid surface as on the other planets. Instead, the hydrogen is gradually squeezed into a dense, hot fluid under increasing pressure. Finally, about 1,800 miles down, a crushing gravitational force (equal to 100,000 earth atmospheres) and temperatures of 12,000°F change the hydrogen and helium into a substance so dense that it behaves like a liquid. Some 12,000 miles down, under a pressure of 3–5 million "atmospheres" and at a temperature of 18,000°F, the hydrogen becomes a metal, in a form unknown on earth. Jupiter may also have a core of iron and other heavy elements, probably no larger than the earth.

While Jupiter's atmosphere is kept constantly churning by its interior heat, one feature of the planet remains almost unchanged. That is the mysterious Great Red Spot in the southern hemisphere. The Red Spot is some 17,000 miles long by 8,500 miles wide. It drifts slowly around the planet, staying generally in the same latitude. Its color sometimes fades to a gray and then returns to its red-orange state. Some scientists think the Red Spot is a long-lived storm that will eventually disappear. Others think that it is a concentration of methane, ammonia, and hydrogen—the characteristic gases of earth's primordial atmosphere.

SATURN

Named for the Roman god of time, the beautiful ringed planet Saturn is the solar system's second largest planet. Saturn's rings are made up of billions of tiny solid particles. They extend outward form 7,000 miles to 171,000 miles above the planet's surface. They are on the plane of the planet's equator, tipped to the orbit at an angle of 26.8 degrees. The rings rotate about the planet, the inside moving at a faster speed than the outer edge.

It is believed that Saturn's interior is composed of a core of rock covered by a mantle of ice. This in turn is surrounded by a dense atmosphere of compressed hydrogen, topped with clouds of methane and ammonia. At 886 million miles from the sun, Saturn has extremely low temperatures. It is probable that there is no solid surface for thousands of miles under the cloud layers we see from earth. In this respect, Saturn may be quite similar to Jupiter.

Pioneer 11, which has already observed Jupiter, will make the first spacecraft instrument observations of Saturn in 1979.

URANUS

Uranus, named for the Greek god of the heavens, was discovered by Sir William Herschel in 1781. It is located almost 1.8 billion miles from the sun. The methane, ammonia, and hydrogen which make up the planet are primarily in a solid state, due to the −300°F temperature.

The planet has five small moons. Uranus appears greenish when seen through the telescope, probably because of its atmospheric methane. In March 1977, scientists at Cornell University and Arizona's Lowell Observatory observed what seems to be a system of rings, in the space between the planet and its five moons.

NASA astronomers will have the opportunity to tell more about Uranus, because the

Pioneer program is scheduled to send an unmanned U. S. spacecraft past the planet in 1985.

NEPTUNE

Uranus and Neptune are often called the twin planets, even though the latter is more than one billion miles farther from the sun. They are similar, though, in size (roughly 30,000 miles in diameter) and composition.

When it was discovered that Uranus did not travel in its regular orbit at all times, astronomers figured that there had to be some object whose gravity pulled Uranus off its path. Astronomers calculated the probable position of such an object—and thus found the planet Neptune in 1848.

Neptune takes 165 years to travel around the sun. The planet has 2 moons; the larger one, Triton, is slightly larger than our moon. Named for the ancient Roman god of the sea, Neptune appears in a telescope as a small greenish disk, much like Uranus. Methane and hydrogen have been detected, but there appears to be no gaseous ammonia as on Uranus. This is probably because Neptune's temperature of $-350°F$ is far below ammonia's freezing point.

PLUTO

The *perturbations* (variations in the regular orbit) of Uranus were not completely explained by the discovery of Neptune. Therefore, astronomers looked for further explanation, in the form of another planet. Finally in 1930 an American astronomer, Clyde Tombaugh, discovered the ninth planet after examining a series of telescopic photographs.

An accurate orbit of the "new" planet was plotted, and it was found to be the only orbit not lying in the same approximate plane. Pluto takes 248 years to revolve around the sun; in the process, it crosses the orbit of Saturn once and that of Uranus and Neptune twice. Pluto has no atmosphere, and the planet is so cold

The variations in regular orbit of Uranus (perturbations) led a number of astronomers to believe that gravitational pull was influencing Uranus. In 1930 Clyde Tombaugh discovered the ninth planet, after examining a series of telescopic photographs. This photo shows the planet as viewed from the 24-inch telescope at the Lowell Observatory, Flagstaff, Arizona.

(below $-350°F$) that its gases are frozen solid.

Pluto was selected as the name for the "newest" planet since Pluto was the Roman god of darkness and the underworld. The planet Pluto is very dark indeed—at a distance of 3.67 billion miles from the sun.

Chapter 6. Study Guide Questions

1. Name the nine planets in order from the sun.

2. What gravitational force keeps the plan-

ets in their orbits? What is the plane of the ecliptic?

3. What type of timetable is used to keep track of the movement and location of the planets?

4. What is an orbital period?

5. Why do some planets appear at times to be going backwards in their orbits?

6. Which two planets are closest to earth?

7. What information did *Mariner 10* provide us about Mercury?

8. What have recent space probes revealed concerning life on Venus?

9. When do we usually see Venus best, and what do we call it at these times?

10. What planet is called the "red" planet?

11. What are the canali? What has happened to the canali theory since the Mariner probes?

12. How far from the sun is Mars?

13. Compare Mars with the earth as to diameter, atmosphere, and other environmental factors.

14. Compare the polar environments of Mars with those of the earth.

15. What have been the results of the search for life on Mars by U. S. spacecraft?

16. Which planet is the largest of our solar system?

17. Why is manned space travel to Jupiter not possible in the foreseeable future?

18. What is the probable composition of Jupiter?

19. What is the Great Red Spot of Jupiter? Why is the Red Spot of particular interest to scientists?

20. How were the planets Neptune and Pluto discovered?

Vocabulary

planet	orbital period
plane of the ecliptic	corrosive
star almanac	illusion
ephemeris	perturbation
ellipse	Martian winds
retrograde movement	Nix Olympica

Chapter 7. Asteroids, Comets, and Meteors

Between the orbits of Mars and Jupiter there are a multitude of small bodies referred to as *asteroids*. The area in which they orbit the sun is called the *asteroid belt*. They have irregular orbits, but all revolve around the sun in the same direction as the larger planets. Approximately 2,000 of these asteroids have been discovered by astronomers so far, and many have been given names. Some scientists believe there may be 25,000 or more such bodies.

Astronomers long wondered why the large distance between Mars and Jupiter seemed to be without a planet. After several hundred years of looking, in 1801 the first and largest asteroid, Ceres, was found. Orbiting at a mean distance of 257 million miles from the sun, Ceres is only 480 miles in diameter. Other asteroids are considerably smaller, some with diameters less than a mile.

Some astronomers think the asteroids are material that was left over when the solar system was formed some 4.6 billion years ago. Some believe that they are leftovers from a collision of two relatively small planets at some time in the distant past. Still others believe that they are the remnants of a small planet which exploded for some as yet unknown reason. None of the asteroids have any kind of atmosphere. They appear to be little more than irregular chunks of rock and metallic substances.

COMETS

Comets appear as bright streaks of light, sometimes visible without the aid of a telescope. They are the most plentiful bodies in our solar system, perhaps numbering more than 100 billion. They are the travelers of the solar system. Comets wander in elliptical orbits, out of the plane of the ecliptic, far beyond the planet Pluto—but still revolving around our sun.

A comet is believed to be composed of frozen gases and dust, which give off a luminous *dust tail* as the comet streaks through space. When a comet approaches the sun and the earth, it begins to reflect sunlight from its head and dust tail. A hydrogen cloud usually envelops the entire comet.

The part in orbit is called the *nucleus.* The nucleus is probably composed of solid fragments or particles—mostly compounds of carbon, nitrogen, hydrogen, oxygen, and sodium—held together by frozen materials. When the comets come near enough to the sun, the frozen material vaporizes. This vapor forms a halo-like structure around the nucleus, called a *coma.* The coma and nucleus actually form the head. Heads of up to one million miles in diameter have been photographed.

As the comet is heated more, dust and ionized gas particles are pushed away from the head by the pressure of the sun's radiation. They move away and form the *gaseous tail,*

This photograph of the comet Kohoutek was taken by members of the Lunar and Planetary Laboratory photography team at the Catalina Observatory, on 15 January 1974. Kohoutek will not reappear for 75,000 years.

which always points away from the sun. The dust tail appears white, while the gaseous ion tail looks pale blue. Tails more than 200 million miles long have been calculated and observed.

As the comet moves away from the sun, its tail is pushed in front of the head. The tail then either disintegrates or is collected again by the nucleus. The comet will then return to the darkness of outer space.

Every trip around the sun causes them to lose some of their matter. Even though comets are millions of times brighter than the earth, they have little mass. Eventually they break up completely, leaving debris all along the path that was once their orbit. Sometimes the earth crosses a part of a former comet path. The tiny particles then collide with our atmosphere, producing a *meteor shower.*

A comet is usually named for the first person to report its discovery. Probably the most famous comet is Halley's Comet. The British astronomer Edmund Halley computed the orbit of the great comet in 1682. In the process, he discovered that it had the same orbit as comets recorded by astronomers in 1531 and 1607. Halley suspected that all three were the same comet, with a predictable 75-year orbital cycle.

This prediction proved to be correct when the comet reappeared in 1758. Sightings of Halley's Comet have continued into more recent history. The last sighting was in 1910 and the next appearance is expected to be in late 1985 or early 1986.

The most recent major comet to be seen on earth was Kohoutek, in 1973–74. More was learned about comets from its flight than from any other comet to date. As the comet whipped around the sun at 250,000 miles an hour, it was photographed from the *Skylab III* space station. The *Mariner 10* spacecraft, while moving toward Venus and Mercury, sighted and measured the hydrogen cloud enveloping the comet. Because of the Kohoutek observations, astronomers now believe that comets may be formed beyond the planets, circling in gigantic orbits which reach as much as a fifth of the way to the nearest stars. NASA now plans to send up a spaceship to rendezvous with the comet Encke in 1984 and make scientific measurements as it passes through Encke's coma.

An official catalog of comet appearances going back to Halley's appearance in 87 B.C. tells us that there are presently 611 known comets. Of them, 513 "long-period" comets will not return for 200 years or more, if at all. Of the 98 remaining "short-period" comets, 65 have been seen more than once.

METEOROIDS, METEORS, AND METEORITES

A *meteoroid* is a piece of rock or metallic substance orbiting in outer space. Meteoroids by the countless thousands orbit the sun. Some are tiny particles of dust which eventually float down through the earth's atmosphere. Others are rocks and metal chunks, weighing anywhere from a few ounces to many tons. Meteoroids are invisible because of their relatively small size—until, by chance, they are drawn into the earth's gravitational field. Then, as the meteoroid rushes through the atmosphere, it meets great air resistance and heats up from the friction. This causes it to flash brilliantly as it streaks across the sky toward the earth's surface.

When this happens, the meteoroid becomes a *meteor*. Meteors are usually seen only below a 100-mile altitude. Most of these little bodies burn up long before reaching the earth, arriving as tiny cinders of dust. The fiery death of the meteoroid is the streak of light called a meteor or "shooting star."

Occasionally, however, the meteoroid is large enough to withstand the friction, and doesn't burn up completely before it hits the earth. As soon as it hits the ground, it is called a *meteorite*. An extremely large and bright meteor is called a "fireball"; it will probably end up as a large meteorite, landing somewhere on earth.

There are two main kinds of meteorites: stony meteorites called *aerolites*, and iron and nickel ones called *siderites*. Aerolites are much like the stones in the earth, composed of oxygen, silicon, magnesium, and some iron. The siderites, however, are about 90 percent iron, 8 percent nickel, and a mixture of other minerals. Of the meteorites that have been found, aerolites outnumber siderites 2-to-1.

Astronomers believe that meteorites originate from the fragments of a shattered planet within the asteroid belt. Thus an analysis of them can tell us a good deal about the relative abundance of elements in the other planets. The stony meteorites probably came from the former planet's crust, while the iron ones came from the planet's core. Such study has convinced most astronomers and cosmologists that the core of the earth also is composed of iron and nickel.

The largest meteorite ever found in the western hemisphere was discovered in Greenland by Admiral Robert Peary in 1894. It weighs 34 tons and presently is kept in the American Museum of Natural History in New York. A 60-ton siderite has been found in southwest Africa, but it still lies where it landed. The largest meteorites found thus far are siderites.

A third kind of meteorite called a *tektite* has been found in widely scattered parts of the globe. This small meteorite usually weighs between an ounce and a pound. It is composed of a glassy compound having high silicon content, along with oxides of aluminum, magnesium, iron, calcium, sodium, and potassium. Some are nearly transparent, while others come in various shades of green, amber, and brown. Tektites do not resemble any rock or glass substance on earth. Thus they may have come from the interior of a destroyed planet where materials were subjected to extremely high temperatures. Considerable research is being devoted to tektites, for they may solve many mysteries concerning the origin of the solar system.

Chapter 7. Study Guide Questions

1. How is it thought that the asteroids originated?

2. Where are the asteroids located in the solar system?

3. Of what are comets composed?

4. What causes the comet to be luminous?

5. In what respect are comets like planets?

6. What are the two tails of comets composed of?

7. What happens when a comet breaks up, leaving debris which eventually enters the earth's atmosphere?

8. What is the name of the most famous comet? How often can it be seen on earth? When will it next be seen?

9. Which recent comet gave astronomers their most up-to-date comet information?

10. What causes a meteor to be a "fireball?"

11. What happens to most meteors?

12. What are the main kinds of meteorites?

13. What are tektites? Where did they probably originate?

Vocabulary

asteroids	meteoroids
comet	meteors
nucleus	aerolites
meteor shower	siderites
Halley's Comet	tektites
Kohoutek	meteorites

Chapter 8. Studying the Sky

How and where can the student or average citizen study the sky? There are two kinds of facilities that are particularly useful—the *planetarium* and the *observatory*. Everyone should take the opportunity to visit each of these places, whether for general interest and self-education, or for more concentrated study.

A planetarium uses a spherical dome upon which is projected an accurate picture of a section of the night sky. The projector is an intricate optical instrument which can show the appearance of the sky at any time, anywhere in the world. It can also project the names and shapes of the constellations, providing arrows and pointers to call attention to particular objects. The projector has a rotational device which will cause the "sky" to move, just as the real sky does. This apparent turning of the sky can be speeded up or slowed down.

An observatory has a telescope which is used for observation of celestial objects. In an observatory, the actual work of the astrono-

mer—photographing the heavens—is going on.

If we were to take an imaginary trip to an observatory during "working" hours, it would be at night. We probably would have to drive up a high hill or even a mountain to get there. The large research observatories are located in remote places away from the lights, smoke, and smog of the cities. On the mountain top the air is thinner and clearer, eliminating as much atmospheric haze as possible. Ideally, the observatory is built in a location where the weather affords a maximum number of clear nights with "steady atmosphere."

The distinguishing feature of an observatory is its great revolving dome. Through a slit-like opening in this dome, the telescope peers into the night sky. Except for the hum of motors and the click of switches, all is quiet as the astronomers guide the telescope to the desired spot in the heavens. The whole dome can be made to turn to point the telescope at stars or planets anywhere in the sky.

The environment in the dome must be exactly as it is outside. It must be dark, so that the time-exposure photography will not be

The U. S. Naval Observatory's newest installation at Flagstaff, Arizona. This building houses the 61-inch Astrometric reflecting telescope.

interfered with in any way. The temperature in the dome must be the same as outdoors, with no heat, since any warm air escaping through the dome slit would blur the photographs. Thus in winter the astronomer must wear heavy clothing as protection from the frigid cold.

Today the telescope and its fine cameras are often operated by computers. The astronomical photographs are taken on sensitive photographic glass plates instead of on film; glass plates do not curl, and can be stored and handled with greater ease. Time exposures are used because the plate must store up the feeble light received from the stars, perhaps for hours. Such time exposures reveal the movement of the planets, asteroids, meteors, and comets, against a background of stationary stars.

The astronomer is much more than a mere "stargazer." When working with optical equipment one must be an electronics technician, photographer, and in some cases, a computer operator. During the day the astronomer must be a mathematician, physicist, chemist, mechanic, research analyst, and somewhat of an office manager. The library of the observatory maintains a filing system of photographs and written records. Research and laboratory work goes on every working day, and in observatory shops new astronomical instruments are being developed.

TELESCOPES

The telescope is the most important object in the observatory. There are two principal types of telescopes: the *refracting* and the *reflecting* telescopes. Both types of telescopes are fitted with spectrographs to photograph the color spectrum of incoming light.

The magnifying power of a telescope is important only in observing nearby celestial bodies, since the stars can't be magnified. In observing the stars, the light-gathering power of the telescope is all-important. The amount of light a telescope can collect depends entirely upon the area of its main lens (or mirror). The larger the lens or mirror, the brighter the star will appear.

The *refracting telescope* uses two lenses. There is a single convex lens called the *objective lens* at the end of the telescope. This lens forms a reduced, inverted image of the celestial body being viewed. The *eyepiece lens* magnifies the image formed by the objective lens, making the object appear closer. What the telescope does, then, is take a picture (called the objective image) and magnify it so it will be enlarged for easier study.

The largest refracting telescope in the world is located at the Yerkes Observatory at Williams Bay on Lake Geneva, Wisconsin. Operated by the University of Chicago, this refractor has an objective lens with a diameter of 40 inches (102 cm).

Sir Isaac Newton is credited with develop-

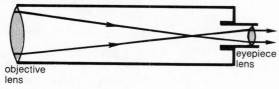
A refracting telescope.

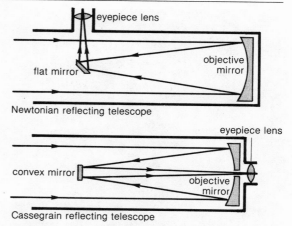

Newtonian reflecting telescope

Cassegrain reflecting telescope

Reflecting telescopes may be Newtonian or Cassegrain. A Newtonian reflector has a small flat secondary mirror, while the Cassegrain has a convex secondary mirror.

ing the *reflecting telescope*, which uses an *objective mirror* in place of the objective lens. This slightly concave mirror forms an image, which is then reflected, by a secondary mirror, to where the eyepiece magnifier is mounted. Secondary reflectors are installed in the telescope tube to avoid the awkwardness of having the eyepiece at the top end. In the Newtonian reflector, a flat mirror reflects the light and brings it to a focus at the side of the telescope.

Another type of reflecting telescope, the Cassegrain reflector, has a convex secondary mirror, instead of Newton's flat one. This mirror causes the light to focus behind the objective mirror. Thus the objective mirror must have a hole in the center to allow light to pass through. The eyepiece can then be placed at the bottom of the telescope tube. Cassegrain reflectors are much more expensive than Newtonian reflectors and are especially designed for telescopes with large mirrors.

The world's largest reflecting telescope is the Hale telescope at California's Mt. Palomar Observatory. That telescope has an objective mirror with a diameter of 200 inches (508 cm).

The discovery of radiation outside the visible spectrum has led to the development of

The U. S. Naval Observatory's 61-inch Astrometric, or distance-measuring, reflector. This instrument is used primarily to determine the distances of faint stars. The timekeepers below the telescope show Universal Time and Sidereal Time, to represent the rotational motion of the earth.

radio telescopes. Radio waves can be reflected and refracted, just as light waves can. In a radio telescope, a dish-like antenna is used to gather the radio waves from space—much as an objective mirror gathers light waves. Astronomers can thus measure and record the characteristics of incoming radio waves.

Radio telescopes must be very large in order to detect faint radio waves from space. Also, because the wavelength of radio waves can be thousands of times longer than those of light waves, radio telescopes must be very large.

Since radio waves are so long, however, radio reflectors don't require the precision of optical telescopes. The mirror on the Hale Telescope, for instance, is polished to a precision of one-millionth of an inch, the tolerance for light waves; but a radio reflector can be made of iron mesh, with a one-half-inch tolerance.

The world's largest steerable reflecting radio telescope dish is at the U. S. Naval Radio Research Station in Sugar Grove, West Virginia. That disk is 600 feet in diameter. Other very large ones are at Eifel Mountain near Bonn, West Germany, 328 feet; and Jodrell Bank in Cheshire, England, 250 feet. The world's largest stationary radio telescope, with a diameter of 1,000 feet, is near Arecibo, Puerto Rico.

A radio telescope traces out changes in the radio energy received as the telescope scans the sky. In this way, a radio map of the sky can be constructed. The radio "star map" or radio source map of the sky does not correspond with an actual map of the stars. This is because the stars themselves are too weak, as sources of radiation, to be picked up at such distances. Radio astronomers have found many huge regions of high-speed gases and the remnants of celestial supernovae explosions, however. Sunspots, as we learned earlier, also give off radio waves, as does the corona of the sun. Radio telescopes have also discovered *quasars*. These objects look no larger than a single star; but they emit hundreds of times more energy than most galaxies.

Special Uses of the Radio Telescope

While radio telescopes normally are used only to receive radio waves, it is possible to modify these devices for other purposes. The radio telescope can direct powerful radio beams at a celestial object, and then receive them when they rebound toward earth. Radio telescopes equipped with such transmitters are often called *radar telescopes*. Because radio waves travel with the speed of light, radar telescopes can furnish accurate data about the

The world's largest radio telescope is the U. S. Navy's 20,000-ton facility near Sugar Grove, West Virginia. Known officially as the Naval Radio Research Station, it will enable Navy scientists to tune in on radio signals coming from stars billions of miles into space. The instrument's aluminum-mesh reflector dish has a 600-foot diameter—twice the length of a football field—and an area exceeding 7 acres.

distance of celestial bodies near the earth. By using various wavelengths, information about the composition of these bodies can be obtained.

Radio-telescope technology has also showed that not all radio waves from space come from swirling, excited gases and celestial bodies. A particular kind of wave was found to emit from the cool, relatively quiet hydrogen clouds strewn throughout space. Mapping these hy-

drogen radio signals has enabled astronomers to pierce the dusty regions of space through which light rarely passes. Such maps told them that our Milky Way is shaped like a pinwheel, and that it rotates, carrying the sun and the planets with it. Until the advent of radio telescopes, scientists only could speculate that this was the case, as it is with many other galaxies.

The same radio-telescope techniques have also found molecules in space. The amino acids, the basis of all living things, were found all through space, by means of the radio telescope. No optical device could have accomplished this feat.

Chapter 8. Study Guide Questions

1. What is a planetarium?
2. What is the principal work of an observatory? When does that work go on?
3. What physical surroundings are usually sought for observatories?
4. Why must the temperature in the dome be the same as that outside of the observatory?
5. Why are glass plates used for photographic work in an observatory?
6. In order to be a competent astronomer, what must the astronomer know—in addition to being able to operate the telescope?
7. Name and describe the two types of telescopes.
8. What part of the refracting telescope actually magnifies the image collected by the objective lens?
9. What is significant about these observatories? A) Yerkes Observatory, B) Mt. Palomar, C) U. S. Naval Radio Research Station, D) Arecibo, Puerto Rico.
10. What does a radio telescope do?
11. Why is the tolerance for error much less on a mirror or lens than on a radio-telescope reflector?
12. What particular astronomical findings have been made possible by radio telescopes?
13. What are quasars?
14. What special findings concerning amino acids were discovered by radio-telescope techniques?

Vocabulary

planetarium	objective lens
observatory	refraction
time-exposure pho-	reflection
tography	atmospheric haze
physicist	tolerance
magnifying power	radio star map
convex lens	quasar
concave mirror	laboratory
eyepiece lens	amino acids

Chapter 9. Satellites

The true beginning of the Space Age was 4 October 1957, when the world's first man-made satellite, *Sputnik I,* was successfully launched by the Soviet Union. *Sputnik I* was followed four months later by the first United States satellite, *Explorer I.* Since then there has been a steady procession of artificial satellites, sent into space on scientific astronomical missions.

A satellite is designed to stay in orbit for a specified amount of time. Then, when its energy of motion dissipates as it comes closer to the earth, gravity will draw it down, perhaps as a fiery meteor. The closer to the earth a satellite travels, and the larger it is, the sooner it will return. We now can send satellites into orbits so high that they will not come down for thousands of years, if ever. Once in orbit—if far enough into space—they will keep on going, just as the moon does.

Satellite orbits are identified by what are called the *elements* of the orbit. These elements describe the size and shape of the orbit, its position in space, and the place of the satellite in the orbit at a particular time. Because these orbital elements change, mainly due to the gravitational pull of the earth, it is necessary to have a system of tracking stations to keep tabs on the satellites.

A true satellite requires no power. It travels in an orbit around the larger body, propelled only by the gravitational force of that body. Once in orbit, it is completely independent of the earth's rotation. It travels in a slow, complicated way, influenced by the sun, the moon, and the earth. Because of these many forces, prediction of future satellite positions is very difficult, even for electronic computers. That is why satellites must be carefully tracked, and their orbits checked and corrected continuously. Governments, therefore, employ many people to keep track of satellites under their control. They use a sort of scoreboard on which the status of each satellite is plotted. The plot includes the name, number, track, and the scheduled time of appearance over selected areas. If satellites were not carefully tracked, they would have little scientific or practical value.

Satellite tracking is now done with special cameras. A series of 12 stations have been set up by the Smithsonian Institution—in Hawaii,

Earth from 22,300 miles in space. Outlines of four continents can be seen, and South America can be seen almost in its entirety.

New Mexico, Greece, Brazil, Ethiopia, Peru, Argentina, South Africa, Spain, India, Australia, and Japan. The communications center for all of these is located in Cambridge, Massachusetts. All stations are connected by teletype so that messages can be sent rapidly. After each station's tracking camera photographs a satellite passage, the exact data identifying the flight is transmitted to Cambridge. The system is accurate to one-thousandth of a second, and the time is printed on each succeeding photograph automatically.

The Uses of Satellites

You might ask, "Why do we go to all the time and expense to send up these satellites?" And that's a fair question. As it turns out, there are at least seven good reasons for putting satellites into orbit today. These reasons are: (1) to gather worldwide weather data (2) to aid long-range rapid communications (3) to aid in air and sea navigation (4) to detect enemy missiles for national defense (5) to provide platforms for space observers and laboratories (6) to assist TV and radio intercontinental relay and (7) to conduct military reconnaissance.

American satellites are named for the particular program in which they are involved. For example, the Explorer satellites are designed to study conditions in space, such as meteors, magnetism, radiations, and temperatures. Discoverer satellites make re-entry studies. The Vanguard series measure the shape and cloud cover of the earth. The Tiros series are concerned mainly with weather observations. The Nimbus satellites are a further advance in meteorology. They provide continuous photography of cloud cover, and do storm tracking, ozone measurements, advance research into infrared, ultraviolet, and visible space regions, and high-resolution earth photography. The "Transit" satellites aid in naval and air navigation, and the "Echo" and "Courier" series serve as communications relays.

The Navy is deeply involved in the field of

A model of the Navy's Transit navigation-aid satellite.

satellite research. Ocean surveillance, navigation, communications, and weather prediction are all important to the Navy—and all can be improved by the use of satellites. Naval astronomical observatories, Navy-sponsored space probes, and naval astronauts participating in the Apollo and Skylab programs—these demonstrate the Navy's deep interest in the field. Of special vital national concern is the satellite program for intercontinental geographic survey. This program, in connection with the navigation program, is vital to the nation's principal war deterrent—the missile-carrying Polaris and Poseidon submarines.

Chapter 9. Study Guide Questions

1. When did the Space Age have its beginning?

2. What were the names of the first U. S. and

Soviet satellites?

3. What is a satellite? What is it designed to do, in general?

4. How and by whom are satellites watched or followed?

5. What are the elements of a satellite orbit?

6. Where are satellite tracking stations located now? How does the communications for these stations function?

7. List seven principal purposes for satellites today.

8. What are some major naval applications to the satellite program? Be able to discuss each.

Vocabulary

tracking station
communications
  relay
ocean surveillance
military reconnais-
  sance

deterrent
geographic survey
high-resolution
  photography
intercontinental
  survey

Electricity and Naval Electronics

Chapter 1. Fundamentals of Electricity

The study of electricity began with the ancient Greeks. They discovered that by rubbing a mineral called *amber* with a cloth, they could create a mysterious force of attraction between the cloth and the amber. They also observed that after they rubbed two different ambers with two different cloths, the two cloths would repel one another—as strongly as they were attracted to amber. These forces were called *electric* (from the Greek word for amber), and the cloths and ambers were said to be *electrically charged*.

Although the Greeks discovered electric force, they couldn't explain it. In fact, it was not until the atomic theory of matter was developed that the true cause of electricity was found. When scientists discovered that atoms were composed of negatively charged particles (electrons) which orbit around positively charged particles (protons), they could explain the phenomenon of electrical charge. Normally there is a balance between the negative charge of electrons and the positive charge of protons. Therefore, under most conditions, an atom will have no charge. But if the number of electrons is increased, the atom will become negatively charged. On the other hand, if electrons are taken away, the atom will have a positive charge. Charged atoms are called *ions*.

One of the fundamental laws of electricity is that like charges repel each other, and unlike charges attract each other. In the atom, the electrons are held in their orbit by the attractive force between them and the protons in the nucleus. In the Greeks' experiments with amber, the cloth picked up electrons from the amber, thus becoming negatively charged. This left the amber with a positive charge— and unlike charges attract one another. See also our explanation of lightning in Unit 6, Chapter 5; lightning is also caused by the attraction of unlike charges.

Electricity, then, is simply the movement of free electrons—that is, of electrons which have been removed from their orbits in atoms. Substances that permit the free motion of a large number of electrons are called *conductors*. Silver, copper, and aluminum wire, in that order, are the best conductors; but copper wire is the most commonly used because it is relatively inexpensive. Electrical energy travels through conductors by the movement of free electrons, migrating from atom to atom inside the conductor. Each electron moves a very short distance to the neighboring atom, where it replaces one or more electrons by forcing them out of their orbits. The replaced electrons repeat the process in other nearby atoms. The movement is thus transmitted through the entire length of the conductor.

Some substances have very few free electrons and are therefore poor conductors. These substances, such as rubber, glass, or dry wood, are called *insulators*. Electricians use good conductors to carry electricity, and use insulators to prevent electricity from being diverted from the wires.

VOLTAGE

The force which causes electricity to move in a conductor is called *voltage* or *electromotive force* (E). There are six basic ways to generate voltage:

1) *Friction.* Voltage can be produced by rubbing two materials together. *Static electricity* is the most common name for this type. It occurs frequently in dry climates, or on days of low humidity.

2) *Pressure.* Voltage can be produced by squeezing crystals such as natural quartz or, more usually, manmade crystals. Compressed electrons tend to move through a crystal at predictable frequencies. Crystals are frequently used in communications equipment.

3) *Heat.* Voltage can be produced by heating the place where two unlike metals are joined. The hot junction where the moving electrons from the two different metals meet is called a *thermocouple.* The difference in the temperature of the two metals determines the amount of voltage; consequently, thermocouples are often used to measure and regulate temperature, as in a thermostat.

4) *Light.* Voltage can be produced when light strikes a photosensitive (light-sensitive) substance. The light dislodges electrons from their orbits around the surface atoms. Voltage produced in this manner is called *photoelectric.*

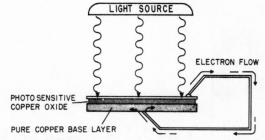
Voltage produced by light.

The *photoelectric cell* is the device which operates on this principle. A plate coated with compounds of silver or copper oxide, which are extremely sensitive to light, can also produce a flow of electrons. Light is used to generate voltage in devices requiring extreme precision—such as television cameras, automatic processing controls, door openers, and burglar alarms.

5) *Chemical Action.* Voltage can be produced by chemical reactions, as in a battery cell. The simple voltaic battery consists of a carbon strip (positive) and a zinc strip (negative), suspended in a container with a solution of water and sulfuric acid. This solution is called the *electrolyte.* The chemical action which results from this combination causes electrons to flow between the zinc and carbon

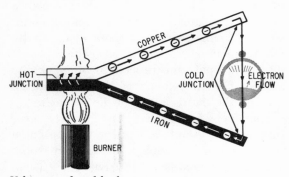
Voltage produced by heat.

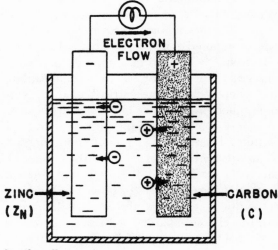
Simple cell.

electrodes. Batteries are used as sources of electrical energy in automobiles, boats, aircraft, ships, and portable equipment.

6) *Magnetism.* Voltage can be produced when a conductor moves through a magnetic field, or vice versa, in such a manner as to cut the field's lines of force. This is the most common source of electric power; it is the method used in electric generators. Usually, a copper wire conductor is moved back and forth through the magnetic field created by a U- or C-shaped electromagnet.

The flow of electrons through a conductor is called *electric current.* Electric current is classified into two general types: direct current and alternating current. *Direct current* flows continuously in the same direction, while an *alternating current* periodically reverses direction. An *ampere* (or *amp*) is the unit used to measure the rate at which current flows. The symbol for current flow is "I."

Every material offers some resistance or opposition to the flow of electric current. The good conductors offer very little resistance, while insulators or poor conductors offer high resistance. The size and composition of wires in an electric circuit are designed to keep electrical resistance as low as possible. A wire's resistance depends on its length, diameter, and composition.

Manufactured circuit elements which provide a definite specified amount of resistance are called *resistors.* Resistance is measured in *ohms.* One ohm is the resistance of a circuit element (or circuit) that permits a steady current of one ampere to flow when a force of one volt is applied to that circuit.

BATTERIES

A battery consists of a number of cells, assembled in a common container and connected to function as a source of electrical power. A cell is the fundamental unit of a battery. A *simple cell* consists of two electrodes, placed in a container holding the electrolyte.

The *electrodes* are the conductors by which the current leaves or returns to the electrolyte. In the simple cell they are carbon and zinc strips, placed in the electrolyte. In the *dry cell* there is a carbon rod in the center and a zinc container in which the cell is assembled. The electrolyte may be a salt, an acid, or an alkaline solution. In the automobile storage battery, the electrolyte is in liquid form; in the dry cell battery, the electrolyte is a paste.

A *primary cell* is one in which the chemical action eats away one of the electrodes, usually the negative. Eventually the electrode must be replaced or the cell discarded. In the case of

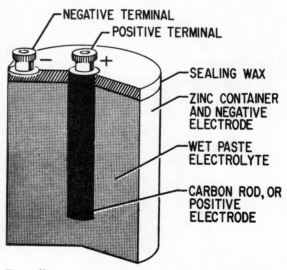

Dry cell, cross-sectional view.

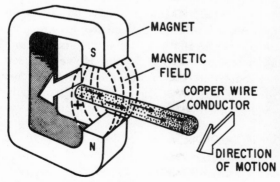

Voltage produced by magnetism.

the common dry cell, as in a flashlight battery, it is usually cheaper to buy a new cell.

A *secondary cell* is one in which the electrodes and the electrolyte are altered by the chemical action that generates current. These cells may be restored to their original condition (recharged) by forcing an electric current through them in the opposite direction to that of discharge. The automobile storage battery is a common example of a battery composed of secondary cells.

In many cases, a battery-powered device may require more electrical energy than one cell can provide. The device may require either a higher voltage or more current—and in some cases both. In such cases it is necessary to combine cells.

There are two ways of doing this. Cells connected in *series* provide a higher voltage, while cells connected in *parallel* provide a higher current capacity. To provide adequate power when voltage and current requirements are both greater than the capacity of one cell, a combination series-parallel network is used.

Series-Connected Cells. Assume that you need a power supply with an electromotive force of 6 volts and a current capacity of $\frac{1}{8}$ ampere. Since a single cell normally supplies

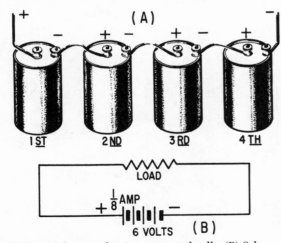

(A) Pictorial view of series-connected cells; (B) Schematic of series connection.

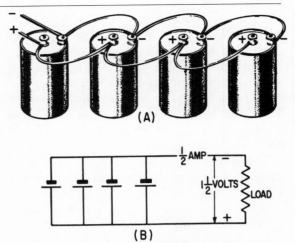

(A) Pictorial view of parallel-connected cells; (B) Schematic of parallel correction.

only 1.5 volts, more than one cell is needed. To obtain the higher voltage the cells are connected in series. The negative electrode of the first cell is connected to the positive electrode of the second cell, the negative electrode of the second to the positive of the third, and so on. The positive electrode of the first cell and negative electrode of the last cell then serve as the real terminals of the battery. With this method, the voltage is boosted 1.5 volts by each cell in the series line. Since there are 4 cells, the total voltage output is 6 volts.

Parallel-Connected Cells. Now assume that you need only 1.5 volts, but $\frac{1}{2}$ ampere of current. (Assume that each cell will supply $\frac{1}{8}$ ampere.) To meet this requirement, the cells are connected in parallel. In a parallel connection, all positive cell electrodes are connected to one another. The voltage is the same as that of one cell—1.5 volts. However, each cell contributes its maximum allowable current of $\frac{1}{8}$ ampere to the line. There are 4 cells, so the total line current is $\frac{1}{2}$ ampere.

Chapter 1. Study Guide Questions

1. Describe the composition of an atom. Which are the positive and negative charged particles?

2. What force keeps the electrons of an atom revolving in regular orbits?

3. How does electricity flow?

4. What substances are the best conductors of electricity? Why?

5. What is an insulator?

6. What is the fundamental law concerning electrical charges?

7. What unit is used to measure electromotive force?

8. What are the six common methods of producing voltage? Describe each briefly.

9. How are crystals used in electricity?

10. What is a thermocouple?

11. Where is the photoelectric cell used?

12. What is the most common use for chemically created electricity?

13. What is the unit of measure for current?

14. What is the unit of measure for resistance?

15. What factors determine the amount of resistance in a conductor?

16. What is an electric cell? What are the principal components of a cell? What is a battery?

17. What is the purpose of combining cells in a battery-powered device?

18. What are the two ways in which cells can be connected to provide electric power? What is the advantage of each way?

Vocabulary

electricity	photoelectric
electronics	current, ampere
electrical conductor	resistance, ohm
insulator	battery, cell
electromotive force	electrolyte
electromagnet	electrode
voltage, volt	series connection
thermocouple	parallel connection

Chapter 2. Simple Electrical Circuits

Whenever two unequal charges are connected by a conductor, a pathway for current flow is created. An *electric circuit* is a conducting pathway, consisting of the conductor and the path through the voltage source. For example, a lamp connected by conductors across a dry cell forms a simple electric circuit. Current flows from the negative (−) terminal of the battery through the lamp to the positive (+) battery terminal, and continues by going through the battery from the (+) terminal to the (−) terminal. As long as this pathway is unbroken, it is a closed circuit and current will flow.

A *schematic* is a diagram in which symbols are used for a circuit's components, instead of pictures. These symbols are used in an effort to make the diagrams easier to draw and easier to understand. Schematic symbols aid the technician who plans or repairs electrical or electronic equipment.

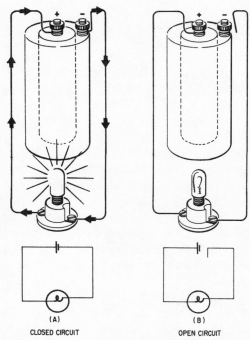

(A)
CLOSED CIRCUIT

(B)
OPEN CIRCUIT

(A) Simple electric circuit (closed) (B) Simple electric circuit (open).

OHM'S LAW

In the early part of the 19th century, Georg Simon Ohm proved that a precise relationship exists between current, voltage, and resistance. This relationship, called Ohm's Law, is stated as follows: The current in a circuit is directly proportional to the applied voltage and inversely proportional to the circuit resistance. Ohm's Law may be expressed as an equation: $I = E/R$ (Equation A).

I = current in amperes
E = voltage in volts
R = resistance in ohms

If any two of the quantities in the equation are known, the third may be easily found.

Example: Circuit 1 contains a resistance of 1.5 ohms and a source voltage of 1.5 volts. How much current flows in the circuit?

Solution:

$$I = \frac{E}{R}$$

$$I = \frac{1.5}{1.5}$$

$$I = 1 \text{ ampere}$$

In many circuit applications the current is known, and either the voltage or the resistance will be the unknown quantity. To solve a problem in which current and resistance are known, the basic formula for Ohm's Law must be transformed to solve for E. Multiplying both sides of the equation by R, the formula for finding voltage is: $E = IR$ (Equation B).

Similarly, to transform the basic formula when resistance is unknown, multiply both sides of the basic equation by R and then divide both sides of the equation by I. The resulting formula for resistance is: $R = E/I$ (Equation C).

SERIES CIRCUITS

If the circuit is arranged so that the electrons only have one possible path, the circuit is called a *series circuit*. The same current flows

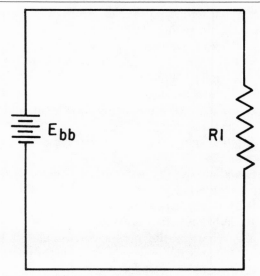

Schematic diagram of a basic circuit. A battery is designated by the symbol E_{bb}; a light bulb is the resistor, and is labeled R_1.

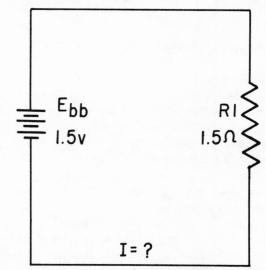

Circuit 1. Determining current in a basic circuit.

through all parts of a series circuit. But it is possible for there to be several different values of resistance and voltage within the circuit. For instance, there might be several light bulbs (resistances) in a single circuit. Then the total circuit resistance (R_T) is equal to the sum of the individual resistances. Thus if three resis-

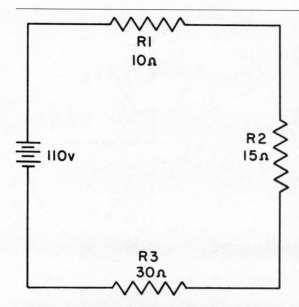

Circuit 2. Finding total resistance in a series circuit.

tors of 10 ohms, 15 ohms, and 30 ohms are connected in a series (see Circuit 2), the total resistance would be calculated as follows:

$$R_T = R_1 + R_2 + R_3$$
$$R_T = 10 + 15 + 30$$
$$R_T = 55 \text{ ohms}$$

As with resistance, the total voltage across a series circuit is the sum of the individual voltage drops in the circuit. Total voltage is called E_T. Thus if there are 2 amps of current going through a circuit with three resistors (20, 30, and 50 ohms) you would first have to use Ohm's Law (Equation B) to solve for the voltage across each resistor; then you would find E_T.

If:
$$E_1 = 40 \text{ volts}$$
$$E_2 = 60 \text{ volts}$$
$$E_3 = 100 \text{ volts}$$

Then:
$$E_T = E_1 + E_2 + E_3$$
$$E_T = 40 + 60 + 100$$
$$E_T = 200 \text{ volts}$$

POWER

Electrical power refers to the rate at which work is being done. Work is done whenever a force causes motion. Therefore, since voltage makes current flow in a closed circuit, work is being done. The rate at which this work is done is called the *electric power rate*, and its measure is the watt—the basic unit of power. Power is equal to the voltage across a circuit, multiplied by the current through the circuit. Using P as the symbol for electrical power, the basic power formula is: $P = IE$ (Equation D). When E is 2 volts and I is 2 amperes, P becomes 4 watts.

When voltage is doubled, and resistance remains unchanged, power is doubled *twice*. This occurs because the doubling of voltage causes a doubling of current (see Equation A), which therefore doubles both of the factors that determine power. In other words, the rate of change of power, in a circuit of fixed resistance, is the *square* of the change in voltage. Thus the basic power formula $P = EI$ may also be expressed as $P = E^2/R$ (Equation E), or $P = I^2R$ (Equation F). (These equations can easily be derived by simple substitution from Equations A and B.)

Each of the resistors in a series circuit consumes power which is dissipated in the form of heat. Since this power must come from the source, the total power must be equal in amount to the power consumed by the circuit resistances. In a series circuit, the total power is equal to the sum of the powers dissipated by the individual resistors. In equation form: $P_T = P_1 + P_2 + P_3$.

Chapter 2. Study Guide Questions

1. What is an electrical circuit?
2. How does electricity flow in a circuit?
3. What is a schematic diagram?
4. Define Ohm's Law. What does it enable us to find?
5. What are the Ohm's Law formulas for finding voltage, current, and resistance?
6. What is a series circuit?
7. What is the unit of measure for power?

8. What are the three formulas for power? Are they related to the Ohm's Law formulas?

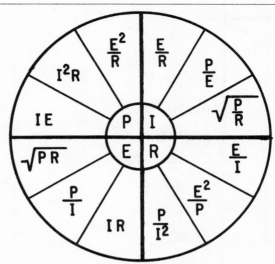

Vocabulary

battery terminal
electric circuit
series circuit
Ohm's Law
inversely propor-
   tional

schematic
directly proportional
applied voltage
power, watt
simple substitution
power dissipation

Summary of basic formulas for Ohm's Law and for power. In each quadrant of the circle are three formulae; each formula can be used to find the unknown factor whose symbol appears in the adjacent quadrant of the central circle.

Problems

Using the summary diagram for Ohm's Law, work out the following problems.

1. A simple series circuit has one 60-watt bulb on a standard 120-volt source of electricity. Using this information, find the following values:
   a. What is the current? $I =$ _____
   b. What is the resistance? $R =$ _____

2. A simple circuit has a 200-ohm resistor in series on a 115-volt battery. Using this information, find the following values:
   a. What is the current? $I =$ _____
   b. What is the power used? $P =$ _____

3. A simple battery-powered circuit has .75 ampere running through a series hookup with one 150-ohm resistor. Using this information, find the following values:
   a. What is the voltage of the battery? $E_{bb} =$ _____
   b. What is the total power used? $P_T =$ _____

4. A series circuit has three resistances of 40 ohms, 60 ohms, and 100 ohms working off a 120-volt battery. Using this information, find the following values:
   a. Total resistance $(R_T) =$ _____
   b. Current $(I) =$ _____
   c. Power dissipated over R_1 $(P_1) =$ _____
   Power dissipated over R_2 $(P_2) =$ _____
   Power dissipated over R_3 $(P_3) =$ _____
   d. Total power $(P_T) =$ _____

5. A series circuit with a 240-volt source has two resistors of 50 ohms and 70 ohms respectively. Using this information, find the following values:
   a. Total resistance $(R_T) =$ _____
   b. Current $(I) =$ _____
   c. Power dissipated over R_1 $(P_1) =$ _____
   Power dissipated over R_2 $(P_2) =$ _____
   d. Total power $(P_T) =$ _____
   e. Voltage over R_1 $(E_1) =$ _____
   Voltage over R_2 $(E_2) =$ _____

6. A series circuit with resistances of 120 ohms and 130 ohms are connected across a battery with .5 amps. Using this information, find the following values:
   a. Total resistance (R_T) _____
   b. Battery voltage (E_{bb}) _____
   c. Voltage over R_1 $(E_1) =$ _____
   Voltage over R_2 $(E_2) =$ _____
   d. What power is dissipated over each resistor?
   Across R_1 $(P_1) =$ _____
   Across R_2 $(P_2) =$ _____
   e. Total power $(P_T) =$ _____
   f. Check: Does $P_T = I \times E_T$?

Chapter 3. Parallel Circuits

A *parallel circuit* has more than one current path connected to a common voltage source. Parallel circuits, therefore, must contain two or more resistors which are not connected in series. Circuit 3 is an example of a basic parallel circuit.

Starting with the voltage source (E_{bb}) and tracing counter-clockwise around the circuit, there are two complete and separate paths in which current will flow. One path runs from the source through resistance R_1, and back to the source; the other runs from the source through resistance R_2, and back to the source.

A single current flows in a series circuit. Its value is determined in part by the total resistance of the circuit. However, the source current in a parallel circuit divides among the available paths, according to the value of the resistors in the circuit. Ohm's Law remains unchanged, however. For a given voltage, current varies inversely with resistance.

The behavior of current in parallel circuits can be illustrated using example circuits with different values of resistance for a given value of applied voltage. Circuit 4 shows a basic series circuit. Here the total current must pass through the single resistor. The amount of current is determined as follows:

$$I_T = \frac{E_{bb}}{R_1} = \frac{50}{10} = 5 \text{ amperes}$$

Circuit 5 shows the same resistor (R_1) with a second resistor (R_2) of equal value connected in parallel across the voltage source. Applying Ohm's law, the current flow through each resistor is seen to be the same as through the single resistor in Circuit 4. These individual currents are determined as follows:

$$I_{R_1} = \frac{E_{bb}}{R_1} = \frac{50}{10} = 5 \text{ amperes}$$

$$I_{R_2} = \frac{E_{bb}}{R_2} = \frac{50}{10} = 5 \text{ amperes}$$

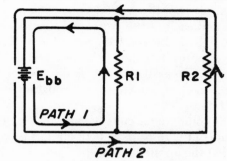

Circuit 3. An example of a basic parallel circuit.

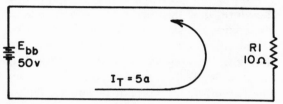

Circuit 4.

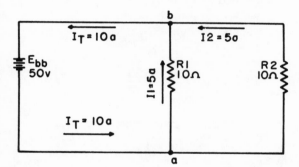

Circuit 5.

It is apparent that if 5 amperes of current flow through each of the resistors, there must be a total current of 10 amperes drawn from the source. The total current of 10 amps leaves the negative terminal of the battery and flows to point "a." Since point "a" is a connecting point for the two resistors, it is called a *junction*. At junction "a" the total current divides into two smaller currents of 5 amperes each. These two currents flow through their respective resistors and rejoin at junction "b." The total current then flows from junction "b" back to the positive terminal of the battery. Thus, the source supplies a total current of 10 amperes and each of the two equal resistors carries one-half the total current. Each of the current paths is called a *branch*. The total current in a parallel circuit is the sum of the current in each branch—or, in equation form: $I_t = I_1 + I_2$.

Now compare Circuits 6 and 7. Notice that the sum of the resistors in both circuits is equal and that the applied voltage is the same value. However, the total current in Circuit 7 is twice the amount in Circuit 6. It is apparent, therefore, that the manner in which resistors are connected in a circuit, as well as their actual resistance value, affects the total current flow. This phenomenon will be illustrated in more detail in the discussion of resistance. For Circuit 7, the amount of current flow in the branch circuits and the total current are determined as follows:

$$I_t = I_1 + I_2 + I_3$$
$$I_t = \frac{E_{bb}}{R_1} + \frac{E_{bb}}{R_2} + \frac{E_{bb}}{R_3}$$
$$I_t = \frac{50}{10} + \frac{50}{10} + \frac{50}{10} = 15 \text{ amperes}$$

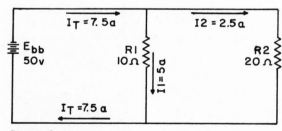

Circuit 6.

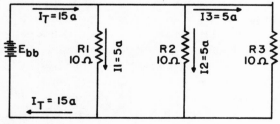

Circuit 7.

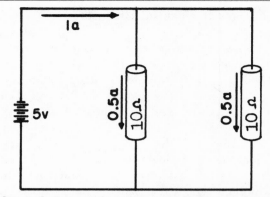

Circuit 8. Two equal resistors connected in parallel.

Parallel Resistance

In Circuit 8, two cylinders of conductive material having a resistance value of 10 ohms (Ω) each are connected across a 5-volt battery. A complete circuit consisting of two parallel paths is formed and current will flow as shown.

Computing the individual currents shows that there is .5 ampere flowing through each resistance. Therefore the total current flowing from the battery to the junction of the resistors, and returning from the resistors to the battery, is 1 ampere. The total resistance of the circuit can be determined by substituting total values of voltage and current into the following equation derived from Ohm's Law.

$$R_t = \frac{E_t}{I_t} = \frac{5}{1} = 5 \text{ ohms}$$

This computation shows the total resistances to be 5 ohms—one-half the value of either of the two resistors.

Since the total resistance of this parallel circuit is smaller than either of the two resistors, the term "total resistance" does not really mean the sum of the two individual resistor values. A better term is *equivalent resistance*. The terms are used interchangeably, but it must be remembered that the equivalent resistance of two parallel resistors is smaller than the resistance of either of the two individual resistors.

There are several methods used to determine the equivalent resistance of parallel circuits. The most appropriate method for a particular circuit depends on the number and value of the resistors. For the circuit with equal-value parallel resistors only, as above, the following simple question is used: $R_{eq} = R/N$ where R_{eq} = equivalent parallel resistance, R = ohmic value of one resistor, and N = number of resistors.

Example: Four 40-ohm resistors are connected in parallel. What is their equivalent resistance?

Solution: $R_{eq} = \dfrac{R}{N} = \dfrac{40}{4} = 10$ ohms

Many circuits have resistors of unequal value connected in parallel. The most common formula used to solve for the equivalent resistance of a number of unequal parallel resistors is the *reciprocal method*. The formula for this method is:

$$R_{eq} = \cfrac{1}{\dfrac{1}{R_1} + \dfrac{1}{R_2} + \cdots\cdots \dfrac{1}{R_n}}$$

Example: Given three parallel resistors of 20 ohms, 30 ohms, and 40 ohms, find the equivalent resistance using the reciprocal equation.

Solution:

$$R_{eq} = \cfrac{1}{\dfrac{1}{R_1} + \dfrac{1}{R_2} + \dfrac{1}{R_3}}$$

$$R_{eq} = \cfrac{1}{\dfrac{1}{20} + \dfrac{1}{30} + \dfrac{1}{40}}$$

$$R_{eq} = \cfrac{1}{\dfrac{6}{120} + \dfrac{4}{120} + \dfrac{3}{120}} = \cfrac{1}{\dfrac{13}{120}}$$

$$R_{eq} = \dfrac{120}{13} = 9.23 \text{ ohms}$$

When all factors in a circuit problem are known except the equivalent resistance, it is possible to solve the problem by simple application of Equation C $(R = E/I)$.

Chapter 3. Study Guide Questions

1. What is a parallel circuit? What must it contain?

2. How is the current flow in a parallel circuit different from that in a series circuit?

3. What is each current path of a parallel circuit called?

4. What does "total resistance" really mean in a parallel circuit?

5. If three 60-ohm resistors are connected in parallel, what is their equivalent resistance?

6. What is the most common formula used to solve for equivalent resistance of a number of unequal parallel resistors in a circuit?

Vocabulary

parallel circuit	equivalent resistance
junction	(total resistance)
branch	reciprocal method

Problems

Using the formulas for Ohm's Law and parallel resistors, solve the following problems.

1. Parallel resistors of 20 ohms and 30 ohms are placed in a circuit powered by a 50-volt battery.
   a. What is the current across R_1? $I_1 = $ _____
   b. What is the current across R_2? $I_2 = $ _____
   c. What is the total current? $I_T = $ _____
   d. What is the equivalent resistance of the circuit? $R_{eq} = $ _____

2. Given three parallel resistors of 75 ohms, 30 ohms, and 50 ohms, find the equivalent resistance using the reciprocal equation. $R_{eq} = $ _____

3. Given three parallel resistors of 40 ohms, 60 ohms, and 80 ohms, find the equivalent resistance using the reciprocal equation. $R_{eq} = $ _____

4. Given three parallel resistors of 15 ohms, 30 ohms, and 45 ohms, find the equivalent resistance using the reciprocal equation. $R_{eq} = $ _____

5. Given three parallel resistors of 60 ohms,

30 ohms, and 20 ohms in a circuit with a 60-volt battery, find the following values:
  a. Equivalent resistance (R_{eq}) = _____
  b. Total current (I_t) = _____
  c. Current across R_1 (I_1) = _____
  d. Current across R_2 (I_2) = _____
  e. Current across R_3 (I_3) = _____
  f. Power across R_1 (P_1) = _____
  g. Power across R_2 (P_2) = _____
  h. Power across R_3 (P_3) = _____
  i. Total power (P_T) = _____
6. Given three parallel lamps drawing 60 watts, 120 watts, and 180 watts respectively from a 120-volt battery, find the following values:
  a. Current in L_1 = _____
     L_2 = _____
     L_3 = _____
  b. Total circuit current (I_t) = _____
  c. Resistance in L_1 = _____
     Resistance in L_2 = _____
     Resistance in L_3 = _____
  d. Equivalent resistance (R_{eq}) = _____
  e. Total power expended (P_T) = _____

Chapter 4. Radio and Radar

The fundamentals of electricity discussed in Chapters 1–3 are the basis of all electronic devices. Many such devices are indispensable to today's Navy, for communication, navigation, and detection. In this chapter, we will examine two types of systems based on the transmission of electromagnetic waves.

RADIO

It has been determined that the speed of radio-frequency (r-f) energy through space is approximately 186,000 miles per second, the speed of light. A radio wave radiates outward from the antenna in the same manner that a wave travels across water into which a rock has been thrown. It consists of a series of crests and troughs, similar to those of a water wave.

There are four important aspects of radio waves: amplitude, wavelength, cycle, and frequency. The *amplitude* is the distance from the average level to the peak or trough of the wave and is a measure of the energy level of the wave. A *wavelength* is the space occupied by 1 cycle and is usually measured in meters, from crest to crest. Each *cycle* is made up of two reversals; the wave moves first in one direction, reverses itself, then returns to the first direction to begin the next cycle. The *frequency* of a radio wave is the total number of complete cycles the electromagnetic wave goes through in a unit of time. The standard measurement of frequency is in *hertz:* 1 hertz = 1 cycle per second. For a radio receiver to get good reception it must be tuned to the same frequency as the transmitter.

Frequencies within the range of 15 to 15,000 hertz are called *audio frequencies* because vibrations of air particles within this range can be detected by a person with good hearing. Above 15,000 hertz are the radio frequencies. The common unit used in speaking of frequencies is the kilohertz (KHz) for 1,000 hertz and the megahertz (MHz) for one million hertz.

The atmosphere through which radio frequencies travel will affect the path the energy follows. Weather or atmospheric conditions

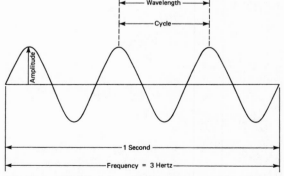

Characteristics of a radio wave, with a frequency of 3 hertz.

can cause variation from the straight path that the waves might otherwise take. These variations are called refraction, reflection, diffraction, and trapping.

Refraction occurs when there is a change in the density of the atmosphere in which the wave is traveling. Take for example a radio wave transiting the atmosphere. Because the atmosphere gradually decreases in density with altitude, the wave is refracted or bent downward. This increases the horizontal distance the wave will have to travel to get out of the atmosphere.

Radio waves are *reflected* from the ionosphere, which is generally from 30–250 miles above the earth. The distance between the transmitter and the point where the reflected sky wave returns to a ground receiver is called the *skip distance.*

Diffraction is the natural bending of radio waves over the horizon. This bending effect is usually weak, but can be detected by a good receiver. Low-frequency waves are bent more readily than high-frequency waves, and so can be intercepted by the enemy at a greater distance.

Trapping is when a temperature inversion in the atmosphere traps cold air close to the earth's surface. Under those circumstances the radio signals may be reflected from the warmer

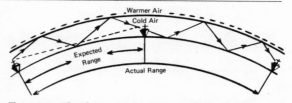

Trapping. The duct acts as a signal wave guide.

air above back to earth a number of times. This will increase the actual range of the transmitted signal. This trapped cold air is called a *duct.* Both the transmitting and receiving antennas must be within the duct.

RADAR

Radar (short for *ra*dio *d*etection *a*nd *r*anging) was developed originally as a means for detecting and ranging on targets in warfare. But it has also become a valuable electronic navigational aid. Radar is based on the principle that electromagnetic waves can be beamed in a straight line, and that part of the transmitted wave will be reflected back, if an object disrupts that wave on its path.

Navy radars are grouped in three general categories: search, fire control, and special. *Search radars* are of two categories: air search and surface search. These are used for early warning and general navigation. Search radars produce detection at maximum range, while

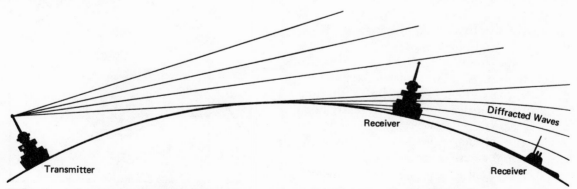

Diffraction is the characteristic bending of radio waves over the horizon (curvature of the earth). It extends the range of low-frequency waves well beyond the rated power of the transmitter, and is an important factor in long-range communication and electronic warfare.

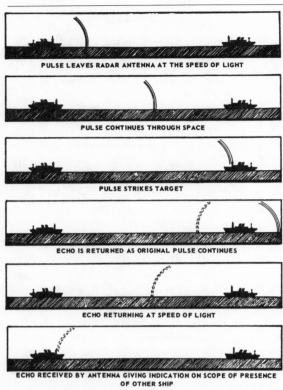

PULSE LEAVES RADAR ANTENNA AT THE SPEED OF LIGHT

PULSE CONTINUES THROUGH SPACE

PULSE STRIKES TARGET

ECHO IS RETURNED AS ORIGINAL PULSE CONTINUES

ECHO RETURNING AT SPEED OF LIGHT

ECHO RECEIVED BY ANTENNA GIVING INDICATION ON SCOPE OF PRESENCE OF OTHER SHIP

The principle of radar operation.

the longer the interval before the echo returns. If a directional device is built to transmit and receive this echo, it can be used to determine the direction, distance, and height of the cliff, since we know the speed of sound.

Radar equipment works on the same principle. Radio waves of extremely high frequency are beamed out, and the radar set is programmed to receive its own echo. This out-and-back cycle is repeated up to 4,000 times per second. If the outgoing wave is sent into clear space, no energy is reflected back to the receiver. But if the wave strikes an object—such as an airplane, a ship, a building, or a hill—some of the energy comes back, at the speed of light, as a reflected wave.

In addition to the power source itself, the typical surface radar is made up of five components. They are the transmitter, modulator, antenna, receiver, and indicator. The *transmitter* consists of a radio frequency oscillator which sends out electromagnetic waves. The *modulator* causes the waves to be emitted as pulses. The *antenna* assembly beams the energy at the target, much as a searchlight is

sacrificing some detail. *Fire control radars* are important parts of gun and missile fire control systems. They are used after a target has been located by search radar. *Special radars* are used for specific purposes, which include: ground-controlled approach (GCA) radar at airfields, carrier-controlled approach (CCA) radar, and height-finding radar.

Radar operates very much like a sound wave or echo reflection. If you shout in the direction of a cliff, you will hear your shout return from the direction of the cliff. What actually takes place is that the sound waves generated by the shout travel through air until they strike the cliff. There they are reflected and some return to the originating spot, where you hear them as an echo. It takes a moment in time between the instant you shout and when you hear the echo. The farther you are away from the cliff,

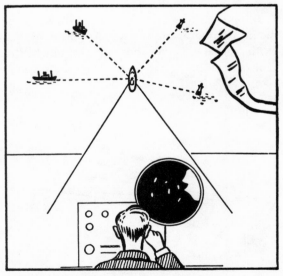

A PPI scope presentation, in the black circle, uses white dots (or pips) to illustrate the contacts viewed visually from the bridge.

beamed. It also can be rotated to scan the surrounding area. In the *receiver*, the reflected radio energy returned from the target is converted to a form that may be presented visually on an *indicator* or scope.

The echoes received by the radar receiver appear as marks of light on an *oscilloscope*, a device similar to a TV screen. It is commonly called a "scope" or PPI (Plan Position Indicator). The scope is marked with a scale of miles, yards, and degrees. It provides a bird's eye view of the area covered by the radar, showing the transmitting ship in the center of the screen. Each time a target is detected it appears as an intensified spot on the scope; thus an observer watching the PPI can tell the range and bearing to the target. Other radars can tell the altitude of incoming aircraft and missiles.

Radar as a Navigational Aid

Because of advances such as radar, the shiphandler can now easily navigate under conditions which otherwise would be very unsafe or impossible. He can maneuver the ship safely at night and in low visibility, in situations where previously it would have been too dangerous. Instead of anchoring until the fog lifts, the modern shiphandler, with the aid of radar and sonar, can maneuver with certainty. Instead of depending upon glimpses of shadowy landmarks and the advice of a navigator who has scant information, the conning officer of today is supported by a specially trained radar team.

The best use of radar in conditions of low visibility is to gain a well-determined position, or *fix*, by radar piloting. A good fix can be obtained by (1) range and bearing of a single object, (2) cross bearing, and (3) two or more ranges. Range and bearing is taken in a manner similar to visual ranges and bearing in piloting situations. The more positively identifiable points which can be determined, and then plotted with accuracy, the more accurate the fix. Two or more ranges provide the most accurate radar fix, presuming the radar is properly calibrated. Good navigational radar targets are isolated rocks, very small islands, sharp points of land, buoys, and offshore lighthouses. Larger targets, such as bigger islands, mountains, and shorelines are much less accurate; even these are better than nothing on a dark foggy night, however, and have helped many a modern navigator.

The accuracy of positions obtained by radar varies with the different types of radar and the skill of the operators. In the majority of circumstances, the accuracy of radar fixes compares favorably with fixes obtained by other means. Limitations exist, however, and these must be thoroughly understood by any navigator or conning officer. Instruments are not foolproof, and the conning officer must not follow the advice of the supporting team without also exercising his own judgment. Beam widths, pulse lengths, mechanical adjustments, and personal interpretations all can cause errors in radar fixes.

Radar has definite advantages, however, when used for navigation. Several of these benefits are listed here:

1) Radar can be used at night and during periods of low visibility, when other methods are unavailable.

2) A fix can be obtained from a single object, whereas a visual fix requires two or more objects.

3) Radar fixes can be obtained rapidly, and the PPI makes available a continuous track of positions.

4) Radar can be used at greater distances from land than visual methods of piloting.

5) Radar is a helpful anti-collision device, both for navigation and ship maneuvering.

6) Radar can be used to locate and track squalls and tropical storms.

Use of Radar in Combat

Just before World War II the development of radar made it necessary to establish a ship-

A midshipman works with the dead reckoning tracer in CIC to provide a good estimated ship's position.

decide which targets to engage, and with what means—aircraft, guided missiles, fire-controlled gunfire. The CO must also decide which way to maneuver to escape or engage incoming enemy ships and aircraft.

Missions in which CIC plays a leading role are: CIC piloting, electronic warfare, antiair warfare, antisubmarine warfare, and intelligence. Special missions include amphibious warfare control, mine warfare control, rescue and assistance, shore bombardment, carrier air operations including control of the combat air patrol, and other surface warfare operations.

Antiair warfare is the tactical use of sensors and weapons to combat airplanes and missiles sent by the enemy. It is a defensive operation, designed to ensure survival of a ship. When intelligence indicates that a formation may be attacked by hostile aircraft, maneuvers are ordered by the officer in tactical command, to put the group in the best defensive formation.

The formation will establish a *surveillance area*, out from the ships along the *threat axis* (the direction from which the enemy is anticipated). Inside of the surveillance area is the initial active defense area, where the *combat air patrol* (CAP) is stationed in order to destroy hostile aircraft. Designated long-range missiles may also be employed in this area. Should the enemy penetrate into the final defense zone of the formation, destruction there must be by surface-to-air missiles and antiaircraft gunfire.

CIC becomes the nerve center during AAW for it must coordinate and display the entire air picture. CIC must evaluate incoming contacts to determine whether they are friendly or enemy. If they are enemy, CIC must direct the CAP in completing a successful intercept. Finally, CIC must coordinate the use of CAP, surface-to-air missiles, and antiaircraft gunfire.

The destroyer's main role since World War II has been to counter attacks by submarines on the main body of a formation. Destroyer types therefore have much specialized equipment used only for locating, classifying,

board clearinghouse, where radar information could be collected and evaluated. As officers and men became more familiar with radar, the functions of this "radar plot" expanded into collecting, processing, displaying, evaluating, and disseminating combat information. With increased experience in air control and fire support, these important control and assist functions were also added. Eventually all warships were equipped with a radar plot, and the Chief of Naval Operations renamed the area the Combat Information Center (CIC).

CIC, then, is the central area from which the modern warship does its fighting. Quite often the commanding officer (CO) assumes a battle station in the CIC, and leaves the executive officer as the senior officer on the bridge. As the evaluator of the myriad of combat information coming into the center, the CO must evaluating, and finally destroying the unseen enemy of the deep. Surface ships and other ASW systems rely principally on sonar to detect submarines. Sonar will be discussed more in Chapter 5 of this unit; but it should be said here that sonar operations are coordinated in the CIC, along with control of the different antisubmarine weapons systems.

Electronic warfare uses highly sophisticated electronics to counter the enemy's radiated electromagnetic waves, and to ensure the proper and effective use of our own. The electronic warfare systems include (1) collection of information regarding the enemy without his being aware, and without divulging our presence; (2) hindering or rendering the enemy's electronic spectrum useless by means of jamming his circuits with electronics countermeasures (ECM); and (3) electronic counter-countermeasures (ECCM), which ensure the proper use of our electronic spectrum—in spite of the enemy's attempts to direct his ECM at our unit.

Chapter 4. Study Guide Questions

1. What are the four main aspects of a radio wave? Define each.

2. What is the standard measurement of frequency? What does this measurement represent? Where do r-f frequencies fall?

3. What are those frequencies within audible range of a person called?

4. What four variations from the straight wave path are caused by atmospheric or weather elements? List a key aspect of each variation.

5. How does the ionosphere affect radio communications? What is skip distance?

6. What effects may a "trapping duct" have on communications?

7. From what phrase is the word "radar" derived? What is the fundamental principle of radar?

8. What are the three general categories of U. S. Navy radars?

9. What are the two categories of search radars and what are they used for?

10. What is radar used to determine?

11. What are the components of a typical radar set?

12. What is the "scope" or PPI? How does a contact appear on the scope?

13. How can radar assist the shiphandler and conning officer?

14. How is a radar fix determined?

15. What type of radar target makes the best reference point for navigational fixes?

16. List in abbreviated form the six principal advantages of using radar in navigation.

17. What is the purpose of CIC?

18. What does the CIC evaluator do?

19. How is antiair warfare (AAW) coordinated in the CIC?

20. What is meant by the term "threat axis?"

21. What has been the main role of the destroyer-type ship since World War II?

22. What are the functions of ECM and ECCM? How do their tasks differ?

23. What is meant by jamming?

Vocabulary

radio frequency energy
wave crests and troughs
amplitude
wavelength
cycle
frequency
hertz (Hz), kilohertz (KHz)
refraction
diffraction
trapping
reflection
atmospheric density
skip distance
temperature inversion

radar
GCA, CCA
fire control radar
oscilloscope
PPI
radar fix
Combat Information Center (CIC)
combat air patrol (CAP)
threat axis
antiair warfare (AAW)
Electronic Warfare (EW)
jamming
electronic countermeasure

Chapter 5. Sonar

The principal method of submarine detection is sonar (short for *so*und *n*avigation *a*nd *r*anging). The earliest sonar device, used in World War I, was a simple hydrophone, lowered into the water and used to listen for the noise created by a submarine. The only indication of a target was an audio tone. Bearing accuracy was doubtful, and ranges were strictly guesswork. But by the end of the war, Allied navies had worked out a system of triangulation (using three ships for best results). This system could pinpoint the location of a U-boat by coordination of hydrophone data.

Today's sonar equipment provides highly accurate ranges and bearings. It can present information both visually (on a scope) and aurally (by sound). In addition, very sophisticated sonars for use in helicopters and fixed-wing aircraft have been developed.

THE PHYSICS OF SOUND

To understand how sonar works, we must first understand some things about sound. Sound travels in the form of waves away from the point of origin—much as ripples travel out in all directions from a pebble tossed into a pond. Echoes are created when the sound waves strike an object of greater density in the surrounding seawater. The waves will not travel through these objects, and some are reflected back to a receiver at the source.

The substance through which sound travels is called a *medium*. The sounds we normally hear travel through the medium of air. In the case of sonar, the sound is traveling through the medium of seawater.

Before sound can be produced, three basic elements must be present. These elements are (1) a source of sound, (2) a medium to transmit the sound, and (3) a detector to "hear" it. In the absence of any one of these elements, there can be no sound.

Any object that vibrates, disturbing the medium around it, may become a sound source. Bells, radio loudspeakers, telephone diaphragms, tuning forks, and stringed instruments are familiar sound sources.

Sound waves are passed along by the material through which they travel. The density of the medium determines the ease, distance, and speed of sound transmission. The greater the density, the greater the speed of sound. The speed of sound through water is about 4 times that through air; through steel it is about 15 times greater than through air.

The detector acts as the receiver of the sound wave. Because it doesn't surround the source of the sound wave, the detector absorbs only part of the wave's energy. Therefore an amplifier is needed to boost the signal's energy.

Having learned something of the theory of sound, let us now look at what happens to an underwater sound pulse. To gain the full benefit of echo-ranging sonar equipment, the sonar technician must be able to recognize the echo returning from a target. Detection of the echo depends on its quality and relative strength, compared with the other sounds which tend to mask it.

Sonar technicians must know (1) what can weaken sound as it travels through water, (2) what conditions in the sea determine the path and speed of sound, and (3) what objects affect the strength and character of the echo.

Transmission losses occur as a sound pulse travels outward from its source. Factors causing these losses are divergence, absorption, and scattering. *Divergence* is simply the natural spreading of the sound wave into a spherical shape as it travels from its source. The further it travels, the more energy it loses. It stands to reason that as the sound pulse goes through water, the water molecules *absorb* some of the energy of the pulse. *Scattering* is caused by the fact that the composition of the sea naturally varies, from place to place and from time to time. Within the medium are many kinds of marine life and particles of foreign matter. As the sound pulse meets each of these particles, a small amount of the sound is reflected away from its direction of movement and is lost. Any scattered energy which happens to come back to the sonar receiver is called *reverberation.*

Additional transmission losses occur as the result of the following causes:

Reflection. When a sound wave strikes the boundary between two mediums of different densities, the wave will be reflected. Reflection takes place whenever the sound hits the boundary between sea and air (sea surface), between sea and bottom, and when it hits a solid object such as a submarine or rock pinnacle. The amount of energy reflected depends on the object's density, size, and shape.

Refraction. Refractions are normally caused by the differences in water temperature in different layers of the sea. The velocity of sound in seawater increases from 4,700 feet per second to 5,300 fps, when the temperature increases from 30° to 85°F. Because of the temperature differences in the sea, the sound does not travel in a straight line; instead, it follows curved paths, which cause bending, splitting, and distortion of the sound beam. When a beam of sound passes from warmer water, where its speed is high, into colder water where it is slower, the beam is refracted toward the area of lower temperature and lower velocity. As the result of refraction, the range at which a submarine can be detected by sound may be greatly reduced, even to less than 1,000 yards.

Quenching. In strong winds and heavy seas, the roll and pitch of the echo-ranging ship make it difficult to keep the sound direction on the target. When this turbulence produces air bubbles in the water, the sound emitted by the ship's sonar transducer may be blanketed, and some of the sound beam may be sent out into the air. This action is known as quenching.

Sound in the Sea

The speed of sound waves traveling through the water is controlled by three conditions of the sea: (1) temperature; (2) pressure, caused by increased depth; and (3) salinity, or the salt content of the seawater.

Temperature is by far the most important of the factors affecting the speed of sound in water. The speed of sound in water increases from 4–8 feet per second, for every degree of change. Since the temperature of the sea varies from freezing in the polar seas to more than 85° in the tropics, and may decrease by more than 30° from the surface to a depth of 450 feet, it is clear that temperature has a great effect on the speed of sound in water.

Sound also travels faster in water under pressure. Pressure increases as depth increases, so the deeper a sound wave is, the faster it travels. Pressure effect is smaller than temperature effect but cannot be neglected, since it increases about 2 feet per second for each 100 feet of depth.

Seawater has high mineral content or *salinity.* The weight of higher-density seawater is about 64 pounds per cubic foot; that of fresh water is only about 62.4 pounds per cubic foot. This variation is the result of the salt content in the seawater. The saltier the water is, the faster the speed of sound in it. In the open ocean the values of salinity normally lie be-

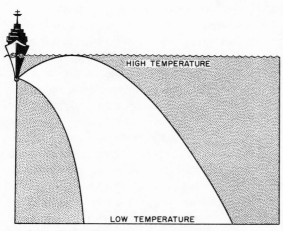

A refracted sound beam.

tween 30–35 parts per thousand, or 3–4 percent of the volume. In regions where rivers pour fresh water into the ocean the salinity values may fall to very low levels. On the other hand, the Mediterranean Sea has a higher salt content than the Atlantic, and the Red Sea and Persian Gulf have salinity which approaches 30 percent. The speed of sound increases about 4 feet per second for each part-per-thousand increase in salinity—a lesser effect than that of temperature, but greater than that of pressure.

THERMAL LAYERS OF THE SEA

Under ordinary conditions the sea has a temperature structure of three levels: a surface layer of varying depth with uniform or nearly uniform temperature (*isothermal*); the *thermocline*, a region of relatively rapid decrease in temperature; and the rest of the ocean, with slowly decreasing temperature down to the bottom. When this structure changes, the path of a beam of sound through the water also changes.

Layer effect is the partial protection from echo-ranging and listening detection that a submarine gains when it submerges below a layer depth—that is, below a point where there is a marked change in temperature. Sometimes a submarine, diving through a sharp thermocline while taking evasive action, loses the screw noises of the enemy ASW ship. Similarly, on the ASW ship, ranges on submarines are reduced greatly when the submarine dives below a sharp thermocline.

DOPPLER EFFECT

You may have noticed the apparent change in frequency or pitch of a train whistle as the train approaches, passes, and departs. Actually, there is no change in frequency; but there is a change to the human ear, because of the relative motion between the source and receiver. As the train comes toward you, the effect is an increase in pitch caused by compression of the waves. As the train moves away, it has a lower pitch because the sound waves are spread farther apart. This phenomenon is known as the *doppler effect*.

This same doppler effect can be used by the sonar technician as he listens to sounds of contacts under the sea. Effective use of doppler comes only with much practice, but it is of extreme importance to the life and safety of both the ASW ship and the submarine.

If the echo from a submarine is not changing in pitch, the sub is either stopped or is crossing the sound beam at a right angle. Its echo has exactly the same pitch as the reverberations picked up from the energy reflected from water particles. There would be no doppler effect.

If the submarine is coming toward the echo-ranging ship, the sound transmission reflected from the approaching submarine is heard at a higher pitch than the reverberations. This would be reported as "doppler up." On the other hand, if the submarine is moving away from the ship, the tone of its returning echo will be lower in pitch than the tone of the reverberations, and the report would be "doppler down."

SONAR SYSTEMS

There are two basic types of sonar systems employed for the detection of targets. They are referred to as active and passive sonars.

Active sonars transmit underwater sound pulses that strike targets and return in the form of echoes. The returned echoes indicate the range and bearing of the target. Surface ASW ships usually employ the active (pinging) mode when seeking out submarines. Active sonar systems also are used by submarines and ships to analyze shorelines, bottom characteristics, and ocean depths. Submarines can switch to active modes to locate ships or other submarines; but this is rarely done since it would give away the transmitting sub's location.

Passive sonars do not transmit sound. They merely listen for sounds produced by the target

The frigate USS *Willis A. Lee* (DL 4) rests in drydock at Boston Naval Shipyard after being refitted with a bow sonar dome.

to obtain accurate bearing and estimated range information. Target detection is achieved at great ranges through the use of highly sensitive hydrophones. Passive sonar is usually associated with submarines, but newer surface ships can employ passive systems in addition to their active sonar. Submarines use passive sonar to analyze the noise of passing ships. ASW aircraft, helicopters, and shore stations also use passive sonar.

DIPPING SONAR AND SONOBUOYS

Sonar equipment called *dipping sonar* can be used by helicopters to detect submerged submarines. The helicopter can hover and lower a hydrophone or pinging transducer into the sea to a depth of about 400 feet, searching a 360° area. After searching, the helicopter hauls in the cable and goes to another spot quickly. When a submarine is detected, the

A Sea King helicopter with dipping sonar dome lowered during ASW exercises.

helicopter can guide in other aircraft or ships to coordinate an attack.

Radio sonobuoys are small expendable floating hydrophone units which are dropped in the area of a suspected submarine by fixed-wing aircraft. They are usually dropped one at a time in a circular pattern around the contact area. An experienced operator, listening for the pitch (doppler) of the radio signals received from each sonobuoy, can estimate the present location and direction of movement of the submarine. The plane can then either attack the submarine with depth charges or bring in ASW surface units.

Most ships also have aboard a *fathometer* for determining water depth under the hull. A sound pulse, directed toward the bottom, is transmitted, and its echo is received back. The fathometer is normally used as a navigational assist, particularly in coming into an anchorage. It also is used regularly in oceanographic research to determine the contour of the sea bottom. Most Navy ships keep their fathometer on continuously, to have an accurate recording of the water depths on their course. The information is automatically recorded by a stylus on a roll of graph paper. This graphic report is sent in to the Defense Mapping

Agency Hydrographic Office for their use in making navigation charts.

SHIPBOARD ASW

Sonar control is the ASW station that maintains a continuous underwater search for submarines. *Underwater battery (UB) plot* is responsible for fire control in an ASW attack. During an ASW attack, CIC, in conjunction with UB plot, takes control of the ship for attack purposes. (The conn is retained by the bridge, as it must ensure safe coordination with the movements of other ships and sonar-dipping helicopters in company.)

The CIC is the key station for coordinating search-attack operations within the ship and between ships. Personnel in CIC will plot, display, evaluate, and disseminate all air, surface, and subsurface contacting information, recommending search plans to the commanding officer.

A destroyer will often work with other kinds of ASW units, such as submarines and carrier- or land-based ASW aircraft. Such combinations improve the chances for success against the elusive modern submarine. In addition,

A flight crew prepares sonobuoys for an antisubmarine mission.

The most effective ASW system is the nuclear-powered attack submarine. Shown here is the USS *Bluefish* (SSN 675).

new ASW ships have computerized tactical data systems aboard in CIC and UB plot. These systems help process all the mathematical information received concerning the submarine, and solve complex maneuvering and fire control problems.

In spite of the tremendous advances in shipboard and aerial ASW, it probably is the ASW nuclear attack submarine which will be most effective in combating enemy submarines in the future. The speed, maneuverability, and underwater endurance of modern nuclear submarines is unequalled. Thus the stealth and swiftness of another submarine, using sophisticated passive sonar and guided missile torpedoes, may be the only consistently effective ASW tactical weapon system.

Chapter 5. Study Guide Questions

1. How was the term "sonar" derived?

2. What was the earliest sonar system used in World War I? How was it made operationally effective?

3. What is meant by visual and aural presentation?

4. How does sound travel?

5. What is the substance through which sound travels?

6. What are the three basic elements necessary for production of sound?

7. What effect does the density of the medium have on sound transmission?

8. Through which medium does sound travel faster—air or water? How much faster? Why?

9. What must the sonar technician be able to do in order to achieve benefit from echo ranging sonar equipment?

10. Explain each of the causes of transmission loss as a sound pulse travels through the water from its source.
   a. divergence:
   b. absorption:
   c. scattering:
   d. reflection:
   e. refraction:
   f. quenching:

11. What are the three conditions of the sea which affect the speed of sound waves in water?

12. What is the most important factor affecting the speed of the sound in water?

13. How does pressure affect sound waves in water?

14. What is the weight of seawater compared to fresh water? What effect does salinity have on the speed of sound in water?

15. Where do the seas have highest salinity content? In what particular bodies of water is the salinity very high?

16. What is the isothermal region? What is the thermocline? How do these layers serve to protect a submarine from detection?

17. How is the doppler effect used by sonar technicians in determining submarine movements under the sea?

18. What are the two types of sonar systems? Which is the most often used by surface ships? Which is the most often used by submarines?

19. Why do submarines rarely use active sonar?

20. How do helicopters use sonar to detect submarines?

21. What are sonobuoys and how are they used?

22. What is the purpose of a fathometer? How is it used for oceanographic purposes?

23. What are the two major sonar stations for shipboard ASW operations? What is the principal mission of each station?

24. Which two stations take control of the ship during ASW attack?

25. What weapons system is probably the most effective in combating enemy submarines? Why?

Vocabulary

sonar	doppler effect
hydrophone	active sonar
triangulation	passive sonar
medium	ASW
sound pulse	dipping sonar
reverberations	sonobuoys
quenching	fathometer
isothermal layer	sonar control
thermocline	underwater battery
echo ranging	(UB) plot

Survival Training

Chapter 1. Introduction to Survival Training

In this day of rapid movement around the world there is more than a passing chance that one day you might find yourself in the unfamiliar surroundings of the arctic, the ocean, a jungle, or a desert, or even a wilderness area within your own state. Impossible, you say? Well, more and more people fly, travel, and go on recreational and hunting trips in remote places. Moreover, both the last two world wars were truly global; and the wars in Korea and Vietnam were fought in extremely harsh environments.

In the military services, the techniques of survival in wilderness areas of every climatic and geographical area of the earth have long been a standard part of training. This has been of special importance for pilot and air crew trainees, all of whom must undergo special survival exercises in desert, rain forest, and wilderness areas. Pilots and special forces organizations have training sites for jungle warfare in Panama, arctic training in Alaska, and desert training in the Southwest. In addition, survival-at-sea procedures are part of basic recruit training in the Navy.

Survival in remote and difficult areas depends largely on resourcefulness. Your chances of success will be greatly increased if you are physically fit, dressed and equipped for all emergency situations, and if you know some woodcraft and outdoor techniques. You must have some basic knowledge of the geography, plants, and animals of the area, and be alert to those things which might harm you. You must learn how to find and prepare foods. And, you must know how to care for your body, how to conserve energy, how and where to sleep, how to make shelter, and how to locate yourself and tell directions.

There are so many different emergency situations which could confront you throughout the globe that it is not possible to lay out a definite survival plan. The best assurance anyone can have, therefore, is to acquire a fundamental knowledge of basic survival information, so you can have some idea of how to meet any emergency which might arise.

Perhaps the most important aspect of survival training is an awareness that needless fears can be eliminated with basic knowledge. Your survival chances are in direct proportion to the knowledge and skill you have, your ability to improvise successfully, and the preparations you made for the possibility of an emergency.

All pilots have survival kits which are designed to meet basic requirements for most circumstances. Special operating units which are assigned to unique environments have equipment and clothing which are prepared for the requirements of their area. Equipment most commonly found in these kits includes the following:

1) Pocket or sheath knife.

2) Waterproof matches or matches in water-proofed container.

3) Waterproof compass.

4) Small pencil flashlight in waterproof case.

5) A small fishing kit.

6) A mosquito head net, especially in the jungle or arctic.

7) First-aid kit.

8) Canteen.

9) Small signaling mirror.

As a general rule, pilots forced down in strange country should stay by the plane, since it is easy for rescue missions to spot, and may provide a good shelter and base for foraging. In enemy territory, however, the plane should be abandoned and destroyed, after any items which will be of value in evasion and survival are removed.

WATER

Water is the most important single factor in determining survival. An individual needs at least a quart of water a day, but this will vary according to the weather and surroundings. People can survive for many days without food, if they have water. In fact, if the body is not overexerted and the climate warm, a person can live off muscle and fat for weeks, as long as water is available.

When very thirsty, sip water slowly and keep intake down. If hot from sun or exercise, avoid drinking very cold or excessive amounts. If the only water available is very cold, such as from snow or ice, warm it in the mouth before swallowing.

When looking for water it is very important to find pure ground water or spring water. Ground water lies below the surface or runoff water; rocks below the water table are saturated with water. Springs occur in places where land contours meet, often near streams or below mountains and hills.

Surface water is often contaminated, especially if it is near villages. This water can be deadly, carrying all sorts of disease germs. If this is the only water available, it must first be boiled for at least three minutes. Rain water is pure, and running water is often safe; but even running water is not safe if it is near or downstream from human habitation.

Along a seashore, drinking water can usually be found by digging near the shore in a depression. This is because rain water seeps seaward as part of the general water cycle (see Unit 6, Chapter 2). If the water which seeps into the dig hole is slightly brackish, the freshest water will be on the surface, since the heavier salty water will sink lower in the hole. Drinking sea water in any quantity when the body is dehydrated can cause death; the kidneys will cease to function when damaged by the high concentration of sodium and magnesium salts.

Water exists even in desert parts of the world, but it may be very difficult to locate unless all indicators of its presence are observed. Converging game trails, presence of some plants, and direction of flight of some birds (especially pigeons and parrots) are generally sound clues to the presence of water. If all other methods fail, certain cacti or young desert trees will furnish some water drops. In the United States, the barrel cactus is a well-known source of water in the deserts of the Southwest. Sap, which is principally water, can be squeezed or sucked out of many roots and stems of plants, and coconut milk from the green nuts is good for fluid intake. In jungle areas, some plants gather falling rain, much like a cup. This water is usually safe to drink.

Drinking impure water is one of the major hazards in tropical and subtropical countries. Such water must be boiled or chemically purified; otherwise there is great danger of contracting dysentery, cholera, typhoid fever, and various parasitic diseases. These diseases in themselves can cause death from high fevers and dehydration; and the weakness and delirium they cause make it impossible to function.

CLIMATE AND FOODS

All food is either plant or animal, and is distributed in each environment according to natural laws. Animals eat plants, and large animals eat smaller animals. Where plant life is scarce, there will probably be little animal life either. Climate is the greatest single factor affecting the abundance and distribution of plant and animal life. A fundamental knowledge of the geographic regions of the earth is valuable in planning and hunting for food sources.

In every continent there are general climatic areas which have the same types of animals and plants. For instance, the grasslands of North America have burrowing animals and hoofed animals, such as prairie dogs and antelope; similar animal types exist on the grasslands of other continents, even if the species are different. Animals that live in and along streams are similar in all like climatic regions, regardless of the continent. Edible plants and animals in foreign countries are found in the same type of places as they are at home—fish and clams in streams, deer in forests, squirrels and birds in woods and grasslands, and so forth.

Wherever animals and birds exist, other animals and birds are nearby, because all species form a link in the natural food chain. For instance, water snakes and kingfishers will certainly indicate the presence of fish, frogs, and crayfish. With the exception of a few kinds of tropical fish, all animals and birds are safe to eat. Additionally, all birds' eggs, amphibians, bee honey, fruits, nuts, seeds, roots, and even many insects such as ants, termites, grubs, and grasshoppers are edible, if properly prepared.

In general, if animals and birds can eat certain seeds, berries, and other plant foods, so can man. It is never wise to eat too much of any strange foods, however. Plants with milky juice should be avoided, for they may be poisonous. Citrus and other fruits often grow wild in tropical highlands, and a wide variety of plantains and bananas are often abundant in lower elevation tropical areas. Blackberries, raspberries, and blueberries are similar throughout the world. Buds and tender young leaves are often nutritious in starch, sugar, oils, and greens. Roots of many plants are usable for food, but normally require considerable preparation and cooking. Edible nuts are the most sustaining of all raw forest foods and are found throughout the world in temperate and tropical climates.

Fishing is probably the easiest, and consequently the best, source of animal food in a survival situation. Bodies of fresh water and streams should be regarded as primary sources of food, so it is generally wise to remain close to water when stranded in any type of country. It is usually best to fish in the early morning or late afternoon, in deep pools where the water is running less swiftly. Natural baits such as grasshoppers, angleworms, crayfish, and bits of other already caught fish work well. Fish can be caught with a variety of set lines, hooks, spears, and even with the bare hands in shallow spots.

Lizards and crustaceans such as crayfish, lobsters, and crabs are all edible. Turtle meat, also, is good to eat in soup. Catching small mammals, such as rabbits, is usually not too difficult to do with snares set across trails or at burrow entrances. Small rodents like mice hide in clumps of grass or under logs and can easily be captured when uncovered. Larger animals like squirrels, coons, and opossums can be driven from holes in trees by smoking them out or capturing them with a noose when they emerge.

Large game hunting will normally require a shooting weapon. Stalking or lying in wait for the animal is necessary, and careful aim required because the shot will frighten animals for a considerable surrounding distance. In the woods, move slowly and stop often; a motionless man with a gun has an immense advantage over a moving animal. It is advisable to keep upwind of large animals, and never become a silhouette on a skyline. Silence is generally the most essential requirement of successful hunting.

SHELTER

Adequate shelter will increase your chances of surviving and greatly reduce physical hardships. Shelter and sleep are as necessary to a stranded person as food and water. A person will tire as quickly from loss of sleep as from lack of food.

Lost or isolated persons should decide on what will be necessary for a safe and comfortable night. In strange country the search for a campsite should begin two hours or more before sunset, for it will be almost impossible after dark. A number of factors should be considered in selecting the campsite:

1) Available food.
2) Good drinking water.
3) Comfortable level site for the bed.
4) Protection from wind and storm.
5) Adequate bedding and shelter material.
6) Protection from floods, wild animals, rock falls, high tides, and cold.

Survival tents made from parachutes can be used to keep out the elements.

7) Concealment from enemies.
8) Absence of insect pests.
9) Firewood.

A minimum amount of time and energy should be expended in making a camp. A natural area well protected from winds should be selected. If this is a cave, it should be carefully examined to see that there are no poisonous snakes and insects. Windbreaks and lean-tos can be constructed with tree branches. If a parachute has been salvaged, a tent which will be largely windproof can easily be fashioned. In the arctic, a small igloo or snow shelter can be constructed, the principal purpose being to break the wind and hold in as much body heat as possible. In the desert it also is necessary to keep out of the wind to reduce dehydration and because, after sundown, the temperature drops rapidly. The hot sand of the day will retain some of its heat if covered with a coat, parachute, or blanket; otherwise it will chill rapidly.

A good bed allows the body to relax completely and insulates against ground chill. It must be dry, smooth, soft, and free of insects. Warmth and comfort are of paramount importance; a cold person cannot relax. Since the ground is cold at night and conducts body heat away, it is necessary to place insulating materials such as evergreen boughs beneath the sleeping area. In the wet jungle it is necessary to sleep off the ground, preferably in a parachute hammock or a jungle bed made of bamboo poles and palm leaves, a foot or two above the surface. Waterproofing can be accomplished in the tropics by heating banana plant leaves one at a time over hot coals and overlapping them on a rack or roof of bamboo stalks. In the arctic or in northern evergreen forests, spruce or hemlock boughs can be made comfortable by inserting all the bough ends into the ground or snow in the same direction, then covering them with feathery evergreen tips or dry leaves and grasses. A fire may be made to reflect heat toward the bed, and hot

Navymen in the Philippine Jungle Training Unit learn to make and relax on jungle beds made of bamboo. The bed is necessary in the hot, wet, tropical jungles.

coals or smoke from green wood will keep away many insects.

ENVIRONMENTAL HAZARDS

Physical and biological hazards often take a heavy toll on persons stranded in the wilds, even when food and water are available. It is necessary to be able to overcome these problems in order to survive. Knowing the dangers and how to surmount them will give an individual confidence, diminish hardships, and lengthen survival time.

Sunburn is a common result of overexposure. It is most common on a mountain snowfield, on open water, desert sands, and beaches. Tropical sunburn is common, but it is easily avoided by getting into the shade of tropical vegetation. Prevention by covering is necessary, for the results of sunburn can be severe. Coconut oil can help to protect skin which is normally exposed to the sun. For sunburn treatment the burn ointment in a standard first-aid kit, or tannic acid derived from boiled dark brown tree barks, can help the burned areas.

Heat stroke and heat exhaustion are common afflictions in the tropics. The loss of salt is a main cause of these problems, so the body's salt and water intake must be maintained at a higher than usual level. Sunstroke or heat stroke is the result of direct exposure to sun; its symptoms are dizziness, nausea, headache, hot and dry skin, and a high body temperature. The best preventives are to keep the head covered or wet and to cool the body and clothing by water immersion. The treatment is to lie in the shade with head slightly higher than the body, drink salty water, and bathe the head and body to cool.

Heat exhaustion is the result of long exposure to the sun. The skin is clammy and temperature is normal or below normal. Treatment is to drink salty water, lie in the shade with head lower than the body, and cover up to keep warm. These symptoms can also occur in high altitudes and very dry, windy areas where sweating is not easily detected, due to its rapid evaporation. If the body requires salt, even a strong salt solution will not taste salty.

Snow blindness is a painful inflammation of the inner side of the eyelids caused by constant exposure to reflection of the sun's rays from snow. Preventive measures include: wearing dark glasses, traveling at night, and blackening eyelids, cheeks, and nose to protect the eyes. Cold water will relieve eye pain. If temporary blindness has resulted, bandages over eyes will probably be necessary. Eye inflammation is a common malady of survivors at sea due to the excessive glare and the exposure to wind, cold, and salt water. Care of the eyes is a vital requirement in any survival situation.

Long exposure to salt water may result in sores and swelling, particularly on legs. Immersion foot is caused by continued immersion of the feet in cold or ice water, or by continued hiking in wet, cold footgear. Pain is followed by swelling and numbness, and blisters and sores may result. Feet must be kept as dry as possible and tight clothing should not be worn, since it will retard circulation and may break the skin.

Nibbling at food is probably the best way to maintain strength under survival conditions. Overeating will upset the regular habits of the body and cause severe headaches and dizziness.

Clothing is the main protection from cold. The clothing must be kept dry. A number of layers of light clothing are generally better than a single heavy garment. This way, layers can be taken off as required to maintain a regular body temperature. All clothing should be loose-fitting. Outer garments should be windproof, but not so airtight as to cause sweating. Control of sweating is essential, for wet clothing conducts heat away from the body and increases chance of freezing. All areas of the body should be kept covered, since exposure of uncovered hands, face, head, and poorly insulated feet will cause sufficient heat loss to chill the entire body and make frostbite on the extremity likely.

BIOLOGICAL HAZARDS

The sources of greatest danger often are the smallest forms of life. While these insects and bacteria may be irritating, their real danger comes in the transmission of disease through their bites. In the services, medical authorities have usually done all in their power to innoculate personnel against the various diseases around the world, especially those in the tropics and those caused by filth from lack of sanitation. Nevertheless, many diseases and parasites cannot be controlled by prior innoculations.

Probably the most common of all disease hazards caused by insects is *malaria,* a tropical disease carried by a certain species of Anopheles mosquito. Injected into the blood stream through the bite of the mosquito, a microscopic protozoan enters the red blood cells, absorbs their contents, and grows to divide into numerous additional individuals which are discharged into the blood stream by rupturing the cell wall.

In the tropics, mosquitoes are much more dangerous than in other localities, as they transmit malaria, yellow fever, dengue fever, and filariasis. In the arctic, there may well be many more mosquitoes, but they do not carry disease. Slow-moving water is required for mosquito-breeding purposes; thus both the heavy rain forest of the tropics and the muskeg swamps of the arctic in the summer are perfect breeding areas for mosquitoes. Mosquito nets are a must in such areas, though improved insect repellents are now available as well.

Flies of many species transmit a variety of diseases and discomforts. Many contaminate food, carry cholera and dysentery; some are vicious biters, or deposit eggs which develop into larvae that infest wounds. Many flies in the tropics carry filarid worms which cause elephantiasis. This disease, for which there is no effective treatment, is caused by minute worms which bore into the lymphatic glands and cause body extremities to swell to huge proportions.

The tsetse fly is found only in central and south tropical Africa; it carries a sleeping sickness which may be fatal. Screwworm flies are found in the American and South Asian tropics. They deposit eggs in wounds, especially around the nostrils of sleeping persons suffering from colds. The larvae burrow into the nasal tissues, causing severe pain and swelling. Fleas, usually carried by rodents, carry plague and endemic typhus. These diseases are usually fatal if contracted. Fortunately, service personnel are innoculated against both plague and typhus. There is also a wide assortment of ticks, lice, fleas, flies, and bugs which can carry disease to human beings as well as make them uncomfortable.

The bites of spiders are normally not dangerous, but the black widow of the southern United States, and other tropical cousins of the same family, can cause severe pain and swelling. The tarantula—the huge spider of the deserts of the Southwest and banana spider of the tropics—though horrible looking, is not poisonous; its bite may cause infection, however. The scorpion, which stings with the spine of its tail, can cause extremely painful wounds, swollen limbs, and illness. In the tropics the huge black scorpion may grow to six or eight inches in length, and can inflict a severe sting which may be fatal to children or persons not in good health. Tropical centipedes are also poisonous, but rarely cause fatal injury. A variety of bees and wasps can inflict extremely painful stings which may vary in severity from one person to the next, depending on individual reaction.

Human parasites such as blood flukes or flatworms are common in the sluggish waters of the tropics and Middle East. These animals live part of their life cycle in snails and then are transmitted to humans through drinking or bathing in infested water. Hookworms are common in the tropics around villages where sanitation is poor; the worms are acquired by going barefooted in such areas. Fungus infections and parasitic skin diseases are common where damp and hot conditions exist, and a lack of regular bathing facilities. Athlete's foot is one example of such disease; it is extremely difficult to cure. Strong soap, immersion in salt water baths, and powdered disinfectants are used for treatment.

Snakes cause concern in some areas of the world, but their danger to man is considerably exaggerated. Poisonous snakes are extremely dangerous, but they usually are timid, moving away from any disturbance. They bite if suddenly surprised or if stepped upon. Two varieties, the king cobra of Southeast Asia and the bushmaster of South America, have been known to attack when their living area is invaded.

Snakes live only in the temperate and tropic regions of the earth. Only in Australia do the poisonous species outnumber the harmless ones. Of about 2,400 species of snakes, some 200 are known to be dangerous to man. While the number of species in the tropics is greater, the danger of snakebite is not much more there than in the United States, where rattlesnakes and water moccasins infest large areas. The exception to this is in India, where every year thousands die from cobra bites due to lack of adequate treatment. An antidote does exist for the Indian cobra bite, but it must be administered very soon after the victim is bitten. There is no antidote for king cobra venom and death usually occurs within 15–30 minutes.

There are three principal groups of dangerous snakes: the *long-fanged snakes* which include rattlesnakes, moccasins, and copperheads of the United States, bushmaster, fer-de-lance, and palm viper of Latin America, and the bamboo snakes of Asia; the *short-fanged snakes* (the most deadly) which include cobras, kraits, several Australian species, and the American coral snake; and the *sea snakes* of the Indian Ocean and southern and western Pacific.

POISONOUS PLANTS

As a general rule, poisonous plants are not a serious hazard, but under certain conditions they are dangerous. Plants may be poisonous to eat or to touch, due to toxic juices or oils; or they may have sting hairs that irritate when they come in contact with the skin.

In the United States the common varieties of poison ivy, poison sumac, and poison oak are irritant contact plants. They cause reddening, itching, swelling, and blistering of affected parts. The best treatment is to wash thoroughly with strong soap as quickly as possible after contact. The ailment must not be scratched or rubbed, for that will only intensify the irritation.

A number of plants of the tropics are poisonous to the touch; some also have berries or fruit which cause blindness if eaten. Probably the most infamous of plant poisons is curare, a byproduct of the strychnine tree. Curare is used on the tips of spears and arrows of South

American tribes. Wounds from such arrows should be treated the same as snake bites.

TRAVELING

One of the first problems when you're stranded in a strange country is to determine your location and what direction you must follow to return to base. By studying charts and maps you can gain the fundamental knowledge which will give you general orientation— for instance, direction of flow of rivers or direction in which ridges run, and any outstanding landmarks.

If you're lost on land it is necessary to sit down and think the situation through first. Panic must be avoided. If possible, view the countryside from a tree or high point to try and find some familiar landmark and to get bearings.

Before going anywhere, you can find north by looking at the sun or stars. Hopefully you will have a compass; this also will help establish a travel route. If you also have a map, orient it with the compass. Orienting a map consists simply of making north on the map coincide with true north. The compass should be placed on the map and the map turned until the north-south grid lines are parallel to the compass needle. Thus map north is the same as compass north. You must remember that magnetic north deviates somewhat from true north; this deviation is minimal in low and middle latitudes, but can be significant in polar regions.

It is unwise to travel by night in strange wooded country except when absolutely necessary. Travel in swamps should never be attempted at night. In open or desert country, however, night may be the only safe time to travel, because of the climate and the possible need to evade an enemy.

It is a good idea to establish a course on the basis of landmarks if possible. Traveling along a river or shoreline is generally wise since it will probably lead you to inhabited areas.

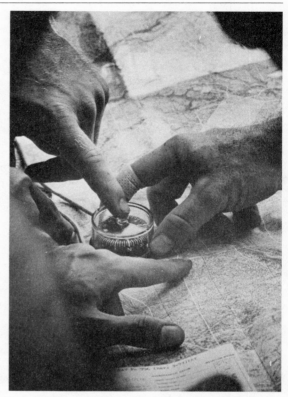

Orienting a map with a compass is a necessary step before plotting a course and setting out to travel in remote areas.

Move in as straight a line as possible and avoid fighting the vegetation. A slow, steady rate of travel with rest as needed will get you much farther in the long run. A fast rate will only serve to exhaust you, make you less alert, and expend valuable water resources in your body.

EVASION

Evasion means traveling through enemy-held territory without being captured. If behind enemy lines, the evader must make use of natural cover and be sure that nothing will reflect light or attract attention. He must stop often to look and listen. When moving he must avoid crossing an exposed spot, and never should silhouette himself against a contrasting background or skyline on a ridge. Travel should be on hard ground or in water, if possible, to prevent leaving footprints.

If danger threatens, all motion should be stopped. This is particularly so in the jungle, where motionlessness is more useful than camouflage. Hiding places in bamboo and rattan thickets, banyan trunks, and brush are plentiful. The best way to lose a pursuer or avoid an enemy is to get off the trails. This makes travel more difficult, but it may be more important to gain concealment than to have easy movement or conserve energy. It is simple to ambush an enemy following a jungle trail, but very difficult to stalk an alerted man in the jungle because of the dense underbrush.

In the jungle, smoke from a small cooking fire can seldom be seen for more than a few hundred feet. A fire at night cannot be detected through the thick growth any further away. Thus, an enemy approaching at night can usually be heard before he is within sight of a small fire.

The allegiance of natives in the area of operations is always somewhat of an unknown factor. At times it may be best to avoid them, but in most cases they will help if you can gain their confidence. The help and friendship they extend to you will be directly proportional to your own good will and good conduct toward them. Never show fear, and treat them as equals. Observe their customs and be eager to learn from them. But be very careful about eating and your personal hygiene in a native village; the danger of disease is greatly increased even if food and shelter is no longer a problem.

Chapter 1. Study Guide Questions

1. Why should more people become acquainted with survival techniques?

2. Why do aviators of the military services have special survival training requirements? Where do naval personnel get their first survival training?

3. What factors will improve one's chances for survival in remote areas?

4. Why is survival planning important to the morale of personnel?

5. When should pilots stay with a downed plane? When should they get away from it as soon as feasible?

6. What is the most important single factor in determining ability to survive?

7. Why should surface water be avoided? What kind of water is safe to drink when in a survival situation?

8. What clues exist to help the survivor find safe drinking water? How can safe water be obtained near the seashore?

9. Why is intake of impure water so dangerous to people?

10. What is the greatest single factor affecting the abundance and distribution of plant and animal life? How does knowledge of the earth's geography figure into survival training?

11. What is a general rule determining edibility of plants and related plant foods? What raw plant or forest food is the most sustaining of all?

12. Why is fishing regarded as a primary food source for the survivor?

13. In order to successfully hunt big game, what is required?

14. What are some reasons why shelter and rest are so important to the survivor? Be able to list a minimum of five or more factors which must be considered when seeking a campsite.

15. What is a jungle bed? Why should a jungle bed or hammock be used when sleeping in tropical forests?

16. What are some common environmental hazards faced by survivors in the jungle? . . . in cold climates? . . . on the sea? What is the difference between heat stroke and heat exhaustion, and how is each treated?

17. What is the most common jungle biological hazard? How is this acquired by man? What are some other tropical diseases carried by insects?

18. What are the more common insect-like creatures which a survivor must avoid?

19. What are human parasites and how do they affect man?

20. Where do snakes inhabit the earth? What is their usual conduct when they sense approach of man?

21. What are the three principal groups of poisonous snakes? How do the poisons of these snake groups affect the victim?

22. What are the three principal poisonous plants in the U. S.?

23. How can pre-mission studying of charts and maps help the surviving members of a downed crew?

24. How can a map be oriented? Why is a slow steady rate of travel better than a fast rate?

25. What is meant by evasion? What are some of the key rules in successful evasion in a jungle environment?

26. How should contact with natives be handled? What is the inherent risk of living with natives, presuming they are friendly?

Vocabulary

survival training	heat stroke
resourcefulness	heat exhaustion
environmental hazard	affliction
	snowblindness
survival kit	malady
forage	immersion foot
overexertion	malaria
ground water	Anopheles mosquito
surface water	filariasis
land contour	elephantiasis
brackish water	tsetse fly
dehydration	plague
tropical, subtropical areas	typhus
	endemic disease
dysentery	scorpion
cholera	centipede
parasitic disease	blood fluke
delirium	antidote
climatic region	venom
snare	contact irritant
jungle bed	evasion
overexposure	landmark

Chapter 2. Jungle Survival

The requirements for survival in jungle areas are basically the same as anywhere else: ability to obtain food and water; to improvise shelters, make fires, and cook foods; to travel; and to overcome or avoid physical and biological hazards encountered. A good woodsman from the temperate zone can quickly adapt to the unique requirements of the jungle.

There are four principal types of jungle: mangrove, along tropical seashores; primary jungle, largely virgin forest; secondary jungle, thick growth coming up from areas once cleared or burned; and high mountain jungle forests. *Mangrove* is usually a swamp of tangled roots and interwoven branches with mud floor, often with a foot or more of water from tides and converging delta streams and rivers. Snakes and crocodiles are common in the mangrove swamps and salt marshes, and mosquitoes, leeches, and other insects are often abundant. A raft is the best means of travel.

Primary jungles are characterized by huge trees and a network of vines. The interior forest floor is often relatively open, because little sunlight can work its way through the dense canopy of trees and vines. There often is little bird and mammal life, except that which exists high in the trees. Therefore the survivor must depend heavily on plants for food.

Secondary jungle is often very dense growth of smaller vegetation. Not so wet, it is often characterized by thorny growth, leathery-leaved plants, and open meadows. Animal trails from larger animals criss-cross the areas heading for waterholes. Villages are usually somewhere in the vicinity.

Swampy jungle of South Vietnam. This is swamp on the edge of mangrove and primary jungle. It is extremely difficult to traverse.

High mountain jungle forests are perhaps the most difficult areas in which to subsist and travel. Rains are often incessant, as are heavy fogs. Insects abound and tree leeches drop from the branches and attach themselves to travelers. Malaria is rampant. Rushing, rock-filled streams are dangerous to cross. The very high humidity saps human strength. During the dry season huge leaves cover the ground and insects are everywhere.

Jungle Travel

Travel in the jungle is hampered primarily by the oppressive heat and the mass of thick vegetation. There is seldom any view, and there are few landmarks for fixes. There is a monotonous sameness which quickly hems in

the traveler and confuses him if he doesn't have a trail or stream to follow. A compass is a necessity. Once a course is set, it is essential to keep to it, even if travel in another direction might seem to be easier.

In jungle travel, following a river is usually advisable. Native and game trails normally follow rivers. It is easier to follow the trail than to try to cut through the jungle, especially if it is full of vines, thorns, and ferns. It may be smart to build a raft and try to float down the river. Bamboo is an ideal material for raft construction.

The jungles of the world are vast, extending thousands of miles across sparsely settled continents. To be able to survive in them requires much travel and long periods of living under

Traveling in dense undergrowth and crossing streams is a part of Navy survival training in the flight program. This group picks its way across a swollen stream.

the most primitive conditions. It requires physical stamina, survival know-how, high morale, and at least a minimum of equipment. Many men did it during World War II in the South and Western Pacific, particularly in New Guinea, the Solomon Islands, the Philippines, and in the Burmese jungles.

A good machete, a lightweight poncho, and malaria drugs are considered essential for jungle survival. It is also extremely helpful to have a small-caliber rifle with ammunition, to shoot animals or birds for food. The lightweight Army jungle hammock with mosquito-net sidewalls is an ideal shelter and bed.

Along with the thorny rattan vines, the insects of the jungle are the greatest annoyance. The best defense against mosquitoes and leeches is proper clothing. Trousers should be long, lightweight, and tucked into boot tops. A shirt should be mosquito-proof, and a hat, water-repellent. Nylon-top boots, with high instep vents to allow water to run out, are the best jungle boots. Wool socks are best. The body must be examined frequently to be sure that leeches or ticks have not become attached.

Despite the abundance of water in the tropical rain forest, drinking water can be difficult to acquire. The best sources of water are the large jungle vines or lianas. Those yielding a clear water are safe to use for drinking purposes. A thick piece of vine 5 or 6 feet long will often yield more than a pint of good quality water.

PLANT FOODS

Fruits and nuts that are used as food by monkeys are usually safe for man to eat. But never eat more than small quantities until their edibility can be established. Palm trees generally are excellent sources of food. Many yield fruits, buds, sugary sap, or stored starch within the trunk. Also, the hearts of the rattan palm vines can be cooked in their outer covering and make good food. Bamboo shoots can be cooked and eaten like the rattans. There is a wide assortment of tropical fruits such as bananas, papayas, mangos, custard apples, limes, and so on, which are excellent eating.

The coconut palm is widely cultivated throughout the tropical world, and grows wild along most tropical seashores. The large terminal bud or cabbage is an excellent vegetable, cooked or raw. The nuts furnish meat and water, and a sugary sap can be obtained by cutting the flower spikes. The nuts are available the year around, and on any one coconut palm the nuts will be in varying stages of maturity. Actually the green nuts are the best because they can be easily opened, have more fluid, and the fluid can be taken in large quantities. The jelly-like flesh of half-grown coconuts is more nourishing, and can be eaten in greater quantity, than the hard oily meat of the mature nuts.

Animal Foods

Fish, crayfish, and mollusks are readily caught in most jungle streams. A gill net is often an excellent means of catching fish. In mangrove swamps and forests, oysters and fish are plentiful. Crabs and lobsters can be speared, trapped, or caught with the hands; the best time to catch them is at night.

Since all species of birds and mammals are edible, the problem is not one of classification, but of catching and killing the game so it can be cooked and eaten. It is very difficult to stalk game in the jungle successfully. It is much more productive to ambush game along a trail or at a water hole. Jungle life is most active during the early morning and late evening just before the sun goes down. It is generally quiet during the heat of the day. Birds can often be found in fruit trees; the noise they make can be heard for a considerable distance. Many kinds of water birds nest in the mangrove trees and their eggs are excellent for eating. Monkeys and wild pigs are also common in many areas.

Chapter 2. Study Guide Questions

1. What are the basic requirements for survival anywhere?

2. What are the four principal types of jungle?

3. What vegetation characterizes each type of jungle?

4. Among the many hindrances to jungle travel, what are the two primary factors making jungle travel difficult?

5. Why is following a river usually advisable in the tropics?

6. During World War II, in what areas did many military personnel find it necessary to practice the art of jungle survival?

7. What type of clothing should be worn in the jungle? Why?

8. How can one easily acquire fresh water in the jungle?

9. What tropical tree is probably the most helpful to a survivor in the jungle?

10. What sea animals are generally abundant in mangrove forests?

11. Since almost all species of birds and animals are edible, what then is the basic problem for survivors as far as these animal foods are concerned?

12. What tactic will probably be the most successful for hunting in the jungle? Why?

Vocabulary

improvise	machete
mangrove forest	poncho
delta stream	rattan palm
primary jungle	liana
secondary jungle	papaya
tree leech	coconut palm

Chapter 3. Survival in Polar and Subpolar Regions

The basic survival problem in the polar regions is keeping warm. The cold allows no trial-and-error experimentation. Keeping warm under emergency conditions in sub-zero temperatures requires specialized clothing and equipment, and a knowledge of controlling heat loss from the body. With the following items and the ability to improvise, a person can successfully cope with most emergency conditions in the cold regions:

1) Heavy underwear (50 percent wool, 50 percent cotton).

2) Intermediate-weight trousers and jacket.

3) Two or three pairs of wool socks.

4) Felt shoe insoles.

5) Shoepacs, felt boots, or mukluks.

6) Fingered gloves and mittens.

7) Outer windbreaker trousers and parka with hood.

8) Dark glasses, matches, and field glasses.
9) Sleeping bag lined with down.
10) Snowshoes, rifle, and ammunition.

Clothing must be kept dry inside and out. The insulating effect of clothing is greatly reduced when it gets damp or wet, when it is not worn loosely, or when the windbreaker is not adequate to stop outside air movement. Cold-weather clothing has thousands of tiny air pockets that trap air warmed by the body and hold it close to the skin.

Footgear sufficiently warm to withstand sub-zero weather should be worn at all times. It is difficult to keep feet warm, because they tend to sweat more readily than other parts of the body, thereby getting damp and cold. Insoles and socks are intended to absorb some of this perspiration; but unless the socks are periodically dried, the feet may become chilled or frozen.

Keeping warm in arctic clothing, in a sleeping bag, in a snow igloo or cave, or in other shelter all satisfy the same need. Air movement must be reduced to a minimum so it can be warmed by body heat or fire. All clothing must be kept dry to prevent heat loss through conduction and through reduced insulating air space.

KEEPING WARM

The critical factor in the far north is cold, not food or water. The prime consideration in polar conditions is how to supplement the protection afforded by arctic clothing, until help comes. The best way to do this is by creating a dead-air space, such as a snow cave, snow house, or bough shelter, and by the use of fire.

In open country a shelter should not be built in a lee as it will tend to be covered by drifting snow. In the mountains or forest, however, a camp can and should be made in a lee. Such a site is generally warmer and snow will be less apt to drift, since the timber will break the wind. Wind is a major factor in keeping a person cold. A snow cave is small and uncom-

Navy traveler in the ice pack. Ice ridges, crevasses, and thin ice make traveling the ice pack a dangerous task.

fortable, but with a sleeping bag and just a candle or small fire it will raise the air temperature much above the outside.

The snowhouse, or igloo, is the ideal cold-weather shelter. It generally is not practical for a single individual to build, but it is adaptable as a permanent camp for a crew of 4 or 5 persons. A well-banked tepee made of a parachute is also an excellent shelter, and especially so in the arctic summer.

A down sleeping bag is essential to the person stranded in polar regions. It will keep a person from freezing, whether or not he has fire or shelter. The bag should be kept dry and fluffed, and should have a water-repellent cover. It should not be placed directly on the snow if insulating boughs or grasses or outer garments are available. The bag should be turned inside-out to dry each day.

The dangers of cold include frostbite and snow blindness. These dangers creep up on a person unnoticed, but they must be anticipated in very cold weather so that survivors can remedy them early. The face is most likely to be frostbitten. When stiffness is discovered, a hand should be removed from a mitten and held over the frozen part until the stiffness is gone. Frozen, cold, or wet feet should not be uncovered unless there is a fire, warm shelter, or sleeping bag to cover them. Snow blindness can be prevented with handmade goggles of bark or cloth designed with small slits for seeing.

Subsistence in Polar Regions

It is essential to have food intake in the polar regions, because food is the fuel for generating body heat. Obtaining food in the arctic should not be too difficult for experienced persons, but it is advisable to have emergency rations in your kit if possible. Living off the land becomes increasingly difficult the further north one goes.

Plants and animals of the arctic region and subarctic forests are pretty much the same. Therefore, living off the land in any of these areas will be basically the same. While plant and animal food is present in this region, it is not always easily available.

North of the Arctic Circle there are musk oxen, wolves, polar bears, hare, foxes, muskrats, lemmings, and seals; there are also birds such as ptarmigans, gulls, owls, geese, ducks, and others. Many of these migrate south during the long arctic winter, but musk oxen and ptarmigan do not. Further south in the pine woods there are many more animals, birds, and plants, including deer, moose, and porcupines, as well as a large number of fur-bearing animals. In the summer the area abounds with birds of many varieties which are nesting, so eggs, in addition to the fowl, are available for food. Seals are the "staff of life" on the arctic ice pack, but exceptional skill is required to spear or shoot them.

Fish are usually plentiful in the streams and lakes of the northland. Salmon are found from spring to fall in coastal streams and rivers from the Pacific Northwest to Alaska and from New England northward. When a fish enters the river and travels upstream to spawn, it can be clubbed and picked out of the streams by hand. Salmon die after spawning, and for a time before this their flesh gets soft and may be poisonous. When the salmon is pink, it no longer is good to eat; select only the silver or white salmon for eating in the wild. Trout, pike, and grayling can be caught in the lakes by fishing through the ice.

Plant foods in the arctic and subarctic may be safely eaten, for few are known to be poisonous. Hemlock juice and buttercups should be avoided, however. There is an abundance of wild berries in the arctic—salmonberry, crowberry, currants, cranberries, strawberries, raspberries, and blueberries often cover many acres in wild growth. In the summer they can easily be picked, and in the winter they can be found frozen on the stalks. Many plants have edible roots which are good after being boiled.

Lichens are the most widespread and surest source of emergency food in the far north. These are mosslike in appearance, and often cover large areas growing on rocks, trees, logs, and in sand and gravel. None are poisonous but some are quite bitter, and will cause internal irritation unless cooked, dried, and recooked.

Travel in Polar Regions

Polar and subpolar regions are vast expanses of largely unexplored, uninhabited territory. Distances alone make travel difficult. It is generally best to stay with a downed plane unless you are fully equipped for polar travel. A person can live for extended periods on the arctic ice pack or in subpolar lands, if skilled in hunting and properly equipped. For extended survival a rifle must be available to kill big game as a major food source.

Problems encountered in polar and subpolar travel vary widely. The problems on polar seas, polar land, forested areas, and mountain regions are all quite different. Basic is the problem of keeping warm and finding food. Generally speaking, spring is the worst season for traveling in polar regions. The snow and ice melt, opening up streams, muskeg, avalanches, and quicksands. Tormenting insects come out in droves.

Deep snow and cold winds are the principal obstacles to winter travel, though winter travel is generally easier than spring travel. Often, snowshoes, skis, or sleds are necessary. Attempting to walk in deep snow without snowshoes is foolhardy, for a person's energy will be quickly used up. It is better to remain in camp than to travel into a cold wind. The wind-chill factor will quickly cause frostbite and chill the lungs, causing death.

Traveling in timbered areas without snowshoes is often impossible because the snow is deep and soft there. Best traveling is on the windswept ridges just below the crest. Steep southern exposures above timberline should be avoided, especially on warmer days or during the warmest part of the day, since that is where and when avalanches are most probable. The greatest danger of avalanche is in the spring, when the thaw starts.

Perhaps the most dangerous part of traveling in winter, other than wind chill itself, is the possibility of falling through thin ice on streams or ponds. Getting wet is extremely dangerous, for death can result very quickly in the frigid weather or wind. The water itself is within a degree of freezing, and so is truly ice water. A person's ability to swim, wade, or hold on in ice water is greatly reduced because the body is so quickly chilled. Crossing deep snow-covered streams is particularly dangerous because the snow is a good insulator. If a heavy snow falls prior to formation of safe ice, the snow blanket will frequently prevent further ice formation. Small swift-flowing streams sheltered by high banks and vegetation are more apt to have thin ice than large windswept bays or rivers.

COLD-WEATHER MILITARY TRAINING

Many military strategists believe that if another war occurs in the near future, it may be fought largely in and over the cold regions of the earth. Great circle navigation routes between the United States and the Soviet Union, the routes for intercontinental ballistic missiles and for manned bombers, traverse the north polar ice cap. United States submarines regularly patrol the Arctic Ocean beneath the polar ice cap.

The new oilfields in Alaska are now beginning to provide significant help to ease the energy shortage in the United States, and dependence on this source is sure to grow. Consequently, these fields and the oil pipeline itself would be targets of great strategic importance to any enemy.

Realistic training programs which instruct airmen in meeting emergency situations in cold regions must be a part of any survival curriculum. The Navy has a continuing expedition in the Antarctic to develop all manner of equipment, fuels, clothing, and tactics which would be applicable to any arctic climate. The health, safety, and morale of military airmen and sailors will depend in large measure upon how thoroughly they have been grounded in polar experience, techniques, and knowledge, and how well their planes are equipped for an emergency landing in the arctic regions.

Chapter 3. Study Guide Questions

1. What is the basic survival problem in the polar regions?

2. In order to keep warm, what is a fundamental requirement for polar survival?

3. How does cold-weather clothing keep a person warm?

4. Why is it so important to keep footwear dry?

5. Where should snow caves or shelters be built in the open? . . . in the forest?

6. What is the most important sleeping gear all pilots must carry aboard their planes in the arctic? Why is it so important?

7. What are two specific dangers of the cold

to the survivor? How should each be prevented?

8. Assuming the survivor has proper clothing and shelter, what is the next essential requirement to keeping warm? Why?

9. What are some of the animals of the Arctic tundra and subarctic forests?

10. What is meant by the term "migration" and how does this affect the arctic food supply?

11. When should salmon not be eaten?

12. What general category of plant food is quite abundant in the arctic? What unique plant growth is the most abundant source of emergency food in the far north?

13. Why is a rifle so important for far northern survival?

14. When is the worst season of the year to travel in the arctic? Why?

15. What special equipments are necessary for winter travel?

16. After wind chill itself, what is the greatest danger of winter travel in the arctic?

17. What do many military strategists feel will be the major area of battle in the event of conflict with the USSR?

18. What is the new U. S. development in the Arctic which would surely be a strategic target early in any polar area war?

19. What are some of the purposes for the United States' exploration and research in the Antarctic?

Vocabulary

polar, subpolar	emergency rations
trial-and-error exper-	realistic training
imentation	ptarmigan
windbreaker jacket	lichens
igloo	sustenance
tepee	muskeg
water-repellent cover	timberline
frostbite	avalanche

Chapter 4. Survival at Sea

Survival at sea depends upon your knowledge, your equipment, your self-control, and your training. You also must exercise a great degree of skill, ingenuity, and resourcefulness. The time to find out as much as possible about survival and rescue at sea is before you abandon the ship or ditch the airplane—not after you find yourself in the water.

SURVIVAL EQUIPMENT

The Navy, Coast Guard, and Merchant Marine have equipped all life boats, rafts, and planes with survival equipment adequate for emergencies at sea. The life preserver is the most important piece of abandon-ship equipment, for it is the surest support in the water, other than a lifeboat. The vest-type preserver is designed to support a man and keep his head out of the water even if he is unconscious. The lifeboat offers the greatest possibility of sur-

vival, because it contains food and water and provides shelter from the elements.

During wartime, each man is issued a life preserver which must be worn or kept readily available at all times. During peacetime, preservers are stowed in ready lockers. Each person should know where his preserver is stowed and how to put it on. This is a regular part of abandon-ship and emergency plane-ditching drills in the Navy.

The two types of Navy life preservers are the inflatable type and the inherently buoyant type. The latter uses fibrous glass pads sealed in plastic waterproof bags that are placed inside an outer canvas cover; it has often been called the Mae West jacket. Leg and body straps keep the preserver in place on the body.

The inflatable preserver is made of lightweight, neoprene-coated nylon. It is carried in a pouch container held around the waist on a web belt. When used, the pouch is pulled around to the front, the preserver is slipped over the head and then inflated, by mouth or by means of a CO_2 capsule. Small waterproof flashlights can be attached to life preservers to aid in finding overboard personnel at night.

A lifeboat may be one of a variety of power-boats or a neoprene-coated fabric boat that is inflated by a CO_2 cylinder or hand pump. The Navy has inflatable boats in a number of different sizes—from 1-man boats up to 15-man boats.

Each boat has an assortment of accessory equipment used to operate the boat itself, and, waterproofed containers of survival equipment. Among the boat gear included are a canopy, sea anchor, lifeline, boarding net, heaving line, rain-catcher tube, radar reflective screen, hand pumps, paddles, a boat repair kit for patching leaks, and a floatable knife. In the survival kits are rations, sea marker dye, flashlight, batteries, signal mirror, whistle, first-aid kit, distress-signal kit, and containers of fresh water. The survival kits in the larger inflatable boats are designed to sustain 15 men for 5 days on regular rations.

Abandon Ship

Having to abandon ship in the middle of the ocean is a traumatic experience. With proper knowledge and training, however, the frightening aspects are greatly reduced. If abandonment becomes necessary, survivors must remain calm; they must not panic or give up hope. The Navy knows the ship is missing and is looking for survivors. Thousands of men have survived ship sinkings, both in wartime and peacetime.

If time permits, the ship will be abandoned in a planned and orderly manner. The routine will have been practiced many times under less trying conditions. If possible, boats will be lowered and inflated and then men will go over the side and get to them as quickly as possible. When preparing to abandon ship, men should get extra clothing and drink extra water before the plunge or debarkation over the side. It is best to go over fully clothed; the life preserver will keep a person afloat, so that swimming, though hindered, will not be unduly difficult for a short distance. The clothing will be needed for any extended stay in a lifeboat on the ocean, for it is essential to keep as warm and as protected from exposure as possible.

Normally crew members should leave from the windward side so the ship will not drift down on them or carry burning oil into their area. They should never dive or jump into the water, because of the danger of hitting debris. It is better to go over on a line, cargo net, or fire hose. If wearing a buoyant preserver, cross your arm over to the opposite shoulder under your chin to prevent neck injury upon hitting the water. If wearing an inflatable preserver, blow it up after getting into the water.

Once in the water you must clear the ship as quickly as possible to avoid being pulled under by a whirlpool effect. Also, a clearance of several hundred feet is advisable to reduce danger of concussion or internal injuries, should there be underwater explosions when the ship goes down. Once away, conserve energy, stay with your shipmates, and get to a lifeboat or raft as quickly as possible. If any debris comes by, hang on to it; it is better than nothing, and may keep you afloat the extra amount of time necessary.

Food and Water

Survival without equipment depends more on fresh water than on food. Without water a person in good health will become delirious in about 4 days and will die within 8 to 12 days. With water, a person can live for weeks without food. As little as 2 or 3 ounces of water a day may be sufficient to keep a person alive for 10 days or more, without causing any permanent body damage. The amount of water and food needed, however, depends upon weather conditions, physical exertion, and individual resistance.

Abandon ship! U. S. soldiers clamber down the sides of the SS *President Coolidge* after the 22,000-ton troop transport struck a mine off a South Pacific island during World War II. Only 2 men were lost out of more than 4,000. Men go over on monkey lines, ropes with knots tied in them to enable hand-over-hand descent.

If you lack water don't eat, because digestion uses up water in the system. It is best to abstain from both food and water for at least the first 24 hours; after that, ration what you have and when that is gone, live off your body fat and protein. One pound of body fat will provide the system with an equivalent of two good meals. The rate at which body fat and protein is converted to heat and energy will depend on the air temperature, activity, and mental state. A person can live longer on stored energy by relaxing the mind and body and by guarding against exposure to extreme temperatures.

Rain, ice, and dew are the only sources of water after canned water rations are exhausted. By keeping clothing damp in warm climates, evaporation of water from the system will be retarded. Dehydration is the real threat; under no circumstances should sea water be used to supplement water intake. That will only aggravate thirst and increase water loss, by drawing body fluids from the kidneys and intestines. This will result in kidney failure, convulsions, and delirium. Rainwater should be collected by any means available, including soaked clothing. Drink all the water you can when running through a rain squall, and catch every bit possible for another day.

The sea is rich in life forms and if fresh water is available there is little danger of starving to death. The problem is to catch the wealth of food which is available. No one at sea should be caught without fishing tackle on his person at all times; but even if this happens all is not lost.

Fish caught at sea are good to eat either cooked or raw; none are likely to be poisonous. Flying fish can be attracted by light at night and will often hit or fall into the boat. Pieces of fish may be used as bait, both for fish and for sea birds. Fish spoil quickly in warm weather so it is necessary to clean and eat them immediately and then dry what is left. Fishing lines can be made from canvas and clothing, and fishhooks can be made from split wood, shoe nails, or bones from birds. It is better to try to catch smaller fish in order to avoid losing the fishing gear.

A grapple or oar should be used to pull in seaweed which may be found floating in the water. Usually a lot of small crabs, fishes, and shrimp will be in the seaweed or sargasso.

All sea birds are edible and nourishing. There are fewer birds in the northern Atlantic and Pacific than in the middle and equatorial latitudes. Sea birds are often found hundreds of miles from shore, and some will cross the oceans behind ships. They can quite easily be lured to hooks with baits made of fish entrails. Often they will land on boats or rafts and can be caught by hand.

Large numbers of birds indicate some kind of land nearby. Most tropical sea birds do not range far from their breeding grounds. Frigate birds and gulls usually indicate that land is near at hand. Cumulus clouds in an otherwise clear sky are likely to have been formed over high or mountainous land, and may be indicative of land below the horizon. Drifting wood or vegetation also is an indication that the boat is approaching land.

The Seashore

The sea beaches and shores of the world contain more food than any other part of the earth. If you are stranded on a seashore in a warm climate, you should have little difficulty sustaining yourself indefinitely. Oysters, mussels, crabs, lobsters, and shrimps are found along all seashores. The best fishing and hunting will be in the tidal pools or in the pools on reefs. Additionally, there usually are many sea birds in the area which will provide both meat and eggs.

In tropical waters there are a few mollusks and fishes which are poisonous and must be avoided. There are dangerous cones and terebras, beautiful shells in which animals with deadly teeth exist. Additionally, there are the parrot fishes, trigger fishes, pufferfishes, and porcupine fishes which have highly toxic flesh. Some sea urchins and fishes have poisonous spines which can cause great pain or death if they inflict a wound.

Dangerous Aquatic Animals

The most dangerous animal of the seas is the shark. At best, sharks are unpredictable and curious; at worst they are vicious maneaters. Barracuda also have been known to attack people in the water. The greatest danger from these animals will be when blood from wounds is in the water, or blood droppings from fish or birds being cleaned for food are present. Hands and feet should not be trailed in the water when sharks or barracuda are thought to be present.

Rays or stingrays are flat fish with powerful venomous tail stingers. One of these stingers can be driven through a person's foot, should the ray be stepped on in sand or mud bottoms in the warm seas. Jellyfish and Portuguese men-of-war can cause painful stings and swelling if one strikes their tentacles when swimming. Survival from the stings is probable, but the paralysis and panic if a person is stung when in the water may result in drowning. The scorpion and stone fishes of the Pacific, and some of the toad fishes of the tropical America, are the most dangerous poisonous fishes. Their venomous spines may produce a sting which causes severe pain and swell, and eventually death. The same treatment which would be afforded a snakebite victim is the best first-aid measure.

TRAINING FOR SURVIVAL

The success of any survival training program depends on the ability of the officer in charge, the amount of time he gets to do the training, and the physical conditions of the area in which the training is given. Advanced base training is very important. The armed forces have continuing programs in which tropical jungle, mountain, and cold-weather training take place. Jungle training is taught in Hawaii, the Philippines, Guam, Florida, and Panama. Centers for cold-weather and arctic training are in Alaska, Colorado, Idaho, and the Pacific Northwest. All services, and particularly the Navy, give extensive training in techniques of airplane-ditching over water.

Chapter 4. Study Guide Questions

1. Upon what four things does a person's success in surviving at sea depend?
2. When must training to abandon ship and survive at sea take place?
3. What are the two categories of life-saving equipment at sea?
4. What two types of life preservers have been developed by the Navy?
5. Why does the lifeboat offer the greatest possibility of survival at sea?
6. Why is it important to abandon ship fully dressed?
7. From which side should crew members abandon a ship? Why should diving or jumping overboard be avoided?
8. What are the particular procedures to be followed with the two kinds of life preservers when abandoning ship?
9. Why must the ship's side be cleared as quickly as possible after leaving the ship?
10. What is meant by the phrase "living off body fat"?
11. How can dehydration be slowed down in warm climates? Why must seawater not be swallowed?

Vocabulary

abandon ship	whirlpool effect
aircraft-ditching	concussion
inherently buoyant life preserver	grapple
	sargasso
inflatable life preserver	tidal pool
	Portuguese-man-of-war
accessory equipment	
debris	venomous spines

Training for survival, these pilots and air crews practice ditching, floating, and lifeboating in the inflatable lifeboat under the watchful instructors' eyes. All pilots must pass this course as a part of their total flight training instruction.

Appendices

NAVY	MARINES	ARMY			AIR FORCE		
MASTER CHIEF P.O.	SGT. MAJOR / MASTER GUNNERY SGT.	STAFF SGT. MAJOR	COMMAND SGT. MAJOR	SPEC. 9	CHIEF MASTER SGT.	CHIEF MASTER SGT. OF THE AF	E-9
SENIOR CHIEF P.O.	1ST SGT. / MASTER SGT.	1ST SGT.	MASTER SGT.	SPEC. 8	SENIOR MASTER SGT.		E-8
CHIEF P.O.	GUNNERY SGT.	SGT. 1ST CLASS		SPEC. 7	MASTER SGT.		E-7
P.O. 1ST CLASS	STAFF SGT.	STAFF SGT.		SPEC. 6	TECHNICAL SGT.		E-6
P.O. 2ND CLASS	SGT.	SGT.		SPEC. 5	STAFF SGT.		E-5
P.O. 3RD CLASS	CORPORAL	CORPORAL		SPEC. 4	SGT.		E-4
SEAMAN	LANCE CORPORAL	PRIVATE 1ST CLASS			AIRMAN 1ST CLASS		E-3
SEAMAN APPRENTICE	PRIVATE 1ST CLASS	PRIVATE			AIRMAN		E-2
SEAMAN RECRUIT	PRIVATE	PRIVATE			BASIC AIRMAN		E-1

Appendix 1. Enlisted Insignia of Rank

NAVY	MARINE CORPS	COAST GUARD	ARMY	AIR FORCE
W-1 WARRANT OFFICER / W-2 CHIEF WARRANT OFFICER	GOLD SCARLET W-1 WARRANT OFFICER / GOLD SCARLET W-2 CHIEF WARRANT OFFICER	W-1 WARRANT OFFICER / W-2 CHIEF WARRANT OFFICER	SILVER BLACK WO-1 WARRANT OFFICER / SILVER BLACK CW-2 CHIEF WARRANT OFFICER	GOLD SKY BLUE W-1 WARRANT OFFICER / GOLD SKY BLUE W-2 CHIEF WARRANT OFFICER
W-3 CHIEF WARRANT OFFICER / W-4 CHIEF WARRANT OFFICER	SILVER SCARLET W-3 CHIEF WARRANT OFFICER / SILVER SCARLET W-4 CHIEF WARRANT OFFICER	W-3 CHIEF WARRANT OFFICER / W-4 CHIEF WARRANT OFFICER	SILVER BLACK CW-3 CHIEF WARRANT OFFICER / SILVER BLACK CW-4 CHIEF WARRANT OFFICER	SILVER SKY BLUE W-3 CHIEF WARRANT OFFICER / SILVER SKY BLUE W-4 CHIEF WARRANT OFFICER
ENSIGN	(GOLD) SECOND LIEUTENANT	ENSIGN	(GOLD) SECOND LIEUTENANT	(GOLD) SECOND LIEUTENANT
LIEUTENANT JUNIOR GRADE	(SILVER) FIRST LIEUTENANT	LIEUTENANT JUNIOR GRADE	(SILVER) FIRST LIEUTENANT	(SILVER) FIRST LIEUTENANT
LIEUTENANT	(SILVER) CAPTAIN	LIEUTENANT	(SILVER) CAPTAIN	(SILVER) CAPTAIN
LIEUTENANT COMMANDER	(GOLD) MAJOR	LIEUTENANT COMMANDER	(GOLD) MAJOR	(GOLD) MAJOR
COMMANDER	(SILVER) LIEUTENANT COLONEL	COMMANDER	(SILVER) LIEUTENANT COLONEL	(SILVER) LIEUTENANT COLONEL

Appendix 2. Commissioned Insignia of Rank

NAVY	MARINE CORPS	COAST GUARD	ARMY	AIR FORCE
CAPTAIN	COLONEL	CAPTAIN	COLONEL	COLONEL
COMMODORE	BRIGADIER GENERAL	COMMODORE	BRIGADIER GENERAL	BRIGADIER GENERAL
REAR ADMIRAL	MAJOR GENERAL	REAR ADMIRAL	MAJOR GENERAL	MAJOR GENERAL
VICE ADMIRAL	LIEUTENANT GENERAL	VICE ADMIRAL	LIEUTENANT GENERAL	LIEUTENANT GENERAL
ADMIRAL	GENERAL	ADMIRAL	GENERAL	GENERAL
FLEET ADMIRAL	NONE	NONE	GENERAL OF THE ARMY	GENERAL OF THE AIR FORCE
NONE	NONE	NONE	AS PRESCRIBED BY INCUMBENT GENERAL OF THE ARMIES	NONE

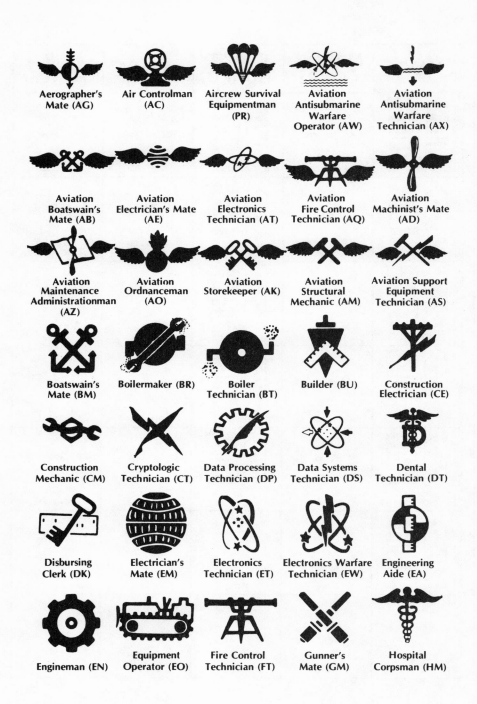

Aerographer's Mate (AG)

Air Controlman (AC)

Aircrew Survival Equipmentman (PR)

Aviation Antisubmarine Warfare Operator (AW)

Aviation Antisubmarine Warfare Technician (AX)

Aviation Boatswain's Mate (AB)

Aviation Electrician's Mate (AE)

Aviation Electronics Technician (AT)

Aviation Fire Control Technician (AQ)

Aviation Machinist's Mate (AD)

Aviation Maintenance Administrationman (AZ)

Aviation Ordnanceman (AO)

Aviation Storekeeper (AK)

Aviation Structural Mechanic (AM)

Aviation Support Equipment Technician (AS)

Boatswain's Mate (BM)

Boilermaker (BR)

Boiler Technician (BT)

Builder (BU)

Construction Electrician (CE)

Construction Mechanic (CM)

Cryptologic Technician (CT)

Data Processing Technician (DP)

Data Systems Technician (DS)

Dental Technician (DT)

Disbursing Clerk (DK)

Electrician's Mate (EM)

Electronics Technician (ET)

Electronics Warfare Technician (EW)

Engineering Aide (EA)

Engineman (EN)

Equipment Operator (EO)

Fire Control Technician (FT)

Gunner's Mate (GM)

Hospital Corpsman (HM)

Appendix 3. Enlisted Rating Specialty Badges

Hull Maintenance Technician (HT)

 Interior Communications Electrician (IC)

 Illustrator-Draftsman (DM)

 Instrumentman (IM)

 Intelligence Specialist (IS)

 Journalist (JO)

 Legalman (LN)

 Lithographer (LI)

 Machinery Repairman (MR)

 Machinist's Mate (MM)

 Master-at-Arms (MA)

 Mess Management Specialist (MS)

 Mineman (MN)

 Missile Technician (MT)

 Molder (ML)

 Musician (MU)

 Navy Counselor (NC)

 Ocean Systems Technician (OT)

 Operations Specialist (OS)

 Opticalman (OM)

 Patternmaker (PM)

 Personnelman (PN)

 Photographer's Mate (PH)

 Postal Clerk (PC)

 Quartermaster (QM)

 Radioman (RM)

 Ship's Serviceman (SH)

 Signalman (SM)

 Sonar Technician (ST)

 Steelworker (SW)

Storekeeper (SK)

Torpedoman's Mate (TM)

Tradevman (TD)

Utilitiesman (UT)

Yeoman (YN)

Bibliography

Books:

Battle Stations! Your Navy in Action. New York: Wm. H. Wise & Co., Inc., 1946.

Bureau of Naval Personnel. *Naval Orientation,* NAVPERS 16138-F. Washington, D. C.: Government Printing Office, 1974.

Clark, Adm. Joseph J., USN (Ret.) and Capt. Dwight H. Barnes, USNR. *Sea Power and Its Meaning.* New York: Franklin Watts, Inc., 1968.

Cope, Harley F. and Howard Bucknell III. *Command at Sea,* Third Edition. Annapolis: U. S. Naval Institute, 1966.

Craighead, Frank C. and John J. Craighead. *How to Survive on Land and Sea.* Annapolis: Naval Institute Press, 1972.

Crenshaw, Capt. R. S., Jr., USN (Ret.). *Naval Shiphandling,* Fourth Edition. Annapolis: Naval Institute Press, 1975.

Friedman, Herbert. *The Amazing Universe.* Washington, D. C.: National Geographic Society, 1975.

Guinness, Alma E., editor. *Joy of Nature.* Pleasantville, N. Y.: The Reader's Digest Association, Inc., 1977.

Herron, W. B., N. P. Palmer, and P. H. Joslin. *Matter, Life, and Energy.* Chicago: Rand McNally and Company, 1972.

James, Leonard F. *American Foreign Policy.* Glenview, Ill.: Scott, Foresman and Company, 1967.

Leadership Support Manual, NAVPERS 15934B. Washington, D. C.: Government Printing Office, 1968.

Lehr, Paul E., Burnett, and Zim. *Weather.* New York: Golden Press, 1975.

Lott, Arnold S., editor. *The Bluejackets' Manual,* 19th Edition. Annapolis: Naval Institute Press, 1973.

Lovette, Vice Adm. Leland P., USN (Ret.). *Naval Customs, Traditions, and Usage.* Annapolis: U. S. Naval Institute, 1967.

MacDonald, Edwin A. *Polar Operations.* Annapolis: U. S. Naval Institute, 1969.

Mahan, Alfred Thayer. *The Influence of Sea Power Upon History 1660–1783.* Boston: Little, Brown and Company, 1963.

Morison, Samuel Eliot. *The Two-Ocean War.* Boston: Little, Brown and Company, 1963.

Naval Education and Training Program Development Center, Pensacola. *Aerographer's Mate 3 & 2,* NAVEDTRA 10363-E. Washington, D. C.: Government Printing Office, 1976.

Naval Education and Training Program Development Center, Pensacola. *Human Behavior and Leadership,* NAVEDTRA 10058-B. Washington, D. C.: Government Printing Office, 1977.

Naval Education and Training Program Development Center, Pensacola. *Introduction to Sonar,* NAVEDTRA 10130-C. Washington, D. C.: Government Printing Office, 1976.

Naval Education and Training Program Development Center, Pensacola. *Naval Orientation,* NAVEDTRA 16138-G. Washington, D. C.: Government Printing Office, 1977.

Naval Education Training Program Development Center, Pensacola. *Quartermaster 3 & 2,* NAVEDTRA 10149-F. Washington, D. C.: Government Printing Office, 1976.

Naval Education and Training Support Command, Pensacola. *A Manual for Navy Instructors,* NAVEDTRA 107. San Diego: Naval Instructional Technology Development Center, 1974.

Naval Training Publications Detachment. *Principles of Guided Missiles and Nuclear Weapons,* NAVTRA 10784-B. Washington, D. C.: Government Printing Office, 1972.

Navy Training Publications Center, NAS Memphis, Millington, Tenn. *Basic Electricity,* NAVPERS 10086-B. Washington, D. C.: Government Printing Office, 1969.

Our Moral and Spiritual Growth Here and Now, NAVPERS 91962. Washington, D. C.: Government Printing Office, 1974.

Pictorial History of the Second World War, Volumes I–IV. New York: Wm. H. Wise and Co., Inc., 1948

Potter, E. B. *The Naval Academy Illustrated History of the United States Navy.* New York: Thomas Y. Crowell Company, 1971.

Potter, E. B. and Chester W. Nimitz, editors. *Sea Power.* Englewood Cliffs, N. J.: Prentice-Hall, Inc., 1960.

Pratt, Fletcher. *The Compact History of the United States Navy,* Third Edition. New York: Hawthorne Books, Inc., 1967.

Principles and Problems of Naval Leadership, NAVPERS 15924-A. Washington, D. C.: Government Printing Office, 1969.

The Readers Digest Association, Inc. *Marvels and Mysteries of the World Around Us.* Pleasantville, N. Y.: The Readers Digest Association, Inc., 1972.

Rice, Capt. William T., USNR (Ret.). *Pearl Harbor Story.* Honolulu: Tongg Publishing Co., Ltd., 1969.

Sagers, Ken W. and Norman Polmar. *Anchors and Atoms.* New York: David McKay Company, Inc., 1974.

Scientific American, Inc. *The Solar System.* San Francisco: W. H. Freeman & Co., 1975.

Snouck-Hurgronje, Jan, editor. *Navigation and Operations.* Annapolis: Naval Institute Press, 1972.

To Use the Sea, Readings in Seapower and Maritime Affairs. Annapolis: Naval Institute Press, 1973.

Training Publications Detachment, Naval Training Support Command. *Basic Military Requirements,* NAVTRA 10054-D. Washington, D. C.: Government Printing Office, 1973.

Training Publications Division, Naval Personnel Program Support Activity. *Navy Space and Astronautics Orientation,* NAVPERS 10488. Washington, D. C.: Government Printing Office, 1967.

Training Publications Division, Naval Personnel Program Support Activity, Washington, D. C. *Quartermaster 3 & 2,* NAVPERS 10151-C. Washington, D. C.: Government Printing Office, 1969.

Training Publications Division, Naval Personnel Program Support Activity, Washington, D. C. *Quartermaster 3 & 2,* NAVPERS 10149-E. Washington, D. C., Government Printing Office, 1971.

Training Publications Division, Naval Personnel Program Support Activity, Washington, D. C. *Quartermaster 1 & C,* NAVPERS 10151-D.

Trinklein, Frederich E. and Charles M. Huffer. *Modern Space Science.* New York: Holt, Rinehart and Winston, Inc., 1961.

U. S. Lifelines, OPNAV 09D-P1 (Revised) Washington, D. C.: Government Printing Office, 1974.

Wolfe, Malcolm E. and others. *Naval Leadership.* Annapolis: U. S. Naval Institute, 1949.

Periodicals:

Annapolis, The United States Naval Academy. Catalog 1977–78.

"Apollo 11 Mission." *National Geographic School Bulletin,* 15 September 1969.

Asimov, Isaac. "The Next Frontier?" *National Geographic,* July, 1976.

Bouffard, Capt. Edward N., USN. "NROTC: Quo Vadis?" *U. S. Naval Institute Proceedings,* July, 1977.

Canby, Thomas Y. "Apollo-Soyuz: Handclasp in Space." *National Geographic,* February, 1976.

Canby, Thomas Y. "Skylab, Outpost on the Frontier of Space." *National Geographic,* October, 1974.

Cane, Capt. Guy, USN. "Sea Power—Teddy's "Big Stick." *U. S. Naval Institute Proceedings,* August, 1976.

Dunn, Col. J. Howard, USMC (Ret.) and Major W. Hays Parks, USMC. "If I become a Prisoner of War. . ." *U. S. Naval Institute Proceedings,* August, 1976.

"First Steps to the Moon." *National Geographic School Bulletin,* 18 March 1968.

Gibson, Edward G. "The Sun as Never Seen Before." *National Geographic,* October, 1974.

High School News Service. *Profile,* October, 1977 Vol. 21, No. 1.

Maloy, Dr. William L. "The Education and Training of Naval Officers: An Investment in the Future." *U. S. Naval Institute Proceedings*, Naval Review Issue, May, 1975

"Mars Observed." *Newsweek*, 1 August 1969.

"Men on the Moon." *Life*, 8 August 1969.

Mitchell, PH1 Terry, USN. "The Science of Forecasting." *All Hands*, July, 1977.

"Moon, Mars and Man." *Newsweek*, 11 August 1969.

Petruska, Lt. A. M., USN. "The Influence of Technology upon Leadership." *U. S. Naval Institute Proceedings*, August, 1976.

Salitter, Cdr. Michael and Cdr. Ulrich Weisser, FGN. "Shallow Water Warfare in Northern Europe." *U. S. Naval Institute Proceedings*, March, 1977.

Skaar, Edwin W., Lt. Cdr. USN. "ASW and the Naval Officer Oceanographer." *U. S. Naval Institute Proceedings*, February, 1978.

Sundberg, JO1 Peter, USN. "Will You Weather the Summer Storms?" *All Hands*, July, 1977.

Weaver, Kenneth F. "Kohoutek, The Comet that Didn't Get Away." *National Geographic*, August, 1974.

Weaver, Kenneth F. "Mariner Unveils Venus and Mercury." *National Geographic*, June, 1975.

Weaver, Kenneth F. "Mystery Shrouds the Biggest Planet." *National Geographic*, February, 1975.

Pamphlets:

Eighty-Third Congress, 1st Session, House Document No. 211. *The United States Constitution, Text with Analytical Index.* Washington, D. C.: U. S. Government Printing Office, 1953.

Excerpts from Radarman 3 & 2, NAVPERS 10144-AE.

Houston, Walter. *Discovering the Moon.* Middletown, Conn: American Education Publications, 1970.

Hynek, Allen. *Exploring the Universe.* Middletown, Conn: American Education Publications, 1971.

NJROTC, A Navy Program for High School Students, NAVEDTRA 37076. Pensacola: Chief of Naval Education and Training, 1976.

Programmed Text, Relations with Juniors, Naval Leadership, Basic (CNABT-P-666). Pensacola: Naval Air Basic Training Command, Code 108, 1966.

Programmed Text, Techniques of Leadership, Naval Leadership, Basic (CNABT-P-668). Pensacola: Naval Air Basic Training Command, 1966.

Recruiting Advertising Department. Navy Career Guide, 1977–1978. Washington, D. C.: Naval Recruiting Command, 1977.

Recruiting Advertising Department. *How to Display and Respect the Flag of the United States.* RAD 71924. Washington, D. C.: U. S. Navy Recruiting Command, 1976.

Schaffter, Dorothy and Dorothy M. Mathews. *The Powers of the President as Commander in Chief of the Army and Navy of the United States.* Washington, D. C.: U. S. Government Printing Office, 1956.

McCain, Adm. John S., Jr., USN. *The Expanding Scope of Sea Power*, NAVPERS 15233. Washington, D. C.: Bureau of Naval Personnel, General Military Training Branch.

Index

"Desert Fox." *See* Rommel.
Destroyer escorts, 55
Détente, 131–132
Deterrent: strength and policy, 132; submarine missile systems, 4
Devotion to duty, 106
Dew, 166
Dewpoint, 158
Dictatorships, rise of, 44–45
Diego Garcia, 14
Diffraction, radio wave, 255
Discipline: conduct ashore, 121–122; consistency with, 166; defined, 112; example of, 113–114; in the Navy, 114; POW camp, 111; "preventive theory" of, 114
Divergence (sonar), 260
Doldrums, 170–171, 173
Dominican Republic, 5
Dönitz, Admiral Karl, 54, 56, 68
Doolittle raid, 72, 73
Doolittle, Colonel James, 72
Doorman, Dutch Admiral Karel, 71
Doppler effect, 262
Dust-cloud hypothesis, 205
Dutch East Indies, 49, 50, 52, 69–71
Dutch Harbor, Alaska, 81

Earth's revolution, winds, 171
Earth's rotation, winds, 169
Eclipse: lunar, 210; solar, 212
Economic equality, 130
Education: ACT, SAT scores, 37; benefits, 29; Class "A" schools, 33; Class "C" schools, 29; "G.I." Bill, 30; Naval Academy curriculum 38; Navy Campus for Achievement, 29; officers', 35–41; postgraduate officers', 29; requirements for, 25–26; service colleges, 29; special training, 33
Eisenhower, General Dwight D., 59, 61, 64, 67, 68; President, 138
Eisenhower (CVN-69), 13
Electricity: defined, 243; origin of term, 243; parallel circuits, 251–252; photoelectric, 244; series circuits, 247–249; static, 244
Electrodes, 245
Electrolyte, 244
Electromagnetic waves, 254
Electronic warfare: countermeasures, 259
Embargo, 49–50
Empress Augusta Bay, Battle of, 84
Energy: solar, 156; tidal, 20
England: colonization by, 4; geographical position, 4; rise to prominence, 3
Enlisted programs, 31–34

Enlistment: advanced pay grade, 32, 34; delayed entry, 32; oath, 122; requirements, 31
Enterprise, 75, 78, 80
Ephemeris, 222
Equal opportunity, 25, 128–130, 133
Equivalent resistance, 252
Ethiopia, conquest of, 45, 47
European Theater, *map*, 59
Evaluator (CIC), 258
Evasion, 274–275
Exosphere, 152–153, 213

Facsimile (FAX), 192–193
Familiarity, 116
Fascism, 130–131
Fathometer, 264
Fifth Fleet, 84
Finances: pay and allowances, 27–28; taxes, 28
Fisheries, 20–21
Fishing, 267, 279, 281, 286
Fix, radar, 257
Fleet Weather Central, 190–194
Fletcher, Admiral Frank Jack, 72
Foehns (Alpine winds), 173
Fog: Aleutian operations, 81; at sea, 166; coastal advection, 166–167; defined, 166; frontal, 168; radiation, 167–168; steam, 167
"Followership," 101
Foreign policy, U. S.: background of, 142; characteristics of, 143–144; U. S. Navy in, 142–143
Fortress Eurpoe (Festung Europa), invasion of, 63
Four-Ocean Challenge, 13–15
France, Vichy, 59–60
Freedom of the seas: doctrine, 19; mission of Navy, 19
Frequency, 254
Friendship, 116
Fronts, weather, 154, 168, 173, 179–181
Frost, 166

Galaxies, 220–221
Galileo, Italian scientist, 148
Gallery, Captain Dan, 56
Geneva Conference on the Seas, 20
Geographic Survey of the World, 10
Geopolitics: defined, 6; history of, 9–10; influence on training and strategy, 11; Japanese militarists and, 10; Mackinder's Theory, 7–8; Mahan's Theory, 6–7; new Soviet theory, 8–9; today, 10–11
Geo-stationary satellites, 192
German–Russian alliance, 10
Giant stars, 217
Gibraltar, Strait of, 16
Gilbert Islands. *See* Tarawa

Gondola, balloon, 203
"Good Neighbor" Policy, 143
Gooseberries, 65, 66
Grand Banks, Newfoundland, 166
Great Depression, 44–45
Greater East Asia Co-Prosperity Sphere, 10
Greenland, 48, 56, 139
Guadalcanal, 78–80
Guadalcanal, Naval Battle of, 80
Guantanamo Bay, Cuba, 15
Guerrilla warfare, 17

Hale Telescope, 235
Halley's Comet, 231
Halsey, Admiral William, 72, 80, 90, 92, 187
Haushofer, General Karl, 10
Heartland. See Mackinder, Sir Halford J.
Heat exhaustion, 271
Heavy weather bill, 195–196
Hedgehog, 55, 56
Helicopters, vertical envelopment, 13
Hewitt, Admiral Kent, 59, 61, 67
Hirohito, Emperor of Japan, 89, 96
History: lessons of, 44; purpose of studying, 43
Hitler, Adolph, 10, 45, 68
Hollandia, New Guinea, 86
Honesty, 120–121
Hornet, 72, 80
Horse Latitudes, 170, 171, 173
Human relations, 101, 115, 116
Human rights. See Democracy
Humidity, 149; relative humidity, 158–159
Hunting, survival, 269, 278, 281
Hurricanes, 184–189; Atlantic tracks of, 185, 186–187; warning system, 189
Hydrologic cycle, 158
Hydrophone, 260. See also Sonar
Hygrometer, 148
Hygroscopic nuclei, 160

Iceland, defense of, 48, 139
Indian Ocean, 17
Indochina, Japanese protectorate, 49
Ingenuity, 107
Initiative, 107
Inland reach of carrier air, 12, 13
Insects, 272–273, 276
Insolation (Incoming solar radiation), 156
Insulators, 243–244
Insurance, 28; Servicemen's Group Life Insurance (SGLI), 28
Intelligence, 72, 78, 85, 96
International Geophysical Year, 149, 151

Intertropical Convergence Zone, 179–180, 184
Ionosphere, 152, 213
Ions, 243
Ironbottom Sound, 78, 83
Isobars, 154–155
Isolationism, 48
Iwo Jima, battle for, 92–94

Japanese militarists, 10, 45
Japanese naval code, 72
Java, 69, 71
Java Sea, Battle of the, 71
Jefferson, Thomas, 132, 136
Jet stream, 151
Johnson, President Lyndon, 138
Jones, John Paul, on motivation, 114
Jungle warfare, 79, 83–84, 86
Jupiter, 227–228

Kamikaze, 92, 94–95
Kavieng, New Ireland, 71
Kellogg–Briand Pact, 44
Kennedy, President John F., 8, 138
Khrushchev, Nikita, Soviet Premier, 9, 131
King, Admiral Ernest J., 52
Kinkaid, Rear Admiral Thomas, 87
Kiska, 77, 81–82
Kjellen, Rudolf, geopolitical author, 9–10
Kohoutek comet, 231
Komandorski Islands, Battle of, 81
Kurita, Vice Admiral Takeo, 87

Langley, 45
Laws, defined, 112
Leadership: defined, 102; philosophies of, 101; qualities of, 105–109, 119; responsibility for, 121–122; training, Naval Academy, 38
League of Nations, 46–47
Leave, 30
Lebanon, 5
"Lebensraum," 10
Lend-Lease Act, 48
Leniency, dangers of, 117
Lenin, Nikolai, 131
Leverrier, U. J., French astronomer, 148
Lexington, 72–73
Leyte: battles for, 91–92; invasion of, 91
Lifeboats, 284
Life preservers, 283–284
Lightning, thunderstorm, 182
Light-year, 215
Lincoln, President Abraham, 137, 139
Lithosphere, 206

Naval ROTC, 38–41
Naval Science Institute, 40
Naval Service: career features, 25; challenge of, 25–26
Navy: in foreign policy, 142–143; job of, 26–27; personnel strength, 26; ratings and career fields, 34; role in world affairs, 141–142
Navy–Marine Corps Team, 13, 16
Navy Weather Service, 191
Nazi Party (Germany), 45
Nebula, -ae, 219
Neptune, 229
Neutrality Patrol, 48, 139
New Guinea, 71, 72, 80, 83–84, 86–87
Nimbus clouds. *See* Clouds; Precipitation
Nimitz, Admiral Chester W., 52–53, 69, 72, 78, 96
Nishimura, Admiral Shoji, 92
Nix Olympica, 226
Normandy, invasion of, 63–67
North Africa, invasion, 58–60
North Atlantic Treaty Organization (NATO), 14, 17
Northern Lights, 152
Nova, -ae, 219
Nuclear power, 13

Obedience, 102–103
Observatory, 233–236
Occluded front, 180–181
Ocean commerce. *See* Maritime commerce
Oceanography, 19–20
Oceans: political and technological developments since World War II, 12–13
Officer Candidate School, 41
Officer programs, 35–41
Ohms, 245
Ohm's Law, 248
Okinawa, Battles for, 94–95
Oldendorf, Admiral Jesse, 92
Omaha Beach, Normandy, 64, 65–66
Operations: Avalanche, 61–62; Anvil, 67; *Husky,* 61; *Iceberg,* 94–95; *Overlord,* 63–67; *Torch,* 58–60
Optimum Track Ship Routing (OTSR), 194
Orbiting Astronomical Observatories (OAOs), 202
Orbits, 222; elements of, 238; of comets, 231; perturbations of, 229
Orders, 104
Oscilloscope, 257
Ozawa, Vice Admiral Jisaburo, 87, 91–92

Pacific Ocean, 14
Pacific Theater, *map,* 71
Pacifism, 44
Palau Islands, 90–91

Panama Canal: bottleneck for trade, 15; locks of, *photo,* 137; Mahan's sea-power concept, 4, 5; treaty concerning, 138
Panay, sinking of, 47
Parallax, stellar, 216
Parallel circuits. *See* electricity
Parasitic diseases, 268, 273
Parsec, 216
Patton, General George, 61, 66, 67
Pay and allowances, 27–28
Pay Entry Base Data (PEBD), 32
Pearl Harbor: attack on, 50–52; base layout, 49
Peleliu. *See* Palau Islands
People's will, 5
Periphery of defense, 15, 139
Personal example, 101, 108–109, 119
Personnel: benefits, 27; dealing with, 115–116; medical care, 28; pay and allowances, 27–28; strength, 26; submarine, 83
Perturbations, orbital, 229
Petroleum: embargo on, 49–50; foreign oil purchases, 19
Phases of the moon, 209–210
Philippine Islands: Japanese conquest of, 52; U. S. return to, 90–91
Philippine Sea, Battle of the, 87–88
Photosphere, 211
Pioneer 10 and *11,* 227–228
Plane of ecliptic, 222
Planetarium, 233
Planets, 221–229
Plankton, commercial use of, 21
Plan Position Indicator (PPI), 257
Plebe, Naval Academy, 38
Pluto, 229
Poland, invasion of, 47
Polar easterlies. *See* Winds
Polar Frontal Zone, 180
Polaris/Poseidon ballistic missile system, 13
Polar operations, 198
Polar survival. *See* Survival
Polk, President James K., 137
Port Moresby, New Guinea, 72, 80
Potsdam Declaration, 96
Power, electric, 249. *See also* Watt
Precipitation: hail, 165–166; rain, 165; rainmaking, 165; snow, 165
President of United States (as CINC), 136–139
Prevailing westerlies. *See* Winds
Prevailing winds. *See* Winds
Preventive theory of discipline, 114
Preventive war philosophy, 140
Prism, spectrographic, 202

Prisoners of War (POW), 110–111; Geneva Convention on, 111
Professional knowledge, 106–107
Promotions, 129
Propaganda, 130
Proto-planet theory, 204–205
Psychrometer, 158–159
Pulsating stars, 218. *See also* Cepheid stars

Quarantine, Cuban, 5, 8–9
Quasars, 236
Quenching, sonar, 261

Rabaul, New Britain, 71, 80, 81, 83–84
Radar, 56, 255–257
Radiation, 152–153, 254
Radio, 254–255
Radio astronomy, 203
Radio telescopes, 236–238
Radius of action, 13
Rain. *See* Precipitation
Rainmaking, 165
Raw materials, 18–19
Rays (moon), 208
Receiver, radar, 256–257
Reconnaissance, 240
Recruiting, 31, 32
Reflection: radio wave, 255; sonar, 261; telescope mirror, 235
Refraction: radio wave, 255; sonar, 261; telescope lens, 235
Relative humidity, 158–159
Resistance, 245
Responsibility: command, 123–124; moral, 101, 105–106
Retirement pay, 28
Retrograde motion, 223
Reverberation, sonar, 261
Rhine River, Navy crossing, 68
Rilles, 208
Rome, capture of, 62
Rome–Berlin Axis, 45
Rommel, Field Marshal Erwin, 58, 60, 61, 63
Roosevelt, President Franklin D., 48, 54, 60, 64, 134, 138, 139–141, 143
Roosevelt, President Theodore, 138
"Rubber Stamp" legislature, 130

Saipan, Mariana Islands, 87
Salamis, Battle of, 5
Salerno, invasion at, 61
Salinity, 261–262
Samar, Battle of. *See* Leyte Gulf

Santa Ana winds, 173
Santa Cruz Islands, Battle of, 80
Satellites, 238–241
Satellite tracking, 239–240
SAT scores, 37
Saturn, 228
Savo Island, Battle of, 79
Scattering (sonar), 260
Schematic diagram, 247
Scholarships: Naval Academy, 36–39; NROTC, 39–41
Seabees. *See* Naval Construction Battalion
Seacoasts, defense of, 4
Sea duty, 27
Sea of Tranquillity, 207–208
Sea-power: defined, 3; in geopolitics, 6–7; in history, 5–6; in national strategy, 22; Soviet, 9
Sea smoke, fog, 167
Seismometer, 208
Self-confidence, 107
Self-discipline, 112–113
Self-evaluation, 119–120
Series circuits. *See* Electricity
Service colleges. *See* Education
Shangri-La, 73
Shelter. *See* Survival
Ship routing (OTSR), 193–194
Sibuyan Sea, Battle of. *See* Leyte
Sicily, invasion of, 60, 61
Sidereal month, 209
Siderites, 232
Siegfried Line, 67
Singapore, port of, 17
Skylab, 212–213
Smith, General Holland, 84
Snakes, 273, 276
Snow. *See* Precipitation
Snow blindness, 271
Socialism, 130
Solar system, creation of, 204–205
Solar wind, 213
Solomon Islands, 78–80, 83
Sonar: active, 262; defined, 260; dipping, 263–264; passive, 262–263; technicians, 260
Sonobuoys, 263–264
Sound: in the sea, 261–263; physics of, 260–261; seawater pressure and, 261; speed of, 261–262
South China Sea, 17
Soviet Mediterranean Squadron, 17
Soviet Union: declaration of war on Japan, 96; economic conditions, 8; fisheries, 20–21; merchant shipping, 18; new geopolitics, 8–9; oceanographic research, 20; pact with Germany, 47; sea power, 9; submarine fleet, 17; World War II supply routes, 57

Uranus, 228–229
U. S. flag ships, 18
Utah Beach, Normandy, 65

Van Allen Radiation Belt, 152, 153, 213, 214
Venus, 222, 224–225
Versailles, Treaty of, 43
Vertical envelopment, 13
Veterans' assistance, 30
Virginia Capes, Battle of, 5
Voltage, 244–245
von Rundstedt, Field Marshal, 63, 68
Vortex, tornadic, 182

War, defined by Clausewitz, 43
Warfare specialties, officer, 29
Warm front, 179, 180. *See also* Fronts
Washington Disarmament treaties, 43, 48
Water. *See* Survival
Waterspout, 183–184
Watt. *See* Power, electric
Wavelength, 254
WAVES, 97

Weather: causes of, 155–157; data reporting, 195; defined, 155; forecasting, 190–192; influence on history, 147–148; maps and charts, 192; route forecast (WEAX), 194; satellites, 189, 192; tactical planning and, 196–197
Welfare and recreation, 114–115
White dwarf star, 217
Willy-willy. *See* Tropical cyclone
Wilson, President Woodrow, 138
Winds, 155; bands, general circulation, 169–170; Beaufort Scale of, 176–177; convergence and divergence of, 169; defined, 169; earth's revolution and, 171; earth's rotation and, 169; highs, 172; lows, 173; monsoon, 174–175; mountain, 173; secondary, 171–172; valley, 173
"Wolfpack" U-boat tactics, 56
"World Island." *See* Mackinder, Sir Halford J.
World War II, 43–99; beginning of, 47; U. S. entry in, 50

Yamamoto, Admiral Isoroku, 50, 72, 76–77, 83
Yerkes Observatory, 235
Yorktown, 72–73, 75, 77
Yorktown, Battle of, 5